# Genesis Curriculum
## The Book of Genesis

Junior Edition

Copyright © 2019 Lee Giles
ISBN-13: 9781731554420

The Scripture translation is my own, a mixture of the NASB of the original lessons, the KJV, and my own wording to try to make it more understandable and easier to follow.

Hugh Ross, "Fulfilled Prophecy: Evidence for the Reliability of the Bible," *Reasons to Believe* website, August 22, 2003, http://www.reasons.org/articles/articles/fulfilled-prophecy-evidence-for-the-reliability-of-the-bible. Reprinted with permission.

## TABLE of CONTENTS

How to Use................................4
Materials List........................7
Daily Lessons..........................9
Course Descriptions..............379
Scope and Sequence Lists....380

## How to Use

Thank you for choosing Genesis Curriculum. I hope you have a great year of learning together. That's what Genesis Curriculum is about, learning together. I hope you will learn right along with your children.

As a homeschool curriculum, I encourage you to make this your own. It's prepared and ready to be picked up and used as is, but you are a homeschooler! You get to adapt it to your family however it works best for you. I will walk you through it and give you some ideas for how to use its sections. You might want to come back to this how-to guide occasionally for some pointers you may have forgotten.

Each lesson is written as an outline. You will basically read through the outline to your children. When a line asks a question, stop and let your children answer before you read the answer I give on the next line. Where I include a (Note:) I'm talking to you, and you can just read that to yourself.

Bible

First is the Bible reading. These readings go directly through the book of Genesis. I did not include questions with the reading. You can just read it and leave it at that, or you can ask your kids to make observations and ask what they think about it. Do they have any questions? You don't have to have the answers. It's good for them to think and to ask questions and to make decisions about what they believe while you are there to guide them. Some of your questions may be answered in the lesson, but you can always research things together and learn together. That's what GC is all about.

I have written the translation being used. It is not a literal word for word translation. I took liberty to delete out some names to make for smoother reading, and to say things like, "he bowed before everyone there," instead of something like, "he bowed in the presence of the sons of Heth, the descendants of Ephron." I tried to be VERY careful to make everything true to Scripture.

Memory Verses

After the reading is a memory verse. They will have one verse a week. These are from all throughout the Bible but are related to the Genesis readings. They will be reviewing these verses throughout the year and asked sometimes to find the verses in the Bible. On the last day of each week you are to "test yourselves" on the memory verse. It's up to you if you want to give a reward to anyone who can say it from memory.

Language

Next comes the language section. This comes in two parts: handwriting/spelling and vocabulary.

Spelling

Spelling and handwriting are the same section, their chance to write something each day. They should always work to write carefully, forming their letters tall or below the line as appropriate. Read the "words to know" one at a time along with the "spelling tip." The tips are to help them spell successfully, so let them have the tips before they write the word. The tips are listed in order. When they misspell a word, point out how many letters they got correct. Praise the positive! If they take it to heart when they get something wrong, you can even use words like, "You got five points on that word!" if the word is six letters long and they got five of them right. Circle the incorrect letter and write the correct letter above or see if you can figure out together what it should be. Then have them write the word the correct way.

Vocabulary

Vocabulary is the next section. This is a word from the day's reading. The verse number is listed with the word, so you can read it in context and see what they can guess for the definition. Ask what the part of speech is. (These will be introduced.) Tell them the part of speech and the definition. You can ask your child to repeat the definition. You could ask them to try to come up with a sentence that uses the word. You can act out the word or the sentence you come up with.

Grammar

As I mentioned, the parts of speech will be introduced and that happens in the vocabulary section. On their workbook pages they will be practicing grammar such as sentence structure, plurals, parts of speech, and basic punctuation. These things are introduced in the writing section.

Lessons

Then we come to the meat of the curriculum. Science and social studies topics follow. Sometimes the lesson is just one or the other, sometimes both. Social studies does have some history, but it is much more social studies, the study of humans and their societies. I have included stories of some of my own experiences and observations from my many years of living overseas, most of which has been among Muslims and much of which has been in a Middle Eastern culture. Both science and history are from a definitively young-earth perspective.

When you come to a question in the curriculum with the answer on the next line, stop and have your kids answer with their thoughts. Then you can read my answer and continue on. They don't have to know the answer. They aren't necessarily meant to know the answer, but in asking you are getting their brains turned on and getting them thinking. Let them guess at answers. They don't have to know the right answer in order to speak up.

Show the pictures I included where applicable. The italicized words are defined in the text. When you read a sentence with an italicized word, you can stop and ask them to repeat the word. If you have just read what it means, have them tell you what it means. These are words that might show up in their review later. At the end of many of these sections there is a "recall" and "explore more." Ask the recall questions and help them answer with hints. The explore more section may have an activity you could do together.

I wanted to point out one more thing about these lessons and topics. They are different each day. They were inspired by the reading that day, so they aren't in order. You will see how certain topics come up repeatedly, so I don't want you to think that you will never see a topic again just because it didn't continue the next day. Since I wrote all of the lessons, I know what has been covered and can weave threads through the lessons, referring to previous things learned. Some topics are covered multiple times from different angles.

### Discussion

The lesson is rounded out with a discussion question. The discussion question is based on the day's lesson. These are open-ended and are meant to make them think. Let each kid give his or her own thoughts and then you can give your own. These aren't right or wrong type questions, so let them express their thoughts without correction. You can give your thoughts, and they will learn from you. This is a great time for instilling wisdom, though some questions are just for fun, like describing a world without gravity.

### Writing

The final section is writing. This will introduce whatever they will be practicing on their worksheet that day.

### Review

Also, one day each week there are no new spelling or vocabulary words. They will have a worksheet to see what they have learned of their spelling and vocabulary words. It's up to you if you want to use this time as an assessment. I just use it as review.

There are five weeks of lessons and then two weeks of review where they will be practicing spelling and vocabulary and completing a worksheet each day.

### Copyright

I decided to not grant photocopy rights. I want to be able to make updates and changes to materials and have everyone use the most recent editions. The workbook is available on our site for printing any extra pages you should need. I've tried to price it so that it's not cheaper to print out. I want to make this easy for you!

# Materials List – not updated for Juniors

Where it's marked extra, it's not something that is needed to complete the lesson. It's in the lesson as something additional you could try. An asterisks* marks when something needs to be cut out. If you don't want to cut those pages from your workbook, they can all be printed from our site, genesiscurriculum.com. You can find them through the Online Support page.

| | |
|---|---|
| 1 | mirror or any shiny surface for reflecting light |
| 2 | mirror, ball that bounces - any size |
| 4 | glass of water, pencil or some other straight object to put in water |
| 41 | (extra) fan, two plates, water |
| 42 | (extra) two sponges (at least one really dry) |
| 50 | cornstarch, water, bowl |
| 51 | food package with label (looking for calorie count) |
| 54 | balloon (only if you want to see it for yourself) (extra) plastic bottle with lid, pen or nail; explore more: short tube/hose, stick |
| 57 | 2 T. white vinegar and ¼ c. skim milk, you can try other types of milk and other acids such as lemon juice and orange juice, (extra) sugar/salt, glass of water |
| 60 | biggest screw you have at home; if you have a toy car where you can see where the wheel is attached to the axle; (extra) stick, short tube/hose, strong tape |
| 63 | *word parts need cutting out |
| 65 | *word strips need cutting |
| 68 | *words and definitions need cutting, zip lock bag (or something to save word cards and definitions in) |
| 76 | pencil with point and eraser (or just a pen), flashlight |
| 83 | (explore more) celery, water and food coloring |
| 87 | (extra) yarn-just a little piece will do |
| 96 | broom (or rake or long-handled scrub brush), string, table that the broom handle reaches across, bucket or basket with handle, something like a big book or weight to go in the basket, (you might need a ruler or wooden spoon and strong tape if your long-handled tool doesn't have a wide place to hold on to securely at the end) See picture on the next page; separately you will need something to act as a wedge such as a long fork or long spoon with a thin edge |
| 97 | ½ teaspoon dry yeast and ½ cup hydrogen peroxide (alternative: steel wool and vinegar to cover it); plastic cup or glass, a thermometer that can measure room temperature if you have one |
| 98 | play dough (clay) in four colors, stick for going through your play dough model (tooth picks or thin skewer, per person) |
| 99 | die (If you don't have one, you could write the numbers 1 through 4 on slips of paper and draw them out randomly.) |
| 107 | measuring tape |
| 117 | rulers with centimeters on them (The kids will be drawing maps and will need to measure centimeters on their papers.) |
| 126 | (extra) baking soda, vinegar (or other acid) |
| 131 | one apple, salt, cooling rack, four cups or bowls that you can do without for the week, plastic wrap and any tape to seal it shut |

| | |
|---|---|
| 132 | 30 minutes of boiling for: spinach, beets, red cabbage, onion skins; hard boiled eggs for dying, a cup for each dye, white vinegar<br>*word parts need cutting out |
| 133 | paper cups, maybe a few per kid so they can make mistakes (They will put holes in them.) |
| 134 | (option 1) baking soda and a variety of things to combine with it for experimentation (solids, liquids, definitely acids like vinegar, orange and lemon juice); (option 2) ice, aluminum foil-could probably use plastic wrap, book, steaming water<br>*word strips need cutting out – Only need one copy today. They will need these words for Day 138. Hold onto what you cut out. |
| 135 | We're going to build a car. Choose your parts. If you can get a variety of sizes of things, then the kids can make different length axles and use different size wheels and test out how it affects the car. You'll need a body: plastic water bottle, toilet paper roll, build a frame out of popsicle sticks, etc. You'll need axles: tooth picks, skewers, hard straws, etc. You will need wheels: bottle caps, wheels from a Lego set, make wheels by slicing off end of toilet paper roll (and then cover openings with masking tape or duct tape.)<br>(extra) rubber band |
| 137 | We're going to draw body diagrams. It would be fun to tape together a bunch of pieces of paper and trace the whole body onto the paper and then draw the bones and organs, etc. onto the body. If you don't want to do this, they will have to draw a body onto a single piece of paper and add in the parts. Just use lines to outline the body to label the parts. |
| 138 | *word strips from Spelling Review 19 (Day 134)  Each person needs their own or they can work in pairs, etc. |

Picture of Day 96 activity

**Day 1 (check Materials List)**

I. Read Genesis 1:1-5.
    1 In the beginning God created the heavens and the earth.
    2 The earth was empty and dark, and the Spirit of God was moving over the surface of the deep.
    3 Then God said, "Let there be light"; and there was light.
    4 God saw that the light was good; and God separated the light from the darkness.
    5 God called the light day, and the darkness He called night. And the evening and the morning was the first day.

II. Memory Verse
- Genesis 1:1
- In the beginning God created the heavens and the earth.

III. Language
- Spelling/Handwriting
  - words to know: God, earth, over, light
  - spelling tips:
    - God is a name so it begins with a capital letter.
    - earth: Begins with the word ear. It begins with the vowels E-A.
    - over: There's an E that makes the O say its name. It has the O sound spelling pattern O_E.
    - light: This uses I-G-H for the I sound.
- Vocabulary/Grammar
  - surface (vs. 2)
  - the outer layer of something (noun)
    - Can you find a smooth surface to run your hand over? The surface doesn't have to be the top. It can be underneath as well. Do you have a table where the surface is smooth on top but not smooth underneath?
  - Surface is a noun because it's a thing. It's something you can touch.

IV. Lesson
- Our first topic is light.
  - God creates light before He creates the sun and the moon and the other stars.
  - God can do anything. He created the laws of physics, the laws of nature, the laws of how this earth survives and operates, but He can also break them at any time. (For example, He causes a heavy metal ax head to float, 2 Kings 6:4-6.)
  - We're going to look more at what He created when He created light.
- What does light do?
  - Jesus is called "the light of the world" (John 8:12).
  - Light is what enables us to see. If you are in a room with no light at all, what can you see?
    - You cannot see anything at all.

- When you are looking at something, what you are seeing is the light that is being reflected off of that object. That light bounces off of the object and hits your eyes. Your miraculous brain puts all those light inputs together into the image you see. And it all happens instantaneously!
- Have you ever reflected light? You can use a mirror or you could try a ring or a watch or any shiny surface. Hold it where a light hits it. Wobble the mirror or other objects and watch the reflection of light move on the wall.

  o What is light?
  - Light is a dance. Light particles, called *photons*, teeny tiny things in our universe, travel in a straight path, while light from them dances up and down in waves. Light is always moving.
    - If you draw a curvy line, up and down and up and down, that's what a light wave does.
  - Light is moving energy. Energy is one of the most important parts of our universe. *Energy* is the ability to do work.
    - So light is moving energy, and in the beginning God created light. I want to tell you something awesome about energy. It cannot be created or destroyed by man! It can only be changed from one form to another. All of the energy that the whole world needs to live and move and have our being was created by God alone on the first day.
    - When people talk of creating energy, they really mean transforming energy. As an example, solar panels don't create energy; they take the sun's energy and convert it into electricity.
  - The sun gives energy to the plants which give energy to the animals that eat them. They give you energy when you eat the animal or plant.
  - Energy keeps us alive. That light keeps us all alive; it gives us all the energy we need to keep on living.

  o Recall: What is light? Light is moving energy. What is energy? Energy is the ability to do work.
  o Explore more: Draw light waves from a light hitting an object and bouncing off. (There are a few blank pages in the back of the workbook for drawing things such as this.)

V. Discussion
  - Jesus calls Himself the light of the world (John 8:12).
  - What do you think Jesus enables us to see with His light?

VI. Writing
  o When you write, you need to make sure your sentences start and end properly. Do you know what I'm talking about?
  o Every sentence begins with a capital letter and ends with a punctuation mark. Mostly that means it ends with a period. But maybe you have something to exclaim! Or maybe you need to ask a question?
  o Make sure you are starting and ending your sentences the right way.
  o Complete Writing Sentences 1 in your workbook.

**Day 2 (check Materials List)**

I. Read Genesis 1:6-10.
   6  Then God said, "Let there be an opening between the waters, and let it separate the waters from the waters."
   7  God made the opening, and separated the waters which were below from the waters which were above.
   8  Heaven is what God called the opening of space He created. And the evening and the morning was a second day.
   9  Then God said, "Let the waters below the heavens be gathered into one place, and let the dry land appear"; and it happened.
   10 God called the dry land earth, and the gathering of the waters He called seas; and God saw that it was good.

II. Memory Verse
   o  Genesis 1:1
   o  In the beginning God created the heavens and the earth.

III. Language
   o  Spelling/Handwriting
      • words to know: dry, seas, good, there
      • spelling tip:
         ▪ dry: When the letter Y comes at the end of a one syllable word, it says I (eye).
         ▪ seas: This is a homophone, a word that sounds like a different word. This is the type of seas you sail a boat on. It has an EA in it to write the E sound. When two vowels are together like that, it's the first one that says its name.
         ▪ good: This has two O's in the middle. This doesn't follow the rule I just told you. Double O has special sounds. The words good and look and took and wood, like the kind you use to build with, all use this kind of double O sound.
         ▪ There is another homophone. This is the kind of there that means that you see something over there. It ends with E-R-E.
   o  Vocabulary/Grammar
      • separate (vs. 6, 7)
      • to move things apart (verb)
         ▪ God moved the waters apart from each other. It was something He did. Actions are verbs.
      • Act it out. What can you separate? You can separate from each other and sit on opposite sides of the room.
      • To write the word separate, just pronounce it: sep – ar – ate. The AR is like in car.

IV. Lesson
   o  Learn the names and locations of the continents. They are found on the Day 2 map of your Map Book.

- Read the ocean names. Learn them if you decide to.
- The Pacific Ocean is also the water on the far-right side of the map in the middle. Why?
- The earth is a ball shape, not flat like a map! The two sides of the map are connected to each other.
    - How many continents are there?
        - seven
    - How many oceans are there?
        - five
    - Explore more: Find where you are on the world map. If you know your heritage, find the general location of that part of the world.

V. Discussion
- What is the point of naming continents and oceans? Who do you think decided where one ended and the other started? Why do you think they decided what they did?

VI. Writing
- On your worksheet today you are going to find verbs, actions that things and people do.
- You can also practice continents.
- Make sure your spelling words are correct. Take another look at them. You can rewrite any word that gave you trouble to practice.

**Day 3**

I. Read Genesis 1:11-13.
   11 Then God said, "Let the earth produce plants, plants with seeds, and fruit trees on the earth producing fruit with seeds in them"; and it happened.
   12 The earth produced plants, which produced seeds of the same kind of plant, and trees bearing fruit with seeds in them each for their kind of tree; and God saw that it was good.
   13 The evening and the morning was a third day.

II. Memory Verse
   o Genesis 1:1
   o In the beginning God created the heavens and the earth.

III. Language
   o Spelling/Handwriting
      - words to know: morning, plants, fruit, seed
      - spelling tips:
         - <u>morning</u>: This has the word OR in it.
         - <u>plants</u>: This ends with the word ants.
         - <u>fruit</u>: There is a U-I that makes the OO sound in this word.
         - <u>seed</u>: This word has a double EE for its E sound.
   o Vocabulary/Grammar
      - produce (verses 11 and 12 – The stress goes on the second syllable.)
      - to make, to cause to come into existence (verb)
      - What's a verb?
         - Verbs are the words that are the actions that things and people do. There are other types of verbs. This type we call action verbs.

IV. Lesson
   o We're going to leave light for today and talk about seeds. Our reading today talked about plants having their own kind of seeds. That means that apples produce apple seeds; those apple seeds grow apple trees. Sunflowers produce sunflower seeds that grow more sunflowers.
   o How do seeds work? They die!
      - When you eat your fruits and vegetables, be on the lookout for their seeds. Some are harder to find than others. Do you know where banana seeds are? What about carrot seeds?
   o Seeds come in many shapes and sizes. Some plants don't have seeds. A potato is its own seed. You just plant a piece of potato in the ground. If you leave a potato out too long it will start to sprout. It's growing a new plant! Onions work that way too.
   o The seed grows inside a plant. Then there are many different ways the seed gets into the ground. They can be planted, but certainly don't have to be. How do you think there are wild flowers and forests?
      - No one planted those. They grew naturally.
      - When a fruit falls off a tree and no one picks it up, what happens to it?

- - - When fruit falls to the ground, the fruit will *decompose*, meaning it becomes rotten and decays. Did you ever see a really icky, squishy fruit or vegetable?
      - Fruit that has turned brown and squishy is decomposing. When it decomposes, it leaves a nice environment for a seed to sprout.
      - This can also happen when an animal eats the fruit but the seed comes out the other end unharmed. It's an already fertilized seed! Gross, but a good way for a seed to get growing.
    - Animals may move seeds purposefully or accidentally.
      - They may pick up the fruit and take it somewhere else to eat it. That would be moving it purposefully.
      - Accidentally, a seed may get stuck to their fur and they may just drag it along with them until it gets knocked off.
    - Some seeds fly away to new locations. Have you ever blown on dandelion seeds to make them fly away?
  - What happens to a seed at this point? The plant has died. The fruit or flower has fallen. It's no longer attached to its life source. The seeds are no longer living and growing. Then what?
    - It's a mystery. God made it that way. Man can't create life; it can only copy life that God has created.
    - Only God brings life from death. He shows us the resurrection in the life of a plant. We get our life because of the death of Jesus.
  - Here's what we do know. We have a dead seed. It gets a burial. It gets under a little bit of soil. What starts happening to the seed?
    - It gets its nutrients, its food, from that very soil it is under. Those nutrients are taken in by the roots of the plant which start pushing out of the seed when it's ready, once the mystery has taken place.
    - While the roots go down deeper into the soil, at the same time, out of the seed green shoots sprout up towards the light.
  - *Germination* is the name of this early growth of a seed plant.
  - The new plant will make its own food from the sun.
    - Be on the lookout for seeds and plant some!
  - Recall: What is happening when fruit decomposes? It's decaying and going rotten. What is happening when animals move seeds? Seeds are being scattered about. What is germination? the early growth of a plant (when the plant is first breaking out of a seed)
  - Explore more: Find some seeds and break them open. What's inside?

V. Discussion
   - Seeds grow plants "after their own kind," meaning the same kind of plant.
   - When we start a new church, we call it a "church plant."
   - What kind of "seeds" do you think need to be planted to grow a church?
   - Remember, a church is not a building! A church is a group of Christians.

VI. Writing
- Complete your workbook page for Day 3.
- Make sure your spelling words are correct. You might want to rewrite any you got wrong to practice.
- Do you remember your continents? Which one is on today's page?
- Finally, you are going to write a sentence. It's important to remember to begin it with a capital letter. It also needs to end with punctuation. What kind of punctuation ends a sentence?
    - a period, exclamation point, or question mark

**Day 4 (check Materials List)**

I. Read Genesis 1:14-19.
   14 Then God said, "Let there be lights in the heavens to separate the day from the night, and let them be for signs and for seasons and for days and years;
   15 and let them be for lights in the heavens to give light on the earth"; and it happened.
   16 God made the two great lights, the greater light to govern the day, and the lesser light to govern the night; He made the stars also.
   17 God placed them in the heavens to give light on the earth,
   18 and to govern the day and the night, and to separate the light from the darkness; and God saw that it was good.
   19 The evening and the morning was a fourth day.

II. Memory Verse
   o Genesis 1:1
   o In the beginning God created the heavens and the earth.

III. Language
   o Spelling/Handwriting
     - words to know: night, heaven, sign, season
     - spelling tips:
       - <u>Night</u> uses the I-G-H spelling pattern for the vowel sound, just like light.
       - <u>Heaven</u> uses E-A like earth does, even though it doesn't say E. Usually when two vowels are together, the first one says its name. But E-A sometimes says the short E as in red.
       - <u>Sign</u> is a hard spelling word. You can think of it as if it was originally sIGHns with an I-G-H and then the H was dropped. Read it after you wrote it. If it says sing, then you mixed up your N and G.
       - <u>Season</u> uses an E-A for the E sound. That's the way E-A is normally used. Season is spelled sea-son, like the son of the sea, the child of the water.
   o Vocabulary/Grammar
     - govern (vs. 16)
     - to rule, to be in control over a group of people (verb)
     - Act it out!

IV. Lesson
   o Today we are back to learning about light but in a little bit different way. Let's talk about stars, and specifically, our sun.
     - God placed the perfect sized star in the perfect location to light and warm our planet. He set it all in motion so that we have night and day and summer and winter and springtime and harvest.
     - God made the star that we call the sun just right to give us what we need. It's not the biggest star. It's little compared to some, but it's just right to give us the light and warmth we need without baking us!

- How fast does light travel? When you turn on a light, how long does it take for the light to fill the room?
  - Not long! Light is the fastest physical thing in our universe. Nothing is faster. It travels at an astonishing 300 million meters per second. Take one giant step forward. That's about one meter. Now do that 300 million times in one second!
- That speed gets the sun's light to us, but how does it warm us?
  - Everything on earth, even those things not on the earth, is made up of a basic building block called the *atom*. They are things you can't see. They build together in different combinations to make something called *molecules*.
    - A famous atom you've probably heard of is oxygen, part of what we breathe. You can't see the air you breathe, but it's full of atoms!
  - We're trying to understand how the sun's light heats the earth. Have you noticed how much hotter it is in the sun than in the shade? Why is that do you think?
    - When light hits those atoms, it gets them excited, which moves them around. That movement is what produces heat. The light is exciting atoms in the ground and in the walls of buildings and in you!
      - Do you get hot when you get excited? Not sure? Run around crazy and see if you warm up. ☺
    - When light hits the atoms, it excites them and gets them moving. Those moving atoms create heat. That heat warms the objects on earth and the earth itself.
- The Bible verses say that the stars in the sky were made for signs, seasons, days, and years.
  - The sun marks 24 hours every day for us by rising and setting.
  - Do you know what the moon marks?
    - It marks months for us, though not precisely the way our calendar does.
  - There's a star called the North Star. What do you think that's used for?
    - It shows people where north is. It's like a compass in the sky to point people in the right direction.
  - We read in the Bible how the wise men saw the sign of a king in the sky. They were among the first worshipers of Jesus because of it.
- Depending on where you are on the earth, the stars look differently. When you are awake, it's dark on another part of the earth and they are sleeping. The stars appear to be in different places.
- Take a look at the world map on Day 2 and find the *equator*. It's the line that goes between the words "Pacific" and "Ocean" and cuts through the top part of South America.
  - It's an imaginary line, but we use it to divide the world in half.
  - We call those halves *hemispheres*. The top half of the map is the northern hemisphere and the bottom half of the map is the southern hemisphere.
  - In which hemisphere do you think most people live?
    - in the northern hemisphere
- Recall: What are the basic building blocks of everything? What's the fastest physical thing in the universe? The equator divides the world into two what?

- atoms
- light
- hemispheres
  - Explore more: Look at the stars. Talk about how it's night on the other side of the world if it's the middle of the day where you are and how in the southern hemisphere it's winter when it's summer in the northern hemisphere.

V. Discussion
  - The Bible talks about walking in the light and not in the darkness. Jesus is the light of the world. If you are walking in the darkness, you are not walking with Jesus. If you are walking with Jesus, you cannot walk in darkness.
  - What do you think it means to walk in the light?
  - What do you think it means to walk in the darkness?

VI. Writing
  - Use the discussion questions as a writing prompt.
  - Can you include a vocabulary or spelling word? Get a high five and/or hug for each one you include.

**Day 5**

I. Read Genesis 1:20.
   20 Then God said, "Let the waters teem with swarms of living creatures, and let birds fly above the earth in the open skies of the heavens."

II. Memory Verse
- Test yourselves.
- Say from memory Genesis 1:1.

III. Language
- Spelling
    - Test yourselves with the words from Days 1-4. You can use your workbook page.
        - God, earth, over, light
        - dry, seas, good, there
        - morning, plants, fruit, seed
        - night, heaven, sign, season
- Vocabulary
    - Test yourselves with the words from Days 1-4. You can use your workbook page.
        - surface – the outer layer of something
        - separate – to move things apart
        - produce – to make, to cause to come into existence
        - govern – to rule, to be in control over a group of people

IV. Lesson
- Today we will learn about birds since we read about God creating them.
- How do you know something is a bird? Name the characteristics of birds.
- Here's my list of what all birds have in common. How does your list compare?
    - feathers, wings, bills/beaks, lay eggs, two legs
    - They do not have to fly. Some birds such as penguins and ostriches do not fly.
    - They are warm blooded, like humans. That means they generate their own body heat.
    - They are *vertebrates*. That means they have a backbone. So do you!
    - A little note about vertebrates and backbones. Each little bone you feel up the spine is called a *vertebra*. By the way, all of them together are *vertebrae*. That's how you write the plural. You say it with an A sound at the end.
- How many different types of birds do you think there are?
    - There are around 10,000 different types of birds. I think God is amazingly creative to make so many different types of animals with so many unique features.
- I want to tell you about a special bird, the eagle.
- Here is a verse about them.
    - Deuteronomy 32:11 Like an eagle that stirs up its nest, That hovers over its young, He spread His wings and caught them, He carried them on His pinions.

- - - Pinions are the outer part of a bird's wings including the flight feathers.
  - - Isaiah 40:31 Yet those who wait for the LORD will gain new strength; They will mount up with wings like eagles, They will run and not get tired, They will walk and not become weary.
- Let's look at these two verses about eagles.
- How does an eagle stir up its nest?
  - First an eagle takes out all of the soft leaves and feathers that it had put in the nest for the babies' comfort.
    - Why do you think it might do that?
    - It needs to teach the baby to fly. It's time for the young bird to leave the nest.
  - Then the mother will hover over the nest, flapping her wings, demonstrating to the young, getting them to copy her. Their first lift off is in the nest with little hops and flaps.
- The second verse talks about eagle's wings and relates it to strength and endurance. Eagles can go up to 75 miles per hour. They also rarely flap their wings on long migration trips. How do you think they can fly so far without flapping?
  - They ride the drafts of wind which hold them up under their large wings which can be up to over a meter long each!
- Our verse today says that God created "swarms of living creatures." In science we talked about what makes something a bird. Well, what makes something living? What is life?
- What things are alive? Name the types of things that are alive.
  - Basically, there are animals and plants. Can you think of what they have in common?
    - Maybe you thought of how they all need energy to live.
- Recall: What are some characteristics of birds? What do all living things have in common? What makes birds a vertebrate?
  - two legs, feathers, wings, beaks/bills, warm-blooded, vertebrates, lay eggs
  - need energy
  - They have backbones.
- Explore more: Choose a type of bird to learn about. What do its eggs look like? What are the differences between the way the male and female look?

V. Discussion
- What makes animals and people different from plants?
- What makes animals different from people?
  - Are animals more important than plants? Are people more important than animals? Why or why not?
- Note: We should care for our world. It's God's creation, but we are only commanded in the Bible to love people. People are most important. Any philosophy that doesn't put people first is not from God.

VI. Writing
- On your worksheet today you can practice your spelling and vocabulary.

**Day 6**

I. Read Genesis 1:21-23.
   21 God created the great sea monsters and every living creature that moves in the water, which was full of them. And God made every bird with wings. The living creatures had babies that were each the same type of animal as the parents. God saw that it was good.
   22 God blessed them to have lots of babies, saying, "Be fruitful and multiply, and fill the waters in the seas, and let birds multiply on the earth."
   23 There was evening and there was morning, a fifth day.

II. Memory Verse
   o Psalm 150:6
   o Let everything that has breath praise the Lord. Praise the Lord!

III. Language
   o Spelling/Handwriting
      - words to know: great, fifth, which, parents
      - The word great ends with the word eat. It's actually the same vowel spelling pattern as your words season and heaven and seas and earth!
      - The word fifth is spelled just as it sounds if you pronounce it really carefully, fif-th.
      - The word which is a question word, which one? Two letters make the W sound.
      - The word parents has two vowels.
   o Vocabulary/Grammar
      - multiply (verse 22)
      - to increase a lot, to become more and more quickly (verb)
         - My love for him multiplied with each passing day.
         - Our rabbits kept multiplying before we had more babies than we knew what to do with.

IV. Lesson
   o We talked about characteristics of birds. Now, let's talk about fish. What do you think makes something a fish? What do all fish have in common? What can you think of?
   o Here's my list.
      - live in water, have fins, have scales
      - They are vertebrates. Do you remember what that means? They have a backbone.
      - They are cold blooded which means their body takes on the temperature of their surroundings.
      - They breathe, take in oxygen, through gills, slits that open on the sides of their bodies.
   o Let me tell you about one amazing fish, the salmon.
      - Salmon are born in a stream. They grow and then make a long journey to the Bering Strait, up near the Arctic Circle in the waters separating Russia from Alaska. They can swim for several years to get there.

- When they arrive, they go back home to where they were born. That means that they have to swim upriver, going opposite of the way the river is flowing. They struggle; they jump up and over waterfalls; they fight their way back to their birthplace. They stop for nothing.
- Why? Because fish obey God, remember? This is what they were created for. They obey their calling despite all the odds against them. They don't let their surroundings or the fact that fish don't swim upstream, against the current, stop them from doing what they are supposed to do.
  - One of our verses today says the God created the "great sea monsters." These are probably related to some of what we know of dinosaurs.
  - Here's one image of sea monsters.

Provided by: http://www.strangescience.net
Originally published in: *Buffalo Land*
Now appears in: *Oceans of Kansas* by Michael J. Everhart

- There has long been a fascination with sea monsters, and stories have been told in many cultures of fierce battles with them in the seas.
  - While most of such stories are considered mythology, since there are so many of these stories, I believe they started somewhere. I believe that sea "monsters" were among the dinosaurs on the earth.
- These animals are since extinct from hunting or changes in their environment. The stories of their impressive frames were passed down and probably changed, as stories tend to be, especially when the stories involve men capturing them or battling them.
  - I will give more evidence for my belief in a future lesson.
- We are still in "prehistory" in the Bible, before records were kept, but we have the Bible as the most accurate record of truth to guide us in knowledge.
- One ancient record we do have is *fossils*. Fossils are the preserved remains of a once living thing.
- Here are some fossil images: bones and a shell in a rock.

V. Discussion
- o What do you think would happen if God hadn't created insects?
  - Imagine the repercussions, the consequences.
  - Would it make the world a better place or a worse place? Why?

VI. Writing
- o Today's vocabulary word was to creep. Was it a noun or a verb? Creeping is something you do. It's an action. That makes it a verb.
- o Nouns can be people, places, or things. So far we've talked about them being things. Find some nouns in the room you are in. Every thing you see is a noun.
- o On your worksheet you'll identify nouns that are things. You'll also be drawing an insect. I hope you remember what makes something an insect.

**Day 8**

I. Read Genesis 1:26.
   26 Then God said, "Let Us make man in Our image, like Us; and let them rule over the fish of the sea and over the birds of the sky and over the cattle and over all the earth, and over every creeping thing that creeps on the earth."

II. Memory Verse
   o Psalm 150:6
   o Let everything that has breath praise the Lord. Praise the Lord!

III. Language
   o Spelling/Handwriting
     - words to know: rule, image, likeness, fish
     - Spelling tips:
       - <u>Rule</u> has the vowel spelling with a silent E at the end of the word. U_E spelling pattern.
       - <u>Image</u> ends with the word age. When a G is followed by an I or an E it has its soft sound. (J instead of G)
       - <u>Likeness</u> is the word like with the suffix, the ending -NESS.
       - The word <u>fish</u> is spelled just like it sounds.
   o Vocabulary/Grammar
     - synonym (rule vs. 26)
     - A synonym is a word of similar meaning. We had the vocabulary word govern. What word in today's verse is a synonym of govern? (noun)
       - rule
       - To rule and to govern mean very similar things. They are synonyms.

IV. Lesson
   o Today we're going to learn about some other creeping things, arachnids. (You say that a-rack-nids.)
     - What are those?
     - The most commonly known arachnid is the spider. What do you know about spiders? What makes them different than insects?
       - My list:
         - Different from insects
           - eight legs
           - no antennae (They have something else for sensing.)
           - two body parts (head and body)
           - none have wings
           - Insects are mostly *herbivores*, meaning they eat plants.
           - Arachnids are mostly *carnivores*, meaning they eat animals.
       - How do you think arachnids might be the same as insects?
         - Same as insects
           - exoskeleton

- invertebrates
- cold blooded
- Can you guess what else might be an arachnid, besides spiders?
  - Here are some: ticks, mites, and scorpions.
- o Spiders build their webs with a strong, fine silk that comes from their abdomen. It is very strong for how thin it is, but you can just knock it down with one swipe.
- o Scorpions are famous for stinging! They have a venomous sting which means they put poison in your body when they sting you. It hurts and can even kill you.
  - They live in hot climate. We had two in our home in Istanbul. One we trapped. One was very small, maybe an inch and a half long, and I squashed it! Yuck again!
- o I asked you on Day 7 what you thought were the repercussions, the consequences, of a world without insects. There would be repercussions because the world was created *interdependent*.
- o Interdependence is how things depend on each other. Let me give you an example.
  - My family loves to eat pizza. It's a big treat. What are we dependent on for that pizza?
    - We are dependent on the store to have workers to make and sell us the pizza.
    - The store is dependent on their ingredient suppliers and their equipment suppliers.
    - They are dependent on the electric and water companies to supply them with electricity and water.
    - The ingredient suppliers are dependent on those who prepare the ingredients.
    - They are dependent on the farmers who are growing the tomatoes for the sauce and the wheat to make the flour for the crust and who are milking the cows that give us the cheese.
    - All of those people are dependent on trucks and truck drivers who carry these ingredients and supplies where they need to go.
    - And the plants are dependent on the sun and the rain or irrigation (watering) system.
    - I'm sure I didn't think of everything. Can you see how there is interdependence? How everything depends on other things?
- o How are you dependent on members of your family? your community? your leaders?
- o Recall: What does interdependence mean? What type of animal is a scorpion?
  - Things are dependent on each other.
  - arachnid
- o Explore more: Learn about a type of arachnid.

V. Discussion
- o God likes it when we rely on Him. He wants us to depend on Him. We should never think that we are alone or need to do something alone. Jesus promises His people that He will always be with us. We are also told that angels are camped out around us. We are not alone.
  - When my daughter was two, she asked why these two men always came on the bus with her and my husband when they went to the Roma community

where we would eventually start a church plant. When she asked, she and my husband were the only ones at the bus stop. We never saw what she saw. We knew they must be angels sent with them.
- o We are dependent on God to take care of us and to provide for us each and every day. That's why we need to be thankful every day.
- o Think of all the ways we are dependent on God and thank Him for each one.
  - Here are some ideas to get you started: the sun, day and night, your functioning body, eyes that know how to clean themselves, your family He placed you in…what are all the ways we are dependent on God just for the food we eat each day?

VI. Writing
- o On your worksheet you'll be finding synonyms, words of similar meaning.
- o Then you'll draw an arachnid.

**Day 9**

I. Read Genesis 1:27-31.
    27 God created man in His own image, in the image of God He created him; male and female He created them.
    28 God blessed them; and God said to them, "Be fruitful and multiply, and fill the earth, and subdue it; and rule over the fish of the sea and over the birds of the sky and over every living thing that moves on the earth."
    29 Then God said, "Look, I have given you every plant that produces seed that is on the surface of all the earth, and every tree which has fruit that has seeds; it shall be food for you;
    30 and to every beast of the earth and to every bird of the sky and to everything that moves on the earth which has life, I have given every green plant for food"; and it was so.
    31 God saw all that He had made, and it was very good. There was evening and there was morning, a sixth day.

II. Memory Verse
    - Psalm 150:6
    - Let everything that has breath praise the Lord. Praise the Lord!

III. Language
    - Spelling/Handwriting
        - words to know: food, surface, male, sky
        - The word food has the U sound spelled with O-O.
        - The word surface ends with the word face. Just like with G, when a C is followed by an I or an E, it has its soft sound. In face, the C says Ssss because it is followed by an E. The beginning of this word starts like surfboard. There are several ways to write the UR sound. This is spelled U-R.
        - The word male is a homophone. This isn't the kind of mail that comes to your mailbox. This is male as in boys and men are male. It is spelled with a silent E at the end.
        - The word sky follows the rules. When a Y comes at the end of a one-syllable word, it has the I sound.
        - Practice syllables. Put your hand under your chin. When you say a word, every time your chin goes down is a syllable. How many syllables do each of your spelling words have?
        - 1, 2, 1, 1
    - Vocabulary
        - subdue (verse 28)
        - to bring under control (verb)
        - How many syllables is subdue?
        - 2

IV. Lesson
    - We have another group of animals to learn about today. You belong to this one! Do you know what it's called?
        - mammals

- You are a mammal. Dogs are mammals. Monkeys are mammals. Rats are mammals. Dolphins are mammals.
- What do you think makes an animal a mammal? What do you think are their characteristics?
- My list:
  - We are vertebrates. We all have spines, backbones.
  - We are warm blooded. We stay about the same temperature whether it's warm or cold outside.
  - We breathe with lungs.
  - We give birth to babies.
  - Mothers have milk for their babies. This sets up a different relationship between mother and child. The child spends more time with its mother and learns survival skills from the mother.
  - This one would be hard to guess from a dolphin, but mammals have hair or fur at some point. Baby dolphins have some whiskers.
- There are more than 4,000 different species of mammals.
  - The smallest is the hog-nosed bat, which weighs 0.05 ounces (1.42 grams).
    - That weighs about as much as one and a half paper clips!
  - The largest is the blue whale, which can be 100 feet long (30.5 meters) and weigh 15 tons (300,000 pounds or 136,000 kilograms). (from http://kids.sandiegozoo.org/animals/mammals, conversions added)
    - That's about the same as seven and a half cars!
- Let's look at sheep because the Bible compares us to sheep.
  - The Bible talks a lot about sheep either following or getting lost.
- Jesus says that His sheep know His voice and follow (John 10:27).
  - I've seen a flock following its shepherd. I didn't even hear him make a noise, but he might have. He just walked past the small flock, they were just standing around, and when he passed, they just turned and followed him. It was so amazing to me.
- Sheep have a very strong *instinct* to follow. They follow the sheep in front of them even if they are leading them into danger. Instinct is a natural reaction you have to do something; you do it with without thinking about it.
  - You blink instinctively when something comes near your eyes. You don't have to decide to blink.
  - Following the leader is instinctive in sheep.
- Here's an interesting sheep fact. Their peripheral vision is so great that they can see behind themselves.
- *Peripheral vision* is what you can see to the sides when you are looking directly forward.
  - How's your peripheral vision? Hold a finger up in front of your face. Stare straight ahead. Move your finger slowly to the side, around the side of your face. How long can you still see it? Make sure you keep looking forward.
- Recall: What are some of the characteristics of mammals? warm-blooded, vertebrates, live babies (as opposed to eggs), moms have milk for their babies, hair
- Explore more: Choose a mammal to learn all about.

V. Discussion (two choices)
    - How are humans like sheep and Jesus like a shepherd?   OR
    - God created a "good" earth. Do you think the earth is still "good"? Why or why not?

VI. Writing
    - On your worksheet today, you'll be identifying which animals are mammals.
    - Complete the Day 9 worksheet in your workbook.

**Day 10**

I. Read Genesis 2:1-3.
   1. Thus the heavens and the earth were completed, and all their armies.
   2. By the seventh day God completed His work which He had done, and He rested on the seventh day from all His work which He had done.
   3. Then God blessed the seventh day and made it holy for Himself, because in it He rested from all His work which God had created and made."

II. Memory Verse
   - Test yourselves on Psalm 150:6.
   - Review Genesis 1:1. In the beginning God created the heavens and the earth.

III. Language
   - Spelling/Handwriting
     - Test yourselves with words from Days 6-10. You can use your workbook.
       - great, fifth, which, parents
       - each, beast, ground, kind
       - rule, image, likeness, fish
       - food, surface, male, sky
   - Vocabulary
     - Test yourselves with words from Days 6-10. You can use your workbook.
       - multiply – to increase a lot, to become more and more quickly
       - creep – to move slowly and carefully, especially in the hopes of not being noticed
       - synonym – word of similar meaning
       - subdue – to bring under control

IV. Lesson
   - We talked about the sun a little on Day 4, about how it lights our world and gives warmth and energy. Today let's talk about the other "light" in the sky; we call it the moon.
   - The moon is really no light at all. It reflects the light of the sun. The sun lights our days and our nights.
   - The sun stands still. We call the sun the center of the solar system. Everything revolves, or *orbits*, around the sun.
   - The moon orbits the earth, meaning it goes around the earth. It draws a circle around the earth. It takes a little less than a month to go around once.
   - From earth we only see one side of the moon.
     - Take three objects for the sun, the moon, and the earth. Have the moon travel around the earth, always facing the earth. The moon never turns its back on the earth.
   - Now what about the different shapes of the moon? We have a new moon, a "thumbnail" moon, a crescent moon, a half moon, a three-quarters moon, and a full moon every month.
     - Can you draw a picture or act out the moon's orbit to figure out what makes us see the moon as these different shapes? Here's a hint. Remember that we

see light. We can only see the part of the moon that the sun's light reflects off of.
- o Did you figure it out? The sun stays still. Only one side of the moon is getting hit with light from the sun.
    - Take your moon. Put the moon between the earth and the sun.
        - Right now, the earth sees the new moon. It's all dark. The earth can't see the side of the moon facing the sun, where the light is. Half of the moon is always lit up by the sun, but earth can't always see that side.
        - Let the moon start orbiting the earth. Stop and observe. What half of the moon is getting light from the sun? What can the earth see of the bright half of the moon? Earth can see part of it, and then finally all of it, and then it starts disappearing again.
        - Can you observe that?
- o Draw a picture of it too if that would help. I think it might.
- o In today's Scripture we read that God rested. He established a day of rest for His people, the Israelites or the Jews, where they could do no work. It was against the law to do any work that wasn't necessary for life. I had a Jewish friend who ripped off toilet paper the day before the Sabbath, the day of rest, so she wouldn't have to work on the Sabbath! When Jesus began His ministry, He spent a lot of time defying Sabbath laws, showing that people are more important than rules.
- o Can I tell you a famous story about rest?
    - Christians used to call Sundays a day of rest and would not work on that day.
    - That's why things are more likely to be closed on Sundays. You don't see that much anymore, but back in 1924, there was an Olympic athlete, a runner named Eric Liddell. He was expected to win the 100-meter race, but he didn't run it. The race was on a Sunday and He wanted to honor God by not working. He went to church instead.
    - His country was upset! (He was British.) He was supposed to win them a gold medal. People didn't understand!
    - He ended up being placed in another race, the 400-meter race, a race four times as long and a race that he hadn't trained for. He won the gold. Someone reminded him that the Bible says God will honor those who honor Him.
- o Recall: What do we call the day of rest? What is it called when the moon goes around the earth or the earth goes around the sun?
    - Sabbath
    - orbit
- o Explore more: Look for pictures of the different phases of the moon. Find out when the moon will rise today and what shape it should see. What are waxing and waning?

V. Discussion
- o What do you think God does when He rests?

VI. Writing
- o On your worksheet today you can practice your spelling and vocabulary.

**Day 11**

I. Read Genesis 2:4-6.
    4   This is the story of the heavens and the earth when they were created.
    5   Now no shrub of the field was yet in the earth, and no plants had sprouted up yet, for the LORD God had not sent rain upon the earth, and there was no one to work in the garden.
    6   But a mist used to rise from the earth and water the whole surface of the ground.

*Genesis 2 is the story of man, beginning with his creation. It's not retelling the whole creation, just the events surrounding man's creation.

II. Memory Verse
- Genesis 1:2
- The earth was formless and void, and darkness was over the surface of the deep, and the Spirit of God was moving over the surface of the waters.

III. Language
- Spelling/Handwriting:
  - Words to know: shrub, sprout, rain, mist
  - Spelling tips:
    - The word shrub has one syllable, so it has one vowel sound.
    - You can hear the word "out" inside sprout.
      - Sprout has the same OU spelling pattern as ground.
    - The word rain has two vowels next to each other making the vowel sound.
    - The word mist is spelled just like it sounds.
- Vocabulary
  - mist
  - a cloud of tiny water droplets near the earth's surface (noun)
  - What is a noun?
    - a person, place, or thing
    - could be the name of a person, place, or thing

IV. Lesson
- Today we're talking about water.
- We learned the word mist. The definition says that mist is a cloud of tiny water droplets. In fact, that's what clouds are, water! Clouds are water in the air, in the form of tiny water droplets. We'll learn more about this in just a minute.
- When there's a mist, you can walk through a cloud. When you are in fog, which is a heavy, thick mist, you are moving through a cloud.
- The verse today says that there was no rain. What makes rain?
  - Rain is part of a water recycling plan God created. Water was created. We cannot make water. All the water we will ever have was created in the beginning. We use the same water over and over again.
- Water on the earth heats up in the sun which *evaporates* it, turns it into a vapor, a gas. The gas floats up.

- You see this when you heat up water on your stove. The water turns into steam and right above the pot is the water vapor. You can see it, but it's a gas at that point, not a liquid. It floats up away from the pot, right?
- The water was heated up and turned into a gas. The gas, or water vapor, travels up. The higher you get in the sky, the cooler it gets. The cool air cools the water vapor and turns it back into water droplets.
- When you see a cloud, you are seeing billions of water droplets. They are so small at this point that there are more than 100 million water droplets in a cubic meter.
  - Stretch your arms out to the side. If you were carrying a box that big with a cloud inside, you would be carrying about 100 million water droplets.
- The water droplets start joining together, getting bigger and bigger. These bigger droplets are easier to see and make the clouds look darker.
  - The droplets at first are too small to even be seen by humans. But as the droplets join together, they get bigger and bigger until they become…? Did you guess what they become?
- They join together to make bigger and bigger drops until they fall as rain. When it rains, that water returns to earth. It was water as a liquid, then as a gas, then as a liquid again. We call this the water cycle.
  - On your worksheet today, you can draw a diagram of the water cycle.
    - water on earth evaporating
    - traveling up as a gas
    - cooling and condensing into water droplets
    - falling as rain

- We need that rain to make things grow. For most of history farming was the main way of life for most people on earth.
- Things were perfect in the beginning.
- We'll read a bit later that God walked with Adam and Eve in the garden. They had a Father talking to them, teaching them.
- Non-biblical histories speak of cavemen who don't even use words to communicate and how it would take thousands of years to develop language and each advancement in how to farm. But we know that Adam and Eve had a Father teaching them!
- Recall: What is the word that describes the process of water heating up and turning into vapor? evaporation
- Explore more: What happens to the evaporated water to make snow instead of rain?

V. Discussion
  - If you were the creator of the earth, what would you have created? What do you think would be the outcome of your new creation?

VI. Writing
  - Today you are going to be fixing sentences in your workbook.
  - A sentence has a subject and predicate.
  - A fragment is just a fragment, a piece, of a sentence.
    - What a cute puppy!
      - That's something you might say, but it's not a sentence. It's just a piece of a sentence.
      - There is no verb.

- The cute, funny kid.
  - That's just the subject. What about it? This isn't a complete sentence.
- Every sentence has one thing wrong with it. Don't forget that all sentences have to begin with a capital letter and end with a period, question mark, or exclamation mark.

**Day 12**

I. Read Genesis 2:7-9.
   7   Then God formed man out of dust from the ground, and breathed into his nostrils, and the man came alive.
   8   God planted a garden toward the east, in Eden; and there He placed the man.
   9   Out of the ground the LORD caused to grow every tree that is nice to look at and that is good for food. He placed the tree of life in the garden, as well as the tree of the knowledge of good and evil.

II. Memory Verse
   - Genesis 1:2
   - The earth was formless and void, and darkness was over the surface of the deep, and the Spirit of God was moving over the surface of the waters.

III. Language
   - Spelling/Handwriting
     - words to know: dust, garden, place, tree
     - Spelling tip:
       - Dust is spelled just like it sounds.
       - Garden has two syllables. Gar is spelled similar to car. Say the end "den" and it will be spelled just like you say it.
       - Place has no S. When a C or G is followed by an I or an E it has its soft sound. That means When a word is spelled with a C-E, like place is, the C says Ssss instead of K.
       - Tree has a double letter for its vowel sound. Can you figure that out?
   - Vocabulary
     - form
     - to create something, to put things together into a shape (verb)
     - You can form your playdough into a ball or a long snake.

IV. Lesson
   - Today we read about God breathing into Adam and giving him breath, life.
   - Let's start learning about our amazing bodies.
   - Today we are going to learn about breathing. In our body it's called the *respiratory system*. That's the system set up in our body that enables us to respire or breathe.
   - All of your body systems act instinctively. You don't have to think about. You just breathe.
   - You take your first breath after you are born. In your mother's womb your lungs were full of amniotic fluid, the liquid you were floating in. Once your body hit the air, you knew it was time to breathe. You just did it.
     - Moms will be interested to learn that the labor process of contractions actually compresses the baby and helps squeeze the fluid out of the lungs so it's ready for that breath.
     - Humans breathe oxygen which we get from the air, but a yet-unborn baby gets its oxygen from its blood. It has extra blood vessels that we don't have.

- All of these changes, to go from fluid to air in the lungs, happen at just the right time, all naturally.
  - Where does the oxygen go? How do you take in oxygen?
    - You take in oxygen through your noses and through your mouths. The air goes through your windpipe.
    - The air then goes into our lungs and our diaphragm.
      - Breathe in deeply. Where do you feel it going? Where do you feel your body expanding? Those places are where your lungs and diaphragm are.
    - Your diaphragm and lungs work together to force air in and out.
  - What happens to the oxygen?
    - The oxygen is used in our blood. When we breathe out, we aren't breathing out oxygen, but gases our bodies don't need.
  - Before we end, I want to look at something called a compass rose. It looks like this.

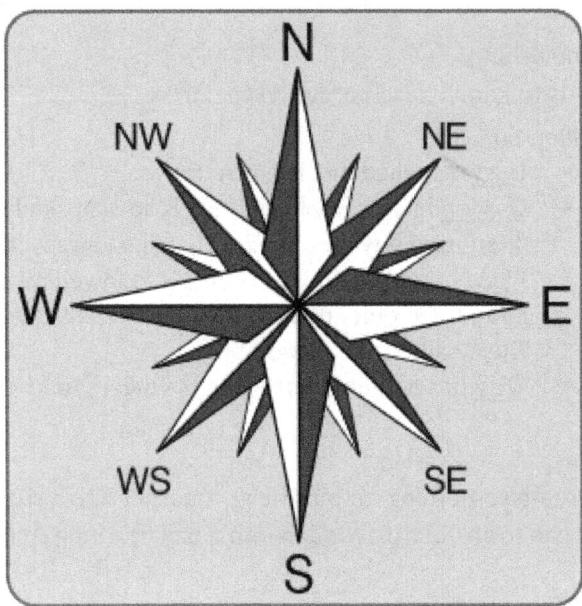

  - The compass rose is the marking on a map that shows which direction is north, south, east, and west. Typically, maps are made with north pointing up.
    - What would a map look like if east was pointing up? south? west?
    - Look at the map for Day 3. The normal way has north at the top. Look at it upside down and sideways. Those are perfectly fine ways to draw a map, just as long as you include the compass rose to tell you which way is north.
    - Before you close the map, find what we call the Far East. Look at the compass rose, if the top of the page is north, where is the east? Find it.
      - We call the area of China and east of it on that map, the Far East.
  - Recall: What does a compass rose tell us? What's the name of the body system that regulates our breathing?
    - respiratory system
    - which way on the map is north

- Explore more: Look up the Far East. What countries are part of it? What are some different things about that part of the world?

V. Discussion
   - Talk about the places you've traveled to. If you want, find them on a map. When have you traveled north, south, east, and west?

VI. Writing
   - Complete your worksheet for today.
   - You are going to be writing a sentence about a place you have visited.
     - For example, I traveled north to visit my grandmother.
   - Make sure your sentence starts with a capital letter and ends with the correct punctuation mark.

**Day 13**

I. Read Genesis 2:10-14.
   10 Now a river flowed out of Eden to water the garden; and from there it split into four rivers.
   11 The name of the first river is Pishon; it flows around the whole land of Havilah, where there is gold.
   12 The gold of that land is good; the bdellium and the onyx stone are there.
   13 The name of the second river is Gihon; it flows around the whole land of Ethiopia.
   14 The name of the third river is Tigris; it flows east of Assyria. And the fourth river is the Euphrates.
   *Note: Some think the flood changed the landscape so that these Eden rivers aren't in the same places today.

II. Memory Verse
   o Genesis 1:2
      • The earth was formless and void, and darkness was over the surface of the deep, and the Spirit of God was moving over the surface of the waters.

III. Language
   o Spelling/Handwriting
      • words to know: name, gold, land, flow
      • Spelling tip:
         ▪ Name is spelled phonetically. The A sound is made with a silent E.
         ▪ Gold has the long O sound but just one vowel. This is similar to kind having a long I sound. Gold is spelled with the word old, which is spelled O-L-D. Bold, fold, and hold are all spelled with that same pattern, so if you can spell gold, you can spell bold, fold, and hold as well!
         ▪ Land ends with the word and.
         ▪ Flow has the same O sound as row and blow. It's written with a vowel and a consonant which can also say, "Ow!"
   o Vocabulary
      • flow (verse 10)
      • to move smoothly and continuously (used as a verb)

IV. Lesson
   o We're not going to learn about rivers flowing today. We will do that another day, but I want to talk about another kind of flow. On Day 12 we learned that the blood in our body transports the oxygen to all of the places it's needed. Let's learn about how the heart works to supply our bodies with blood. This is called the *circulatory system*.
   o The main organ that functioned in the respiratory system was your lungs.
   o The main organ that functions in the circulatory system is your heart.
      • An *organ* is just a piece of the body that is contained in itself and serves a specific function, like the lungs taking in oxygen or the heart pumping out blood.

- o  Place your right hand on your chest. Can you feel your heart beating? If not, run around and then try again.
- o  You can also feel the blood moving through your body. Place two fingers across your wrist and press a little. Do you feel something? (You can also try with two fingers on the side of your neck.)
    - What did you feel? It was a pulse. You didn't feel a constant rush. You felt it and then didn't, felt it, then didn't. We call this our pulse.
        - The smaller the animal (that's you) the faster the pulse.
    - When you felt your heart beating, it was pulsing. Your heart sends out blood in bursts.
- o  With each pulse your heart is beating. What's happening when your heart beats?
    - It's moving blood in and out.
- o  Look at the inside of your wrist. Can you see blueish lines? Those are *veins.* Your veins carry the blood throughout your whole body. It's like a road system in your body. It starts with a large tube at the heart, an artery called the aorta, which sends out the blood with oxygen in it. It branches out to smaller arteries and then capillaries which deliver the blood. The blood then returns through our veins.
    - I used a lot of new words there.
        - Arteries are the main branches of the circulatory system.
        - The aorta is like a highway and the other arteries are the exit ramps.
        - The capillaries are the final destinations.
        - Then veins bring the blood all back home to the heart.
- o  Recall: What's the name of the system in our bodies that regulates our blood flow?
    - circulatory system
- o  Explore more: Learn how blood moves through the heart or just follow the arrows with your finger and follow where the blood enters and leaves the heart.

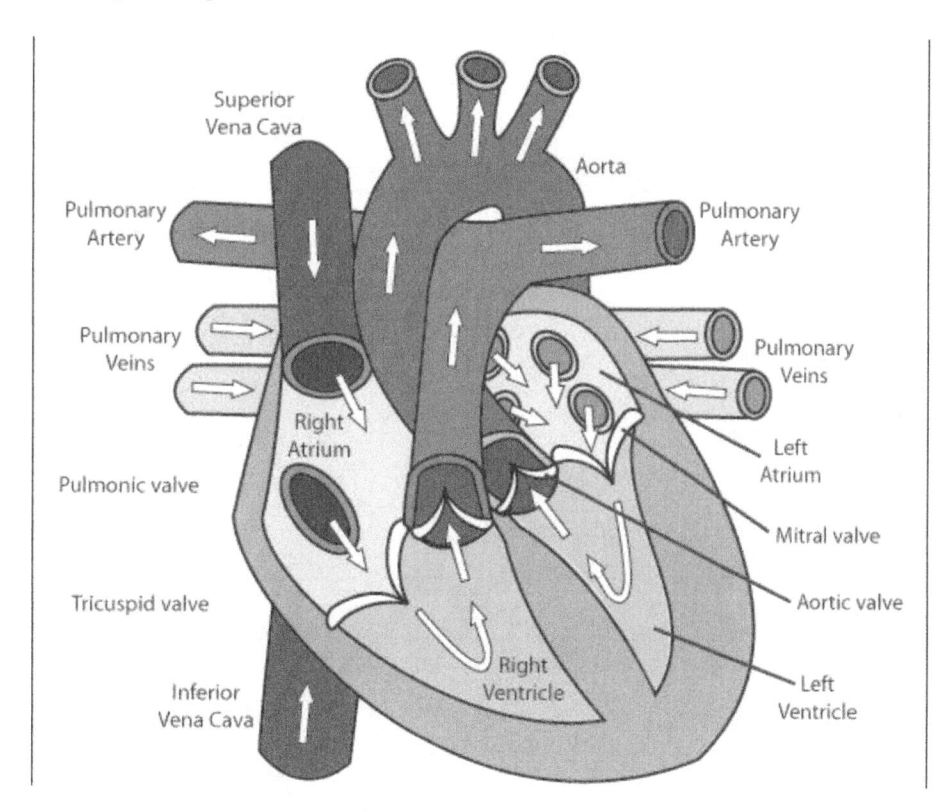

V. Lesson, cont.
- You drew an upside down or sideways map on Day 12. Today make a map of your neighborhood. You can use your workbook page.
- Draw streets. Put on at least some houses. Decide on a symbol for a house.
- You will draw on a compass rose. (Did you figure out the other day which way was north?)
- You will put a key on your map. A key is where you will draw your symbols and write what they mean.
- Do you have a playground or store in your neighborhood? firehouse? Make a symbol for anything you add to your map and add it to your key.
- If you live in the middle of "nowhere," you could have symbols for trees, creek, etc.
- Explore more: If you are feeling ambitious, you could measure some distances in your neighborhood, or even yard, and make your map to scale. It doesn't have to be precise. You could measure in steps.

VI. Discussion
- What do you wish you had in your neighborhood? Why?

VII. Writing
- Complete your worksheet for today.

**Day 14**

I. Read Genesis 2:15-17.
   15  Then the Lord God took the man and put him into the garden of Eden to be its keeper.
   16  The Lord God commanded the man, saying, "From any tree of the garden you may eat as much as you want;
   17  but from the tree of the knowledge of good and evil you must not eat because the day that you eat from it you will die."

II. Memory Verse
   o Genesis 1:2
      - The earth was formless and void, and darkness was over the surface of the deep, and the Spirit of God was moving over the surface of the waters.

III. Language
   o Spelling/Handwriting
      - words to know: die, saying, want, because
      - spelling tips:
         - Die uses two vowels next to each other to make the vowel sound.
         - Saying starts with the word say which has one vowel. It ends like the words day and play.
         - Want ends with the word ant.
         - Because is a tricky word you need to practice, but the good news is that you use it a lot, so you'll get practice with it. It breaks into the syllables be and cause. Cause has three vowels and ends with a silent E.
   o Vocabulary
      - command (verse 16)
      - to give an order in a way that says you mean it (verb)

IV. Lesson
   o The man was the keeper of the garden. What do gardens need to grow?
      - Here's my answer:
         - sunlight: All living things need energy. Plants get theirs from the sun.
         - water: Living things need water.
         - nutrients: Nutrients will help them grow bigger and stronger.
            - Nutrients are found in the soil. We get our nutrition from eating healthy foods full of vitamins and minerals. Plants eat minerals too. They need lots of nutrients just like us.
            - Do you recognize the names calcium, potassium, and iron? They are all things you need and plants need them too.
               o Do you know where we get our calcium from?
                  - It is found in dairy products such as milk.
               o Do you know where we get iron from?
                  - It is found in protein products such as meats.
               o Do you know where we get potassium from?

- It is found in fruits and veggies such as bananas and potatoes.
- *Agriculture* is the practice of farming.
- Early civilizations relied on agriculture, on farming. Do you know what a civilization is? Try to define it.
  - A civilization is a group of people that are organized in how they live and interact together.
  - They relied on farming to supply their food to survive.
- Take a look in your Map Book for Day 14. The area between the two rivers, the Euphrates and the Tigris, is known as "the cradle of civilization."
  - What do you think that term means? What's a cradle?
  - A cradle is used for babies. This is where civilization was in its infancy. It's where the first cities were born.
- Cities sprouted along rivers. Why do you think?
  - Water is necessary for life, right?
  - With water to support large numbers, large numbers of people could gather together in one place.
- The area that we are talking about, between the rivers, is known as the Fertile Crescent.
  - Look at the last map for Day 14 to find it. The Fertile Crescent is crescent shaped, though it looks more like a boomerang really. It stretches from the northern part of the Nile, across Israel, and over the area of Mesopotamia, and covering the land surrounding and between the Euphrates and the Tigris.
- What do all those areas have in common?
  - Water!
  - Water is what makes that area *fertile*. That means the land is good for farming. It's easy to grow crops there.
- Recall: Why is it called the Fertile Crescent? What is agriculture?
  - Fertile means land that it is good for farming. The crescent-shaped area of land is around water which makes the ground ideal for growing crops.
  - farming
- Explore more: See what modern-day countries are part of the Fertile Crescent, or start to grow something. What would make your soil fertile?

V. Discussion
- God made man to cultivate the land. Why does God make man work for a living? Why doesn't God just create the food ready to go?

VI. Writing
- On your worksheet today, you will be writing sentences, commands. Here are some examples. They all end in an exclamation point. You aren't asking them nicely. You are commanding them, letting them know they better do it right now!
  - Go to your room!
  - Come here now!
  - Put it down here!
  - Throw away your trash!

**Day 15**

I. Read Genesis 2:18-20.
   18  Then God said, "It is not good for the man to be alone; I will make him a helper, someone suited just for him."
   19  Out of the ground the Lord God formed every animal that lived on land and every bird that lived in the sky, and brought them to the man to see what he would call them; and whatever the man called a living creature, that was its name.
   20  The man gave names to all the cattle, and to the birds of the sky, and to every beast of the field, but for Adam there was not found a helper just right for him.

II. Memory Verse
   o Test yourselves on Genesis 1:2.
     • The earth was formless and void, and darkness was over the surface of the deep, and the Spirit of God was moving over the surface of the waters.
   o Review Psalm 150:6.
     • Let everything that has breath praise the Lord. Praise the Lord!

III. Language
   o Spelling/Handwriting
     • Test yourselves on the spelling words from Days 11-14. You can use the spaces on your worksheet.
       ▪ shrub, sprout, rain, mist
       ▪ dust, garden, place, tree
       ▪ name, gold, land, flow
       ▪ die, saying, want, because
   o Vocabulary
     • Test yourselves on your words from Days 11-14.
       ▪ mist – a cloud of tiny water droplets near the earth's surface
       ▪ form – to create something, to put things together into a shape
       ▪ flow – to move smoothly and continuously
       ▪ command – to give an order

IV. Lesson
   o In the verses we read today, Adam names all of the animals. We have names for all of the animals too.
   o To make it easy for scientists to know what they are talking about, a very specific pattern of classifying animals was developed. To *classify* is to arrange into categories.
   o We've actually been talking about animal *classes* when we were talking about mammals, reptiles, birds, etc.
   o Here's an example. You'll notice that the kingdom is animals. This classification system is not just for animals. We use it for all living things.
   o (Note: Read each category name and classification and then everyone can guess what the animal is based on the new information in each level. With each new level, they will receive more information and can change their guess.)

Kingdom: Animal
Phylum: Vertebrate
Class: Mammal
Order: Carnivore
Family: Cat
Genus: Panther
Species: Tiger

- o   Here are some of the orders of mammals.
    - primates: includes monkeys
    - mammals with pouches: includes kangaroos
    - insect-eating mammals: includes shrews
    - flying mammals: just the bats
    - rodents, includes squirrels: there are about as many of these as the rest combined
    - carnivores: includes dogs, anything that eats meat
    - even-toed hoofed animals: includes the gazelle
- o   There is also a plant kingdom. We'll get to that another day, but I want to talk more about farming today.
- o   People were settled in Mesopotamia in order to farm since about 4000 BC. This agricultural society relied on water from the river to *irrigate*, or water their crops. They got the water to their fields by digging ditches between them and the river.
- o   A main crop would have been wheat and barley. What would those crops have been used for?
    - Those are grains and are used for making bread products. Their bread may not have been anything like we know it. It was likely flat.
    - Here is the work they put into eating a piece of bread.
        - Grain has to be planted and tended.
        - When the grain is ready, ripe, it is cut down.
        - Grain is then bundled up.
        - Grain is then threshed, beaten about. Nowadays threshing is done by machine, but then it wasn't. During threshing the grain falls off of the stalk.
        - Grain is gathered and then it is winnowed. To winnow grain, it is tossed up and the wind blows away the chaff, the little bits of straw. This is making the grain pure for consumption (that's eating!) Grain can be poured back and forth while the wind does its job. Jesus talks about a winnowing fork (Matthew 3:12). It was used to toss grain up into the wind. The kernels of wheat would fall back down and the chaff would be blown away.
        - Grain is then ground into flour on a flat rock using another rock as the grinding tool.
        - Then it's ready to use for cooking.
        - How important do you think grain was to their lives? How much of their lives do you think revolved around grain?
        - We'll learn later that the Egyptians used bread as currency (as money). Can you understand why it would be valuable?

- o Recall: What does it mean to classify something? How did ancient peoples irrigate their fields?
  - arrange it into categories
  - To irrigate the land means to water it, so that's when they dug ditches to carry water from the rivers to their land.
- o Explore more: You could learn the classification of a favorite animal, or create an irrigation system either for your plant (can you send water down through a straw?) or just to move water. You don't have to dig a ditch to do it.

V. Discussion
- o Do you think you could name every animal? Rename an animal and tell why you chose the name.

VI. Writing
- o Choose one of your writings from Days 12-14 to edit.
- o Read it out loud to look for things that don't make sense, don't flow, or just don't sound right.
- o Look for spelling mistakes. Check for correct capitalization and punctuation.
- o Check that your sentences have subjects and predicates.
- o You can use an editing checklist to help you look for problems.
- o Have someone older than you check it over once you've fixed it. (You can fix it by just making marks on the page to note changes.)
- o Listen to their corrections and suggestions and make changes to your writing.
- o Make a final draft. Rewrite it or type it.

**Day 16**

I. Read Genesis 2:21-25.
21   So the Lord God caused a deep sleep to fall upon the man, and he slept; He took one of his ribs and then closed him up.
22   The Lord God took the rib from the man and used it to form a woman, and brought her to the man.
23   The man said, "This is now bone of my bones, and flesh of my flesh; she shall be called woman, because she was taken out of Man."
24   For this reason a man shall leave his father and his mother, and be joined to his wife; and they shall become one flesh.
25   And the man and his wife were both naked and were not ashamed.

II. Memory Verse
- Romans 3:23
- For all have sinned and fall short of the glory of God.

III. Language
- Spelling/Handwriting
  - words to know: bone, join, sleep, ashamed
  - spelling tips:
    - Bone is spelled with a silent E.
    - Join has an O-I that spells the OY sound.
    - Sleep is spelled with a double letter. (Hint: Think of all the ways you could write the E sound.)
    - Ashamed follows the rules. The A sound is made with a silent E. Say the word in parts as you spell it.
- Vocabulary
  - ashamed  (verse 22)
  - feeling very embarrassed and guilty over something you did that was bad (adjective)
    - An adjective is a word that describes. Ashamed describes a person and how they are feeling.
  - Maybe you have felt ashamed if you called someone a bad name when you were angry.

IV. Lesson
- We're going to learn about the skeletal system. The skeletal system is all of your bones and how they fit together to hold you up! What bone did we read about in our Scriptures today?
- I'm sure you figured out that it was a rib.
  - Try to count how many ribs you have. Maybe lying down would make it easier. How many did you come up with?
  - People have 24 ribs, 12 on each side. (Men don't have one less rib; Adam lost one, but he had been created with a complete set and his kids of course were born complete.)

- Those rib bones are part of what we call the *rib cage*. Why do you think God created a cage inside of us? What is the cage guarding?
  - Your ribs are a protection for your heart and lungs.
- You have 206 bones. You have lots of small bones in your toes and fingers. In fact, you have 27 bones in just one hand.
  - The smallest bone is actually in your ear and measures just two and a half millimeters in length. How big is that?
  - The largest bone is called the *femur*. Can you guess which bone is that?
    - It's your thigh bone.
- You have another bone that's made to protect an organ like the rib cage protects your heart and lungs. Feel your head. It feels hard. What bone is under there?
  - It's called your *skull*.
  - Why do you think it's important to have a thick, solid skull?
    - Your skull protects your brain. Your skull has an important job!
- One last question...what would you look like without bones?
  - You would be nothing but a blob on the ground!
- Before we end our lesson, I want to tell you about some marriage traditions. What do two people do in your country in order to marry?
- My family lived for seven years both in Macedonia and in Turkey. Here are some of their wedding traditions.
- In Macedonia there are numerous traditions as part of the wedding ceremony.
  - Symbolic foods are prepared and everything is done by ritual.
  - There is a ritual haggling over the "price" of the bride.
  - There are superstitions over who the new couple's children will look like based on things that happen that day.
  - The bride's family can wail when she leaves the house, mourning the loss of their daughter. This is really a fake thing done for display. The bride is supposed to look sad that she is leaving her family.
- The Roma weddings in Macedonia last seven days.
  - The bride is "bought" with gifts from the husband's family. The groom's family buys everything, even the woman's wedding dress for her.
- In Turkey there are two days to a wedding, two parties.
  - The first party is for when the bride is decorated with henna; she gets a painted tattoo.
  - The second day is the wedding celebration. There is lots of dancing at both parties. On the second night the couple stands up front and everyone pins money to their clothing. The bride is dressed in a fancy dress, but it does not have to be white.
- Recall: What's the name of the biggest bone in your body and where is it? What's the name of the bone that protects your brain?
  - femur, thigh bone
  - skull
- Explore more: Learn some bone names or look at pictures of skeletons.

V. Discussion
  - Today's question. What is marriage?

VI. Writing
- o We have learned that things are nouns. Other things can be nouns as well. Places are nouns. Here are some places: the beach, the grocery store, the park. They are places and they are nouns.
- o Find the places in the sentences and mark them as nouns. Look for things too!

**Day 17**

I. Read Genesis 3:1-7.
   1. Now the serpent was sneakier than any beast of the field which the Lord God had made. And he said to the woman, "Did God really say, 'You may not eat from any tree of the garden'?"
   2. The woman said to the serpent, "We may eat from the fruit of the trees of the garden;
   3. but God said, 'You may not eat the fruit from the tree in the middle of the garden or touch it, or you will die.'"
   4. The serpent said to the woman, "You surely will not die!
   5. For God knows that when you eat from it your eyes will be opened, and you will be wise like God, knowing good and evil."
   6. When the woman saw that the tree was good for food and delightful to look at, and that the tree's fruit would make them wise, she took a piece of fruit and then ate it; and she gave a piece of fruit to her husband with her, and he ate.
   7. Then the eyes of both of them were opened, and they knew that they were naked; so they sewed fig leaves together and made themselves coverings.

II. Memory Verse
   - Romans 3:23
   - For all have sinned and fall short of the glory of God.

III. Language
   - Spelling/Handwriting
     - words to know: sew, open, piece, together
     - spelling tips:
       - <u>Sew</u> is a word that trips up foreigners I know. Sew is spelled like the word new, so they pronounce it sue. This is one you just need to memorize how it's spelled.
       - <u>Open</u> is a combination of O and pen.
       - <u>Piece</u> is spelled following the rules, but it's a little tricky. It follows the rule that I comes before E except after C. The E sound is spelled with an I and an E. Which comes first? The S sound is made with a C. A C followed by an I or an E has its soft sound, so C says S instead of K.
       - To spell the word <u>together</u> just say the parts. To- Ge- Ther  Each syllable always has at least one vowel (A-E-I-O-U).
   - Vocabulary
     - serpent (verse 1)
     - snake (noun)
     - Serpent and snake are synonyms (words with similar meaning).

IV. Lesson
   - We've learned that water brings life. Sin brings death. Let's stick with life. We mentioned the Tigris and the Euphrates. Where are they?
     - They are in the Fertile Crescent.
   - What do you know about rivers?
     - All rivers begin and end somewhere. Do you know where all rivers end?

- All rivers run into the seas and oceans.
- All that moving water is headed towards the seas and oceans. It's a good thing there is evaporation. Why?
    - Evaporation takes water out of the ocean and back into the sky. If water didn't evaporate out of the ocean, what would happen as all that river water kept going into the ocean?
    - The oceans would overflow. Sea level would go up and cover land and houses!
  - We use the term "sea level" when we talk about how high ground is. Mountain peaks are a certain number of miles (kilometers) above sea level. Why are there few land areas below sea level? (There are things below sea level, such as tunnels, but in general land is above sea level.)
    - The water would flow over it. Think of it this way. Picture a bathtub with water in it. That's sea level, where the water comes up to. What happens to anything that goes below the water level?
      - It's covered in water. That's why most land is above sea level. Anything below sea level has to have a barrier, some sort of wall keeping the water out.
  - All rivers run down to sea level.
  - So why do rivers run down to sea level? The key word is down. Sea level is the lowest point.
    - *Gravity* pulls everything on earth downward towards the earth.
    - Gravity is what makes things fall down when there's nothing to hold it up. It's also what holds you to the earth! Did you ever think about how you need to be held down so you wouldn't float away?
  - Find the two largest rivers in the world, the Nile and the Amazon. People argue over which is longest. Look in Egypt in Africa using the Middle East map from Day 16. You can find the Amazon on the South America map for Day 17. Hint: Look for where they empty out into the sea and ocean.
    - There's a dispute over which is longer.
  - We've talked about how early civilizations relied on rivers for life. Check out the Cities and Rivers map for Day 17. The rivers are blue. The big cities are marked with black dots. Are the biggest cities still near rivers? Why or why not? What do you think?
    - Now look at the map showing rivers in comparison to the state boundaries. Do you think rivers played a role in creating boundaries of territories?
  - There is also a *topographical* map of America for Day 17; that's a map that shows elevation.
    - The key is hard to read but the bottom is the lowest elevation and the top of the key shows the color for the highest elevation.
  - Recall: What's the name of the type of map that shows elevation? What's the lowest level of land that's not under water? What pulls everything down towards earth?
    - topographical
    - sea level
    - gravity
  - Explore more: If you like, you could make a clay model of a topographical map. You would build up where the land has a higher elevation.

V. Discussion
- o What would the world be like without gravity?

VI. Writing
- o Complete your worksheet for today.
- o You are going to draw a picture showing a river flowing. It needs to start high, maybe on a mountain, and then flow down to the ocean.

**Day 18**

I. Read Genesis 3:8-21.
   8 In the evening, Adam and Eve heard the sound of God walking along in the garden, and the man and his wife hid themselves in the trees to hide from God.
   9 Then the Lord God called to the man, "Where are you?"
   10 He said, "I heard You in the garden, and I was afraid because I was naked; so I hid myself."
   11 And He said, "Who told you that you were naked? Have you eaten from the tree that I commanded you not to eat from?"
   12 The man said, "The woman You gave to be with me, she gave me the fruit, and I ate."
   13 Then the Lord God said to the woman, "What is this you have done?" And the woman said, "The serpent deceived me, and I ate."
   14 The Lord God said to the serpent,
   "Because you have done this,
   you are more cursed than any other animal;
   On your belly you will go,
   And dust you will eat
   All the days of your life;
   15 And I will put hatred
   Between you and the woman,
   And between your children and hers;
   Her children will bruise you on the head,
   And you will bruise him on the heel."
   16 To the woman He said,
   "I will greatly multiply
   Your pain in childbirth,
   Your husband will rule over you."
   17 Then to Adam He said, "Because you have listened to the voice of your wife, and have eaten from the tree about which I commanded you, saying, 'You shall not eat from it';
   Cursed is the ground because of you;
   You will work hard to grow food
   All the days of your life.
   18 "Both thorns and thistles it shall grow for you;
   And you will eat the plants of the field;
   19 By the sweat of your face
   You will eat bread,
   Till you return to the ground,
   Because from it you were taken;
   For you are dust,
   And to dust you shall return."
   20 Now the man called his wife's name Eve, because she was the mother of all the living.
   21 The Lord God made garments of skin for Adam and his wife, and clothed them.

II. Memory Verse
   o Romans 3:23
   o For all have sinned and fall short of the glory of God.

III. Language
- o Spelling/Handwriting
    - words to know: children, head, face, command
    - spelling tips:
        - <u>Children</u> starts with the word child. Pronounce it slowly and carefully to spell it.
        - <u>Head</u> starts like the word heaven. Two letters are making that short E sound.
        - <u>Face</u> you have written before, at the end of the word surface.
        - <u>Command</u> has a double letter and ends with the word and.
- o Vocabulary
    - deceive (verse 13)
    - make someone believe something that isn't true (verb)
    - You can deceive your parents by letting them believe you cleaned up the mess when really it was a sibling that did it.

IV. Lesson
- o Today we're going to talk about serpents, but first, let's talk about reptiles.
- o What is a reptile? What makes one animal a reptile and another animal not? Think about it. What's your list of reptile characteristics?
- o Here's my list:
    - They are vertebrates. What does that mean?
        - It means they have a backbone.
    - They are cold-blooded. What does that mean?
        - They need to get their warmth from the sun. Their bodies take on the temperature of their environment.
    - They have dry, scaly skin. Scales are like small sections of skin put together. In some animals they overlap and in others they don't. Why do you think they have scaly skin?
        - One purpose for their skin is to be armor for the animal, providing protection.
    - They lay eggs on land. Their eggs have a soft shell. That's different than bird eggs. For instance, you know that chicken eggs have a hard shell that we have to crack to open.
- o Now let's talk about snakes, the serpent from our story.
- o Snakes are reptiles, so they are cold blooded and vertebrates. Their backbone is very bendable!
- o They are carnivores. What does that mean?
    - They only eat animals, not plants. What animals do you think they eat?
        - Snakes consume a variety of items including termites, rodents, birds, frogs, small deer and other reptiles. Snakes eat their prey whole and are able to consume prey three times larger than the diameter of their head because their lower jaw can separate from the upper jaw. To keep prey from escaping, snakes have rear-facing teeth that hold their prey in their mouths.
        (from http://www.defenders.org/snakes/basic-facts)

- - Snakes range from tiny to huge, from just four inches to thirty feet long. That long snake is called a python. It can eat things like a small deer, but it only has to eat once a year. Snakes don't have to hunt daily.
  - Snakes live in a variety of habitats. They can live in the desert, on the prairie, in forests, and even underwater.
    - Most snakes, though, live in tropical weather, the hot and humid forested areas of the world.
  - A *venomous* snake is a poisonous snake. It injects a poison into its prey when it bites.
  - How can you tell a venomous snake from a non-venomous snake?
    - There are a lot of ideas about this, but with so many exceptions, they aren't very helpful. In America, poisonous snakes are mostly very big and fat. If the snake has a rattle on its tail, it's venomous. The rattle shakes to warn you to back off. If you are bitten and there are fang marks, two closely set puncture wounds, then it was a poisonous snake. A ragged cut would be from a regular snake. Only venomous snakes have fangs. Venomous snakes also have broad heads.
  - Recall: What are some characteristics of reptiles?
    - vertebrates, cold-blooded, dry and scaly skin, lay eggs on land
  - Explore more: You could look at maps at where snakes live, or it might be fun to measure 4 inches and 30 feet. How big are those snakes?

V. Discussion
  - The snake in the story today talked. Eve blamed the snake for her sin. Was Eve responsible for her sin or was it not her fault? Do you ever blame others when you've done something wrong?

VI. Writing
  - Complete your workbook page for today.

**Day 19**

I. Read Genesis 3:22-24.
22 Then the Lord God said, "Look, the people have become like God, knowing good and evil. Now, they might reach out, and take fruit from the tree of life, and eat, and live forever."
23 So, the Lord God sent him out of the garden of Eden, to work on the land from which he was taken.
24 God drove Adam and Eve out; and at the east of the garden of Eden He stationed the cherubim and the flaming sword which turned every direction to guard the way to the tree of life.

II. Memory Verse
- Romans 3:23
- For all have sinned and fall short of the glory of God.

III. Language
- Spelling/Handwriting
  - words to know: station, look, become, might
  - spelling tip:
    - <u>Station</u> ends with T-I-O-N. The I in T-I-O-N does the job of the silent E and makes the A say its name.
    - <u>Look</u> has the same vowel combination as good.
    - <u>Become</u> is the words be and come put together.
    - <u>Might</u> has the same spelling pattern as night and light, two words you've already had. If you can spell night or light, you can spell might.
- Vocabulary
  - to station (verse 24)
  - to put someone in a position in a particular place for a particular purpose (verb)
    - (Note: Have your child station you in a particular place for a particular purpose. You can decide if you want to fulfill your purpose!)

IV. Lesson
- We've been learning about different types of animals. I want to also learn about where they live.
- An animal's home environment is called its *habitat*. An animal habitat is the environment where it can get the food, water, and shelter it needs for survival.
- When I say there are 10,000 species of a certain type of animal, that's not an exact number. The truth is that we can't count the number of animal species out there. There are probably more than 30 million insect species alone!
  - And each animal has its own habitat, its home.
  - These homes, however, intersect and overlap.
  - They can be grouped together into certain types of habitats. We call the broad characteristics of the habitats, *biomes*.
  - Here's a list of the world's major biomes.
    - grasslands

- tundra, in polar regions
- deserts
- mountains
- salt water
- fresh water
- coral reefs
- rainforests
- deciduous forests
- coniferous forests
  - *Deciduous* trees are broadleaf trees, the kind that lose their leaves in winter.
  - *Coniferous* trees are pine trees. They have needles.
    - Why do we call coniferous trees evergreens?
      - They stay green in the winter unlike deciduous trees where the leaves change color when the weather cools.

- What is necessary in a habitat? Every animal has different requirements. The Monarch butterfly for instance, is an herbivore, but it only eats milkweed plants. That's a requirement for its habitat.
  - Let me tell you something amazing about the Monarch. Those butterflies living in America travel to Mexico, to a specific region. This is similar to the salmon all knowing where to go in the Arctic Circle.
  - The parents leave and die, but the babies hatch and know where to go to head to their parents' home in America!
  - They have a very specific habitat that sustains them, most notably the presence of the milkweed plant.
- When we look at different *biomes*, the characteristics of large habitats, remember that God made it all specifically as well. It all works together: the environment, the climate, the plants, the animals, etc. all work together and depend on each other. They are interdependent.
- Another thing we're dependent on is the calendar. You can decide later if you agree with that, but first, I want to explain how we talk about time.
- We count years from before and after Jesus was born, sort of.
- We use the symbols AD and BC next to year numbers.
  - AD stands for the Latin, Anno Domini, or in the year of the Lord.
  - BC stands for Before Christ. One is in Latin and the other English because BC came much later. When the division of the calendar was created, I guess maybe only the present and the future were considered important.
- In this system there is no year zero. There is no bull's-eye zero date when Jesus was born.
- Before Jesus was born we count down to His birth, like counting down to a rocket launch. Here's a mini timeline to help you answer the questions. (Note: Show your child where each date would be on the timeline to help them answer.)

3000 BC        2000 BC        1000 BC        1BC    1AD        1000 AD        2000 AD

- Which is more recent: the year 2000 BC or the year 500 BC?

- 500 BC is more recent.
- Which is older? A civilization that was around 3000 BC or 2000 BC?
  - 3000 BC is older.
- When you get to 1 BC, the next year is 1 AD. Then we start counting up.
  - Which is older: 7 AD or 500 AD?
    - 7 AD is older.
  - Which is more recent: 1700 AD or 2000 AD?
    - 2000 AD is more recent.
- Recall: What does BC stand for? What is a habitat?
  - Before Christ
  - the home of a living thing
- Explore more: What habitats are in your yard or in your house?

V. Discussion
- How important is a calendar? Is it good that we have one? What would the world be like without one? What if every country or every state had their own calendar? (Note: Ethiopia has their own calendar. It's years off of ours. My Ethiopian friend says it's because they started counting as soon as they heard about Jesus. Think of the story about the Ethiopian eunuch.)

VI. Writing
- Complete your workbook page for today.
- You will be putting years in order and drawing a habitat. Think about what animal you would like to draw.

**Day 20**

I. Read Genesis 4:1-7.
1. Now the man and his wife Eve had a son, Cain, and she said, "I have gotten a male child with the help of the Lord."
2. Then Eve gave birth to his brother Abel. Abel became a shepherd, a keeper of flocks, but Cain was a farmer.
3. So it came about after a time that Cain brought an offering to the Lord of the fruit of the ground.
4. Abel brought of the first young animals of his flock and of their fat portions. The Lord was pleased with Abel and his offering;
5. but Cain and for his offering He was not. So Cain became very angry, and his face showed it.
6. Then the Lord said to Cain, "Why are you angry? Why are you upset?
7. If you do the right thing, won't you be smiling again? And if you do not do what is right, sin is crouching at the door and wants you to join him, but you must not."

II. Memory Verse
- Test yourselves on Romans 3:23.
  - For all have sinned and fall short of the glory of God.
- Review Genesis 1:2.
  - The earth was formless and void, and darkness was over the surface of the deep, and the Spirit of God was moving over the surface of the waters.

III. Language
- Spelling/Handwriting
  - Test yourselves on your words from Days 16-19.
    - bone, join, sleep, ashamed
    - sew, open, piece, together
    - children, head, face, command
    - station, look, become, might
- Vocabulary
  - Test yourselves on your words from Days 16-19.
    - ashamed – feeling very embarrassed and guilty over something you did that was bad
    - serpent – snake
    - deceive – make someone believe something that isn't true
    - to station – to place someone in a particular place for a particular purpose

IV. Lesson
- We're going to look at one of the major biomes today, the desert.
- We've talked about the Fertile Crescent. That land is fertile because of its location along water, but it's really a desert region. That's why the whole region wasn't known as fertile.
- What do you know about the desert?
- Here are some things to know about the desert.

- What defines a desert is that it has very little rain. We call cold weather deserts the tundra.
- Today I'm talking about hot-weather deserts. They will usually have less than 10 inches (25 cm) of rain each year.
- Is there life in the desert?
    - Yes. There are living things created to survive in what we would consider to be a harsh environment.
    - They still need water, but God has made a way. Many animals get water from plants. The most famous desert plant is the cactus.
        - Instead of leaves, it has spines, sort of like scales for a plant. These are close to the plant and reduce the exposure to wind and sun which lessens how much water is lost to evaporation.
        - A cactus stores water in its stem which is very large compared to other plants. Think of how a cactus stem compares to the stem of a flower!
    - One desert animal is the ostrich.
        - The ostrich is a very fast bird, on the ground. It cannot fly, but it can run as fast as a car on the highway.
        - Since ostriches can't fly, they are nomads, wandering from place to place to find food and water, not settling in one certain location.
            - Actually, a lot of their water comes from food. There is water inside all living things, and so the ostrich gets water from the things it eats.
  - Like the ostrich, Cain was a nomad, a wanderer.
  - In an agricultural society people have to stay put. Farming takes place in one location. Your farmland can't be packed up and taken with you! People settled where there was good land for farming, where it was fertile.
  - When people settled, they set up homes, businesses, places of worship, etc.
  - Nomads didn't. They wandered about without any permanent home. They traveled with tents for their shelters that could be taken down and carried along. They may have used camels to carry loads.
  - Nomads often had herds. They would drive their animals on to find more food for them. When they'd cleared an area, they could move on.
  - They could also have been involved in *trade*. Trade is buying and selling without money. They could take items gained in one area and take them to new places. They could trade one thing for another and in that way introduce new ideas, materials, foods, spices, fabrics, etc. to different areas.

- o  Recall: What is a nomad? How could they have helped develop civilization? What makes something a desert?
    - a wanderer
    - By trading they could introduce new ideas and materials into areas.
    - very little rainfall
- o  Explore more: Learn about nomadic people such as the Bedouins or about a desert plant or animal.

V. Discussion
- o  Look at verse 7 from today's Scripture reading. What should have Cain done?

VI. Writing
- o  Your worksheet today is for your spelling and vocabulary.

# Day 21

I. Read Genesis 4:8-12.
   8   Cain told Abel his brother. And it came about when they were in the field, that Cain came against his brother Abel and killed him.
   9   Then the Lord said to Cain, "Where is Abel your brother?" And he said, "I do not know. Am I my brother's keeper?"
   10  He said, "What have you done? The voice of your brother's blood is crying to Me from the ground.
   11  Now you will be cursed from the ground, which has opened its mouth to receive your brother's blood from your hand.
   12  When you farm the land, it will no longer produce food for you; you will be a wanderer on the earth."

II. Memory Verse
   o   1 Corinthians 10:13
   o   No temptation has overtaken you but such as is common to man; and God is faithful, who will not allow you to be tempted beyond what you are able, but with the temptation will provide the way of escape also, so that you will be able to endure it.

III. Language
   o   Spelling/Handwriting
       - words to know: Cain, came, brother, farm
       - spelling Tips:
           * <u>Cain</u> is a name. All names begin with a capital letter. It has the same vowel spelling pattern as rain, where two vowels together make the first one say its name.
           * The next word is in the past tense. It tells us about something that already happened. He came over here yesterday. <u>Came</u> ends with a silent E.
           * The word <u>brother</u> ends like the word together. Remember that every syllable has to have a least one vowel. The beginning of the word says, "bro."
           * The word <u>farm</u> has the AR sound just like garden. If you can spell "gar," then you can spell "far."
   o   Vocabulary
       - wanderer (verse 12)
       - A wanderer is someone who wanders. To wander means to move around, not really with any specific direction.

IV. Lesson
   o   Let's go to a different biome today. Let's learn about the frozen desert, the tundra.
   o   The most famous tundra environment is Antarctica. It's a continent with no country. It's used only for scientific exploration and a little sightseeing.
       - Do you know what shape Antarctica is?

- It's located at the South Pole. On a map it's a strip of land across the bottom, but on a globe, and in real life, it's more like a circle covering the bottom of the earth. Take a look at the map for Day 21.
- The opposite end of the earth, on top of the globe, is the Arctic. That's the location of the North Pole.
- The northern and southern hemisphere have opposite seasons, so when it is summer in the North Pole, it is winter in the South Pole.
- In the dark of winter, the tundra can reach temperatures of -130 degrees Fahrenheit (90 degrees below zero in Celsius). The highest ever recorded temperature is 58 degrees Fahrenheit (14 degrees Celsius).
- Just like the hot deserts, the tundra has very little *precipitation*, or what falls from the sky, and of course what does come is snow.
- Is there plant life in Antarctica?
  - While most of the continent is solid ice, the coastal areas, which are the warmer areas, can sustain green life during the short summer. In Antarctica you can find moss and lichen mostly. You say lichen, liken.
  - When my family visited Finland, a cold-weather climate, the ground was very spongy to walk on in places because of moss and lichen (pictured).

- What animals do you think live in Antarctica?
  - There are several kinds of seals, whales, and penguins there as well as the albatross, a bird.
  - The most famous of the penguins is the emperor penguin, which is the largest of them all, standing at over three feet tall.
  - It's the only animal of Antarctica that has babies in winter. The father protects the penguin egg, holding it on top of his feet and covering it with the folds of his belly. He stands like that for two months to keep his baby alive.
  - The mother is off feeding during this time. Then the mother will return and take the egg and the father will get to go eat. This happens right around the time the egg hatches.
  - To survive the harsh winter, the dad penguins huddle together, all squeezed in. They don't do anything except keep their babies warm. They fast for months.
- Most of the green on Antarctica is found on its *peninsula*.
  - Look at the map of Antarctica for Day 21.
  - The peninsula is the part that sticks out (on the upper left).

- - The definition of peninsula is that it has water on three sides.
    - That's different than an island which has water on all sides.
  - Look at the map of America on Day 20. Can you find another peninsula? What about on the world map on Day 2? (Note: Look on the maps before continuing.)
    - America has a sunny one in the southeast. Much of the state of Florida is a peninsula.
    - The country of Italy is another famous peninsula.
  - Recall: What is the name of an area of land that has water on three sides? What is precipitation?
    - peninsula
    - what falls from the sky (rain, snow, etc.)
  - Explore more: Maybe you'd like to learn more about emperor penguins, or maybe glaciers would be interesting to you to learn about.

V. Discussion
  - In what ways are we responsible to be our brother's keeper? In what ways are we not responsible?

VI. Writing
  - Peninsula and precipitation are both nouns, both things.
  - Cain, one of our spelling words today, was a person. A person is also a noun.
  - Wanderer was our vocabulary word. A wanderer is a person. Any person is a noun.
  - On your worksheet today, you'll find nouns that are things and that are people.

**Day 22**

I. Read Genesis 4:13-15.
   13 Cain said to the Lord, "My punishment is too hard!
   14 Lord, You have driven me away from my land; and I will be hidden from your face. I will be a wanderer on the earth, and whoever finds me will kill me."
   15 So the Lord said to him, "Therefore whoever kills Cain, vengeance will be taken on him sevenfold." And the Lord appointed a sign for Cain, so that no one finding him would kill him.

II. Memory Verse
   o 1 Corinthians 10:13
   o No temptation has overtaken you but such as is common to man; and God is faithful, who will not allow you to be tempted beyond what you are able, but with the temptation will provide the way of escape also, so that you will be able to endure it.

III. Language
   o Spelling/Handwriting
      - words to know: hard, said, away, find
      - spelling Tips
         ▪ The word hard has the same AR sound as farm.
         ▪ The word said is one you just have to learn how to spell it. You'll use it a lot in writing and you'll read it often. The vowel sound is made with an A-I.
         ▪ The word away is written a – way. Way is spelled with the same pattern as say. You have already had saying as a spelling word, so you can spell say.
         ▪ The word find has the same spelling pattern as kind. We've already had kind as a spelling word, and if you can spell kind, you can spell find.
   o Vocabulary
      - vengeance (verse 15)
      - revenge (noun)

IV. Lesson
   o Do you think Cain had anything else to fear besides man? Did humans have to fear wild animals back then? Do you think Cain ran into a dinosaur? We talked about reptiles before. Let's look at these largest of reptiles.
      - The largest reptiles we know of are the dinosaurs which are *extinct*, which means none live any more. The stories that exist in cultures around the world of sea monsters and fire-breathing dragons, though possibly exaggerated, began with real encounters I believe.

      One interesting thing to note is that there are universal stories of giant reptiles. These stories have been told in different cultures, in different regions of the world, and through different centuries, yet all of these people have similar stories. Evolution scientists say that dinosaurs lived millions of years before humans and that they never had contact. If that were true, how did these stories begin? They didn't learn about dinosaurs from fossils. Fossils of dinosaurs were not found until hundreds of years after these stories were told.

- o Since I'm talking about supposed dinosaur myths, let's talk about mythology in cultures. What is a myth?
    - a myth is a make-believe story
- o Some call the Bible mythology. I don't.
- o Some would call stories of fire-breathing dragons mythology. It's likely such stories have been changed and exaggerated as time goes on, which is what happens with oral histories, where new generations learn history through storytellers.
- o Do you know any myths from your culture?
- o In America we have the myth of Paul Bunyan.
    - Paul Bunyan is the tale of a frontiersman who was so big and strong he could do anything. He is told to have cleared much of western America for the pioneers.
    - One of the stories is about how he found Babe, his blue ox. It was blue because he found it in the blue snow. Why was the snow blue?
        - "Well now, one winter it was so cold that all the geese flew backward and all the fish moved south and even the snow turned blue. Late at night, it got so frigid that all spoken words froze solid afore they could be heard. People had to wait until sunup to find out what folks were talking about the night before."
        (*Babe the Blue Ox* retold by Schlosser http://americanfolklore.net/folklore/2010/07/babe_the_blue_ox.html)
    - The most famous mythology comes from Greece. The stories revolve around a number of gods who had Zeus as their ruler. He was called the god of the sky and thunder and ruled from Mount Olympus (in Greece).
    - Let me tell you one of the Greek myths that is sometimes referenced in literature. The character is Achilles.
        - In the story, Achilles is the best Greek fighter among those fighting against the Trojans.
        - He could only be harmed in one area, his Achilles tendon.
            - Above your heel run your finger up. Do you feel a line going up from your heel? That's it.
        - The myth is that his mother dipped him in a special river that made him invincible, except she was holding him by the back of his heel.
        - In battle he was hit by an arrow, where?
        - When we say that something is our Achilles' heel, we are saying that it is our downfall. It's what caused us to fail.
- o Recall: What is a myth? What does it mean if an animal is extinct?
    - a made-up story
    - The animal is no longer in existence. They all have died.
- o Explore more: Read a Paul Bunyan story. (You can search online for a kid's story of Paul Bunyan read aloud.) You could, of course, learn about some dinosaurs. Specifically, you could see what you can learn about what the Bible calls "behemoth."

V. Discussion
- o Did Cain have the right to argue with God about his punishment? Was God wrong to protect Cain? What do you think it says about God that He does protect Cain?

VI. Writing
- o Today you are going to write sentences using the word said.
- o You are going to tell what someone else said.
- o There are examples on the page.

**Day 23**

I. Read Genesis 4:16-20.
   16   Then Cain went out from the presence of the Lord, and settled in the land of Nod, east of Eden.
   17   Cain's wife gave birth to Enoch. Cain built a city and called the name of the city Enoch, after the name of his son.
   18   Now to Enoch was born Irad, and Irad became the father of Mehujael, and Mehujael became the father of Methushael, and Methushael became the father of Lamech.
   19   Lamech took to himself two wives: the name of the one was Adah, and the name of the other, Zillah.
   20   Adah gave birth to Jabal; he was the father of those who dwell in tents and have livestock.

   *Jabal, was he in agriculture or was he a nomad?

II. Memory Verse
   o 1 Corinthians 10:13
   o No temptation has overtaken you but such as is common to man; and God is faithful, who will not allow you to be tempted beyond what you are able, but with the temptation will provide the way of escape also, so that you will be able to endure it.

III. Language
   o Spelling/Handwriting
     - words to know: father, city, tents, two
     - spelling Tips:
       - The word <u>father</u> does not have an O. The ER sound at the end of a word is most often spelled the same way. You've spelled it in the words over, together, and brother.
       - The word <u>city</u> follows two spelling-pattern rules. When a C is followed by an E or an I, it will have its soft sound, S. When a word of more than one syllable ends with a Y, the Y has the E sound.
         - Words that are longer than one syllable and end with an E sound, probably end with a Y.
         - All rules are broken sometimes, but these are the general rules.
       - <u>Tents</u> is a plural noun. Just make tent plural by adding one letter.
       - <u>Two</u> has a funny spelling. This is a homophone. It sounds just like other words, but it is spelled differently. This isn't, "I want to go to the store too." This is the number two. It is spelled with three letters. The middle one is silent. This is one you just have to learn how it is spelled. Use it in your writing to practice.
   o Vocabulary
     - presence (verse 16)
     - being there, whether seen or not  (noun)

IV. Lesson
   o Cain was the father of those who cared for livestock. Livestock are farm animals, usually referring to things like horses and cows. What type of animals are those?

- mammals
  o We're going to look at another mammal today, one that's mentioned in the Bible.
  o Do you remember the things that make an animal a mammal, that make you a mammal?
    - (Note: You can look back to Day 10 if you want to check.)
  o The animal we're going to learn about today is the gazelle.
  o Gazelles can go anywhere easily, even up a mountain slope, even escaping those chasing after it.
  o So, what makes the gazelle move so easily? Let's see if we can find out. What can you observe about gazelles from these pictures?

Picture info: "תמונה 1108" by avishai teicherUser:Avi1111 - Own work. Licensed under Public domain via Wikimedia Commons - http://commons.wikimedia.org/wiki/File:%D7%AA%D7%9E%D7%95%D7%A0%D7%94_1108.jpg#mediaviewer/File:%D7%AA%D

- The second picture is an ancient mosaic of a mountain gazelle. The picture was found in Israel.
- What did you observe about its body, legs, and feet? How do you think those things might help it be fast and agile?
- Let me tell you some things you can't observe.
  - There are 19 species of gazelle, most live in the plains of Africa and Asia, but there are gazelles that live in mountains. They are in the same family as sheep. They range in size from about two to five feet tall.

- They have smaller hearts, which need less oxygen, which helps them with their endurance, being able to run longer.
- Gazelles don't run. They pronk or stott. It's a leap where they spring from all four feet.
- Did you notice the hooves in the mosaic?
  - They protect their feet, helping them run faster and go on all sorts of land and rock.
- All of this makes for speeds of up to 60 miles an hour. (That's nearly 100 km/hr.) That's about the speed of a car on a highway. But not only that, they can maintain a fast speed without having to stop. This means they can outrun fast predators who have to stop and catch their breath! Their coasting speed is half their sprinting speed, which is probably about as fast as your parents drive near your home.
- Gazelles live in the wild. Livestock are animals that people control.
- In what ways do people rule over animals?
  - Here are some I thought of:
    - pets
      - They have become man's friend, but live in their homes under their control. Pets are *domesticated;* they are tame, not wild. People use animals for companionship or entertainment.
    - working animals
      - Another type of domesticated animal are animals that work for humans. This includes animals such as horses, oxen, and camels that carry people or loads or pull wagons or carts. There are other working animals such as animals in shows. Have you ever seen a dog do tricks for money? People use animals for their profit.
    - farm animals
      - These are also domesticated animals. While some farm animals work, others are for producing wool, milk, eggs or meat. People have the power to kill animals and eat them.
- Recall: What is the name for an animal that is tame, not wild? What are some special things about the gazelle?
  - domesticated
  - pronk, fast, hooves
- Explore More: Learn about animal training or try it out! Watch videos of gazelles pronking or look up a related animal, such as the antelope.

V. Discussion
- What would you name your parents or describe them as, for instance, the father of those who dwell in tents and have livestock?

VI. Writing
- Today you are going to write plurals.
- Plurals are when there is more than one.

- Today you are going to write the letter S on the ends of the nouns to make them plural.
- Plus, it will give you practice spelling the number two!

**Day 24**

I. Read Genesis 4:21-24.
   21 His brother's name was Jubal; he was the father of everyone who played the lyre and pipe.
   22 As for Zillah, she also gave birth to Tubal-cain, who made tools of bronze and iron; and the sister of Tubal-cain was Naamah.
   23 Lamech said to his wives,
   "Adah and Zillah, Listen to my voice,
   You wives of Lamech, Pay attention to my speech,
   For I have killed a man for wounding me;
   And a boy for striking me;
   24 If Cain is avenged seven times,
   Then Lamech seventy-seven times." *What kind of person is Lamech?

II. Memory Verse
   o 1 Corinthians 10:13
   o No temptation has overtaken you but such as is common to man; and God is faithful, who will not allow you to be tempted beyond what you are able, but with the temptation will provide the way of escape also, so that you will be able to endure it.

III. Language
   o Spelling/Handwriting
      - words to know: tools, seven, time, also
      - spelling Tips:
         - Tools is a plural noun. The vowel sound is made with a double letter.
         - Seven has two Es and no other vowels. It looks like it should say "see-ven."
         - Time has a silent E.
         - Also ends with the word so. It has four letters. The "all" part just has one L.
   o Vocabulary
      - strike (verse 23)
      - to hit suddenly with a lot of strength (verb)

IV. Lesson
   o The man today made tools out of iron and bronze.
   o Bronze is made from other elements. It is made of copper and tin mixed together.
   o What do tin, copper, bronze, and iron all have in common?
      - They are metals.
   o We know they are useful for tools. Do you know what else bonze is used for?
      - Bronze and brass are both made from copper and are often used to mean the same or similar thing. There may be bronze or brass fixtures in your home. It's used in architecture.
      - It's a useful metal around things that can catch on fire because it doesn't cause sparks like some other metals.
      - It is used in sculptures and has been used in coins as well.

- In ancient times bronze was used to make weapons.
  - What is iron used for?
    - Iron is used to make other metals, similar to how bronze is made of copper and tin.
    - You may have an iron skillet in your home.
    - Iron is useful to plants. It's a nutrient that keeps them healthy.
    - Iron keeps you healthy too. Iron, in fact, is needed to carry oxygen through your blood.
      - Meats have a lot of iron. Some greens have a lot of iron, such as spinach.
  - I also want to look at a metal mentioned in Genesis 2, gold.
    - Gold is a pure substance. It can be broken down to a single atom of gold.
    - Gold is considered a *precious metal*. What does it mean if we call something precious?
      - It means it has great value.
    - Gold is the only yellow metal. It's also very malleable, meaning it can be bent and stretched and hammered into different shapes (which is how we get our gold jewelry). Gold can even be made into threads for sewing and hammered so thin that it can be eaten!
      - I've never eaten gold, but if I did, it wouldn't taste like anything, but it's not toxic, meaning it's safe to put in your mouth.
  - There's a period in history known as the Bronze Age. It's considered to be around 3300 BC through 1200 BC.
  - It's the period of history when people started making bronze tools instead of using stone tools.
    - It happened at different points for different civilizations. It happened earliest in the part of the world we've looked at so far, in Mesopotamia.
  - The end of the Bronze Age came because people started making tools with another metal. Can guess which one?
    - Iron
  - The flood probably happened around 2300 BC, so that happens during this period. Abraham was around 2000 BC, so he was alive during this period.
  - It was a period of history where there were big new inventions.
    - It was the start of using written communication. Civilizations developed ways of writing.
    - It was when the wheel was invented.
  - Recall: What does it mean if a metal is precious? What marked its beginning and end?
    - valuable
    - the discovery of bronze, the discovery of iron as a use for tools
  - Explore More: What are other precious minerals? Look up archeology tool finds.

V. Discussion
  - What would be your saying you'd want to be known for?

VI. Writing
  - On your worksheet today, you'll write plurals again.
  - Then you design a tool. What tool would you want to have?

**Day 25**

I. Read Genesis 4:25-26.
   25 Eve gave birth to a son, and named him Seth. She said, "God has given me another child in place of Abel, for Cain killed him."
   26 To Seth, to him also a son was born; and he called his name Enosh. Then men began to call upon the name of the Lord.

   *Think about this time period. People are living a long time and having lots of children. Some are farmers (like Abel) and are establishing agricultural areas, and others are nomadic (like Cain) and are herders. God had not yet given permission to kill and eat animals, but we read of Lamech who killed men and children who messed with him. It seems likely someone like that might kill an animal! What do you think it was like then? Today we read how they began to call on God. What was happening before then? What happened after that? What do you think? What do you wish you knew about this time period?

II. Memory Verse
   - Test yourselves.
     - Say 1 Corinthians 10:13 from memory.
   - Review Romans 3:23.
     - For all have sinned and fall short of the glory of God.

III. Language
   - Spelling/Handwriting
     - Test yourselves on your words from Days 21-24. You can use your worksheet for this.
       - Cain, came, brother, farm
       - hard, said, away, find
       - father, city, tents, two
       - tools, seven, times, also
   - Vocabulary
     - Test yourselves on your words from Days 21-24. You can use the worksheet activity for this.
       - wanderer – someone who wanders - To wander means to move around, not really with any specific direction.
       - vengeance – revenge
       - presence – being there, whether seen or not
       - strike – to hit suddenly with a lot of strength

IV. Lesson
   - People started to call on the name of the Lord. People throughout history have called on many different gods, including the sun and moon.
   - Why do you think ancient people worshiped the sun and the moon?
     - The sun and the moon seemed so powerful and magical to ancient people.
   - Ancient peoples around the world had ceremonies to honor these celestial bodies and to scare away whatever might harm them.

- It's extremely sad. The Bible talks about those who worship the creation instead of the Creator. How much greater is the one who made the creation!
- Even more foolish are those who worship statues that they call gods. The statues are made with human hands, but they sacrifice to them and pray to them.
- Satan takes advantage of these false religions and uses his demons to act among the worshipers. They may see supernatural things, but they aren't from God!
- They are tormented by fear. Our God tells us to be free from fear!
  - Those caught in false religions feel the constant need to please or appease their false god.
- They need to know that the one true God gives salvation as a free gift and desires us to love Him, not sacrifice to Him.
- They need to know there is a God who loves them and wants to be with them and who will care for them as opposed to gods who don't care about human life.

o That's one way to tell true religion from false religion. True religion loves people. People are most important.
o Let's stay out in outer space for a science lesson.
o We talked about stars and the sun and moon which are all part of the heavens. Let's talk about what else is out there in the universe.
o The Sun, Moon, and Earth are part of what is known as our Solar System. Earth is a planet. There are eight planets in our solar system with a couple of dwarf (smaller) planets as well. The sun is at the center, meaning all of the planets orbit around the sun. That's our *solar system*, the planets and moons that orbit our sun. Earth is the only planet that humans can live on. Any farther from the sun and it would be too cold, any closer, too hot. It perfectly rotates to give us day and night, and orbits to give us the seasons of the year.
o I'm going to tell you the order of the planets. Pay attention and then name which planet is the closest and farthest. The order of the planets, from the closest to the farthest from the sun is: Mercury, Venus, Earth, Mars, Jupiter (the biggest), Saturn (known for the rings around it), Uranus, and Neptune. The most famous dwarf planet is Pluto because it comes next and used to be considered one of the planets.
  - Did you catch which is closest to the sun?
    - Mercury is a mere 36 million miles from the sun (58 million kilometers.)
  - Which planet is the farthest?
    - Neptune is the farthest from the sun. It's 2.8 billion miles away from the sun (4.5 billion kilometers). Pluto is even farther.
o Our sun, which is a star, is part of the Milky Way galaxy; the Milky Way has over 200 billion stars in it. That's what a galaxy is, a group of stars.
  - Astronomers, those who study the stars and planets, have observed 80 galaxies. It's hard to imagine just how big our universe is!
    - Think of it this way. It's like the room you are sitting in is a galaxy. A piece of dirt in the room is the sun. How small would you be then?
o Recall: What is a solar system? What is a galaxy?
  - rocks orbiting a star (planets and moons orbiting a star like the sun)

- a group of stars
  - Explore more: Look at pictures of the Milky Way. Look for something that shows the relative size of things in the universe.

V. Discussion
  - When have you called upon the Lord?

VI. Writing
  - On your worksheet today, you'll be doing the spelling and vocabulary review.

**Day 26**

I. Read Genesis 5:1-2.
   1 This is the book of the generations of Adam. In the day when God created man, He made him in the likeness of God.
   2 He created them male and female, and He blessed them and named them Man in the day when they were created.

II. Memory Verse
   - Review Genesis 1:1. Can you say it from memory?
   - Find it in the Bible. (This shouldn't be hard!)
   - "In the beginning God created the heavens and the earth."

III. Language
   - Spelling
     - Have a spelling bee. (Parent: Read a word from Day 5's worksheet. Choose one they didn't have trouble with. Have them spell it out loud.)
     - If you want to do a spelling activity here are ideas.
       - Write words with sidewalk chalk.
       - Write words with invisible ink.
       - Write words by pressing down and then reveal them by coloring lightly over the words.
       - Color a page and then color over it in black. Write the words by scratching off the black.
       - Write the words with letters cut out of magazines.
       - Write the words with yarn.
       - Write the words in the air or on each other's back.

IV. Lesson
   - Complete the worksheet for Day 26.

**Day 27**

Genesis 5:3-5.
- 3 When Adam had lived one hundred and thirty years, he became the father of a son in his own likeness, according to his image, and named him Seth.
- 4 Then the days of Adam after he became the father of Seth were eight hundred years, and he had other sons and daughters.
- 5 So all the days that Adam lived were nine hundred and thirty years, and he died.

II. Memory Verse
  - Review Psalm 150:6. Can you say it from memory?
  - Find it in the Bible.
  - "Let everything that has breath praise the Lord. Praise the Lord!"

III. Language
  - Spelling
    - Have a spelling bee. (Parent: Read a word from Day 5's worksheet. Choose one they didn't have trouble with. Have them spell it out loud.)
    - If you want to do a spelling activity here are ideas.
      - Write words with sidewalk chalk.
      - Write words with invisible ink.
      - Write words by pressing down and then reveal them by coloring lightly over the words.
      - Color a page and then color over it in black. Write the words by scratching off the black.
      - Write the words with letters cut out of magazines.
      - Write the words with yarn.
      - Write the words in the air or on each other's back.

IV. Lesson
  - Complete the worksheet for Day 27.

**Day 28**

I. Read Genesis 5:6-7.
    6  When Seth had lived 105 years, he became the father of Enosh.
    7  After he became the father of Enosh, Seth lived 807 years and had other sons and daughters.

II. Memory Verse
- Review Genesis 1:2. Can you say it from memory?
- Find it in the Bible.
- The earth was formless and void, and darkness was over the surface of the deep, and the Spirit of God was moving over the surface of the waters.

III. Language
- Spelling
    - Have a spelling bee. (Parent: Read a word from Day 10's worksheet. Choose one they didn't have trouble with. Have them spell it out loud.)
    - If you want to do a spelling activity here are ideas.
        - Write words with sidewalk chalk.
        - Write words with invisible ink.
        - Write words by pressing down and then reveal them by coloring lightly over the words.
        - Color a page and then color over it in black. Write the words by scratching off the black.
        - Write the words with letters cut out of magazines.
        - Write the words with yarn.
        - Write the words in the air or on each other's back.

IV. Lesson
- Complete the worksheet for Day 28.

**Day 29**

I. Read Genesis 5:8-10.
   8  Altogether, Seth lived a total of 912 years, and then he died.
   9  When Enosh had lived 90 years, he became the father of Kenan.
   10 After he became the father of Kenan, Enosh lived 815 years and had other sons and daughters.

II. Memory Verse
   o Review Romans 3:23. Can you say it from memory?
   o Find it in the Bible
   o For all have sinned and fall short of the glory of God.

III. Language
   o Spelling
      - Have a spelling bee. (Parent: Read a word from Day 10's worksheet. Choose one they didn't have trouble with. Have them spell it out loud.)
      - If you want to do a spelling activity here are ideas.
         - Write words with sidewalk chalk.
         - Write words with invisible ink.
         - Write words by pressing down and then reveal them by coloring lightly over the words.
         - Color a page and then color over it in black. Write the words by scratching off the black.
         - Write the words with letters cut out of magazines.
         - Write the words with yarn.
         - Write the words in the air or on each other's back.

IV. Lesson
   o Complete the worksheet for Day 29.

**Day 30**

I. Read Genesis 5:11-14.
   11 Altogether, Enosh lived a total of 905 years, and then he died.
   12 When Kenan had lived 70 years, he became the father of Mahalalel.
   13 After he became the father of Mahalalel, Kenan lived 840 years and had other sons and daughters.
   14 Altogether, Kenan lived a total of 910 years, and then he died.

II. Memory Verse
   - Review 1 Corinthians 10:13. Can you say it from memory?
   - Find it in the Bible.
   - No temptation has overtaken you but such as is common to man; and God is faithful, who will not allow you to be tempted beyond what you are able, but with the temptation will provide the way of escape also, so that you will be able to endure it.

III. Language
   - Spelling
     - Have a spelling bee. (Parent: Read a word from Day 15's worksheet. Choose one they didn't have trouble with. Have them spell it out loud.)
     - If you want to do a spelling activity here are ideas.
       - Write words with sidewalk chalk.
       - Write words with invisible ink.
       - Write words by pressing down and then reveal them by coloring lightly over the words.
       - Color a page and then color over it in black. Write the words by scratching off the black.
       - Write the words with letters cut out of magazines.
       - Write the words with yarn.
       - Write the words in the air or on each other's back.

IV. Lesson
   - Complete the worksheet for Day 30.

**Day 31**

I. Read Genesis 5:15 -17.
    15  When Mahalalel had lived 65 years, he became the father of Jared.
    16  After he became the father of Jared, Mahalalel lived 830 years and had other sons and daughters.
    17  Altogether, Mahalalel lived a total of 895 years, and then he died.

II. Memory Verse
    o   We're going to learn Genesis 1:3.
    o   Then God said, "Let there be light"; and there was light.

III. Language
    o   Spelling
        - Have a spelling bee. (Parent: Read a word from Day 15's worksheet. Choose one they didn't have trouble with. Have them spell it out loud.)
        - If you want to do a spelling activity here are ideas.
            - Write words with sidewalk chalk.
            - Write words with invisible ink.
            - Write words by pressing down and then reveal them by coloring lightly over the words.
            - Color a page and then color over it in black. Write the words by scratching off the black.
            - Write the words with letters cut out of magazines.
            - Write the words with yarn.
            - Write the words in the air or on each other's back.

IV. Lesson
    o   Complete the worksheet for Day 31.

**Day 32**

I. Read Genesis 5:18 -20.
   18  When Jared had lived 162 years, he became the father of Enoch.
   19  After he became the father of Enoch, Jared lived 800 years and had other sons and daughters.
   20  Altogether, Jared lived a total of 962 years, and then he died.

II. Memory Verse
   o  Genesis 1:3.
   o  Then God said, "Let there be light"; and there was light.

III. Language
   o  Spelling
      • Have a spelling bee. (Parent: Read a word from Day 20's worksheet. Choose one they didn't have trouble with. Have them spell it out loud.)
      • If you want to do a spelling activity here are ideas.
         ▪ Write words with sidewalk chalk.
         ▪ Write words with invisible ink.
         ▪ Write words by pressing down and then reveal them by coloring lightly over the words.
         ▪ Color a page and then color over it in black. Write the words by scratching off the black.
         ▪ Write the words with letters cut out of magazines.
         ▪ Write the words with yarn.
         ▪ Write the words in the air or on each other's back.

IV. Lesson
   o  Complete the worksheet for Day 32.

**Day 33**

I. Read Genesis 5:20-24.
   20 Altogether, Jared lived a total of 962 years, and then he died.
   21 When Enoch had lived 65 years, he became the father of Methuselah.
   22 After he became the father of Methuselah, Enoch walked faithfully with God 300 years and had other sons and daughters.
   23 Altogether, Enoch lived a total of 365 years.
   24 Enoch walked faithfully with God; then he was no more, because God took him away.

   *Enoch was one of two people in the Bible who never physically died before going to be with the Lord. The other was Elijah. God just took them. What's the Bible's description of Enoch?

II. Memory Verse
   o Genesis 1:3.
   o Then God said, "Let there be light"; and there was light.

III. Language
   o Spelling
       • Have a spelling bee. (Parent: Read a word from Day 20's worksheet. Choose one they didn't have trouble with. Have them spell it out loud.)
       • If you want to do a spelling activity here are ideas.
           ▪ Write words with sidewalk chalk.
           ▪ Write words with invisible ink.
           ▪ Write words by pressing down and then reveal them by coloring lightly over the words.
           ▪ Color a page and then color over it in black. Write the words by scratching off the black.
           ▪ Write the words with letters cut out of magazines.
           ▪ Write the words with yarn.
           ▪ Write the words in the air or on each other's back.

IV. Lesson
   o Complete the worksheet for Day 33.

**Day 34**

I. Read Genesis 5:25 -29.
   25 When Methuselah had lived 187 years, he became the father of Lamech.
   26 After he became the father of Lamech, Methuselah lived 782 years and had other sons and daughters.
   27 Altogether, Methuselah lived a total of 969 years, and then he died.
   28 When Lamech had lived 182 years, he had a son.
   29 He named him Noah and said, "He will comfort us in the labor and painful toil of our hands caused by the ground the Lord has cursed."

II. Memory Verse
   o Genesis 1:3.
   o Then God said, "Let there be light"; and there was light.

III. Language
   o Spelling
      - Have a spelling bee. (Parent: Read a word from Day 25's worksheet. Choose one they didn't have trouble with. Have them spell it out loud.)
      - If you want to do a spelling activity here are ideas.
         ▪ Write words with sidewalk chalk.
         ▪ Write words with invisible ink.
         ▪ Write words by pressing down and then reveal them by coloring lightly over the words.
         ▪ Color a page and then color over it in black. Write the words by scratching off the black.
         ▪ Write the words with letters cut out of magazines.
         ▪ Write the words with yarn.
         ▪ Write the words in the air or on each other's back.

IV. Lesson
   o Complete the worksheet for Day 34.

**Day 35**

I. Read Genesis 5:29 -32.
   29  He named him Noah and said, "He will comfort us in the labor and painful toil of our hands caused by the ground the Lord has cursed."
   30  After Noah was born, Lamech lived 595 years and had other sons and daughters.
   31  Altogether, Lamech lived a total of 777 years, and then he died.
   32  After Noah was 500 years old, he became the father of Shem, Ham and Japheth.

   *I repeated verse 29. When was the ground cursed? Did you notice how old Noah was before he had children? Here are the other ages listed for when fathers had their first son: 130, 105, 90, 70, 65, 162, 65, 187, 182. Noah was 500. It reminded me of Abraham and Hannah as well as Zacharias and Elizabeth, all who had to wait for a child. It seems to be a pattern in the Bible. Why do you think God might choose to make His people wait?

II. Memory Verse
   o  Can you say Genesis 1:1-3 from memory?
      1  In the beginning God created the heavens and the earth.
      2  The earth was formless and void, and darkness was over the surface of the deep, and the Spirit of God was moving over the surface of the waters.
      3  Then God said, "Let there be light"; and there was light.

III. Language
   o  Spelling
      - Have a spelling bee. (Parent: Read a word from Day 25's worksheet. Choose one they didn't have trouble with. Have them spell it out loud.)
      - If you want to do a spelling activity here are ideas.
         - Write words with sidewalk chalk.
         - Write words with invisible ink.
         - Write words by pressing down and then reveal them by coloring lightly over the words.
         - Color a page and then color over it in black. Write the words by scratching off the black.
         - Write the words with letters cut out of magazines.
         - Write the words with yarn.
         - Write the words in the air or on each other's back.

IV. Lesson
   o  Complete the worksheet for Day 35.

**Day 36**

I. Read Genesis 6:3-4.
   3   The Lord said, "My Spirit will not put up with people forever, because they are just flesh; however, they will live one hundred and twenty years."
   4   The Nephilim were on the earth in those days, and also afterward, when the sons of God married the daughters of men, and they had children. Those were the mighty men who were of old, men of renown.

II. Memory Verse
   o  1 John 1:9
   o  If we confess our sins, He is faithful and just to forgive us our sins and to cleanse us from all unrighteousness. (KJV)

III. Language
   o  Spelling/Handwriting
      • words to know: mighty, twenty, forever, sons
      • spelling tips:
         ▪ You just need to add one letter onto might to turn it into mighty. When a Y is on the end of a two-syllable word, it has the E sound.
         ▪ The word twenty ends with the same sound as mighty.
         ▪ The word forever is the words for and ever put together. That's for as in, "This is for you."
         ▪ The word sons is plural. What do you need to add onto the word son to make it plural? Sun is a homophone. This isn't the sun in the sky.
   o  Vocabulary
      • renown (verse 4)
      • fame, lots of people know you and talk about you (noun)

IV. Lesson
   o  The men of renown in our reading were "mighty men," men of supernatural strength, so today for science let's learn about strength. We've learned about several of our body's amazing systems. Today we'll learn about another, our *muscular system.*
   o  Our muscular system is all of our muscles and how they work together with tendons, joints and bones to make our body move. Before even our muscles can do anything at all, what do they need?
      • Energy because that's the ability to do work.
      • How do muscles get the energy they need to work?
   o  Our bodies get energy from food. Muscles use energy created from our food by a chemical process.
      • This process takes our food and changes it into the energy we need to move.
   o  Without muscles our skeletal system just sits there, our heart can't beat, and our lungs can't take in air. None of those other body systems function unless we have muscles to make them work. Your heart is pumped by muscles. Muscles work to expand your lungs to let in air. Your bones walk, sit, jump, climb, and do everything else by muscles. You eat with muscles; you blink with muscles. You even have muscles

in your forehead. That's how you can raise your eyebrows. Move your face in different ways to try to figure out some of the different places you have muscles.
- o We're going to back up because there's a lot going on to make your muscles move!
- o What are the building blocks that everything on earth is made of?
    - Atoms are the building blocks of everything physical in the universe.
- o Trillions and trillions of atoms make up just one cell in the human body. *Cells* are the building blocks of the body. You have brain cells, skin cells, blood cells, and all sorts of other kinds of cells that make up your body.
    - Each cell has about 100 trillion atoms in it and there are about 100 trillion cells in your body.
- o Muscles are made up of cells just like everything in your body.
- o Our muscle cells are long and thin. Many of these combined together make our muscle fibers.
    - A fiber is threadlike. Your clothing is made from fibers; maybe today you are wearing cotton fibers.
- o These fibers are in bundles. The bigger the muscle, the more bundles.
    - Packed in with the muscles are blood vessels which carry to the muscles the energy they need. There are also nerve endings which we haven't talked about yet. They deliver messages from the brain.
- o To make energy going to your muscles, your body needs oxygen.
    - Do you remember how blood gets oxygen?
        - The heart pumps blood out to the lungs to get oxygen and then the oxygenated blood returns to the heart and is sent through your body. Some of that blood goes to your muscles and delivers the oxygen it needs to make more energy.
- o We'll continue with the muscular system for our next lesson because we haven't even gotten to how they move yet!
- o Recall: What's the name of the system that moves your body?
- o Explore more: Experiment with your muscles. Learn the word contract and relax and make your muscles do those things. Where can you find muscles in your body?

V. Discussion
- o If you were to create a mythical character, who would it be and what would the character be able to do?

VI. Writing
- o On your worksheet today, you'll start with writing a question. A question is a sentence that asks something. A question always ends with a question mark.
- o You'll also be looking for body parts that are controlled by muscles. There's an eye, a hand, a heart, lungs, and some mouth parts. What do you think your muscles move? (Note: All of them!)

**Day 37**

I. Read Genesis 6:5-12.
   5   The Lord saw how wicked the human race had become, and that every human thought was evil.
   6   The Lord was sorry that he had made human beings on the earth, and his heart was deeply troubled.
   7   So the Lord said, "I will wipe from the face of the earth the human race I have created—and with them the animals."
   8   But Noah found favor in the eyes of the Lord.
   9   This is the account of Noah and his family. Noah was a righteous man, blameless among the people of his time, and he walked faithfully with God.
   10  Noah had three sons: Shem, Ham and Japheth.
   11  Now the earth was corrupt in God's sight and was full of violence.
   12  God looked on the earth, and saw it was corrupt; for everyone had corrupted their way upon the earth.

II. Memory Verse
   o  1 John 1:9
   o  If we confess our sins, He is faithful and just to forgive us our sins and to cleanse us from all unrighteousness. (KJV)

III. Language
   o  Spelling/Handwriting
      • words to know: animal, every, saw, eyes
      • spelling tips:
         ▪ The word <u>animal</u> has three vowels but only two different ones.
         ▪ The word <u>every</u> starts like your spelling word forever ends.
         ▪ The word <u>saw</u> actually ends the way your spelling word away begins.
         ▪ The word <u>eyes</u> has two letter E's and a Y. It almost looks like two eyes around a nose.
   o  Vocabulary
      • corrupt (verse 11)
      • being willing to do something wrong in order to get something for yourself (adjective)
      • An adjective describes a noun. The people are corrupt. Corrupt is describing the people.
      • How would you describe yourself? Words like cute, funny, loveable, and clever are all adjectives. They are words that describe.

IV. Lesson
   o  We're going to continue with muscles. We've gotten energy to the muscles by using stored ATP and by using glucose and oxygen to create more. Now what does that energy enable the muscles to do?
   o  Muscles move by *contracting*. The fiber bundles slide together, stacking up.
      • Scrunch up your face. How many different muscles can you feel contracting?

- Contract lots of different muscles in your body. How can you make the muscles at the base of your thumb contract?
  - The opposite motion is when a muscle relaxes. Contract and relax different muscles in your body. Feel your muscles with your hands. What do you feel happening? Can you feel a muscle get shorter and longer?
  - Maybe the easiest place to see your muscle stack up and then flatten again is in your biceps. That's the muscle you flex when you bend your elbow.
  - Muscles move our bones, but they aren't attached to the bones. They are attached to something called *tendons*.
  - Tendons are strong and flexible but they can't stretch. This combination allows them to be pulled by the muscle. It's attached to the muscle on one end and to the bone on the other end. When the muscle contracts and tugs on the tendon, it pulls the bone along with it.
    - This isn't an exact demonstration of how tendons work, but you could pretend your pen or pencil is a tendon. Two people can hold onto its two ends. One hand holding the pencil is the muscle and the other is the bone. The muscle contracts and pulls on the tendon. What happens to the bone?
    - Next time you are eating chicken drumsticks, look for bones, muscles and tendons. Tendons are the white strings you will find. The bone I'm sure you can find. What's the muscle?
      - The meat you are eating! The strings of meat are bundles of muscle fibers.
  - Muscles don't have to be attached to bones. Can you find muscles in your body not attached to bones?
    - They can be attached to your skin which is how you can smile!
  - You control the muscles we've been talking about, but you don't have control over all of your muscles. There are *involuntary muscles*, which are muscles that work instinctively, without your thinking about it. They work without you controlling them.
  - Your heart muscles squeeze and pump your blood through your body without you having to think about it. Your muscles expand your rib cage and let in air so that you can breathe, without your thinking about it. Those are involuntary muscles.
  - There are lots of involuntary muscles. Can you think of other things your body does without your thinking about it?
    - One way involuntary muscles work is to take the food you eat and get it through your body. Once you swallow your body takes over.
  - Another way your muscles work involuntarily is by your *reflexes*. You can close and open your eyes voluntarily, meaning you can choose when you want to open and close them. But the same muscles can work by reflex, which is what happens when you blink. Your body does it without your having to think about it. It's a reflex God gave us to protect us. It protects our eyes.
  - Can you think of any other reflexes you have?
    - Sneezing is a reflex.
    - You pull your hand away from something hot without having to decide you should.
    - What about your response to a tickle?

- Shivering is also a reflex.
  - Recall: What are involuntary muscles? What attaches muscles to bones?
    - muscles that work without us controlling them
    - tendons
  - Explore more: Think about involuntary muscles as you go throughout your day and your voluntary ones. You use muscles constantly. Maybe you could watch a video about how muscle fibers get bigger and how they stack up and relax.

V. Discussion
  - God called Noah's generation violent. How do you think God would describe your parents? How would He describe you?

VI. Writing
  - Complete your worksheet for today.
  - You are going to write adjectives, words that describe the nouns.

**Day 38**

I. Read Genesis 6:13-22. FYI: a cubit is a form of measurement. Things like an inch and a meter are forms of measurement.

13 Then God said to Noah, "The end of all people has come before Me; because of them, the earth is filled with violence; and see now, I am about to destroy them with the earth.
14 Make an ark of gopher wood for yourself; you will make rooms in the ark, and will cover it inside and out with pitch.
15 This is how you will make it: the length of the ark three hundred cubits, its breadth fifty cubits, and its height thirty cubits.
16 You will make a window for the ark, and finish it a cubit from the top. Set the door of the ark in the side of it, and make it with lower, second, and third level decks.
17 Look, I myself am bringing the flood on the earth, in order to destroy all living things made of flesh from under heaven; everything that is on the earth will die.
18 But I will establish My covenant promise with you; and you will enter the ark—you and your sons and your wife, and your sons' wives together with you.
19 And of every living thing made of flesh, you will bring two of every kind into the ark, to keep them alive with you; the two will be male and female.
20 Of the birds after their kind, and of the animals after their kind, of every creeping thing of the ground after its kind, two of every kind will come to you to keep them alive.
21 As for you, take for yourself some of all food which is good for eating, and gather it for yourself and it will be for food for you and for them."
22 Noah did according to all that God had commanded him.

II. Memory Verse
- 1 John 1:9
- If we confess our sins, He is faithful and just to forgive us our sins and to cleanse us from all unrighteousness. (KJV)

III. Language
- Spelling/Handwriting
  - words to know: end, people, them, rooms
  - spelling tips:
    - The word <u>end</u> is spelled almost like the word and. It starts with a different vowel sound, so it starts with a different vowel.
    - The word <u>people</u> is a strange word you just have to practice spelling. It ends with a silent E, but it also has an O in the word. Here's the rule it follows, when two vowels are together, the first says its name. People has an EO and together they make the first says its name, E.
    - The word <u>them</u> is the word "the" with one more letter added on.
    - The word <u>rooms</u> is plural. There's a double letter making the vowel sound.
- Vocabulary
  - establish (verse 18)
  - to create something intended to last (verb)

IV. Lesson
- o Today we are going to learn about density.
  - A dense object is filled with a lot of stuff. The more stuff crammed into a space, the denser it is. The more spread out stuff is, the less dense it is.
  - A dense object is not good at floating, so a boat needs to be less dense.
    - If I gave you a golf ball and a ping pong ball, which are similar in size, which do you think would float?
      - The ping pong ball would float because it's full of air.
      - So, which is denser, the ping pong ball or the golf ball?
        - The golf ball is denser because it has more weight for its size and because it has more "stuff" in it instead of being full of air.
    - A ping pong ball floats because it is less dense than water. A golf ball sinks because it is denser than water.
- o We can also talk about density when we look at countries and their populations.
- o Let me give you an example before we look at a map of population density.
  - Right now, in the room where you are sitting there are a certain number of people. You are probably a little spread out. You aren't too densely packed in. Now, if you all got up and sat on the same side of the room. Would you be a little more densely packed in? (Note: Go ahead and actually move and see.)
    - What if you all got up and sat on the same chair? (Go for it!)
    - The number of people never changed. The population of your room didn't change. The population density changed. How much room each person had changed. That's what is described by the term *population density*.
- o Take a look at the Day 38 population density map. The darker the spot on the map, the more people there are that live in that country compared to the size of the country. What do you notice?
- o Do you know which countries are the darkest, meaning having the highest number of people per square kilometer (mile)?
  - The country with the highest *population density* is Bangladesh. Bangladesh is the small country to the right of India. India is the dark brown peninsula sticking into the Indian Ocean. There are nearly 3,000 people living in each square mile of Bangladesh. (That's more than 1,000 per square kilometer.)
- o Why do you think Russia and other northern countries have a very low population density?
  - Their cold climates create areas of snow and ice where few people live. Russia, Canada, and Greenland have large areas of land where no one lives. Moscow is a very crowded city in Russia, but as a whole, the country of Russia has a low population density because of its frozen tundra.
- o Why do you think Australia might have a low population density? You can look at the Australia map for an idea. It's in the Map Book for Day 38.
  - That brown land in Australia is arid or semi-arid land. That means it's really dry. Australia has a large desert. With a large desert, there is a large amount of land with few people living in it which lowers the population density for the whole country.
- o Recall: What is density? What does population density refer to?

- the amount of stuff something has in it for its size, a dense object's molecules are more tightly packed in
- how many people live in an area compared to the size of the area
  - Explore more: Your family can practice population density by playing Sardines. ☺ That's hide and seek where one person hides and when you find that person you hide there with them.

V. Discussion
- God gives Noah a task. He gives Noah responsibilities. He has to build a boat. He has to gather up food to bring. God sends the animals. God provided the plans for the boat. What is God responsible for and what are we responsible for in our lives? Where's the line between taking responsibility and trusting God to take care of things for us?
  - (Note: Here's one thought. Noah was to bring food on the ark for himself, his family, and his animals. He had no idea how long they would be on the ark. He didn't have means of keep the food good all that time. There was no way he could have provided food for them all. He did what he was asked, as best as his humanness allowed, and God took care of the rest. God must have protected and preserved the food. And He must have multiplied it, never letting it run out.)

VI. Writing
- Complete your worksheet for today.
- Fill in the missing sounds for the words.

**Day 39**

I. Read Genesis 7:1-16.
   1. Then the Lord said to Noah, "Enter the ark, you and all your family that lives with you, for you alone I have seen to be righteous before Me in this time.
   2. You will take with you seven of every clean animal, a male and his female; and of the animals that are not clean two, a male and his female;
   3. also of the birds of the sky, by sevens, male and female, to keep them alive in all the earth.
   4. Because in seven more days, I will send rain on the earth for forty days and forty nights; and I will wipe off the earth every living thing that I have made."
   5. Noah did everything just how the Lord had commanded him.
   6. Now Noah was six hundred years old when the flood of water came over the earth.
   7. Then Noah and his sons and all their wives entered the ark because of the flood.
   8. Clean animals and animals that are not clean and birds and everything that creeps on the ground,
   9. they all went into the ark to Noah by twos, male and female, as God had commanded Noah.
   10. It came about after seven days, that the water of the flood came on the earth.
   11. In the six hundredth year of Noah's life, in the second month, on the seventeenth day of the month, on that day all the fountains of the great deep gushed out of the earth, and the floodgates of the sky were opened.
   12. The rain fell upon the earth for forty days and forty nights.
   13. On the very same day Noah and Shem and Ham and Japheth, the sons of Noah, and Noah's wife and the three wives of his sons with them, entered the ark,
   14. they and every kind of beast, and all types of cattle, and every kind of creeping thing that creeps on the earth, and every type of bird, all sorts of birds.
   15. So they went into the ark to Noah, by twos of all living animals.
   16. Those that entered, male and female of all animals, entered as God had commanded Noah; and the Lord closed the door behind them.

II. Memory Verse
   o 1 John 1:9
   o If we confess our sins, He is faithful and just to forgive us our sins and to cleanse us from all unrighteousness. (KJV)

III. Language
   o Spelling/Handwriting
      • words to know: seven, alive, wives, life
      • spelling tips:
         ▪ The word seven ends with the word even. It has the name Eve in the middle of it.
         ▪ The word alive ends with the word live. It ends with a silent E.
         ▪ The word wives has the same spelling pattern as the word alive.
            • It is the plural of wife. The F changed into a V to form the plural.
         ▪ The word life has the same vowel spelling pattern as alive and wives. It ends with a silent E.

- Vocabulary
    - righteous (verse 1)
    - doing what is right (adjective)

IV. Lesson
- Today we read about them coming onto the ark by twos, male and female of all flesh.
- Males and females are in many ways similar to each other. They each have a muscular system and skeletal system and each breathes with lungs that take in oxygen for their blood to create energy for their bodies to be able to do work.
- There are many differences as well, even in places you might not expect, like in their brains. Male and female brains are created differently from each other; their brains were made to think differently. That's how God created them.
- However, there is no difference in males and females in who's smarter.
- Everyone can grow smarter. You exercise your brain just like you exercise muscles. That's why it's good to learn. You are exercising and growing your smart muscles. ☺ Every time you don't know something and then learn about it, you just got smarter. So, the next time you make a mistake, be thankful for the chance to get smarter.
    - You have the chance to learn something from your mistake and make yourself that much smarter.
- The other day we talked about boats. What do you think the first boats were like?
    - The first boat was maybe just a log.
    - Canoes, which were just hollowed out logs, and rafts, or logs tied together, probably were also early types of boats.
- We've learned that ancient civilizations grew up around water because life needs water. Their lives revolved around the rivers and seas, so we can be sure that water was used for transportation as well.
- Rivers were the first highways as roads had not been built yet. Water travel was an easier alternative for transporting goods, making rivers ideal for trade.
- Early Mesopotamian boat design included a sail that was square in shape and fixed into place. If the wind changed direction, the sail couldn't be changed. Oars would be used to row back against the wind.
- What can you observe about boats in Mesopotamia in this ancient artwork? How is it made? How was it used? etc.

From: http://www.egyptorigins.org/mesoboats.htm

- The design was simple. They couldn't carry much. It looks like two workers were guiding the boat and taking the owner of the goods wherever he was headed.

- o Recall: What were some first types of boats?
  - logs made into rafts or canoes
- o Explore more: Do you want to build a model?

V. Discussion
- o Think about how you have been made unique. What qualities do you have that make you, you? How are you different from your siblings? Do you react differently in situations? Do you find different things funny? Do you like to be around people or to be alone? Do you like different types of subjects or games? Make observations about yourself and your family members.

VI. Writing
- o Complete your worksheet for today.
- o You are going to add the silent E to change the words.
- o Then you are going to design a boat.

**Day 40**

I. Read Genesis 7:17-24.
   17  Then the flood came over the earth for forty days, and the water increased and lifted up the ark, so that it rose up above the earth.
   18  The water covered the earth, and the ark floated on the surface of the water.
   19  The water poured out more and more over the earth, until all the high mountains everywhere under the heavens were covered.
   20  The water continued to fill the earth another fifteen cubits higher, and the mountains were covered.
   21  All of the animals that moved on the earth died, birds and cattle and beasts and every swarming thing that swarms upon the earth, and all mankind;
   22  of all that was on the dry land, everything that had the breath of the spirit of life died.
   23  In this way God wiped out every living thing that was on the face of the land, from man to animals to creeping things and to birds of the sky, and they were wiped out from the earth; and only Noah was left, together with those with him in the ark.
   24  The water gained and held its place over the earth one hundred and fifty days.

II. Memory Verse
   o Test yourself on 1 John 1:9.
      • If we confess our sins, He is faithful and just to forgive us our sins and to cleanse us from all unrighteousness. (KJV)
   o Review Genesis 1:3.
      • Then God said, "Let there be light"; and there was light.
      • Can you say verses 1-3?

III. Language
   o Spelling/Handwriting
      • Test yourselves on your words from Days 36-39. There are lines on your worksheet for this.
         ▪ mighty, twenty, forever, sons
         ▪ animal, every, saw, eyes
         ▪ end, people, them, rooms
         ▪ seven, alive, wives, life
   o Vocabulary
      • Review and test yourselves on these words. There's a worksheet activity for this.
         ▪ renown – fame, lots of people know you and talk about you
         ▪ corrupt - being willing to do something wrong in order to get something for yourself
         ▪ establish – to create something intended to last
         ▪ strive – to make a great effort to achieve something or to struggle

IV. Lesson
   o Today we are going to learn about floods.
   o What is a flood?

- A flood is an overflowing of a large amount of water over what is normally dry land.
- There isn't a flood every time it rains. The water seeps into the ground or goes down drainage systems. What do you think might be some causes of floods?
    - The ground can completely fill up in an area so that water can't get absorbed down into the ground any longer. Any more water forms a puddle. If there's a whole lot of extra water, you've got a flood. This can happen from a lot of rain coming all at once, or it can happen by it raining steadily over days or even weeks.
    - One flooding risk is clogged drains. Have you ever gotten a clogged drain in your home? Hopefully it didn't cause a flood, but what happens?
        - The sink or the tub starts filling with water.
        - That can happen with a clogged drain on a street. If too much trash or debris gets in the drain, it can clog it up so that water stops getting through or not much can get through. The water backs up and fills the street.
    - In 2011 an earthquake caused a tidal wave to rise up in the ocean and crash down over land causing a horrific flood. That event is called a *tsunami*, an earthquake triggering a large wave. The wave reached heights of over 130 feet (40 meters).
    - Floods can be sudden and destructive, but God is in control of the weather, and God can prepare you for it and get you out if need be. He's trustworthy, even if terrible things are happening. We never need to be afraid. We can know He's not forgotten about us and loves us and is taking care of us.
- We know the flood in the Bible happened. We've talked about how myths from different cultures developed from somewhere. They grow into something outlandish and far-fetched, but there was an original experience that started the story.
    - The Bible's stories are not myths. They are different because the original stories were written down and preserved. We know the stories haven't changed over time.
- Another one of such myths is that of the flood. There are stories of an ancient flood that wiped out the earth told all around the world. These myths involve many different features as cultures have sought to explain how an all-consuming flood could have happened. Many involve their gods.
    - How did a story of a great flood get to ancient cultures on six continents?
    - After the flood who's alive?
        - It's just Noah's family.
    - Their descendants cover the earth now. The remembrance of the flood remained as they told the story over and over through the generations, but the facts got lost along the way. Cultures added their own understanding of the gods and nature.
- Here's a little piece of the Mayan flood story.

"This is not what I had in mind,"

       says Heart-of-Sky.
       And so it is decided to destroy
       these wooden people.

       Hurricane makes a great rain.
       It rains all day and rains all night.
       There is a terrible flood
       and the earth is blackened." (from http://www.jaguar-sun.com/maya.html)

- o Recall: What's a tsunami?
  - when an earthquake causes a huge wave
- o Explore more: Where are areas near you that get flooded? Why?

V. Discussion
- o Why the flood? Why did God do it? Did He make a mistake in creating the earth? All of history is the story of God loving man. He creates him. Man sins, separating him from God. God redeems the situation so that man can be with Him because God is love. How does the flood move forward God's redemption plan and the story of Christ? How does the flood show God's love for the world? "For God so loved the world…" (John 3:16)

VI. Writing
- o On your worksheet today, you'll be doing the spelling and vocabulary review.

**Day 41 (check Materials List)**

I. Read Genesis 8:1-5.
   1. But God remembered Noah and all the beasts and all the cattle that were with him in the ark; and God caused a wind to pass over the earth, and the water started going down.
   2. Also the fountains of the deep and the floodgates of the sky were closed, and the rain from the sky was held back;
   3. and the water went down steadily from the earth, and at the end of one hundred and fifty days the water decreased.
   4. In the seventh month, on the seventeenth day of the month, the ark settled on the top of Mount Ararat.
   5. The water decreased steadily until the tenth month; in the tenth month, on the first day of the month, the tops of the mountains could be seen.

II. Memory Verse
   o Romans 6:23
   o For the wages of sin is death, but the free gift of God is eternal life in Christ Jesus our Lord.

III. Language
   o Spelling/Handwriting
      • words to know: Noah, remember, were, water
      • spelling tips:
         ▪ Noah is a name so it begins with a capital letter.
         ▪ Remember is a long word but you can spell it by breaking it into parts, into syllables, re – mem- ber. Each syllable always has a vowel. Each syllable always has one vowel sound. In this word each syllable has just one vowel and in each syllable it's an E.
         ▪ Were is one of those words you just have to learn. It has the same spelling pattern as the word there that you've already had, as in it's over there.
         ▪ Water also isn't exactly spelled as it sounds. It looks like it could say wait-er. It has five letters and ends like remember. Usually when a word ends with an -er sound, it's spelled E-R.
   o Vocabulary
      • decrease (verse 3)
      • to become less or to make something become less (verb)

IV. Lesson
   o In today's Scripture we read that God sends a wind over the earth which causes the water to start going down; it's receding, subsiding, and decreasing.
   o Wind is one thing that aids evaporation. Wind makes evaporation happen faster.
      • What is evaporation?
         ▪ Evaporation is when liquid turns into gas form. Water turns into water vapor when it becomes a gas. Where does water go once it turns into vapor?
      • It travels up. What happens when it gets high?

- It cools off and condenses into water droplets which then combine together to make rain.
- Evaporation is occurring at all times. It's a continuous process. It never stops. The amount of rainfall and snowfall is equal to the amount of water that is evaporating from the earth. Why?
  - It's all the same water, right? It just goes round and round in a cycle. It's the same amount because it's the same water.
- When we talked about the water cycle before, we learned that when water heated up it turned into water vapor and rose.
- A liquid, like water, does need heat from a hot day to turn into a gas. That heat can come from the energy in the water molecules themselves. A tiny drop of water doesn't need a whole lot of energy to create the heat necessary to escape its liquid home and become a gas.
- There are a few things at work in the process of evaporation.
  - We've already talked about heat and its role in evaporation.
  - Do you remember learning about how light warms the earth?
    - It excites the molecules and gets them moving. That movement creates the heat which warms the earth and us.
- Moving molecules are what's happening during evaporation. Some of those molecules are colliding together. The crash creates heat, and that can be enough heat to transform one water molecule to escape as a gas.
  - You can act this out if you are careful not to hurt each other when you collide! Everyone is a water molecule and is moving around. When two of you collide, one escapes the bunch as water vapor.
- Knowing this about collisions, how do you think wind aids evaporation?
  - The wind moves the molecules around causing more collisions. More collisions make the water evaporate more quickly.
- In our Scripture reading today there was a specific location mentioned, where the ark came to rest. What's the location's name? (Note: If they don't know, read verse 4.)
  - Ararat
- Ararat is located in Turkey. Find it on the map for Day 41. (Note: If you are having trouble, it's far to the east on the border with Iran.)
- Many people have been looking for Noah's ark. Some think you can see the outline of it from above, that the ground, having covered it, shows its shape. Others claim to have found wood from the ark, but it's always suspicious because people use the area to make money off of tourists.
- Do you have questions about Noah and his ark? What questions would you like to know the answers to?
  - I can answer a few questions.
- When did this happen?
  - Using the ages given in the Bible, we think the flood happened maybe around 2300 BC.
- I know some kids like to ask if dinosaurs were on the ark.
  - How big are reptiles when they are born?
    - They come from eggs, so pretty small.
  - Reptiles continue to grow their whole lives. Do humans?

- - No, little kids usually think that the older you get the bigger you are because it's true for kids, but by the time you are an adult, you are no longer growing taller.
  - Many young dinosaurs could have easily fit on the ark.
  - One last question: how long was Noah in the ark?
    - We can figure that out from what the Bible tells us. He went into the ark when he was 600 and left one year and ten days later. With the way they counted months by the moon, that would be 370 days.
  - Recall: Where is Mount Ararat? What are some things that affect how much and how fast water evaporates?
    - Turkey
    - heat, wind
  - Explore more: You could set up an experiment. Set up two plates with a little puddle on each. Aim a fan at one of them and see which evaporates completely first.

V. Discussion
  - Noah was on the ark for a year. Do you think he and his family wondered if the water would really ever go away? (I wonder if it ever rained again in that year!)
  - Do you think you could trust God and patiently wait for something that long?
  - What do you think it was like waiting for the water to go down?
  - Do you think the waiting got easier or harder after it landed on the top of the mountain? (It landed in the 7th month, and they didn't get out until the 2nd month. There were not quite halfway through the wait yet.)

VI. Writing
  - Complete the worksheet for today.
  - You are going to write names today. What do all names begin with?
    - a capital letter

**Day 42 (check Materials List)**

I. Read Genesis 8:6-19.
   6   Then after forty days, Noah opened the window he had made in the ark;
   7   and he sent out a bird, a raven, and it flew here and there until the water was dried up.
   8   Then he sent out another bird, a dove, to see if the water was gone from the face of the land;
   9   but the dove found no resting place for the sole of her foot, so she returned to Noah in the ark. Noah put out his hand and took her and brought her back into the ark.
   10  So he waited seven more days; and again, he sent out the dove from the ark.
   11  The dove came to him toward evening, and in her beak was a freshly picked olive leaf. So Noah knew that the water was gone from the earth.
   12  Then he waited another seven days, and sent out the dove; but she did not return to the ark.
   13  Now it came about in the six hundred and first year, in the first month, on the first of the month, the water was dried up from the earth. Then Noah removed the covering of the ark, and looked, and saw the surface of the ground was dry.
   14  In the second month, on the twenty-seventh day of the month, the earth was dry.
   15  Then God spoke to Noah, saying,
   16  "Go out of the ark, you and your wife and your sons and their wives.
   17  Bring out with you every living thing that is with you, birds and animals and every creeping thing, that they may have lots of children, and be fruitful and multiply on the earth."
   18  So Noah went out with his sons and all their wives.
   19  Every beast, every creeping thing, and every bird, everything that moves on the earth, went out by their families from the ark.

II. Memory Verse
   o  Romans 6:23
   o  For the wages of sin is death, but the free gift of God is eternal life in Christ Jesus our Lord.

III. Language
   o  Spelling/Handwriting
   o  words to know: made, window, bird, foot
      - spelling tips:
        - The word made has a silent E.
        - The word window starts with the word win and ends with the same vowel spelling pattern as your spelling word flow.
        - The word bird has an i helping make the "er/ir" sound.
        - The word foot has a double letter for the vowel sound like your spelling words food and look.
   o  Vocabulary
      - remove (verse 13)
      - to take away, to get rid of (verb)

IV. Lesson
- We're going to continue with water today. When the water levels went down, where did the water go? We know that some of it evaporated and traveled up. But that's not the only thing that happens to water. Where else do you think the water might have gone?
    - Down!
- What pulls water down, just like everything else on earth?
    - gravity
- Gravity pulls water down into the earth. It goes into the soil and fills in the spaces between rocks. When something gets completely full, we say it is saturated.
- When the ground is saturated with water, and it no longer has a place to go, it can puddle on top of the land, but what about the water under the ground? If it's already down underground but it can't go any farther, what do you think happens to it?
    - It can pool up underground.
- We call the water that fills the soil and the spaces between the rocks, *groundwater*. That's an easy-to-understand term. Groundwater is the water in the ground.
- How do people get water from the ground?
    - Wells are dug to reach where water has pooled up underground and to draw up water. The water we need for life, right?
- Life not only needs water, but it needs fresh water. We can't drink the salty water of the ocean.
- If salt water is found in the oceans and seas, where do you think fresh water is found?
    - Fresh water is found in streams, lakes, and underground. The water gets replenished when it rains.
- Groundwater is an important part of the water cycle. The water underground is always moving, though sometimes very slowly. Do you remember what water is always moving toward?
    - Water is always moving towards the lowest point. Water can get pulled in any direction but mostly it's joining streams and making its way to the oceans and seas.
    - Water can move down by gravity and it can even flow up!
- Did you realize that even fish living in the salty ocean need fresh water to survive?
    - Think about this. If you put a plate of salt water out, what would happen? You can try it if you like, but it will take time because the water has to evaporate.
        - The water evaporates but the salt doesn't. The salt gets left behind.
        - What does that mean for the ocean? Can you figure it out?
            - I know because I make soup, and I add salt to the water. If I let the water boil down too much, then the soup gets really salty.
            - That's what would happen to the ocean. Water is evaporating from the oceans. If it wasn't replaced with fresh water, the oceans would get too salty to live in!
            - There's a sea called the Dead Sea. Why is it called that?
                - It's too salty for animals to live in. It's so dense you can sit in it and float!

- Recall: What is water called that is in the ground?
  - groundwater
- Explore more: You can use a sponge or two to see how rain becomes ground water.
  - Place one sponge on top of another.
  - Pour water onto the top one. What happens over time?
    - The water will get pulled down into the bottom sponge. The top will dry out (like the dry ground that you walk on).
  - Can you make the bottom sponge saturated?

V. Discussion
  - What do you think you would be feeling leaving the ark after a year? They were in a new place because the ark traveled. Their home was gone anyway. The world looked different. They were all alone. Everything must have been very green from all the water. What do you think it would have been like?

VI. Writing
  - Complete the worksheet for today.
  - Our vocabulary word was remove. On your worksheet instead of adding a silent E, you are going to remove it. What word do you make?

**Day 43**

I. Read Genesis 8:20-9:7.
   20 Then Noah built an altar to the Lord, and offered burnt offerings of every clean animal on the altar.
   21 The Lord smelled the soothing aroma; and the Lord said to Himself, "I will never again curse the ground because of humans, for their hearts are evil from the time they are young; and I will never again destroy every living thing, in this way.
   22 "While the earth exists,
   Planting and harvesting,
   And cold and heat,
   And summer and winter,
   And day and night
   Will not stop."
   1 And God blessed Noah and his sons and said to them, "Be fruitful and multiply, and fill the earth.
   2 Every beast of the earth and every bird of the sky will fear you; along with everything that creeps on the ground, and all the fish of the sea, I give them to you.
   3 All animals will be food for you; I give all to you, just as I gave plants to you to eat.
   4 Only you shall not eat animals with its blood.
   5 I will require your blood, and from every animal I will require their blood. I will require the life of every living thing.
   6 "Whoever kills a man,
   He will be killed by a man,
   Because man was made in the image of God.
   7 "As for you, be fruitful and multiply;
   Populate the earth and multiply in it. Fill the earth with lots of people."

II. Memory Verse
   - Romans 6:23
   - For the wages of sin is death, but the free gift of God is eternal life in Christ Jesus our Lord.

III. Language
   - Spelling/Handwriting
     - words to know: clean, eat, thing, again
       - The word <u>clean</u> has the same E sound spelling pattern as your spelling words each and beast.
       - The word <u>eat</u> has the same vowel spelling pattern.
       - The word <u>thing</u> is a useful word. Two letters make the beginning sound; three letters make the ending sound.
       - The word <u>again</u> starts with the word "a" and ends with the word gain, which has the vowel spelling pattern of rain.
   - Vocabulary
     - require (verse 5)
     - to need, to say that something has to be done (verb)

IV. Lesson
- o We've learned that when we eat meat, we are eating muscle. In today's verses we read that they were told they can eat meat; before this they were only told they could eat plants. It's probably good that Noah's family didn't have the temptation to eat the animals that they were supposed to help be safe from the flood!
- o We use heat when we cook meat. Can you think of ways heat causes changes in food?
    - Here's my list:
        - We use heat to boil water which changes water from a liquid to a gas.
        - Heat also changes liquids into a solid. Can you think of when that happens?
            - That's what happens when a cake batter turns into a cake.
            - It happens when eggs are cooked.
- o Solids, liquids, and gases are what we call the stages of matter. Matter is the word we give to all the stuff in the world that takes up space.
    - Water is one of the easiest things to think about when we talk about the stages of matter because it can pretty easily be in all three states.
    - How does water become a solid?
        - It freezes into ice.
    - We've already talked about water as a liquid and a gas.
- o Water is still water in all three stages. It is still made up of water molecules. Water as a liquid, a gas, and a solid are all made up of $H_2O$ molecules. The difference is how much those molecules are moving.
    - When do you think the molecules are moving fastest: in a gas, a liquid, or a solid?
        - Molecules move fastest in a gas.
    - When do you think the molecules are moving slowest?
        - Molecules move slowest in a solid. There is very little movement in solids, but there is movement in the molecules.
        - Are you surprised that the molecules are still moving in a solid?
        - In fact, water can evaporate from ice. It's much slower, but it does happen. Things are happening!
        - Whatever you are sitting on right now is moving under you! That's a strange thought!
- o Noah sacrificed the animals to God. In the New Testament, Jesus sacrifices Himself for us.
- o The Old Testament points us to Jesus in many ways. The ark itself is a picture of Christ's salvation. Sinners will face the wrath of God, the flood is an example of God's wrath, God showing His anger. The only way to be saved from God's wrath is to enter through the door to salvation. The only way to be saved from the flood was to enter through the door of the ark. The only way to be saved from God's wrath against sinners is to enter into salvation through faith in Jesus Christ.
    - Jesus said, "I am the door; if anyone enters through Me, he will be saved." (John 10:9a)
- o Recall: What are the three main stages of matter? gas, liquid, solid
- o Explore more: You can observe water in all three states of matter. You can read about Jesus being the final sacrifice in Hebrews 10.

V. Discussion
- Is God's wrath something to fear?

VI. Writing
- Complete your worksheet for today.
- You are going to draw water in different states.

**Day 44**

I. Read Genesis 9:8-17.
   8  Then God spoke to Noah and to his family, saying,
   9  "Now, I Myself establish My covenant promise with you, and with your descendants;
  10  and with every living creature that is with you, every animal of the earth.
  11  I establish My covenant promise with you; never again will all life be cut off by the water of a flood. There will never again be a flood to destroy the earth."
  12  God said, "This is the sign of the covenant promise which I am making between Me and you and your descendants and with every living creature;
  13  I will set My rainbow in the cloud, and it shall be for a sign of a covenant promise between Me and the whole earth.
  14  When I bring a cloud over the earth, the rainbow will be seen in the cloud,
  15  and I will remember My covenant promise, which is between Me and you and every living creature; and never again will the water become a flood to destroy every living thing.
  16  When the rainbow is in the cloud, then I will look at it, to remember the everlasting covenant promise between God and every living creature that is on the earth."
  17  And God said to Noah, "This is the sign of the covenant promise which I have established on the earth."

II. Memory Verse
- Romans 6:23
- For the wages of sin is death, but the free gift of God is eternal life in Christ Jesus our Lord.

III. Language
- Spelling/Handwriting
    - words to know: myself, never, making, between
    - spelling tips:
        - <u>Myself</u> is the words my and self combined.
        - <u>Never</u> ends just like forever which you have already practiced.
        - <u>Making</u> is a form of the word make. To change make into making, you take off the silent E and add on I-N-G.
        - <u>Between</u> is the words be and tween put together. There are three vowels and they are all the same. The last letter is an N.
- Vocabulary
    - descendants (verse 9, 12)
    - all the children that are born from you and from your children and from your children's children, etc. (noun, plural noun)
        - You have no descendants yet, but you are the descendant of your parents and grandparents.

IV. Lesson
- When light separates, we see the rainbow of colors that makes up light. Do you know what the colors of the rainbow are?
    - We remember them by the name, Roy G. Biv. It's an acronym. Each letter stands for a color.

- The colors are: red, orange, yellow, green, blue, indigo, violet. Indigo is a dark blue.
- You can make a rainbow by placing a glass of water by a window where the sun is shining through.
  - The light is being bent when it hits the water, slowing down the light rays. The different colors get slowed at different speeds and separate.
- Isn't it fascinating that "white" light is actually all the colors mixed together?
  - Black isn't all the colors mixed together; black is the absence of light. That's why it's pitch black when there is no light.
- So, we know what makes a little rainbow. What makes a big rainbow in the sky? How does it get its shape?
  - What is the light hitting that is slowing it down and causing it to bend?
    - If you don't know, here's a hint. When does a rainbow occur?
    - Rainbows occur usually at the end of a rain. The light is hitting the water droplets in the air. We don't see a rainbow the whole time it's raining because it's cloudy. We need the clouds to break for the sun to shine light. The light hits the water droplets and bends.
  - But why the perfect rainbow shape?
    - When light hits the water, it bends in a predictable way. If you stick your pencil in a cup of water, it will appear bent in the same way every time you do it.
    - When light hits the water drops in the sky, it bends in a predictable way.
- In the Scripture reading today, we read about one of God's covenants with man. A covenant is an agreement, a pact. It's two people, or groups of people, coming together and making an agreement.
  - Usually there are terms. Each says what they promise to do. If you do these things, then I will do these things, and you sign the legal document and you've made a covenant.
  - In this passage God is making a pact with mankind, all of us.
- God's covenants are very important. He can never break His covenant. The Bible says that if we are faithless, He is still faithful. (2 Tim. 2:13)
  - God's word is binding. He cannot lie. He is always faithful. We can trust His promises.
- What's God's promise in today's reading?
  - He says He will never again destroy the world with a flood. He gave us a sign of His promise. When it rains, we are reminded of His promise that He's been faithful to.
- What are the covenants in the Bible? Actually, the word testament, as in Old and New Testament is the Latin word for covenant. The whole Bible is God's promise to us. It's His word to us that He plans to keep!
- In the Bible there are promises to everyone and there are promises to certain people and there are promises to Israel. God's promise that the earth would never be flooded like that again was made to all people for all time.
- Recall: What is a covenant? What are the colors of the rainbow?
  - a binding agreement between two people or groups of people

- o Explore more: If you haven't yet, put a glass of water where it can get sunlight coming through it. Try to make a rainbow. You can also stick things like pencils in the water to see them bend. That's called refraction. The colors of light travel at different speeds. That's why they separate when they bend. A rainbow is actually a circle. The horizon makes it so we only see an arch.

V. Discussion
- o What promises has God made that you can believe in and wait for to see fulfilled?

VI. Writing
- o Complete the worksheet for today.
- o You are going to draw a rainbow. Make sure you know the order. Red goes on top!

**Day 45**

I. Read Genesis 9:18-10:32.
   18   Now the sons of Noah who came out of the ark were Shem, Ham, and Japheth. Ham was the father of Canaan.
   19   The whole earth was populated from the three sons of Noah.
   20   Then Noah began farming and planted a vineyard.
   21   He drank wine and became drunk, and uncovered himself inside his tent.
   22   Ham, the father of Canaan, saw his father's nakedness, and told his two brothers outside.
   23   But Shem and Japheth took a cloak and laid it upon both their shoulders and walked backward and covered their father's nakedness; they kept their faces turned away, so that they did not see their father's nakedness.
   24   When Noah woke up, he knew what his youngest son, Ham, had done to him.
   25   So he said,
   "Cursed be Canaan, Ham's son;
   A servant he will be to his brothers."
   26   He also said,
   "Blessed be the Lord,
   The God of Shem;
   And let Canaan serve him.
   27   "May God give Japheth more and more land,
   And let him live in the tents of Shem;
   And let Canaan serve him."
   28   Noah lived three hundred and fifty years after the flood.
   29   Noah died when he was nine hundred and fifty years old.
   1    Now these are the records of the generations of Shem, Ham, and Japheth, the sons of Noah; and sons were born to them after the flood.
   ...
   32   ... and out of these the nations were separated on the earth after the flood.

II. Memory Verse
   o   Test yourselves on Romans 6:23.
       • For the wages of sin is death, but the free gift of God is eternal life in Christ Jesus our Lord.
   o   Do you remember 1 John 1:9?
       • If we confess our sins, He is faithful and just to forgive us our sins and to cleanse us from all unrighteousness. (KJV)

III. Language
   o   Spelling/Handwriting
       • Test yourselves on the words from Days 41-44.
         ▪ Noah, remember, were, water
         ▪ made, window, bird, foot
         ▪ clean, again, eat, thing
         ▪ myself, never, making, between
   o   Vocabulary
       • Test yourselves on the words from Days 41-44.
         ▪ recede – to go back or gradually diminish

- abate – to lessen, reduce, or remove
- intent – intention, purpose, what someone is determined to do
- successive – coming after another

IV. Lesson
- Do you know your family tree? How far back do you know your *ancestors*, those in your family who lived earlier? Has anyone in your family studied them?
- I have a relative who has researched my family.
  - I learned that the Sarchet family (Sar-shay, my mother's father's family) fled France because of religious persecution and founded the Isle of Guernsey.
  - There was also a Sarchet who was part of the Underground Railroad, helping runaway slaves get to freedom.
- Create a family tree.
  - You will be at the bottom along with your siblings.
  - You will connect above you to your parents. They will each connect to their siblings and above them to their parents.
  - Use your parents, grandparents and other relatives to make your family tree as big as possible. Learn some family history in the process.
- If you are American, can you learn when your family first arrived in America? Where did they come from?
- Almost every American is an *immigrant*, or someone who came from another country.
  - Why is America a country of immigrants?
  - We call Native Americans, Native Americans because they were native to the land. They were the first ones living there.
  - Europeans showed up on their boats and started claiming territory. Those first pilgrims were immigrants, just like all those who came after them.
- Recall: What is an ancestor? What is an immigrant?
  - a person you are descended from, you are the descendant of your ancestors
  - someone who came from another country
- Explore more: Interview the oldest living members of your family. What can you learn about their childhood life? What can you learn of your family history? If you learn about when your family first came to America, learn about what was happening in the country where they came from and why they might have left.

V. Discussion
- What's special about your family?

VI. Writing
- Complete your worksheet for today.
- You'll be checking on how well you remember your vocabulary and spelling.

**Day 46**

I. Read Genesis 11:1-9.
   1 Now in the whole earth everyone spoke the same language and used the same words.
   2 It came about as they moved east, that they found a flat area of land and settled there.
   3 They said to one another, "Let's make bricks." And they used brick for stone, and they used tar for mortar to stick the bricks together.
   4 They said, "Let's build ourselves a city, and a tower whose top will reach into the sky, and let's make a name for ourselves, otherwise we will be scattered over the face of the whole earth."
   5 The Lord came down to see the city and the tower which they had built.
   6 The Lord said, "Look, they are one people, and they all have the same language. And this is what they began to do, and now nothing they decide to do will be impossible for them.
   7 Come, let's go down and confuse their language, so that they will not understand one another."
   8 So the Lord scattered them over the face of the whole earth; and they stopped building the city.
   9 Therefore the city was named Babel, because there the Lord confused the language of the whole earth; and from there the Lord scattered them over the face of the whole earth.

II. Memory Verse
   o Genesis 1:4
   o God saw that the light was good; and God separated the light from the darkness.

III. Language
   o Spelling/Handwriting
      • words to know: everyone, same, words, let's
         ▪ The word everyone is the words every and one combined. You've already learned every. One is the word for the number one. It starts with an O and ends with a silent E. It has three letters.
         ▪ The word same ends with a silent E.
         ▪ The word words has the word OR inside of it. It is a plural noun. There is more than one word.
         ▪ The word let's has an apostrophe.
   o Vocabulary/Grammar
      • babble (vs. 9)
      • to talk nonstop in a way that you aren't even listened to or understood (verb)
      • the speech of someone who talks that way (noun)

IV. Lesson
   o Today we read about them trying to build a building to heaven. They wanted to "make a name" for themselves.
      • People are still doing this today, wanting to make a name for themselves by having the tallest building.
      • In Istanbul they advertise that they are building the world's tallest building in Europe. It gets them attention. (The funny thing is that they are building it in Asia.)

- 
  - 
    - Part of the city of Istanbul is in Europe, and part is in Asia. Most of the country of Turkey is in Asia, but a corner of it is in Europe. When we lived in Istanbul, we could wake up in Europe and have breakfast in Asia. ☺
    - You can find it on the map for Day 41 of Mount Ararat. You can see a blue river line which divides Europe from Asia right at Istanbul (on the left).
- The pyramids were the earliest buildings at which the world marveled.
- Long after came the cathedrals of Europe with fancy spires that poked at the sky.
- It wasn't until the invention of steel and Andrew Carnegie creating a process to make it efficiently and to sell it cheaply that what we know as skyscrapers were built.
  - The Empire State Building in New York City has held the title of world's tallest building longer than any other. It was opened in 1931 and was 1,250 feet tall (381 meters).
  - The tallest buildings before the skyscrapers were around 500 feet (152 meters).
- The difference in skyscrapers was the steel. Before steel, buildings had strong exterior walls. But they could only support so much weight.
  - If your family stood around holding the edges of a bed sheet, you are all strong enough to support it to keep it off the ground.
  - But what's happening in the middle of the sheet?
    - Need to see it? Grab a sheet or blanket and hold it.
      - The middle sags down. It needs support.
  - The older buildings were made with bricks and stone that created strength on the outside of the building.
  - Steel gave interior support to a building; it put the strength on the inside.
- Steel is made from iron.
  - Iron is strong but it can break, which isn't good when it's holding you up in a tall building!
    - Maybe in your house you have iron and stainless-steel pots or pans and you can feel and see the difference.
- Iron is an element. It can't be broken down into other things. It's pure. Like gold is gold, and oxygen is oxygen. When you break down iron, you just get iron atoms.
- Steel has a lot of properties making it perfect for building skyscrapers.
- What do you think are good qualities for a building material for a very tall building?
  - It's strong. It doesn't break.
  - It's durable which means it lasts a long time.
  - It's malleable which means it can be shaped in different ways, but it still needs to be sturdy.
- Steel can be made into wire, into sheets for the body of cars, and into the steel beams in buildings.
- What other metal have we learned about that was malleable?
  - gold
  - But we don't eat steel! Do you think it would break your teeth to try?
- Let me leave you with a picture of the 2014 tallest building in Dubai. Look at it compared to the tall buildings surrounding it. How does steel make it possible to build such a tall building?

- Recall: What metal is steel made from?
  - iron
- Explore more: Learn about the properties of iron or the method of creating steel.

V. Discussion
   - I find it amazing that God says that man would be able to do anything they put their mind to.
   - Do you think anything is possible? If you could put your mind to something and make it happen, what would it be?

VI. Writing
   - Complete your worksheet for today.
   - You are going to be putting apostrophes into words. You had a spelling word with an apostrophe, let's. It's short for let us. The apostrophe lets us combine two words into one.
   - Here's another example.
     - We say, "I'm coming!" instead of "I am coming." We combine I and am into one word, I'm.

**Day 47**

I. Read Genesis 11:29-12:9.

29 Abram and Nahor each married. The name of Abram's wife was Sarai; and the name of Nahor's wife was Milcah, who was Haran's daughter.

30 Sarai was barren; she had no child.

31 Terah took his son Abram and Sarai, along with his grandson Lot the son of Haran; and they left together from Ur of the Chaldeans to enter the land of Canaan. They went as far as Haran, and settled there.

32 Terah lived to be two hundred and five years; and Terah died in Haran.

1 Now the Lord said to Abram,
"Go out from your country,
And from your relatives
And from your father's house,
To the land which I will show you;

2 And I will make you a great nation,
And I will bless you,
And make your name great;
And so you will be a blessing;

3 And I will bless those who bless you,
And the one who curses you I will curse.
And in you all the families of the earth will be blessed."

4 Abram left as the Lord had commanded, and Lot went with him. Abram was seventy-five years old when he departed from Haran.

5 Abram took Sarai his wife and Lot his nephew, and all their things and people which they had accumulated in Haran, and they set out for the land of Canaan. That's how they came to the land of Canaan.

6 Abram passed through the land as far Shechem, to the oak of Moreh. Now the Canaanites were living in the land then.

7 The Lord appeared to Abram and said, "To your descendants I will give this land." So, Abram built an altar there to the Lord.

8 Then he went from there to the mountain on the east of Bethel, and pitched his tent. There he built an altar and called upon the name of the Lord.

9 Abram journeyed on toward the Negev.

*In verses 2 and 3 we read one of those covenants, where Abraham is told he will be blessed and will be a blessing and that he will be a great nation. In verse 7 Abraham is promised the land of Canaan for his descendants, but right now it's full of Canaanites. Canaanites are descendants of Canaan, Noah's cursed grandsons.

II. Memory Verse
- Genesis 1:4
- God saw that the light was good; and God separated the light from the darkness.

III. Language
- o Spelling/Handwriting
  - verse 1
  - words to know: passed, pitched, child, Lot
  - spelling tips:
    - The word <u>passed</u> is the past tense of the verb to pass. First write the word pass, as in, "Please pass the ketchup." Then add the two letters needed to make it past tense as in, "At the picnic yesterday, we passed the ketchup back and forth all afternoon until the hot dogs and hamburgers were all gone."
    - The word <u>pitched</u> has three letters making the CH sound. They are T-C-H.
    - The word <u>child</u> you can spell. It's the beginning of the word children.
    - The word <u>Lot</u> is a name so what does it begin with?
      - a capital letter
- o Vocabulary/Grammar
  - accumulate (verse 5)
  - gather or get more and more (verb)

IV. Lesson
- o What kind of home did Abraham have?
  - Why do you think it's important to have a tent? If it's a flimsy structure, what purpose does it serve?
  - Abraham is wandering in a desert area. Shelters protect from the sun, the wind, the heat. In other climates they protect from rain and snow and the cold. They're a refuge from the elements which can be more threatening than a lack of food or water.
  - Humans can live for forty days without food and three days without water, but they grow weak when they don't have them for long.
  - However, if the weather conditions are bad, a human might only survive for hours without shelter.
- o So how would you build a shelter if you needed to? First, we need to decide why we're building a shelter. It needs to protect us from the elements. We want to shield ourselves from rain, wind, heat, and cold. What about the first, rain? What would protect us from rain?
  - We need something with a roof. If you had the equipment, a plastic tarp would work. If not, leaning branches together and then covering them with leaves is an alternative.
- o How would you defend against wind?
  - In this case you'd need something with walls. It seems like a similar thing would work if you could set it up against the wind. Leaves could blow away, so maybe leafy branches would work better or many twigs intertwined in the branches.
- o How would you defend against sun?
  - Mostly you need a roof, a covering to produce shade if you can't find shade where you are. It should also have space and be open so that air can blow through. It should also be near water.

- How would you defend against cold?
  - The shelter should be small to hold in your heat. It should be able to be closed so that your body heat can warm the space.
    - Did you ever get in bed and it was so cold and then after a little bit it warmed up?
    - The blankets don't have magical warming powers. Their job is to hold in the heat your body already has.
- Why did Abraham have to live in a tent?
  - He lived in a tent because he had to move around and a tent can be packed up and carried with you.
- Follow Abraham's route together using the Day 47 color map and the map in your workbook. You can draw a line to show his route.
  - Here are the locations.
    - He begins in Ur. This is in Mesopotamia.
    - His family settles in Haran.
      - Abraham leaves from there but his father stays because we read that he dies there.
        - From there God calls him to leave. He's 75 years old at this point.
    - He goes through Shechem in Canaan.
      - What do you notice about this area of the map?
      - It's green! It's fertile land. What does that mean?
        - It's good for farming.
    - He builds an altar on a mountain between Bethel and Ai. (Bethel on the west and Ai on the east.)
      - This is just under Shechem on the map.
      - By the way, Jerusalem is just south of that. They are all close together on the map.
    - Then he continues on to Negev.
  - He would have probably kept near water as he traveled.
    - Ur is on the Euphrates. Haran is between the Euphrates and the Tigris. Shechem is near the sea. The Negev region has two seas on its borders.
    - We also read that he traveled to Egypt, but don't know exactly where. We only know that he crosses the Negev region into Egypt but doesn't go farther than the Nile.
- Recall: Who was told to leave his home and that God would bless him? Why do we need shelter?
  - Abraham
  - to protect us from the elements
- Explore more: It would be fun to build a mini shelter out of sticks and leaves or a bigger one out of branches if you have access to them. See what you can rustle up. Decide what you need to protect against.

V. Discussion
- o Do you always like to know where you are going and what you are going to be doing? Would it be easy or hard for you to trust God to take you somewhere without telling you why or where or what?

VI. Writing
- o You've already completed today's workbook page!

**Day 48**

I. Read Genesis 12:10-20.
   10  Now there was a famine in the land. Abram went down to Egypt to stay there because the famine was severe where he had been.
   11  When he came near to Egypt, that he said to Sarai his wife, "I know that you are a beautiful woman;
   12  and when the Egyptians see you, they will say, 'This is his wife'; and they will kill me.
   13  Please say that you are my sister so that I may live on account of you."
   14  When Abram came into Egypt, the Egyptians saw that the woman was very beautiful.
   15  Pharaoh's officials saw her and praised her to Pharaoh; and the woman was taken into Pharaoh's house.
   16  Pharaoh treated Abram well for her sake; and gave him sheep and oxen and donkeys and camels and male and female servants.
   17  But the Lord struck Pharaoh and his house with great plagues because of Sarai, Abram's wife.
   18  Then Pharaoh called Abram and said, "What have you done to me? Why did you not tell me that she was your wife?
   19  Why did you say, 'She is my sister,' so that I took her for my wife? Here is your wife, take her and go."
   20  Pharaoh commanded his men to send Abram on his way with his wife and all that belonged to him.

II. Memory Verse
   o  Genesis 1:4
   o  God saw that the light was good; and God separated the light from the darkness.

III. Language
   o  Spelling/Handwriting
      - verse 14
      - words to know: donkeys, woman, tell, severe
      - spelling tips:
        - For <u>donkeys</u> you are spelling the plural form, meaning more than one donkey. You need to add an S. If a Y has a vowel before it, then the Y stays and you can just add an S.
        - <u>Woman</u> is the singular noun, just one. It ends with the word man and the plural, women, ends with the plural of man, men.
        - <u>Tell</u> is spelled like well and even spell.
        - The word <u>severe</u> is your vocabulary word for today. I thought you could try to spell it so that you could use it in a story you write some time. It has three vowels and they are all the same. Remember that every syllable has at least one vowel. Severe ends with a silent E.
   o  Vocabulary/Grammar
      - severe (verse 10)
      - intense, extreme (adjective)
      - What does this adjective describe?
        - the famine

IV. Lesson
- o Today's lesson is about famines. Do you know what a famine is?
  - A famine is when there is not enough food for everyone.
  - This doesn't mean if you run out of food at your party that you are experiencing a famine. A famine is a lack of food day after day.
- o The famine in our reading today was severe. What do you think a severe famine would be like compared to a regular famine?
  - It probably means that a lot of people didn't have food or that people didn't have food for a long time.
- o What do you think could be some causes of famines?
  - Famines are caused by either a lack of food or a lack of access to food, meaning you can't get the food that's there.
  - One cause of famine is leaders who keep food or take food from the people they are supposed to serve and protect.
    - When the Communists took over China in 1949, 45 million people died of famine because the government kept food from them.
    - Hundreds of thousands were killed because they were Christians.
- o Apart from governments keeping food from their own people, let's look at other causes of famine.
- o Food comes first from the farm, so things that would hurt the crops could cause famines. What would hurt a farm?
  - Crops can be destroyed by the weather, by plant diseases, or by animals.
- o What weather conditions might destroy crops or keep them from growing?
  - Droughts are when there is little to no rain. Plants and animals need water to survive, so droughts can kill crops.
  - Floods are the opposite problem. Floods are too much water and can also kill plants.
  - If it gets too cold and the plants freeze, that will kill them.
- o Did you know plants could get diseases? Have you ever heard of one?
  - I don't know much about plant diseases, but just like people can get sick from bacteria, plants can get sick from bacteria too.
  - There are more bacteria in your body than there are cells. Bacteria can be good for your body.
  - What we call "germs" refers to living things, too small for us to see. They are bacteria, viruses, and fungi that make us sick and make plants sick too.
  - When we are sick, we can often get others sick by spreading bacteria.
    - That's why we wash our hands, to wash off bacteria that might have gotten on them from touching others or other things that might have had germs.
    - When a plant gets sick, it can spread bacteria too. Farmers have to be on the lookout for sick plants and get them away from the others. If a disease spreads, it can destroy a whole crop. No crops means no food.
- o One final cause of famine that I mentioned is animals destroying crops.
  - One that I know about is the boll weevil. Cotton grows in what we call bolls, the protective covering that the cotton grows inside of. In America the bug

was feared in the southern states where cotton was the main crop produced and was how most people made their money.
- The boll weevil is in the animal kingdom and in the class of insect. It's just over half a centimeter long.     1 cm
- It's a tiny beetle.   (actual size)
- It devastated farms which solely produced cotton.
  - Farming seems so fragile! You can see how reliant on God farmers are.
  - Recall: What is a famine?
    - when there is not enough food for everyone on a continuing basis
  - Explore more: Learn about different types of plant diseases or bugs that affect crops.

V. Discussion
  - What do you think of the idea of Communism that everyone is equal and that everyone should give to the common cause?
  - Why doesn't it work? Why did it kill 45 million people?
  - Is there a way to make it work?

VI. Writing
  - Complete your worksheet for today.
  - You are going to be making words plural and adding adjectives.

**Day 49**

I. Read Genesis 13.
1. So Abram went up from Egypt to the Negev, he and his wife and Lot and everyone and everything with him.
2. Abram was very rich in livestock, in silver and in gold.
3. He went on his journey from the Negev as far as Bethel, to the place where he had been at the beginning,
4. to the place where the altar was which he had made there before; and there Abram called on the name of the Lord.
5. Now Lot, who went along with Abram, also had flocks and herds and tents.
6. And the land could not sustain them there together. They had too many herds between them.
7. There was arguing between the herdsmen of Abram's livestock and the herdsmen of Lot's livestock.
8. So Abram said to Lot, "Please let's not argue, nor our herdsmen, for we are family.
9. The whole land is before you. Please separate from me; if you go to the left, then I will go to the right; or if you go to the right, then I will go to the left."
10. Lot looked around and saw all the valley of the Jordan, that it was well watered everywhere like the garden of Eden—this was before the Lord destroyed Sodom and Gomorrah.
11. So Lot chose for himself all the valley of the Jordan, and they separated from each other.
12. Abram settled to live in Canaan, while Lot settled in the cities of the valley, as far as Sodom.
13. Now the men of Sodom were extremely wicked and sinners against the Lord.
14. The Lord said to Abram, after Lot had separated from him, "Now lift up your eyes and look from the place where you are, northward and southward and eastward and westward;
15. for all the land which you see, I will give it to you and to your descendants forever.
16. I will make your descendants as the dust of the earth, so that if anyone can count and number the dust of the earth, then your descendants can also be numbered.
17. Arise, walk about the land, for I will give it to you."
18. Then Abram moved his tent and came by the oaks of Mamre, which are in Hebron, and there he built an altar to the Lord.

II. Memory Verse
  - Genesis 1:4
  - God saw that the light was good; and God separated the light from the darkness.

III. Language
  - Spelling/Handwriting
    - words to know: before, family, are, well
      - The word <u>before</u> starts with the words be and for.
      - The word <u>family</u> has how many syllables? The first syllable ends with the word am. The next syllable is just one letter. The last syllable has a letter that makes an E sound, but it's not an E. What letter makes the E sound when it ends words with more than one syllable?

- The word <u>are</u> is one you just have to learn. It doesn't sound the way it looks. This is "are" as in "where are we?"
- The word <u>well</u> has the same spelling pattern as your spelling word tell.
  - Vocabulary/Grammar
    - sustain (verse 1)
    - support physically or mentally (verb)

IV. Lesson
  - What do you think it means that the land couldn't sustain Lot and Abraham and their families and livestock, which is all their animals?
    - It means that there wasn't enough of what they needed. They needed grass for their animals. The herdsmen were fighting, so they probably would have been fighting over grazing land or water, the two things their animals needed most. When Lot chooses land, he picks what appears "well-watered."
  - We have a word that we use today to talk about something being able to support us for the indefinite future. The word is sustainability.
    - The suffix ABLE means to be able to do something. *Sustainability* is the ability to be sustained.
  - The land couldn't sustain Abraham and Lot. The way they were living was *unsustainable*.
  - Usually we use the term unsustainable and sustainable in relation to something we're doing. For instance, it's unsustainable to cut trees down faster than new ones can grow. Cutting down trees at a fast pace is an unsustainable practice. Eventually we'd be out of trees.
  - Can you think of things we, us humans, are doing that we couldn't possibly just keep doing forever and ever?
    - The biggest thing that comes to my mind is throwing away trash. It happens in many forms. Do you know where trash goes when it's taken away?
      - It goes to the trash dump. What would happen if we just keep piling up and piling up trash in the dump?
        - It would eventually (in a long time) fill the earth! It's unsustainable.
    - Some things decompose and break down into the ground. Other things, like plastics, just sit there in the ground. Still others, like batteries, leak poison into the ground. Can you think of why that would be dangerous?
      - Do you remember groundwater? That poison gets into the groundwater, which is water we drink and what plants and animals drink as well.
    - This is why we have recycling programs. It keeps trash out of the dumps. It reuses the materials. You can also reuse things instead of throwing them away.
    - In Macedonia I saw a dump truck dump a full load of trash into a river. Factories dump their waste into rivers around the world. In America there have been court cases against companies who have done this. They poison the water and local families get sick from it.

- When they test our water, it shows traces of medicines in it! Everything that gets into the water gets spread around and not even water treatment plants can clean out everything people dump in. It's unsustainable to just keep dumping poisons into the water supply.
  - Let's look at the other side, what we call sustainable practices, doing things in a way that we'll be able to continue doing them in the future.
    - Recycling is a sustainable practice. If we can use things and then recycle them, we can use them again and again.
      - How can you recycle at home? How can you reuse things?
    - One source of sustainable energy is solar power. Have you ever seen solar power in use?
      - We use solar panels to convert, or change, the light's heat into electricity.
  - Recall: What is sustainability? What is an example of an unsustainable practice?
    - the ability to be sustained, to keep supplying what is needed
    - dumping trash in dumps
  - Explore more: Plan together how you can be a better earth protector.

V. Discussion
  - We talked today about sustainability. Do you think it's important? God created the earth and gave man rule over the land. Does that make us responsible? He's going to destroy the earth one day and we're going to have a new earth, so does it matter what happens to it before it's destroyed? What do you think?
    - My opinions! I think sustainability is a very good thing. There's no reason to be wasteful when it's not necessary. The earth is God's creation and He gave it to us. We should care for it, not destroy it. The biggest threat to the earth is sin. It's greed and selfishness, not pollution. That's just one ugly product that greed and selfishness produce. There are those who say we need fewer people so that there are fewer people hurting the earth. I've already warned you that any philosophy that puts anything before people is not from God. God loves us more than He loves the trees! When looking into sustainability, be careful to stay away from that which belittles the value of human life.

VI. Writing
  - Complete today's worksheet.
  - You are going to be drawing pictures of sustainable and unsustainable practices. What does that mean?

**Day 50 (check Materials List)**

I. Read Genesis 14:1-3, 10-16.
- 1 And it came about that the king of Elam and his three allies
- 2 made war with five kings including the kings of Sodom and Gomorrah.
- 3 All these came as allies to the valley of the Salt Sea, known as the Dead Sea.
- ...
- 10 Now the valley of the Salt Sea was full of tar pits; and the kings of Sodom and Gomorrah ran away from the battle, and they fell into them. But those who survived fled to the hill country.
- 11 Then the others took all the goods of Sodom and Gomorrah and all their food supply, and left.
- 12 With them they also took Lot, Abram's nephew, and his possessions because he was living in Sodom.
- 13 Then someone snuck away and told Abram the Hebrew.
- 14 When Abram heard that his relative had been taken captive, he led out his trained men, born in his house, three hundred and eighteen, and went in pursuit to rescue Lot.
- 15 He divided his forces to sneak up by night, he and his servants, and defeated them. They ran away and Abram's men chased them to north of Damascus.
- 16 Abram brought back all the goods, and also brought back Lot and Lot's family and possessions.

II. Memory Verse
- o Genesis 1:4
- o God saw that the light was good; and God separated the light from the darkness.
- o Review Romans 6:23.

III. Language
- o Spelling/Handwriting
    - Test yourselves on the words from Days 46-49.
        - everyone, same, words, let's
        - passed, pitched, child, Lot
        - donkeys, woman, tell, severe
        - before, family, are, well
- o Vocabulary/Grammar
    - Test yourselves on the words from Days 46-49.
        - babble – to talk nonstop in a way that you aren't even listened to or understood
        - accumulate – to gather, to get more and more
        - severe – intense, extreme
        - sustain - support physically or mentally

IV. Lesson
- o There's a war going on in today's reading. There are allies and foes. There are kidnappings and rescues. Don't get bogged down in all of the names and miss the action!
    - Who was kidnapped and who was the rescuer?

- Lot and his family were kidnapped, and Abraham and his servants and their families were the rescuers.
- We read in verse 10 that the kings of Sodom and Gomorrah fall into tar pits.
    - It sounds like they died in the tar pit because the rest of the verse says that those who survived fled.
- Reading about the tar pits made me curious about them. I knew what tar is, but I didn't know of anywhere in the world where you can just fall into something like a pit of tar.
- First things first, what is tar?
    - I don't really have a good definition of tar. It's black sticky stuff; often it's made from coal. We might use it to glue on roof tiles.
- However, when I started researching this, I learned that what people call tar pits are technically asphalt lakes. Do you know what asphalt is?
    - That's the hot black sticky stuff they pour to make roads. The lakes are just the black sticky stuff, not the gravel rocks mixed with it like our streets are made of.
- It turns out there are tar pits still around today. One is even in America, in Los Angeles, California. *Paleontologists*, those who study ancient fossils, have dug up many ancient animals from there. Why do you think there were so many animal bones found in the tar pit?
    - Animals would get stuck in the tar. They would get stuck and not be able to get out. If they got far enough in, they could sink into it.
    - Also, weak animals attract prey, so I would think when one animal got stuck, it would attack animals thinking they had found an animal in trouble that would make easy prey. Then those animals would get stuck too!
    - Here's a picture. From a distance it can just look like a body of water. But look at the thick sticky stuff clinging to the stick and stretching all the way to the ground.
- Have you ever heard of quicksand? Tar pits make me think of quicksand.
    - Quicksand is sand that acts like a liquid in that you can sink into it, but it's also sort of like a solid in that you can get stuck in it.

- o   Do you want to make quicksand? Maybe it would be a little like getting stuck in a tar pit.
    - You'll mix a 16 oz. box of cornstarch (about 450 grams) with 1-2 cups of water. Start with a half cup of water and slowly add more until it has the consistency of honey.
    - The faster you move in quicksand, the worse off you are. Try moving your hand fast in the quicksand you made. Is it harder to move quickly? Drop something in and try to rescue it. Does the quicksand/tar pit seem to hold onto it?
    - When you are done, dump it into a plastic bag and throw it away. Don't goop up your drain.
    - This experiment is from stevespanglerscience.com if you want to see a video of it.
- o   Recall: What do paleontologists study? What is a tar pit full of?
    - fossils
    - asphalt
- o   Explore more: Learn the word viscosity. How does it relate to tar pits and quicksand and the science experiment?

V. Discussion
- o   Do you think you could be brave enough to go on a rescue mission like Abraham?

VI. Writing
- o   Make sure your worksheet is complete for today.
- o   You'll be checking your spelling and vocabulary today.

**Day 51 (check Materials List)**

I. Read Genesis 14:17-24. (When this begins, it's talking about Abraham returning from his rescue mission battle.)
   17 Then after his return from the defeat of the kings, the king of Sodom went out to meet him at the King's Valley.
   18 And Melchizedek king of Salem brought out bread and wine; now he was a priest of God Most High.
   19 He blessed Abram and said,
   "Blessed be Abram of God Most High,
   Possessor of heaven and earth;
   20 And blessed be God Most High,
   Who has delivered your enemies into your hand."
   Abram gave Melchizedek a tenth of all.
   21 The king of Sodom said to Abram, "Give the people to me and take the goods for yourself."
   22 Abram said to the king of Sodom, "I have promised to the Lord God Most High, to whom belongs heaven and earth,
   23 that I will not take even a thread or anything that is yours, for fear you would say, 'I have made Abram rich.'
   24 I will take nothing except what the young men have eaten, and the share of the men who went with me; let them take their share.

II. Memory Verse
   o Genesis 26:4
   o I will multiply your descendants as the stars of the heaven, and will give your descendants all these lands; and by your descendants all the nations of the earth shall be blessed.

III. Language
   o Spelling/Handwriting
      • words to know: return, went, out, meet
      • spelling tips:
         ▪ <u>Return</u> ends with the word turn. The sound ER can be made with an E-R, I-R, or U-R. This is made with the U. The RE at the beginning is just two letters.
         ▪ <u>Went</u> is spelled just like it sounds.
         ▪ The word <u>out</u> you have already spelled in the word sprout.
         ▪ The word <u>meet</u> is a homophone. This is the kind of meet where you meet someone new, not the kind of meat you eat. The meat you eat is spelled with the same vowel pattern as eat. The meeting-someone-new meet is spelled with a double letter.
   o Vocabulary/Grammar
      • deliver
      • rescue, save (verb)
      • other definition: to hand over

IV. Lesson
- o Abraham doesn't want to take away any glory from God and doesn't want anyone else claiming they made "Abram" rich.
- o He takes nothing but the food they had eaten.
    - What is a share of food? How much does a man eat in a day or need to eat in a day? What about a kid? How much food do you think is enough? How much do you think is too much?
- o Why do we need food?
    - We know that our body gets its energy from food. It's an important part of how God made our bodies to work.
    - Growing bodies need more and more energy as they get bigger. Babies don't eat very much. They don't need as much energy.
- o We measure how much food energy we are taking in by something called *calories*. One calorie will produce one unit of energy in our bodies.
    - Go look at a food package in your kitchen. What does it say is the number of calories in it?
    - In other countries the word calories is sometimes translated as energy.
- o So how many units of energy do we need? Any guesses?
    - It's different for everyone because we use up different amounts of energy. If you run around all day, are you using more energy than someone watching TV or playing video games all day?
        - Yes! If you are running around, you would need more food than a kid just sitting around.
        - If we don't use up the energy we consume, the energy that we eat, then the energy turns into fat. You gain fat by eating more food energy than you use up.
    - I will give you some general numbers of how many calories you need, but just remember these aren't exact numbers of how much you in particular need to eat.
        - Kids need about 1500 calories a day.
        - As they get to be about eleven years old, they need 2000 calories.
        - Teenage boys need 3000 calories a day.
    - Remember that your need for calories grows with you. It's not that when you turn eleven then all of a sudden you need more calories. When you are going through growth spurts, a time when you are growing quickly, you will eat more. You need the energy to grow!
- o Calories are good things for your body. Your body runs on their energy. Calories are only bad when you are taking in too many. Let me give you a few examples of how many calories are in your food. (Note: You may want to let them guess the number of calories for the food.)
    - 144       can of Coke
    - 108       homemade biscuit
    - 68        slice of bread
    - 240       package of M&Ms
    - 110       Cheerios (1 ¼ cups)
    - 51        homemade chocolate chip cookies
    - 140       goldfish, 45 crackers

- 377     one cup of soft vanilla ice cream
- 188     one slice of cheese pizza, Dominos
- 111     one scrambled egg with butter and milk
- 80     apple
- 71     orange
- 117     one cup of apple juice
- 406     extra-crispy chicken thigh from KFC
- 520     quarter-pounder with cheese from McDonald's
- 288     4 ounces of lean ground beef
- 190     a serving of salted peanuts

- One thing you shouldn't do from this list is think, I should drink soda instead of eating peanuts because peanuts have more calories!
    - That would be very wrong thinking. Soda provides calories but nothing else. We call them "empty calories."
    - Your body needs more than calories; it needs nutrition, things like calcium which makes bones strong and vitamin A which helps our eyesight.
    - Peanuts provide iron, among other nutrients, which helps get oxygen to where it's needed in our bodies.
- Recall: What is a calorie?
    - a measurement of food energy
- Explore more: How about tracking your calories for a day? Think about what you've already eaten today and write it down with your best estimate as to how many calories it was. Tomorrow look at it compared to the average numbers for a child (or adult!) You'll need to use the internet to get more information for this.

V. Discussion
- Melchizedek takes out bread and wine. Communion is a time when we remember Jesus' death on the cross. What do you think of when you remember Jesus' sacrifice on the cross? Even before the cross Jesus sacrificed for us by giving up heaven to come to earth. What all did He give up or sacrifice for you?

VI. Writing
- Complete your workbook page for today.
- You will be writing the names of places. There are directions and examples on your page. (Note: You can help out by talking about the street, city, and state you live in. You may need to help with spelling those!)

**Day 52**

I. Read Genesis 15:1-18.
- 1 After these things the word of the Lord came to Abram in a vision, saying,
  "Do not fear, Abram,
  I am your shield;
  Your reward will be very great."
- 2 Abram said, "O Lord God, what will You give me, since I am childless, and the heir of my house is my servant?"
- 3 And Abram said, "Since You have not given me a child, a servant born in my house is my heir."
- 4 Then the word of the Lord came to him, saying, "This man will not be your heir, but your own child will be your heir."
- 5 And He took Abram outside and said, "Now look toward the heavens, and count the stars, if you are able to count them." And He said to him, "That's how many descendants you will have, so many that you couldn't even count them."
- 6 Then he believed in the Lord; and God saw it as righteousness in Abram.
- 7 And He said to Abram, "I am the Lord who brought you out of Ur, to give this land to you."
- 8 Abram said, "O Lord God, how may I know that it will be mine?"
- 9 So He said to Abram, "Bring Me a three-year-old heifer, and a three-year-old female goat, and a three-year-old ram, and a turtledove, and a young pigeon."
- 10 Then Abram brought all these to Him and cut them in two, and laid each half opposite the other; but Abram did not cut the birds.
- 11 The birds of prey came down upon the carcasses, and Abram drove them away.
- 12 Now when the sun was going down, a deep sleep fell upon Abram; and terror and great darkness came over Abram.
- 13 God said to Abram, "Know for certain that your descendants will be strangers in a land that is not theirs, where they will be slaves for four hundred years.
- 14 But I will also punish the nation who makes them slaves, and when they come out, they will come out with many possessions.
- 15 As for you, you will die in peace; you will be buried at a good old age.
- 16 Then in the fourth generation they will return here, when the timing is just right."
- 17 When the sun had set and it was very dark, there appeared a smoking oven and a flaming torch which passed between the pieces.
- 18 On that day the Lord made a covenant with Abram, saying,
  "To your descendants I have given this land,
  From the river of Egypt as far as the great river, the river Euphrates."

II. Memory Verse
   - Genesis 26:4
   - I will multiply your descendants as the stars of the heaven, and will give your descendants all these lands; and by your descendants all the nations of the earth shall be blessed.

III. Language
   - Spelling/Handwriting
     - words to know: old, three, year, you
     - spelling tips:

- The word <u>old</u> you have spelled before in the word gold, so if you can spell gold, you can spell old.
- The word <u>three</u> has a double letter making its vowel sound.
- The word <u>year</u> has the same vowel spelling pattern as seas and each.
- The word <u>you</u> just needs to be memorized, but it rhymes with its spelling; it's spelled Y-O-U.
  - Vocabulary/Grammar
    - heir (verse 3)
    - the person who will inherit property, money, or position title after a person leaves a position or dies (noun)

IV. Lesson
  - We're going to learn more about rivers today. Look at the Day 52 map of the Mississippi River. What do you notice?
    - It kind of looks like a tree, how it branches out, and then those branches can branch out as well.
  - Today we're going to learn about those different parts of a river and how they happen.
  - A river begins with the *headwaters*. A river could begin with a spring bubbling up from underground. It could begin in a wet, marshy area with a large amount of snow melting. It could begin where thousands of streams all come together, or maybe it starts with just a trickle of water coming from a pond.
    - From what you've learned about elevation and sea level, where are the headwaters of the Mississippi River?
      - They are up in Minnesota.
  - Can you think of any reason why the headwaters of a river are important?
    - Anything that happens to the water at the beginning will affect everything downstream.
  - A *tributary* is a river whose water goes into another river. A large river is getting lots of its water from tributaries. Now look at the Mississippi River map again. Which rivers are the tributaries?
    - The large Mississippi River is getting its water from the rivers that connect to it. Some of those tributaries have tributaries that feed into them.
  - The *channel* is the path the river takes. What do river channels look like?
    - A river can go straight through a valley with high rock cliff walls on each side of it. Some rivers curve back and forth. Some rivers even crisscross themselves like a braid. The channel can be wide or narrow. Each river is unique.
  - How do you think a river's channel gets curvy?
    - *Erosion* wears away dirt and rocks and sand from one spot is deposited, or dropped off, in another spot on the other side of the channel. Little by little a river can change its own shape.
      - Maybe you'd like to come up with a way to act that out, using people or props for the sediment, to show how the river changes shape.
    - In fact, rivers are always changing.
  - The riverbank is the land right next to the river.

- o The mouth of the river, or the river *delta,* is where the river slows down and fans out as it empties into the sea or ocean or lake. Where's the mouth of the Mississippi?
    - If you look at the Day 20 map of America's wetlands (says Rivers and State Boundaries), you can see the fan-ish shape of the Mississippi's delta.
    - On the Day 47 map of the Middle East, you can see the green fan shape at the Nile's delta. Why is it green there?
        - It's fertile. Things grow easily there because of all the water.
- o Recall: Draw a picture of a river. Label the headwaters, a tributary, the riverbank and the delta. You can use your workbook for this.
- o Explore more: Take a look at the other maps for Day 52 and talk about what they show. Abraham was promised land for his descendants. We're not exactly sure where that is, but we're pretty sure they've never had the full land. The maps show modern borders or countries and territories, the rivers mentioned in the reading, Palestinian territory, and proposed borders to Israel based on Scriptures.

V. Discussion
- o Do you think Israel will ever live in the land described as being given to Israel? Do you think they should? When Jesus comes back to Israel to rule the world, who will live in Israel do you think? Would you want to be there?

VI. Writing
- o Complete your worksheet for today.
- o You will be writing words that have the same vowel spelling pattern as three.
- o There is also a place for your river picture.

**Day 53**

I. Read Genesis 16-1-6.
   1. Now Sarai, Abram's wife, had not had any children, and she had an Egyptian maid named Hagar.
   2. So Sarai said to Abram, "Look here, the Lord has prevented me from having children of my own. Please take my maid as a wife; perhaps I will receive children through her." And Abram listened to his wife.
   3. After Abram had lived ten years in Canaan, Abram's wife Sarai took Hagar the Egyptian, her maid, and gave her to her husband Abram as his wife.
   4. And Hagar conceived and became pregnant; and when she saw that she had conceived, Hagar despised Sarai and looked down on her.
   5. And Sarai said to Abram, "This is your fault that Hagar treats me wrongly now. May the Lord judge between us to see who is at fault."
   6. But Abram said to Sarai, "Look, she is your maid; you have the power to decide what to do to her." So Sarai treated Hagar harshly, and Hagar ran away.

II. Memory Verse
   - Genesis 26:4
   - I will multiply your descendants as the stars of the heaven, and will give your descendants all these lands; and by your descendants all the nations of the earth shall be blessed.

III. Language
   - Spelling/Handwriting
     - words to know: maid, wrong, power, your
     - spelling tips:
       - The word maid is a homophone. This is the kind of maid that cleans a house, not something you put together. This kind of maid does not have a silent E.
       - The word wrong ends with a similar spelling pattern to I-N-G words. It just uses an O. If you can spell wrong, you can spell song and gong and long.
       - The word power has the word OW inside of it. It's the same spelling pattern used in flow, but here it says Ow! Remember that every syllable must have at least one vowel. How many syllables are in this word?
         - 2
         - That ER ending syllable can't just be an R. It must have a vowel.
       - The word your is just like your word you from Day 52 except it ends with one extra letter. Your is a homophone as well. It sounds like you're which means you are. This kind of your means that something belongs to you, like your bike.
   - Vocabulary/Grammar
     - prevent (verse 2)
     - to keep something from happening (verb)

IV. Lesson
- We read that Hagar conceives a child.
- The word conceive means to become pregnant. It also means to dream up or to think up. Ideas are conceived. I think that's neat that the word has those two meanings. Each child is conceived by God. He has a bright idea. He forms the child and plans its future.
- Psalm 139:13 says, "For You formed my inward parts; You wove me in my mother's womb."
    - The womb is where a baby grows. When a mommy's belly grows big it's not because her stomach is getting big. She didn't eat the baby!
- The womb is lower on her belly than her stomach. Only women have a womb. God created them to carry babies and to care for them.
- God makes every baby from a piece of the mother and a piece of the father. That's why children look like their parents. They are made from them.
- Women have eggs in their bodies, but not like chicken eggs; they don't have shells. Each egg is actually a single cell, the biggest type of cell in a woman's body. The egg cells can barely be seen by the human eye, while all other cells are *microscopic*, meaning you need a microscope to see them. There are more than a million of these eggs in each woman.
    - Why so many? I don't know! I guess God wanted to be able to choose just the right one when the time comes. Actually, even a little girl has these eggs inside of her. Girls are born with them. A little girl can't have a baby because her body doesn't get ready to have a baby until she's a teenager and there has to be a father, but God prepared her for when the day comes.
- When God chooses the right time, a piece of the father is joined with the egg cell and that is called conception. A new baby has been conceived in God's mind and in the woman's body.
- In about nine months that baby grows from just an idea and a cell to a baby you can hold in your arms, a baby that was made in God's image. If you are in a hurry to get taller, just remember that every adult you see used to be almost microscopic!
- Let me tell you one more thing about being in your mother's womb. Do you know why you have a belly button?
    - You were connected to a piece of your mother when you were in her womb. That's how you got your food and oxygen. You were connected by what's called the umbilical cord. After you were born, it was cut to separate you and then what was left of it still attached to you fell off, leaving you with a cute button. Your belly button can remind you of how your mom took care of you even before you were born!
- Remember that God is the one who conceived you. You were God's bright idea. He made you on purpose! He says: "For I know the plans I have for you," says the LORD. "They are plans for good and not for disaster, to give you a future and a hope." (Jeremiah 29:11 NLT)
- Recall: What does it mean to conceive? What is microscopic?
    - to become pregnant or think up a plan or idea
    - can only be seen with a microscope
- Explore more: There are neat videos that show the growth of a baby in the womb.

V. Discussion
- o In the end Jesus will come and rule. What kind of laws do you think Jesus will establish when He rules on earth?

VI. Writing
- o Use the discussion question as a writing prompt.
- o You are going to be writing sentences today.

**Day 54 (check Materials List)**

I. Read Genesis 16:7-13. (Today's reading picks up after Hagar has run away from Sarah because she was being treated harshly.)
   7 Now the angel of the Lord found Hagar by a spring of water in the wilderness.
   8 He said, "Hagar, Sarai's maid, where have you come from and where are you going?" And she said, "I am running from my mistress Sarai."
   9 Then the angel of the Lord said to her, "Return to your mistress, submit yourself to her authority and obey Sarai."
   10 The angel of the Lord also said to her, "I will multiply your descendants so much that they will be too many to count."
   11 Then the angel of the Lord said to her,
   "Behold, you are expecting a child,
   And you will have a son;
   And you will name him Ishmael,
   Because the Lord has paid attention to your troubles.
   12 "Ishmael will be a wild donkey of a man,
   He will fight with everyone,
   And everyone will fight against him;
   And he will live to the east of his brothers."
   13 Then she called the Lord who spoke to her, "You are a God who sees"; and she questioned, "How am I even alive after seeing Him?"

II. Memory Verse
   o Genesis 26:4
   o I will multiply your descendants as the stars of the heaven, and will give your descendants all these lands; and by your descendants all the nations of the earth shall be blessed.

III. Language
   o Spelling/Handwriting
      • words to know: angel, spring, sees, trouble
      • spelling tips:
         ▪ The word angel is put together with the words an and gel.
         ▪ The word spring has only one syllable, so there is only one place where there is a vowel sound. It's made with just one vowel, just like it sounds.
         ▪ The word sees is a homophone of a word you have already spelled, seas like the oceans. This is, "He sees you hiding there." It has a double letter making the vowel sound.
         ▪ The word trouble is a trickier word. It has two syllables, so it has two places with vowels. The first syllable uses the same vowel spelling pattern as the word out. The last two letters are the same as in your spelling word people.
   o Vocabulary/Grammar
      • authority (verse 9)
      • the person or organization in power, in control, with the right to give orders (noun)
      • other definition: something that causes pain and suffering (noun)

IV. Lesson
- In our story today, Hagar is by a spring of water.
- Do you remember what the headwaters of a river are?
  - They are the beginning of a river.
- On Day 52 I told you that the headwaters of a river might begin by a spring bubbling up.
- Do you remember what groundwater is?
  - It's the water stored and moving underground.
- We use wells to get water from underground, but sometimes the water comes up to us in the form of a spring.
- Can you demonstrate how to spring? (Note: I'm talking about the jumping up kind of springing.)
  - The water does something like that. It shoots up and then comes back down.
  - Springs are another part of the water cycle. Can you describe the water cycle?
    - Water goes in a cycle, a circle. It goes up through evaporation and transpiration from plants. It comes down as rain. That's the basic cycle.
    - Most evaporation occurs from the ocean which is where most water ends up as it is pulled by gravity down to sea level.
- There are different types of springs. The most common are from groundwater finding its way to the surface through cracks in rocks. What happens to the rock as water keeps pushing its way through?
  - It erodes. It wears away at the rock little by little. The water opens its way, more and more, until you have water pouring out of a rock.
  - Growing up, my family used to take jugs and fill them up with water from a local spring.
  - These kinds of springs are the type that begin streams.
    - In the summer my kids make water squirters by poking a hole in the lid of a plastic bottle. Maybe your parents will let you try it. You can create a small stream by letting water flow out of your bottle-spring.
    - If you turned the bottle sideways and pointed it a little down, gravity would begin to pull water out of the hole. What happens when the bottle is squeezed?
      - It shoots out the water. When you are squeezing the bottle, you are applying pressure.
      - If you squeeze it gently, with low pressure, then the water comes out slowly. If you squeeze it hard, with high pressure, then what happens?
        - It shoots out farther.
- In our story today, who is by the spring?
  - Hagar is there but she is also met by the angel of the Lord. I know I am familiar with all of the stories in the Bible where the Lord guides His people and helps them. I think of Abraham and Moses and Joshua and Gideon. But I don't think of Hagar. Here is someone in Scripture who has a divine encounter. She obeys and goes back. Here is part of the prophecy she is given. I think the rest of it is probably talking just about Ishmael or his household, not his far-removed descendants. It says:

- God will multiply her descendants so that they will be too many to count.
- She will have a son to be named Ishmael which means God listens or God will hear.
- Ishmael is the father of the Ishmaelites. We will come across them later. He is the father of the Arabs.
- Isaac, Abraham's next son, is the father of the Jews.
  - Both Jews and Arabs trace their lineage through Abraham.
- Look at the Day 54 map of Arab nations. Where's Israel?
  - It's the little spot that's not green, but surrounded by green, along the Mediterranean Sea.
- There are over well over 400 million Arabs in the world today. Half are under 25 years old which means their population is only getting bigger and bigger.
  - There are over 21 million Jews.
- All of the numbers change daily (minute by minute), so in a way, they are too numerous to count!
- Recall: What is it called when water wears away at rocks?
  - erosion, Water is eroding the rock.
- Explore more: There is one more map for Day 54. You could look at that. There are technically more Christians than Muslims, but most of the Christians are ethnically Christian, born into it, and don't know Christ as Savior. (Also, not all Arabs are Muslims and not all Muslims are Arabs.) Do you have any rocks that have been collected at home, or could you go out looking for rocks? Can you find rough and smooth rocks? A smooth rock has faced more erosion. Its rough edges have been worn away by water, by rubbing against things the ground and other rocks.

V. Discussion
  - What do you think of God blessing Ishmael and making his descendants even more numerous than Isaac's?

VI. Writing
  - Complete your worksheet for today.

**Day 55**

I. Read Genesis 16:15-17:8 and verse 15.
   15 So Hagar bore Abram a son; and Abram called the name of his son, whom Hagar bore, Ishmael.
   16 Abram was eighty-six years old when Hagar bore Ishmael to him.
   1 Now when Abram was ninety-nine years old, the Lord appeared to Abram and said to him,
   "I am God Almighty;
   Walk before Me, and be blameless.
   2 "I will establish My covenant between Me and you,
   And I will multiply you exceedingly."
   3 Abram fell on his face, and God talked with him, saying,
   4 "As for Me, My covenant is with you,
   And you will be the father of a multitude of nations.
   5 "No longer shall your name be called Abram,
   But your name shall be Abraham;
   For I have made you the father of a multitude of nations.
   6 I will make you very fruitful, and I will make nations of you, and kings will come forth from you.
   7 I will establish My covenant between Me and you and your descendants after you throughout their generations for an everlasting covenant, to be God to you and to your descendants after you.
   8 I will give to you and to your descendants after you, the land of your journeys, all the land of Canaan, for an everlasting possession; and I will be their God."
   15 Then God said to Abraham, "As for Sarai your wife, you shall not call her name Sarai, but Sarah shall be her name.

II. Memory Verse
   o Genesis 26:4
      • I will multiply your descendants as the stars of the heaven, and will give your descendants all these lands; and by your descendants all the nations of the earth shall be blessed.
   o Review Genesis 1:4.
      • God saw that the light was good; and God separated the light from the darkness.

III. Language
   o Spelling/Handwriting
      • Test yourselves on the words from Days 51-54.
         ▪ return, went, out, meet
         ▪ old, three, year, you
         ▪ maid, wrong, power, your
         ▪ angel, spring, sees, trouble
   o Vocabulary/Grammar
      • Test yourselves on the words from Days 51-54.
         ▪ deliver – to rescue, save

- heir – the person who will inherit property, money, or position title after a person leaves a position or dies
- prevent – to keep something from happening
- authority – the person or organization in power, in control, with the right to give orders

IV. Lesson
- o In our reading today Abram's name changes to Abraham. His wife Sarai will get her name changed to Sarah. What's in a name?
- o In the Old Testament we are often told the meanings of names.
  - Ishmael was named for God listening.
  - Abraham means father of a multitude.
  - The name Sarah means princess.
  - Abraham and Sarah will have a son named Isaac which means "he laughs." Abraham and Sarah both laugh when they are told they will have a son.
  - One of the cities we have come across is Salem. It later becomes the city of Jerusalem, the capital city of Israel. It was named for the Canaanite god, Salem. In Hebrew, though, the same name translates to peace. Jerusalem means foundation of peace.
- o Here are some other biblical names and their meanings.
  - Samuel – heard of God
  - Peter – rock
  - Andrew – manly
  - Anna – grace
  - Nathaniel – gift of God
  - Ruth – friend
  - Rachel – ewe, which is a female sheep
- o Rachel doesn't seem to be this way, but in Nathaniel, Samuel and Ishmael, the EL at the end of their names is referring to God, like in eloHEEM. That made me think that the name Israel also ends in EL.
- o The nation of Israel also has a significant name. It means who prevails with God, or triumphant with God.
- o Recall: What does Abraham mean? What does Sarah mean?
  - father of a multitude
  - princess
- o Explore more: Maybe you'd like to look up the meanings of your names. Some can be weird! How are you like or not like your name's meaning?

V. Discussion
- o Abraham was 86 when Ishmael was born and 99 when God renewed the promise about his descendants. He will be 100 when Isaac is born, the child promised from the beginning. Do you understand Abraham thinking Ishmael was the answer to God's promise? Do you think he ever doubted if that's what God had intended? Do you think you could wait so many years and still believe it could happen?

VI. Writing
- o Your worksheet should be complete for today.
- o You have a place for spelling and vocabulary.

**Day 56**

I. Read Genesis 17:9-21.
   9   God said to Abraham, "Now as for you, you must keep My covenant, you and your descendants that come after you.
   10  This is My covenant, that every male among you must be circumcised.
   11  It will be the sign of the covenant promise between Me and you.
   12  And every male among you who is eight days old shall be circumcised.
   13  A servant who is born in your house or who is bought with your money must also be circumcised; My covenant will be in your flesh for an everlasting covenant.
   14  But a male who is not circumcised, that person must be cut off from his people because he has broken My covenant."
   15  Then God said to Abraham, "As for Sarai your wife, you shall not call her name Sarai, but Sarah shall be her name.
   16  I will bless her, and indeed I will give you a son by her. Then I will bless her, and she shall be a mother of nations; kings of peoples will come from her."
   17  Then Abraham fell on his face and laughed, and said in his heart, "Will a child be born to a man one hundred years old? And will Sarah, who is ninety years old, bear a child?"
   18  And Abraham said to God, "Oh that Ishmael might live before You!"
   19  But God said, "No, but Sarah your wife will have a son, and you will call his name Isaac; and I will establish My covenant with him for an everlasting covenant for his descendants after him.
   20  As for Ishmael, I have heard you; I will bless him. He will become the father of twelve princes, and I will make him a great nation.
   21  But My covenant I will establish with Isaac, whom Sarah will have around this time next year."

II. Memory Verse
   o   2 Corinthians 1:20
   o   For as many as are the promises of God, in Him they are yes; therefore also through Him is our Amen to the glory of God through us.
       • (Here's the version I gave my younger kids. All the promises of God are "yes" and "amen" in Christ Jesus.)
       • We know that the answer is "yes" from God if it's something He's promised, so we can say, "Amen, so be it."

III. Language
   o   Spelling/Handwriting
       • words to know: nine, twelve, Sarah, next
       • spelling tips:
           ▪ We have two numbers we are spelling today. The first is <u>nine</u>. It ends with a silent E. That's how the I is saying its name.
           ▪ The second number is <u>twelve</u>. It ends with a silent E. The E doesn't really do anything, but does it look really strange without it?
           ▪ The next word is a name, so what does it begin with? <u>Sarah</u> has two vowels that are both the same. It ends with a silent H.
           ▪ The last word is <u>next</u>. It is spelled just like it sounds, so say it carefully.

- Vocabulary/Grammar
  - intercept (I just chose this for today.)
  - blocking something from getting to where it's supposed to go (verb)

IV. Lesson
  - We know a little of ancient surgical practices. Read these laws from Babylon, the most famous city from Mesopotamia.
    - 215. If a physician makes a large incision with an operating knife and cures it, or if he opens a tumor (over the eye) with an operating knife, and saves the eye, he shall receive ten shekels in money.
    - 217. If he is the slave of someone, his owner shall give the physician two shekels.
    - 218. If a physician makes a large incision with the operating knife, and kills him, or opens a tumor with the operating knife, and cuts out the eye, his hands shall be cut off.
  - What can you learn from these laws?
    - Surgery was a risky business. It seems like ten shekels must have been a lot of money if they were willing to risk losing their hands! We can also see how a slave's life wasn't valued as much.
      - There's a sermon called "Ten Shekels and a Shirt" that's one of my favorites. You can find it on sermonindex.net. You can find its transcript online too. It's based on the Bible story about Micah being hired to be the priest to a false god. He received ten shekels of silver and food and clothing. That was his yearly wage, so maybe ten shekels for one surgery was a really good deal.
  - Those laws come from the *Hammurabi Code*. It was written by the ruler of Babylon in the 1700s BC.
    - God gives His law to Moses and Israel in the 1400s BC. Which came first?
      - Hammurabi's Code was written first.
    - There have been even older laws found. A tablet with laws written on them was found in an ancient Syrian city. It is said to date in the 2400s BC.
  - Some of the laws include:
    - That a man's wife or children be sold as slaves to work for three years to pay his debts. (BTW: This is still done today in places. Is it fair that the man isn't taken as a slave instead?)
    - If a woman doesn't do her work around the house, she is to be thrown into the Euphrates River. She may or may not make it back to the shore.
    - If a builder builds a house that collapses and kills the owner, the builder is put to death.
  - There is a strong sense of an "eye for an eye, and a tooth for a tooth" that is similar to the Old Testament law which makes some think that Moses copied the code.
    - However, just from the laws I described above, I hope you can already see important differences. An eye for an eye is about justice, making things right, being fair. Where is the justice in selling your wife or child to pay for your debts?
    - In every culture there were the same issues of lying, stealing, murder, etc. and every culture had to find a way to deal with it and bring about justice.

- The main difference with the law that God gave Moses and his people, is that it is the only one that was spiritual in nature. It wasn't just about how people should deal with other people in different situations. It was about the root cause of the problems, sin.
- The law of God was about sin and our need to live righteously. We are to worship one God only. We are not to make idols.
- And a big difference is that the Hammurabi Code offers no forgiveness. The law given by God provided means of receiving forgiveness and restoration, making things right with God.
- And what about selling your wife and children as slaves to work for three years to pay your debt?
    - Not in the law of Moses.
    - There is mention of selling yourself as a slave, and every 7th year debts were forgiven and slaves were set free. There are also other provisions to help the poor, so they wouldn't find themselves in such desperate situations.
  - Recall: What is the name of the code of law written in Babylon in the 1700s BC?
      - Hammurabi's Code
  - Explore more: Read more of the code. What can you learn about Hammurabi?

V. Discussion
  - If you could make your own laws, what laws would you change? What laws would you create?

VI. Writing
  - Complete your worksheet for today.
  - You are going to write sentences by using a noun and a verb.

**Day 57 (check Materials List)**

I. Read Genesis 18:1-8.
   1. Now the Lord appeared to [Abraham] by the oak trees, while he was sitting at the tent door in the heat of the day.
   2. He looked up and saw three men there standing opposite him; he jumped up and ran to meet them and bowed down in front of them,
   3. and said, "My Lord, if you are pleased with me, please do not leave just now. I am Your servant.
   4. Please let a little water be brought so that you can wash your feet, and rest yourselves under the tree;
   5. and I will bring a piece of bread, that you may eat and get refreshed; after that you can continue on, since you are here visiting Your servant." And they agreed.
   6. So Abraham hurried into the tent to Sarah, and said, "Quickly, prepare three servings, use fine flour, knead it, and make bread cakes."
   7. Abraham also ran to the herd, and took the best calf and gave it to the servant, who hurried to prepare it.
   8. He took curds and milk and the calf which he had prepared, and placed the meal before them; and he was standing by them under the tree as they ate.

II. Memory Verse
   - 2 Corinthians 1:20
   - For as many as are the promises of God, in Him they are yes; therefore also through Him is our Amen to the glory of God through us.
     - (All the promises of God are yes and amen in Christ Jesus.)

III. Language
   - Spelling/Handwriting
     - words to know: trees, sitting, heat, day
     - spelling tips:
       - Trees is the plural of tree. You've already had tree, so I hope you know how to spell it!
       - The word sitting has a double letter. We keep the vowels apart with two letters to keep the second one from making the first say its name. We want it to say sitting, not sighting.
       - The word heat has the same vowel spelling pattern as seas and season.
       - The word day has the same vowel sound spelling pattern as your words saying and away.
   - Vocabulary/Grammar
     - opposite (verse 2)
     - having a position on the other side, or being completely different (adjective)
       - An adjective describes something. On your worksheet today, you are going to write opposites. You had day as your spelling word. What's the opposite of day? You could say night.

IV. Lesson
- o Whenever I read today's passage in the Bible, I always wonder how long it took them to prepare this meal for the guests. Did you think that must have taken a long time to get the meal ready?
    - The bread was probably a flat bread, which means the dough wasn't fermented. They didn't have to wait for it to rise!
- o We get a little glimpse of hospitality in Abraham's culture. I think, in some ways, it's similar to cultural experiences I've had overseas among Muslims.
- o First, what would you describe as the hospitality practices of America, or wherever you are from?
- o What about if three strangers showed up at your door? What is the cultural expectation of hospitality?
    - I would say in America, we certainly wouldn't just invite three strangers in to sit and eat! We would stand at the door talking, being polite, hopefully.
    - Even if someone we know comes by, we find out at the door what's up, why they came, if they need something.
    - Guests would call before coming over. They would be offered something to drink or something to eat if there's food right there. Guests are free to turn it down. They wouldn't be expected to stay long and they would be given our attention while in our home.
    - Hospitality in America is making someone feel at home, that they should feel comfortable to help themselves to whatever.
- o What are some differences between your culture and what we observe in this story of Abraham's culture?
    - Abraham's guests couldn't have called ahead, but even today in Muslim cultures it can be considered rude to call before you visit someone. It's questioning their hospitality. Of course, you would be welcome!
    - Abraham doesn't ask why they've come.
    - Abraham leaves his guests to rush around and organize a meal.
    - They are served instead of welcomed to "help themselves."
- o I have literally been left sitting alone in a room for a long time while a meal was prepared for me. In one Muslim home in Istanbul, the kids and I were put into one room while my husband and the man of the house were taken into another room. I sat alone with my kids while she made dinner and served the men. I found out later they had chicken. The woman finally came and set up a small round table that stood just inches off the floor. We sat on the floor around the table and ate a pile of boiled whole potatoes.
    - There are a lot of cultural differences just in that one story. The men and women are treated differently. Which got more respect?
        - the men
    - What was the main point of the hospitality?
        - the food
        - to serve food is to show hospitality
- o To reject food offered you is a major offense in many cultures.
- o Some Muslims will say that they will invite you in, and you can stay three days before they will ask you why you came. That's certainly a different approach to hospitality.

It's not weird to end up spending the night at someone's house where you are visiting.
- Americans don't like to intrude or inconvenience others, but in a Muslim culture hospitality is expected.
- In a hospitality culture, there's a "fight" every time you try to leave someone's house. It's their duty to try to get you to stay. Even if they want you to go, they will insist you stay.
    - They will also always invite you over even if they don't really want you to come. My friend taught me how to read peoples' eyes and smiles to see if it was a real offer to visit.
    - This is part of their culture. Hospitality is so important in a Muslim culture that they have to offer it. It doesn't occur to them to not offer hospitality. It's built into them through the culture that they've been brought up in.
- They will also insist you eat, basically forcing food on you. It's polite to say no when offered something, so it means nothing to them when you turn down food because everyone says no when something is offered. They will give it to you anyway, and basically yell at you to eat it. They aren't being mean; they are being hospitable in their culture.
- There have been many a hungry and thirsty foreign exchange student in America who turned down food they wanted because they were following their own culture's rules for politeness.
    - In America we tend to say what we mean and accept other's answers. If we offer and they say they don't want it, then we don't give it to them.
- Recall: How did Abraham show hospitality?
    - He served a meal to his guests.
- Explore more: Choose a culture to learn about its hospitality rituals.

V. Discussion
- What is hospitality? The Bible says to show hospitality without complaint (1 Peter 4:9). Romans 12:13 says to "practice" hospitality. How is your family practicing it? How can you do a better job of it?

VI. Writing
- Complete your worksheet for today.
- What's the opposite? That's what you are going to have to decide for your worksheet today.

**Day 58**

I. Read Genesis 18:9-15.
   9 Then the visitors said to Abraham, "Where is your wife, Sarah?" And he said, "There, in the tent."
  10 The Visitor said, "I will certainly come back at this time next year; and Sarah your wife will have a son." Sarah was listening at the tent door, which was behind him.
  11 Now Abraham and Sarah were old, very advanced in age; Sarah's body was no longer able to have children.
  12 Sarah laughed to herself, saying, "After I have become old, shall I have pleasure of becoming a mother, Abraham old as well?"
  13 And the Lord said to Abraham, "Why did Sarah laugh, saying, 'Could I really have a child, when I am so old?'
  14 Is anything too difficult for the Lord? At the set time I will come back, at this time next year, and Sarah will have a son."
  15 Sarah denied it however, saying, "I did not laugh" because she was afraid. And the Visitor said, "No, but you did laugh."

II. Memory Verse
- 2 Corinthians 1:20
- For as many as are the promises of God, in Him they are yes; therefore also through Him is our Amen to the glory of God through us.
    - (All the promises of God are yes and amen in Christ Jesus.)

III. Language
- Spelling/Handwriting
    - words to know: visit, wife, come, back
    - spelling tips:
        - <u>Visit</u> ends with the word sit.
        - <u>Wife</u> ends with a silent E.
        - <u>Come</u> ends your spelling word become.
        - <u>Back</u> has four letters.
- Vocabulary/Grammar
    - deny (verse 15)
    - refuse – to say no to something – to say you won't (verb)

IV. Lesson
- Today Sarah thinks she is too old.
- What happens as we age? Name some things.
- Let's see what you know about old age.
    - Based on what you learned about calories, do you think your grandparents need fewer calories than you? Do they need fewer calories than your parents?
    - They do need fewer calories than your parents, and maybe you, if you are pre-teen or a teenager.
    - Why?

- They use less energy. Their bodies use calories more slowly. They also are probably less active.
- Do you think that after the age of forty, a lot of people have trouble seeing small things that are very close to them?
  - They do. Have you ever seen people hold something farther away from themselves to be able to read it?
  - The scientific word for the eye condition is presbyopia. What happens is that the lenses in your eyes start having trouble focusing. Basically, the eye is losing its flexibility. Probably a lot of body parts start to lose their flexibility!
- Do you think your brain starts to shrink when you are in your twenties?
  - It does! Your brain will reach its maximum size in your early twenties.
  - However, you can still actually improve your memory with age, even with a shrinking brain. The key is to keep your brain active, so never stop learning!
- Do you think kids' voices are the hardest to hear when you get older?
  - Yes, little kid voices are higher pitched which makes them harder to hear as your hearing starts to decline.
  - You have hairs in your ears that vibrate and send the sound waves to your brain. They can become less sensitive with age.
- Do you think that people shrink as they get older?
  - They do! Men can tend to lose an inch of height and women tend to lose two inches.
- Do you think your nose keeps growing as you age?
  - No, it doesn't. But your ears do!
  - These questions and answers were chosen and rephrased from http://www.webmd.com/healthy-aging/rm-quiz-aging-body.
- And what about Sarah? She thinks she is too old to have children. Age is the most important factor in whether or not a woman will have a baby. Those eggs I told you about start to get too old. Only 3% of the egg cells are still okay by the age of 40. Sarah's body told her she was long past being able to have a child. But God doesn't have to follow the laws of nature! By waiting, He made the birth miraculous instead of just unexpected.
- Abraham is told a prophecy, that Sarah will have a son. It will be just one more year until it's fulfilled.
- How many prophecies do you think there are in the Bible and how many have been fulfilled?
  - According to the "Reasons to Believe" website, there are about 2500 prophecies in the Bible and about 2000 of those prophecies have been fulfilled.
  - We are still waiting on some, which means we are in the middle of the story! It's not the end yet.
- Explore more: Read about fulfilled prophecies (maybe from the website mentioned) or come up with a brain training regimen to keep you and your parents sharp.

V. Discussion
- Do you think of the Bible as something that happened long ago or do you ever think of yourself as being part of God's story? If there were chapters written about your life

or about your family, what chapters of the Bible would they resemble? Would it be a story of God's faithfulness or of rebellion or of discovery?

VI. Writing
- o Complete your worksheet for today.
- o Write sentences with nouns and verbs.

**Day 59**

I. Read Genesis 18:16-33.

16 Then Abraham's three visitors stood up and looked down toward Sodom; and Abraham was walking with them to send them off on their way.

17 The Lord said to the two other visitors, "I should not hide from Abraham what I am about to do,

18 since Abraham will become a great and mighty nation, and in him all the nations of the earth will be blessed.

19 For I have chosen him, so that he may command his children and his household after him to keep the way of the Lord by doing what is right and acting justly, so that the Lord may bring about all He has said about Abraham."

20 And the Lord said, "The outcry against Sodom and Gomorrah is great, and their sin is very serious.

21 I will go down now, and see if they have done what I have heard; and if not, I will know."

22 Then the other two visitors turned away from there and went toward Sodom, while Abraham was still standing before the Lord.

23 Abraham came near and said, "Will You destroy the righteous with the wicked?

24 Suppose there are fifty righteous within the city; will You destroy it and not spare the city for the sake of the fifty righteous who are in it?

25 Far be it from You to do such a thing, to kill the righteous with the wicked, so that the righteous and the wicked are treated alike. You would never do that! The Judge of all the earth will deal justly."

26 So the Lord said, "If I find in Sodom fifty righteous within the city, then I will spare the whole place because of them."

27 And Abraham replied, "Now, I have been brave to speak to the Lord, although I am nothing.

28 Suppose the fifty righteous are five less, will You destroy the whole city because of five?" And He said, "I will not destroy it if I find forty-five there."

29 He spoke to Him yet again and said, "Suppose forty are found there?" And He said, "I will not do it for the sake of the forty."

30 Then he said, "Lord, please do not be angry, and I will speak; suppose thirty are found there?" And He said, "I will not do it if I find thirty there."

31 And he said, "Now, I have continued to brace in speaking to the Lord; suppose twenty are found there?" And He said, "I will not destroy it on account of the twenty."

32 Then he said, "Please Lord, do not be angry, and I will speak only once more; suppose ten are found there?" And He said, "I will not destroy it on account of the ten."

33 As soon as He had finished speaking to Abraham the Lord left, and Abraham returned to his place.

II. Memory Verse
- 2 Corinthians 1:20
- For as many as are the promises of God, in Him they are yes; therefore also through Him is our Amen to the glory of God through us.
    - (All the promises of God are yes and amen in Christ Jesus.)

III. Language
- Spelling/Handwriting
  - words to know: ten, thirty, fifty, forty-five
  - spelling tips:
    - The word <u>ten</u> is spelled just like it sounds. It starts the word tents, which you've already had as a spelling word.
    - The word <u>thirty</u> is spelled like it sounds as well except that the "ER" sound can be made with E-R, I-R, and U-R. Thirty is spelled with an I.
    - The word <u>fifty</u> is also spelled how it sounds. You just have to say it carefully.
    - The word <u>forty-five</u> is one word. You write forty and then a hyphen, a little dash line, and then the word five. Five ends with a silent E. The vowel sound in the first syllable in forty is spelled with the word OR.
- Vocabulary/Grammar
  - return (verse 33)
  - to go back to where you came from, to bring back something you took from a place (verb)

IV. Lesson
- Today's reading seems to be about righteousness and justice.
  - Those are two character traits of God. He is righteous, meaning He does what is right. And He is just, meaning He acts fairly.
  - The Bible tells us that the punishment of sin is death. It would be just for us all to die. But God is more than just just. ☺ God is merciful and gracious and compassionate. That's why we should always show gratitude because He saves us from our just punishment, one that we deserve.
- Sodom and Gomorrah will soon receive a just punishment for their sins, but what stands out to me is verse 19. "For I have chosen [Abraham], so that he may command his children and his household after him to keep the way of the Lord by doing righteousness and justice, so that the Lord may bring upon Abraham what He has spoken about him."
- God has made promises. He has to keep His promise. Here it says that Abraham needs to teach his children to do justice and to live righteously so that He can give him what is promised.
  - God can be very confusing to us. He doesn't have a brain like ours that aches when we try to understand how He works.
  - In order to fulfill His promises to His people, they have to live according to His ways. He has to fulfill His promises, so He has to ensure that there are always some of His people living according to His word.
- We call this group, the remnant. There is always a remnant, a group that hasn't forgotten God and hasn't stopped living according to His ways.
- Noah was a remnant. He was the one living righteously when everyone else was bent on violence and evil.
- The remnant will always exist. Throughout Israel's history, we see the remnant shrink and then grow repeatedly. In Romans 11 we are told that believers are now part of Israel, God's people. There will always be believers, and I think there will always be a remnant of Jewish people as well.

- o A remnant is what is left over from something larger. You can have a remnant of fabric after you are done with a sewing project, some scraps that weren't used. Let's look at Romans 11 to see what we can learn about God's remnant. It's something we should always want to be part of.
    - Here's Romans 11:3-5. This is Paul writing. He starts by quoting Elijah from 1 Kings 19.
        - "Lord, they have killed Your prophets, they have torn down Your altars, and I alone am left, and they are seeking my life." But what is the divine response to him? "I have kept for Myself seven thousand men who have not bowed the knee to Baal." In the same way then, there has also come to be at the present time a remnant according to God's gracious choice.
    - What was happening here? What does Elijah say in his prayer?
        - Elijah thinks he's all alone, that he is the only one left who worships God and not idols.
        - What does God assure him?
            - There's a remnant. There are 7,000 men who haven't worshiped idols.
            - This, we are told, is by God's grace. We are all saved by God's grace. Justice says we should all die. By grace He made a way for us to receive forgiveness and the power to overcome sin.
- o So, although Abraham must teach his children to live righteously and justly, it's by God's grace that Abraham can, and it's by grace that Abraham even knew God, and it's by grace that His promises will be fulfilled because His grace will ensure there will always be a remnant following Him.
- o Recall: What is the name for the people who remain faithful to God when everyone else falls away?
    - the remnant
- o Explore more: What other stories about God's remnant can you find in the Bible? What does Revelations have to say about the remnant?

V. Discussion
- o Are you part of the remnant today? How has God's grace made a way for you to be part of the remnant?
- o There are ways His grace has worked for all of us, but there are special ways He shows grace in each individual life. What are your family's stories of how God's grace brought you to Him and into the remnant, those left on earth who still live by faith in God and His Son Jesus Christ?

VI. Writing
- o Complete the worksheet for today.
- o You are going to write a thank you letter today. We need to thank God for His grace that makes all good things possible.

**Day 60 (check Materials List)**

I. Read Genesis 19:1-2.
   1. Now the two angels who had been with the Lord came to Sodom in the evening as Lot was sitting at the gate of the city. When Lot saw them, he rose to meet them and bowed down with his face to the ground.
   2. And he said, "My lords, please come to my house, and spend the night, and wash your feet; then you can get up early and go on your way." But they said, "No, we will spend the night in the square."

II. Memory Verse
   - Test yourselves on 2 Corinthians 1:20.
     - For as many as are the promises of God, in Him they are yes; therefore also through Him is our Amen to the glory of God through us.
     - (All the promises of God are yes and amen in Christ Jesus.)
   - Review Genesis 26:4.
     - I will multiply your descendants as the stars of the heaven, and will give your descendants all these lands; and by your descendants all the nations of the earth shall be blessed.

III. Language
   - Spelling/Handwriting
     - Test yourselves on words from Days 56-59. (worksheet)
       - nine, twelve, Sarah, next
       - trees, sitting, heat, day
       - visit, wife, come, back
       - ten, thirty, fifty, forty-five
   - Vocabulary/Grammar
     - Test yourselves on the words from Days 56-59. (worksheet)
       - intercept – blocking something from getting to where it's headed
       - opposite – having a position on the other side
       - deny – refuse
       - return – to go back to where you came from

IV. Lesson
   - Sodom was in ancient Mesopotamia. Another city there that we've read about but not studied is Babel. That's where they built the tower of Babel. We know it as the city of Babylon. It was mentioned in one of the fulfilled prophecies that we read about on Day 58.
   - Babylon has many references in Scripture, and they are all bad. It's not only the location of the tower of Babel, but it's where Daniel was thrown into the lion's den and where Shadrach, Meshach, and Abednego were thrown into the fiery furnace.
     - Babylon was controlled by many different empires. One of its kings was Hammurabi who wrote the law code we looked at on Day 56. Do you remember any of Hammurabi's Code?
     - While he was in charge, Babylon became the largest and most important city in Mesopotamia.

- - Hammurabi was a skilled leader and was able to unite all of Mesopotamia under Babylon's rule and named it Babylonia.
  - Babylon is known for being the location of one of the seven wonders of the ancient world, the hanging gardens. Here's one artist's image of it. We don't know exactly what it looked like.

  - The gardens were said to have been built by King Nebuchadnezzar, the one who has the dream that Daniel interprets (Daniel 2). This puts the garden's creation at around 600 BC. Is that before or after Abraham's time?
    - It's long after. We're just talking about Babylon today, not Abraham's time.
  - The hanging gardens weren't hanging down from somewhere. They were up high, though, instead of being in the ground. I think they were probably much higher than is shown in this picture.
    - The gardens are described as terrace after terrace going upward like steps. Pillars were hollow and filled with earth so that "trees of the largest size" could be planted (according to one ancient description, unmuseum.org/hangg.htm).
  - It was new and modern. No one had ever seen anything like it, a garden in the sky! I switched around social studies and science today so that you could learn about the garden and then learn about how they made it work.
  - Why was the "hanging" garden such a marvel?
    - They had figured out new things. There was engineering at work.
  - What does a garden need?
    - It would need soil and water and sun.
  - There was plenty of sun. It was the desert. What would provide the water?
    - the Euphrates River
  - But somehow the water would have to get from the river to the top terrace. Soil would also have to be transported to the different levels, but only once. Water would have to be delivered regularly, especially in a desert climate.
  - Here are pictures of a few of what we know as the simple machines, tools that make work easier. Which do you think might be useful in some way to deliver water to the gardens? How could they be used?

- The first is a pulley. On other days you'll learn more about the first two.
  - The pulley is used for lifting. The top is fixed in place up high. Something is lifted onto the hook. Can you think of a way this might be used in transporting water to the highest levels of the garden? (Note: We don't know how they watered the garden. There is no right or wrong answer. Let them imagine.)

Cropped Image original by Welkinridge

- Another simple machine is the wheel and the axle. In the well picture to follow, the wheel is the circle with spokes. The axle is the log looking thing that has the rope wrapped around it.
- How does this wheel and axle work to lift water?
  - You turn the wheel to raise and lower the bucket.
- How could this be used to get water way up high from a river?
  - We don't know for sure how they did it. Since they couldn't bring water straight up from the river, maybe an irrigation ditch brought water to outside the garden walls. Something like this could then lift water to each level.

- One other simple machine that carries water is the screw. Do you have any screws in your home?
    - If you do, get it and run your finger along the groove. What do you notice?
        - It goes up and up and up.
    - That's how a screw can carry water. As it turns, the water is pushed up along the groove. Let's look at some pictures.
- I'm going to show you one more picture; this is of a screw. In order to carry water somewhere the screw needs a tube or trough to hold the water and the screw forces it upwards.

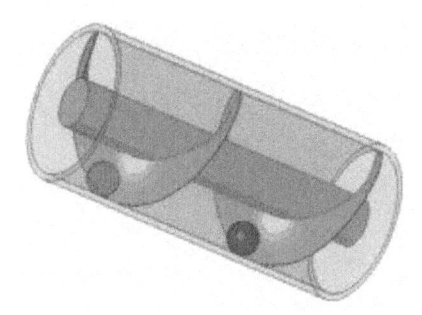

- Recall: What ancient city became the largest in Mesopotamia?
    - Babylon
- Explore more: If you have a piece of hose or tube that you could try it with, you can wrap it around a stick and tape it into place. Stick one end in a bucket of water. Hold your stick at an angle and turn your screw.

V. Discussion
  - If you were hired to be the architect and engineer to design the newest wonder of the world, what would you make?

VI. Writing
  - Complete your worksheet today if you haven't already.
  - There is just spelling and vocabulary for today.

**Day 61**

I. Read Genesis 19:3-4.
   3  Yet Lot begged them, so they went with him into his house; and Lot prepared a feast for them, and baked unleavened bread, and they ate together.
   4  Before they went to sleep, the men of the city, the men of Sodom, surrounded the house, both young and old, all the people from every quarter;

II. Memory Verse
   o Review 1 John 1:9.
   o If we confess our sins, He is faithful and just to forgive us our sins and to cleanse us from all unrighteousness. (KJV)

III. Language
   o Spelling
      - Have a spelling bee. (Parent: Read a word from Day 40's worksheet. Choose one they didn't have trouble with. Have them spell it out loud.)
      - If you want to do a spelling activity here are ideas.
         - Write words with sidewalk chalk.
         - Write words with invisible ink.
         - Write words by pressing down and then reveal them by coloring lightly over the words.
         - Color a page and then color over it in black. Write the words by scratching off the black.
         - Write the words with letters cut out of magazines.
         - Write the words with yarn.
         - Write the words in the air or on each other's back.

IV. Lesson
   o Complete the worksheet for Day 61.

**Day 62**

I. Read Genesis 19:5-7.
   5 and they called to Lot and said to him, "Where are the men who came to you tonight? Bring them out to us that we may have relations with them."
   6 But Lot went out to them, and shut the door behind him,
   7 and said, "Please, my brothers, do not act wickedly.

II. Memory Verse
   o Review Romans 6:23.
   o For the wages of sin is death, but the free gift of God is eternal life in Christ Jesus our Lord.

III. Language
   o Spelling
      - Have a spelling bee. (Parent: Read a word from Day 40's worksheet. Choose one they didn't have trouble with. Have them spell it out loud.)
      - If you want to do a spelling activity here are ideas.
         - Write words with sidewalk chalk.
         - Write words with invisible ink.
         - Write words by pressing down and then reveal them by coloring lightly over the words.
         - Color a page and then color over it in black. Write the words by scratching off the black.
         - Write the words with letters cut out of magazines.
         - Write the words with yarn.
         - Write the words in the air or on each other's back.

IV. Lesson
   o Complete the worksheet for Day 62.

**Day 63 (check Materials List)**

I. Read Genesis 19:8.
   8 I have two daughters who have not had relations with man; please let me bring them out to you, and do to them whatever you like; only don't harm these men, since I am giving them shelter."

II. Memory Verse
   o Review Genesis 1:4.
   o God saw that the light was good; and God separated the light from the darkness.

III. Language
   o Spelling
      - Have a spelling bee. (Parent: Read a word from Day 45's worksheet. Choose one they didn't have trouble with. Have them spell it out loud.)
      - If you want to do a spelling activity here are ideas.
         - Write words with sidewalk chalk.
         - Write words with invisible ink.
         - Write words by pressing down and then reveal them by coloring lightly over the words.
         - Color a page and then color over it in black. Write the words by scratching off the black.
         - Write the words with letters cut out of magazines.
         - Write the words with yarn.
         - Write the words in the air or on each other's back.

IV. Lesson
   o Complete the worksheet for Day 63.

**Day 64**

I. Read Genesis 19:9-11.
   9 But they said, "Move aside." Then they said, "This man came to Sodom as a stranger, and already he is acting like a judge; now we will treat you worse than them." So they pressed hard against Lot and came near to break the door.
   10 But the visitors reached out their hands and brought Lot into the house, and shut the door.
   11 They struck the men who were at the door with blindness, all of them, so that they gave up trying to get into the house.

II. Memory Verse
   o Review Genesis 26:4.
   o I will multiply your descendants as the stars of the heaven, and will give your descendants all these lands; and by your descendants all the nations of the earth shall be blessed.

III. Language
   o Spelling
      - Have a spelling bee. (Parent: Read a word from Day 45's worksheet. Choose one they didn't have trouble with. Have them spell it out loud.)
      - If you want to do a spelling activity here are ideas.
         - Write words with sidewalk chalk.
         - Write words with invisible ink.
         - Write words by pressing down and then reveal them by coloring lightly over the words.
         - Color a page and then color over it in black. Write the words by scratching off the black.
         - Write the words with letters cut out of magazines.
         - Write the words with yarn.
         - Write the words in the air or on each other's back.

IV. Lesson
   o Complete the worksheet for Day 64.

**Day 65 (check Materials List)**

I. Read Genesis 19:12-13.
   12 Then the two men said to Lot, "Whom else have you here? A son-in-law, and your sons, and your daughters, and whomever you have in the city, bring them out of the place;
   13 for we are about to destroy this place, because their outcry has become so great before the Lord that the Lord has sent us to destroy it."

II. Memory Verse
   o Review 2 Corinthians 1:20.
   o For as many as are the promises of God, in Him they are yes; therefore also through Him is our Amen to the glory of God through us.
   o (All the promises of God are yes and amen in Christ Jesus.)

III. Language
   o Spelling
      - Have a spelling bee. (Parent: Read a word from Day 50's worksheet. Choose one they didn't have trouble with. Have them spell it out loud.)
      - If you want to do a spelling activity here are ideas.
         - Write words with sidewalk chalk.
         - Write words with invisible ink.
         - Write words by pressing down and then reveal them by coloring lightly over the words.
         - Color a page and then color over it in black. Write the words by scratching off the black.
         - Write the words with letters cut out of magazines.
         - Write the words with yarn.
         - Write the words in the air or on each other's back.

IV. Lesson
   o Complete the worksheet for Day 65.

**Day 66**

I. Read Genesis 19:14.
   14 Lot went out and spoke to his sons-in-law, who were to marry his daughters, and said, "Get up, get out of this place, for the Lord will destroy the city." But he appeared to his sons-in-law to be joking.

II. Memory Verse
   o Say 1 John 1:9 from memory.
      • If we confess our sins, He is faithful and just to forgive us our sins and to cleanse us from all unrighteousness. (KJV)
   o Review Genesis 1:1.
      • In the beginning God created the heavens and the earth.

III. Language
   o Spelling
      • Have a spelling bee. (Parent: Read a word from Day 50's worksheet. Choose one they didn't have trouble with. Have them spell it out loud.)
      • If you want to do a spelling activity here are ideas.
         ▪ Write words with sidewalk chalk.
         ▪ Write words with invisible ink.
         ▪ Write words by pressing down and then reveal them by coloring lightly over the words.
         ▪ Color a page and then color over it in black. Write the words by scratching off the black.
         ▪ Write the words with letters cut out of magazines.
         ▪ Write the words with yarn.
         ▪ Write the words in the air or on each other's back.

IV. Lesson
   o Complete the worksheet for Day 66.

**Day 67**

I. Read Genesis 19:15-16.
   15 When morning dawned, the angels urged Lot, saying, "Get up, take your wife and your two daughters who are here, or you will be swept away in the punishment of the city."
   16 But he hesitated. So the men seized his hand and the hand of his wife and the hands of his two daughters, for the compassion of the Lord was upon him; and they brought him out, and put him outside the city.

II. Memory Verse
   o Say from memory Romans 6:23.
   o For the wages of sin is death, but the free gift of God is eternal life in Christ Jesus our Lord.
   o Review Psalm 150:6.
   o Let everything that has breath praise the Lord. Praise the Lord!

III. Language
   o Spelling
      - Have a spelling bee. (Parent: Read a word from Day 55's worksheet. Choose one they didn't have trouble with. Have them spell it out loud.)
      - If you want to do a spelling activity here are ideas.
         - Write words with sidewalk chalk.
         - Write words with invisible ink.
         - Write words by pressing down and then reveal them by coloring lightly over the words.
         - Color a page and then color over it in black. Write the words by scratching off the black.
         - Write the words with letters cut out of magazines.
         - Write the words with yarn.
         - Write the words in the air or on each other's back.

IV. Lesson
   o Complete the worksheet for Day 67.

**Day 68 (check Materials List)**

I. Read Genesis 19:17-18.
  17 When the angels had brought them outside, one said, "Escape for your life! Do not look behind you, and do not stay anywhere in the valley; escape to the mountains, or you will be destroyed."
  18 But Lot said to them, "Please no, my lords!

II. Memory Verse
  - Say from memory Genesis 1:4.
  - God saw that the light was good; and God separated the light from the darkness.

III. Language
  - Spelling
    - Have a spelling bee. (Parent: Read a word from Day 55's worksheet. Choose one they didn't have trouble with. Have them spell it out loud.)
    - If you want to do a spelling activity here are ideas.
      - Write words with sidewalk chalk.
      - Write words with invisible ink.
      - Write words by pressing down and then reveal them by coloring lightly over the words.
      - Color a page and then color over it in black. Write the words by scratching off the black.
      - Write the words with letters cut out of magazines.
      - Write the words with yarn.
      - Write the words in the air or on each other's back.

IV. Lesson
  - Complete the worksheet for Day 68.

**Day 69**

I. Read Genesis 19:19-20.
   19 "I have found favor in your sight, and you have shown me mercy by saving my life; but I cannot escape to the mountains, for the disaster will find me there;
   20 look, this town is near enough to flee to, and it is small. Please, let me escape there (is it not small?) that my life may be saved."

II. Memory Verse
   o Say from memory Genesis 26:4.
      - I will multiply your descendants as the stars of the heaven, and will give your descendants all these lands; and by your descendants all the nations of the earth shall be blessed.
   o Review 1 Corinthians 10:13.
      - No temptation has overtaken you but such as is common to man; and God is faithful, who will not allow you to be tempted beyond what you are able, but with the temptation will provide the way of escape also, so that you will be able to endure it.

III. Language
   o Spelling
      - Have a spelling bee. (Parent: Read a word from Day 60's worksheet. Choose one they didn't have trouble with. Have them spell it out loud.)
      - If you want to do a spelling activity here are ideas.
         - Write words with sidewalk chalk.
         - Write words with invisible ink.
         - Write words by pressing down and then reveal them by coloring lightly over the words.
         - Color a page and then color over it in black. Write the words by scratching off the black.
         - Write the words with letters cut out of magazines.
         - Write the words with yarn.
         - Write the words in the air or on each other's back.
      - Some of the words could go into more than one pile. It's okay whichever it is placed in. The possible arrangements are in the answer key.

IV. Lesson
   o Complete the workbook page for Day 69.

**Day 70**

I. Read Genesis 19:21-22.
   21 He said to Lot, "I will allow it and will not destroy the town you are going to escape to.
   22 Hurry, escape, for I cannot do anything until you arrive there."

II. Memory Verse
   o Say from memory 2 Corinthians 1:20.
      - For as many as are the promises of God, in Him they are yes; therefore also through Him is our Amen to the glory of God through us.
      - (All the promises of God are yes and amen in Christ Jesus.)
   o Review Romans 3:23.
      - For all have sinned and fall short of the glory of God.

III. Language
   o Spelling
      - Have a spelling bee. (Parent: Read a word from Day 60's worksheet. Choose one they didn't have trouble with. Have them spell it out loud.)
      - If you want to do a spelling activity here are ideas.
         - Write words with sidewalk chalk.
         - Write words with invisible ink.
         - Write words by pressing down and then reveal them by coloring lightly over the words.
         - Color a page and then color over it in black. Write the words by scratching off the black.
         - Write the words with letters cut out of magazines.
         - Write the words with yarn.
         - Write the words in the air or on each other's back.

IV. Lesson
   o Complete the workbook page for Day 70.

**Day 71**

I. Read Genesis 19:23-25.
   23  The sun was up by the time Lot arrived at his safe town.
   24  Then the LORD poured fire and brimstone on the cities of Sodom and Gomorrah,
   25  and the Lord destroyed those cities, all the valley, and its inhabitants and everything that lived there.

II. Memory
   o   Joshua 24:15
   o   "[If it is disagreeable in your sight to serve the LORD,] choose for yourselves today whom you will serve: [whether the gods which your fathers served which were beyond the River, or the gods of the Amorites in whose land you are living;] but as for me and my house, we will serve the LORD."
   o   I put brackets [] in the verse in case you want to leave out the middle. Everyone worships a god. When they say they don't believe in any god, they make themselves god, relying on themselves to make decisions, to provide for themselves and to take care of themselves. Everyone has to choose whom it is that they will serve.

III. Language
   o   Spelling/Handwriting
       • words to know: sun, safe, town, fire
       • spelling tips:
           ▪ Sun is a homophone. This is the kind of sun in the sky that lights and warms the earth.
           ▪ Safe is spelled with a silent E.
           ▪ Town has the word OW in the middle of it, like power.
           ▪ Fire is also spelled with a silent E.
   o   Vocabulary
       • inhabitant (verse 25)
       • someone who lives in a place (noun)

IV. Lesson
   o   We've been reading the story of Lot. There are many strange things in his story. When the men are wanting to hurt Lot's visitors, the visitors, really angels, make them blind.
   o   We see something by seeing the light reflecting off of it. The black part of your eye is called the *pupil* which is really a hole in your eye. It lets in the light.
       • When someone is blind, something has gone wrong with letting in light, getting light to the back of the eye, or with the light receivers that take the light and send it onto your brain to tell it what is being seen.
       • Here's a diagram of what an eye looks like. Where's the pupil?

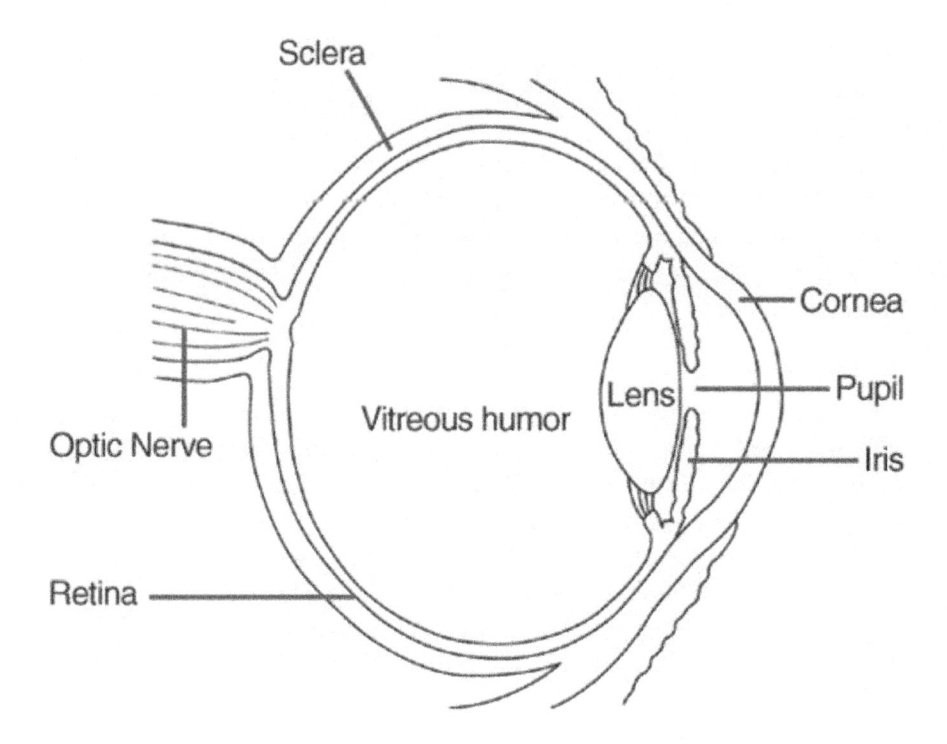

*Eye diagram with labels: Sclera, Cornea, Lens, Pupil, Iris, Vitreous humor, Optic Nerve, Retina*

- o  We saw some more culture at work in the story of Lot that we've been reading. Why was Lot sitting at the gate? He bows to the men entering the city, enables them to wash their feet, and protects them even more than family.
- o  Have you heard the story of the US soldier in Afghanistan being taken in by an Afghan family? The Afghan family faced death threats, had their business burned, and were forced from their home for taking in an American.
    - • What did they do? They showed hospitality. The Afghan man said, "By rescuing and keeping him safe for five nights in our home we were only doing our cultural obligation." (http://www.thedailybeast.com/articles/2013/11/08/the-afghan-village-that-saved-navy-seal-marcus-luttrell.html)
    - • The father risked the lives of his family in order to protect the one he had taken into his home. Does that sound familiar to the story of Lot?
- o  Lot offers water to his guests so that they can wash their feet.
    - • Walking through desert areas in sandals makes for dirty feet. It can also lead to cracked and bleeding feet and washing them can protect them and bring relief.
    - • In the New Testament we read about Jesus washing the disciples' feet (John 13). Jesus also points out when He's not offered water to wash his feet (Luke 7:44).
- o  When Lot first greets the angels, he bows to them. Not just any bow, he puts his face to the ground. We would see that as worship, but Lot is not reprimanded for doing so as the angel reprimands John for bowing down to worship before him (Revelation 19:10).
    - • Lot's bow wasn't one of worship. He did not know they were angels. Abraham didn't send a text message letting Lot know they were coming.
- o  We call this kind of bow a kowtow. (Note: Kow is said cow, and tow rhymes with cow.)

- It involves kneeling and putting your forehead to the ground. It was used in ancient Asian cultures. It is not really used today apart from martial arts and formal, traditional ceremonies.
    - There is still bowing in Asian cultures. Japan especially is known for bowing. People greet each other with bows and how far you bow shows your respect. Anyone older than you is shown more respect, so try bowing to your parents today. They can return the bow with a head nod forward since you are beneath them!
    - Learning about bowing makes me wonder how the church in Japan treats it. Do they all bow the same to each other and see each other as equals?
- We don't know why Lot was "sitting in the gate." This wasn't a little fence gate. Cities had huge thick walls. The gates had a gatehouse that was a meeting place and often a courthouse. We don't know if Lot was just looking to see who was coming or if he was on duty watching those coming to learn their business in the city.
- Recall: What's the name of the bow that involves kneeling and putting your head to the floor? kowtow
- Explore more: Learn about Afghan culture.

V. Discussion
- Did you notice that the men in the Bible story are still trying to get into the house even after they've been struck blind? The Bible talks about people being "given over" to their sin. It becomes an addiction. You have to have it. Is there anything in your life that has a hold on you? It could be television or internet or talking back or getting angry. We shouldn't be addicted to anything. The way free from addiction is through Jesus and repentance.
    - What has ever had a hold on you where you felt like you had to do it?
    - What has it caused you to do wrong in order to do it?
    - What are you going to do about it?

VI. Writing
- Complete today's worksheet.
- You are going to be working with words with OW like town.

**Day 72**

I. Read Genesis 19:24-26.
   24  Then the LORD poured fire and brimstone on the cities of Sodom and Gomorrah,
   25  and the Lord destroyed those cities, all the valley, and all the inhabitants and everything that lived there.
   26  But Lot's wife, from behind him, looked back, and she became a pillar of salt.

II. Memory Verse
   o  Joshua 24:15
   o  "[If it is disagreeable in your sight to serve the LORD,] choose for yourselves today whom you will serve: [whether the gods which your fathers served which were beyond the River, or the gods of the Amorites in whose land you are living;] but as for me and my house, we will serve the LORD."

III. Language
   o  Spelling/Handwriting
       • words to know: from, lived, everything, salt
       • spelling tips:
           ▪ The word from is spelled with an O.
           ▪ The word lived is the past tense of live. Live is spelled just like LIVE, which you spelled in the word alive.
           ▪ The word everything is made up of the words every and thing. The Y at the end of every makes an E sound because every has more than one syllable.
           ▪ Salt has the same vowel as the word ALL. Can you hear the word all inside of salt?
   o  Vocabulary/Grammar
       • pillar (verse 26)
       • a tall, relatively thin structure that is used to support a building or decorate it (noun)

IV. Lesson
- Lot has to flee from Sodom. He goes to a small town named Zoar which means small. It is close enough that he just walks there, quickly.
    - Lot and his daughters are refugees after they leave their home.
- A *refugee* is someone who is forced to leave their country due to their life being in danger. This is the technical definition, though there are many considered refugees in their own countries like Lot was. They have lost their homes and are reliant on others to protect and provide for them until they can do so for themselves.
- Many refugees are known as war refugees, though there is often more at work.
    - In recent years millions of Christians have fled Middle Eastern countries because while the country was at war, they were a particular target of one side or the other. Those against Christianity were taking advantage of the war as an excuse to kill Christians. Many fled for their lives, leaving their homes, businesses, and most of their belongings.
- I know many refugees with sad stories.
    - One woman's whole family was killed before she decided to leave her home. She walked from Ethiopia to Lebanon and then was basically made a slave when she tried to work as a housekeeper. She eventually made it to Turkey where she was put in prison and treated horribly.
    - When one family fled Syria in 2013, they said goodbye to each other before they walked the final stretch to the border, even though they were all together. They knew that they would be shot at as they tried to get across the border and didn't know if they would all survive. (They did.)
    - Another family left Pakistan because they were targets of religious persecution. They had an uncle killed and one of their teenagers was beaten to the point of needing hospitalization.
        - They flew to Turkey, had their passports confiscated, and were trapped. They could not travel without passports so they couldn't leave; their new country, though, won't accept them as citizens. They thought the United Nations would help them, but the UN was slow to recognize them as refugees, so they received no help.
            - After seven years they were recognized as refugees and after nine years were moved to America!
        - I know several people who have been waiting over a decade for the UN to place them in a country accepting refugees.
- The UN's job is hard because there is a constant flow of refugees. In 2014 the reported number was over 50 million refugees. Half of those are reportedly children. Guess what continent produces the most refugees?
    - The majority come from Africa.
    - Many refugees are placed in camps. Refugee camps are sort of like prisons with more freedom to move around, but only within the camp. They are supposed to be cared for there and protected. They are given food and shelter, but there is a lack of any family space, education, or job opportunities. They are stuck. Refugees are often trapped where they fled to.
- One famous story of refugees is that of The Lost Boys of the Sudan. Muslim militias attacked Christian villages, slaughtering everyone. Children were left alone and

walked on foot across two countries to get to Kenya. They grew up in camps. Eventually the US took in a few thousand of them and settled them into American life.
- I know someone who was a volunteer to help a few of them learn how to live in America. She talks of how they were overwhelmed by the choices offered and confused about what kind of work the dogs did since in America they were fed so well. (A whole aisle at the grocery store with food just for dogs???)
  - At the time of writing this, I have neighbors who are refugees from Syria. They have started a school for Syrian children. Because of the war in their country, many young children had never even started school. They lost three years of education. Adult refugees are the teachers, the cooks, the cleaners, and the helpers, and child refugees are the students. It's a little piece of hope in a grim situation.
  - Recall: What is a refugee? someone who has to flee their home country to save their lives (technically Lot didn't flee his country, but they had to leave everything and flee their home town—It's much harder when you are in a new country with a different language!)
  - Explore more: Learn about the refugee situation in the world. Can you chart where they are and where they came from?

V. Discussion
  - If someone told you that an angel said you had to abandon your home and belongings and flee, would you be willing to go?
  - How hard do you think it would be to leave your home and go to another country?
  - The Bible actually says a lot about foreigners. They are easily oppressed and taken advantage of, so they have a special place in God's heart. Just like we are admonished to care for widows and orphans, we are told to love the "strangers" in our midst. Here's one verse, Leviticus 19:34. "The stranger who resides with you shall be to you as the native among you, and you shall love him as yourself, for you were aliens in the land of Egypt; I am the LORD your God."

VI. Writing
  - Complete your worksheet for today.
  - Design and draw your own pillars. Pillars are nouns. Nouns are people, places, and things. You can add a person and place to your drawing as well.

**Day 73**

I. Read Genesis 19:27-29.
    27 Abraham got up early in the morning and went to the place where he had been with the L ORD;
    28 and he looked down toward the cities of Sodom and Gomorrah, and toward all the land of the valley, and he saw smoke coming from the land like the smoke of a furnace.
    29 That's how it happened when God destroyed the cities of the valley, that God thought of Abraham, and sent Lot out of the destruction.

II. Memory Verse
- Joshua 24:15
- "[If it is disagreeable in your sight to serve the LORD,] choose for yourselves today whom you will serve: [whether the gods which your fathers served which were beyond the River, or the gods of the Amorites in whose land you are living;] but as for me and my house, we will serve the LORD."

III. Language
- Spelling/Handwriting
  - words to know: early, been, with, smoke
  - spelling tips:
    - Early starts with the word ear. What letter makes the E sound at the end of the word?
    - Been has a double E.
    - With is spelled just like it sounds.
    - Smoke is spelled like it sounds and ends with a silent E.
- Vocabulary
  - furnace (verse 28)
  - a metal stove where something is burned to produce heat (noun)

IV. Lesson
- Fire and brimstone destroyed the cities and inhabitants of the valley for their sin against God.
- Today let's talk about the brimstone which rained out of heaven with fire and caused the smoke rising from the cities.
  - Brimstone is an ancient word for sulfur. Sulfur is another element, like gold, oxygen, iron, hydrogen, and carbon. They aren't made up of different types of atoms. Sulfur is made up of only sulfur atoms.
- While we're talking about elements and atoms, this would be a good time to look at what makes the atoms different from one another.
- What are atoms?
  - They are the building blocks of everything physical in the universe. What in the room you are in is made up of atoms?
    - Everything you can see and even some of what you can't see, like the air.
  - Everything is made up of atoms in different combinations.
  - When atoms join together, what do they make?

- molecules
- What atoms make up a water molecule?
  - H₂O (Two hydrogen atoms and one oxygen atom make up one water molecule.)
- What we call the *elements* are the atoms, the atoms that build together into different molecules. Each element is different from the others and cannot be broken down into anything else. Gold is only made of gold atoms. Oxygen is only oxygen atoms. Carbon is only carbon atoms. They are elements.
- Is water an element?
  - No, it's a made of molecules, hydrogen and oxygen atoms together.
- Is steel an element?
  - No, it's an alloy, a mixture. It's iron and carbon (and can be mixed with other metals as well).
- In the back of your map book I put a chart of the elements. It's called the periodic table. There is another one in the back of your workbook.
  - Before we look at it, guess the scientific symbol for sulfur.
    - It's just the letter S.
- Find on the periodic table these elements: oxygen, sulfur, carbon, and hydrogen.
- What do you notice on the chart along with the symbols and the names of the elements?
  - There are numbers too. Lots of different numbers. On the color chart at the back of your map book, there is a box in the middle that tells about some of those numbers.
  - The main number at the top of each box (on our charts) is its *atomic number*. What do you notice about those?
    - They go in order. That's how the elements are placed, in order of their atomic number.
      - So, what is it? It's the number of protons in the atom.
      - Basically, the difference between the elements is how many of these protons are inside of the atom!
        - That's pretty crazy isn't it? Think about it. The difference between oxygen and chlorine is that one has nine more protons than the other!
- Use the periodic table to answer the following questions.
  - How many protons are in hydrogen? (Hint: Find its atomic #.)
    - Hydrogen has one proton.
  - Take a look at the diagram of carbon with an atomic number of 6.
- Recall: What is a molecule?
  - A molecule is made up of atoms. Atoms bind together to make a single molecule.
- Explore more: Build an H₂O molecule. Find two things that you can connect, like raisins, erasers, pretzel sticks, paper clips, etc.

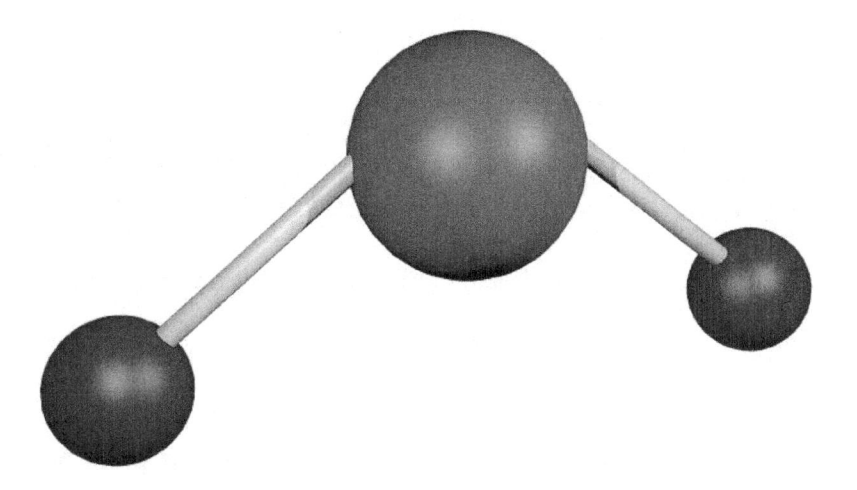

V. Discussion
- In verse 29 in today's reading it seems to say that Lot and his daughters (could have been his whole family) were saved because of Abraham. Did you ever think that your prayers could save a family? God's love for you can reach to those you love.
- Thinking of that, who should you be praying for?
    - People you know and people you don't know.
    - What about those in prison for their faith?
    - Who can you reach with God's love through prayer?
- What could you pray for them?
    - How do you think your prayers could change their lives?

VI. Writing
- Complete your worksheet for today.
- List names of people you want to pray for. Each name is a proper noun. A noun is a person, place, or thing. A proper noun is the name of a person, place, or thing.

**Day 74**

I. Read Genesis 20:1-3.
   1. Abraham traveled from there to the land of the Negev, and settled there; then he stayed in an area with a king named Abimelech.
   2. Abraham said about Sarah his wife, "She is my sister." So king Abimelech sent and took Sarah.
   3. But God came to Abimelech in a dream of the night, and said to him, "You are a dead man because you took a married woman."

II. Memory Verse
   - Joshua 24:15
   - "…Choose for yourselves today whom you will serve: …but as for me and my house, we will serve the LORD."

III. Language
   - Spelling/Handwriting
     - words to know: now, took, dead, dream
     - spelling tips:
       - The word <u>now</u> has one vowel. If you remember how to spell cow, you can spell now.
       - The word <u>took</u> has a double vowel.
       - The word <u>dead</u> has the same vowel spelling as your spelling word head.
       - The word <u>dream</u> has the same vowel spelling pattern as beast and each.
   - Vocabulary/Grammar
     - settle (verse 1)
     - to stay in one place (verb)

IV. Lessons
   - Abraham's wife was taken away. We don't really know exactly what happened to Lot's wife. This rock in Israel is known as "Lot's Wife" pillar. It is made of rock salt, the mineral form of sodium chloride (NaCl). It's located on what's called Mount Sodom.

(Photo By Wilson44691 (Own work) [Public domain], via Wikimedia Commons)

- Find Na and Cl on the periodic table. What are their elements and what are their atomic numbers?
    - sodium 11
    - chlorine 17
- Mount Sodom is located to the west of the Dead Sea. The whole mountain is made of sodium chloride. What's that?
    - salt
    - It is a mountain of rock salt. That's the stuff they put on the ground to melt ice in the winter.
- Mount Sodom has caves. In one of them Lot hid with his daughters.
    - The next picture is someone's photograph of a salt cave in Mount Sodom. (By Wilson44691 (Own work) [CC BY-SA 3.0 http://creativecommons.org/licenses/by-sa/3.0)], via Wikimedia Commons)

- There are other stories in the Bible involving caves. What do you think are some ways they were used?
    - to hide (Joshua 10:17, 1 Samuel 13:6)
    - as a prison (Joshua 10:18)
    - to live in to be protected (Judges 6:2)
    - as a bathroom (1 Samuel 24:3)
    - Caves were also used as graves. Abraham will bury Sarah in a cave.
- Caves are part of our history. Maybe you've visited famous caves near where you live. They are considered landmarks in some areas.
- Recall: What is Mount Sodom made of? rock salt; Where is it located? west of the Dead Sea; Name a few ways caves have been used. living, hiding, prison, bathroom, grave
- Explore more: What are the most famous caves? You could research Petra.

V. Discussion
- Like Lot's daughters, Abraham sins in a kind of desperation. Don't make decisions when you are feeling desperate! Call out to God and wait for His peace so that you can see your situation more clearly.
- Has there ever been a time you felt desperate? Did you take action? What was the result?

VI. Writing
- Complete the worksheet for today.
- Ask your parent a question. Write the question and answer. Spell the words as best you can. If you get some spelling corrected, celebrate every letter you did spell correctly!

**Day 75**

I. Read Genesis 19:12-16. This is a review reading.

12 Then the two men said to Lot, "Whom else have you here? A son-in-law, and your sons, and your daughters, and whomever you have in the city, bring them out of the place;

13 for we are about to destroy this place, because their outcry has become so great before the Lord that the Lord has sent us to destroy it."

14 Lot went out and spoke to his sons-in-law, who were to marry his daughters, and said, "Get up, get out of this place, for the Lord will destroy the city." But he appeared to his sons-in-law to be joking.

15 When morning dawned, the angels urged Lot, saying, "Up, take your wife and your two daughters who are here, or you will be swept away in the punishment of the city."

16 But he hesitated. So the men seized his hand and the hand of his wife and the hands of his two daughters, for the compassion of the Lord was upon him; and they brought him out, and put him outside the city.

II. Memory Verse
- Joshua 24:15
- "[If it is disagreeable in your sight to serve the LORD,] choose for yourselves today whom you will serve: [whether the gods which your fathers served which were beyond the River, or the gods of the Amorites in whose land you are living;] but as for me and my house, we will serve the LORD."

III. Language
- Spelling/Handwriting
  - Test yourselves on words from Day 71 to Day 74.
    - sun, safe, town, fire
    - from, lived, everything, salt
    - early, been, with, smoke
    - now, took, dead, dream
- Vocabulary/Grammar
  - Test yourselves on words from Day 71 to Day 74.
    - inhabitant – someone who lives in a place
    - pillar – a tall, relatively thin structure that is used to support a building or decorate it
    - furnace – a metal stove where something is burned to produce heat
    - settle – to stay in one place

IV. Lesson
- We are told that the cities in the valley were going to be punished. Here are some other stories of how God punishes.
- Achan and his whole family are swallowed whole in a sinkhole because Achan disobeyed and stole gold and silver from Israel's enemies which God commanded to be destroyed.

- - Because of his sin, all of Israel was punished. Their covenant was broken and they no longer had His blessing because of Achan's sin. Israel lost their next battle and tens of thousands of Israelites died in battle.
    - Israel partners with God to get rid of the sin in their midst. Achan and his family are killed and God's blessing is restored.
  - God uses enemy armies to conquer Israel when they need disciplining to cause them to repent. Then God punishes the foreign armies for what they did to the Israelites.
  - In Revelation it talks about Mystery Babylon being destroyed by God for her many sins.
  - We have already seen God destroy the whole earth. That was a punishment on everyone except Noah.
  - What observations can you make from all we've learned? Who is punished? How are they punished? Who is saved from punishment?
    - Those who sin against God are punished. Many are killed giving them no chance of repentance. God saves those who are righteous and those closest to them. Lot is saved for his own righteousness and for Abraham's sake. Lot's daughters are saved for Lot's sake.
  - How do discipline and punishment differ?
    - Sometimes they can look the same, like being conquered in battle. But when your life is spared, you have the chance to repent.
  - How does this next verse relate to discipline and punishment? First you should know that pruning is cutting branches, trimming them down which actually encourages them to grow more. With that in mind, how is this verse related to discipline and punishment? "He cuts off every branch in me that bears no fruit, while every branch that does bear fruit he prunes so that it will be even more fruitful." John 15:2 (NIV)
    - The cutting and pruning are like punishment and discipline.
    - Which is which?
  - Cutting off a branch is like punishment. It's basically killed. The branch can't grow any more if it's not attached to a tree. It's dead wood. Pruning is like discipline. Part of the branch is cut off, but the branch still lives and having been cut will enable it to grow more.
  - Did you notice that pruning and cutting both look the same? They both involve cutting off much of the branch. They look almost the same, but they have a different purpose.
    - Why should we want to avoid God's punishment?
    - Why should we want God's discipline?
  - Explore More: What are other Bible stories of God's punishment? What about Acts 5? Why do you think God punishes instead of disciplines?

V. Discussion
  - God is patient and loving, but He does punish those who sin against Him and against His people. It may be instantly, it may be on earth, it may be after death, but it will happen. We also see how whole groups of people are punished. Families are punished. Cities are punished. Countries are punished. It's important who you are united with! When we become Christians, we become citizens of heaven and members of the body of Christ. That's who we should stand with.
  - Who are you "aligned" with? Does that protect or endanger you?

- o God is still just and can work it out for the individual among the group (as He does with Lot and Noah, but they still lost their homes and their lives as they knew them because of the sins of those around them.)
- o Do you ever look at the wars in the world and consider that God is using them as punishment and discipline?

VI. Writing
- o Complete your worksheet today if you haven't yet.
- o There is a place for spelling and vocabulary practice to see what you know.

**Day 76 (check Materials List)**

I. Read Genesis 20:6-8.
    6   Then God said to Abimelech in the dream, "Yes, I know that with integrity you took Sarah for yourself. I have kept you from sinning against Me because I did not let you touch her.
    7   Now give Abraham back his wife, for he is a prophet, and he will pray for you and you will live. But if you do not, you will die, you and all who are yours."
    8   So Abimelech got up early in the morning and called all his servants to come, and he told them all these things, and everyone was very afraid.

II. Memory Verse
    - 2 Peter 3:9
    - The Lord is not slow about His promise, as some count slowness, but is patient toward you, not wishing for any to perish but for all to come to repentance.

III. Language
    - Spelling/Handwriting
        - words to know: yourself, pray, who, afraid
        - spelling tips:
            - The word yourself is the words your and self combined.
            - The word pray has the same vowel spelling as day.
            - The word who is spelled with an O as its one vowel. It has three letters. It begins like the other question words: what and where and why and when.
            - The word afraid has the same A sound spelling pattern as rain.
    - Vocabulary/Grammar
        - integrity (verse 5)
        - the character quality of holding to strong moral principles (noun)
        - Name two prepositions and two objects in this phrase from today's reading.
            - in the integrity of my heart
            - Answers: in, of; integrity, heart
        - What is the possessive adjective in the phrase? (in the integrity of my heart)
            - my

IV. Lesson
    - Abimelech rises early in the morning.
    - Today, let's look at how the earth's rotation causes the sun to rise each morning and how the earth's orbit causes that time to change every single day.
        - Where my family lived in Turkey, during the Muslim holiday of Ramadan a cannon is shot off at sunset each night. The people are supposed to fast from food and drink all day between sunrise and sunset. The booming of the cannon means you get to eat. (It's a neat cultural experience. The roads are empty. Everything is quiet. Everyone is at home waiting to eat. If it's summer, then the windows are open and you only hear the clink-clink of silverware coming from all sides once they are allowed to eat.)
        - The interesting thing, though, is that every day the cannon goes off about a minute later or earlier, depending on the time of year. Their fast is at least a

half hour shorter or longer by the end of the month than when they began, that's how much longer or shorter the day got as the month wore on.
- o Have someone shine a flashlight at you as you turn in a circle. That's sunrise and sunset. When the light is in your face, that's day. When you can't see the light, that's night. As you turn around, when you first see some light, that's sunrise. In 24 hours the earth turns around one time giving everyone day and night.
- o The change in time each day is caused by the earth's orbit, the path it travels around the sun. Look at the picture. (By following Duoduoduo's advice, vector image: Gothika. ([1]) [GFDL (http://www.gnu.org/copyleft/fdl.html) or CC-BY-SA-3.0 (http://creativecommons.org/licenses/by-sa/3.0/)], via Wikimedia Commons)

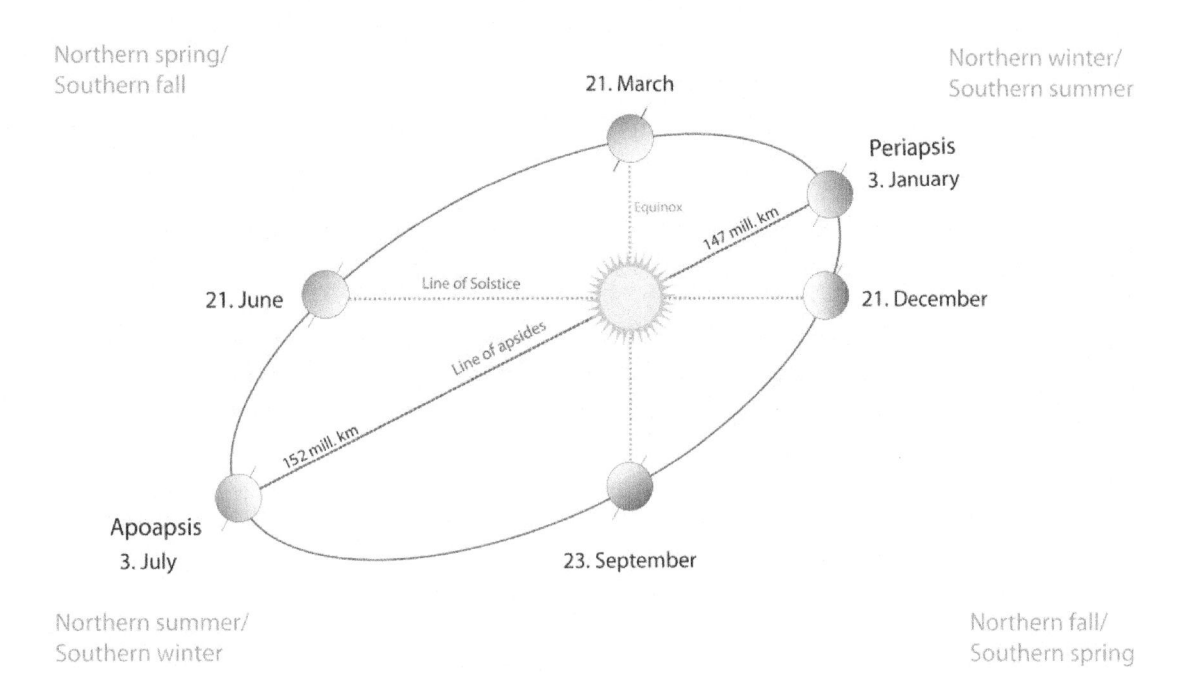

Northern spring/ Southern fall — 21. March — Northern winter/ Southern summer

Periapsis
3. January

21. June — 21. December

Apoapsis
3. July — 23. September

Northern summer/ Southern winter — Northern fall/ Southern spring

- o Make observations about the earth's orbit around the sun.
  - Its shape is an ellipse. That makes the earth closer at some points in the orbits. That doesn't really affect the earth's temperature. Once you're 150 million kilometers away from something, a couple more million doesn't change much.
- o Let's act out the earth's orbit. Do you remember what the imaginary line through the earth is called?
  - the axis
  - The axis is the key to the changes in sunrise and sunset times.
- o What is the earth doing on its axis?
  - It's rotating on its axis. It spins like a top and the axis is the handle.
- o You'll notice in the picture that the axis isn't up and down; it's not vertical.
  - Choose a pencil or pen to be your earth's axis.
  - Hold it upright. We'll call the top of the eraser (or flat end) the North Pole. We'll call the point the South Pole.
- o The earth spins at a pretty constant speed. When the earth turns around once, that's a full day, 24 hours. Since that part just stays the same, you don't really need to act

that out. We need to figure out what causes the changes we notice as the seasons change. The days are longer in summer and shorter in the winter. Let's observe why.
- Use your flashlight. Tilt the top end of your axis stick toward the sun. Now don't change the position of your hand. Stay just like that! (You could also use a ball or if you had an inflatable globe, that would work!)
- Which pole is getting all the light? (They can point on your prop.)
  - The North Pole
- Which pole is getting no light?
  - The South Pole
- Which pole is having summer?
  - The North Pole
- Which pole is having winter?
  - The South Pole
- When the North Pole is having summer, is it warm or cold in the northern hemisphere?
  - warm
- When the South Pole is having winter, is it warm or cold in the southern hemisphere?
  - cold

o Now start your orbit. Keep facing the same wall of the room, but walk in an ellipse around the sun. Stop when neither end of your axis is pointing towards the sun at all.
- What seasons are the two hemispheres experiencing? These are the in between months.
  - spring and fall

o Continue your orbit. Stop when the South Pole (bottom of your stick) is pointing in the direction of the sun.
- What season is the southern hemisphere experiencing?
  - summer
- What season is the northern hemisphere experiencing?
  - winter
- Where is there no light or hardly any?
  - the North Pole

o Can you see that the North Pole went from having all the light to no light?
- It's most dramatic on the poles where in summer the sun doesn't set and in winter the sun doesn't rise, but we all experience the changing daylight hours to varying degrees depending on where in the world we live.

o Recall: What's the imaginary line that the earth rotates around? axis; What does Earth orbit? Sun; What shape is the earth's orbit around our sun? ellipse; What about the earth's axis causes the sun to set earlier or later (same thing that causes the seasons)? It's tilted so that parts of the earth are either pointing towards or away from the sun.

o Explore more: Learn why the poles are colder than the equator. Here's a website that might help. (http://www.hko.gov.hk/education/edu06nature/ele_srad_e.htm)

V. Discussion
  o What holidays where you live bring everyone together? What's the value in having holidays that everyone joins in?

VI. Writing
- o Complete your worksheet.
- o Draw the earth's orbit. Where are you on the earth you drew? When is it summer there (on your picture)?

**Day 77**

I. Read Genesis 20:9-18. This is the continuation of the story of Abimelech taking Sarah.
   9  Then Abimelech called Abraham and said to him, "What have you done to us? And how have I sinned against you, that you have lied to me?"
   10 And Abimelech said to Abraham, "What did my kingdom do against you, that you have done this thing to us?"
   11 Abraham said, "I thought that you didn't fear God and that you would kill me because of my wife.
   12 Besides, she actually is my sister, the daughter of my father, but not the daughter of my mother, and she became my wife.
   13 I asked Sarah a favor, to tell everyone that I am her brother."
   14 Abimelech then took sheep and oxen and male and female servants, and gave them to Abraham, and restored his wife Sarah to him.
   15 Abimelech said, "You may settle in my land wherever you please."
   16 To Sarah he said, "I have given your brother a thousand pieces of silver; it shows that you have not committed any sin and before everyone you are cleared of any wrongdoing."
   17 Abraham prayed to God, and God healed Abimelech and his wife and his maids, so that they had children.
   18 For the Lord had closed all the wombs of the household of Abimelech because of Sarah, Abraham's wife.

II. Memory Verse
   o 2 Peter 3:9
   o The Lord is not slow about His promise, as some count slowness, but is patient toward you, not wishing for any to perish but for all to come to repentance.

III. Language
   o Spelling/Handwriting
       • words to know: thousand, please, clear, sister
       • spelling tips:
           ▪ The word thousand has the word sand at the end of it. It starts with the word thou. The vowel sound is the same spelling as in the word out.
           ▪ In the word please, there is a silent E, but there are also two vowels making the E sound. It's the same vowel spelling pattern as in the words each and beast.
           ▪ The word clear has that same E sound spelling pattern. It ends just like your spelling word year.
           ▪ The word sister ends just like water.
   o Vocabulary/Grammar
       • restore (verse 14)
       • to bring something back to its normal condition (verb)

IV. Lesson
- Today we're going to learn about one of the animal gifts Abraham received, oxen.
    - The first thing that comes to mind when I think of oxen is the Oregon Trail! When my kids would act out the Oregon Trail, some kids would always have to be the oxen.
- Oxen is the plural of the word ox. They are related to cows; they are kind of like cousins. We don't eat them, though, like most of us do cows. We use them for work.
- Look at this ancient drawing of oxen and then a modern picture of them being used.
- Below is a picture from India. (By Antônio Milena/ABr. [CC BY 3.0 br (http://creativecommons.org/licenses/by/3.0/br/deed.en)], via Wikimedia Commons)

- How are oxen used?
  - They are used in farming. Even today they are used to pull ploughs like in that drawing.
  - They are also used to pull carts.
- This isn't from our reading today, but I mentioned the Oregon Trail. It was one place where oxen were used to pull loads.
- In the first half of the 19th century, the US government was interested in opening up the western part of the country. About a third of what we know as America had just been bought from France in a trade known as the Louisiana Purchase. The new land covering the entire center of the country needed to be explored and settled.
  - Take a look at the map showing America at the time of the Louisiana Purchase. It's in the map book for Day 77. The original colonies along the east coast were states. Other areas east of the Mississippi River were considered "territories." Florida and much of the southwest belonged to Spain.
- The US government sent out a team to establish a colony in what was known as Oregon country.
  - It was a long road in between, literally.
  - The Oregon Trail from Independence, Missouri to Willamette Valley, Oregon covered about 2000 miles (3200 km).
    - Take a look at the Oregon Trail map for Day 77 in the map book.
    - Independence, Missouri is known as a jumping off point, or where people joined others to head off on the trail.
  - Consider that most people had to walk that distance; they walked halfway across America.
  - The oxen pulled their wagons full of supplies. They didn't carry people for the most part.
- The Oregon Trail was the path taken by those wanting to *migrate* west. Can you hear the connection between the words migrate and immigration? It's easier to see it than to hear it. To migrate means to move from one place to another, especially traveling a far distance and often to find work.
  - Early migrants to Oregon had to clear the path for others, again, literally. They chopped down what was in their way and made roads for the wagons.
- It wasn't only hard physically; it was a dangerous trip. Can you think of dangers they might have faced on the way?
  - The most common cause of death was disease.
  - Another common cause of death was accidents, especially gun accidents. People were accidently shot or their guns malfunctioned.
    - Those travelling west were afraid of Native Americans, even though for the most part they didn't need to be. They bought and brought guns even if they weren't experienced in using them. Inexperience isn't the best idea around weapons.
  - But even with all that, the most dangerous part of the trip was crossing rivers. Can you guess why?
    - There were no bridges yet.
    - They would have to walk across the rivers or float across. Walking across could work if it wasn't too deep and if the water wasn't flowing to quickly. People could get swept away.

- To float across they balanced their wagons on rafts or canoes. It was difficult and not uncommon for a wagon to tip over and fall into the water.
            - Native Americans were hired to help with the crossings of either kind.
            - Oxen had to walk or swim to the other side. Sometimes Native Americans would help by pulling the front animals by reigns so that the others would follow and they could help pull the load across.
                - This was dangerous for oxen as well and it was also possible for them to drown if the waters were too rough.
        - Recall: Where was the jumping off point for the Oregon Trail? Are oxen cows? What makes them valuable?
            - Independence, Missouri
            - no
            - They pull heavy loads.
        - Explore more: Learn more about the Oregon Trail. There are lots of stories. Why were they going west?

V. Discussion
   - Abraham made an assumption about Abimelech that proved to be false. Abraham decided that Abimelech didn't have the fear of God, but we read about Abimelech's integrity before God. The problem with assumptions is that we often don't know they are wrong, or we don't find out they are wrong until later.
   - Can you remember a time when you made an assumption? You probably make them all the time! Can you remember a time when you made a false assumption? What happened?
   - How can you keep from making false assumptions?
   - (Note: Another discussion topic is how God opens and closes wombs.)

VI. Writing
   - Complete your worksheet for today. Make a drawing like the ancient one of the oxen. Your ox doesn't need to be farming.
   - Then write a sentence about what your ox is doing.

**Day 78**

I. Read Genesis 21:1-8.
   1. Then the Lord did for Sarah as He had promised.
   2. So Sarah conceived and Abraham had a new son in his old age, at just the time God had said.
   3. Abraham and Sarah called their son Isaac.
   4. Then Abraham circumcised his son Isaac when he was eight days old, as God had commanded him to do.
   5. Abraham was one hundred years old when his son Isaac was born.
   6. Sarah said, "God has given me laughter; everyone who hears will laugh with me."
   7. And she said, "Who would have said to Abraham that Sarah would nurse children? Yet I have given him a son in his old age."
   8. The child grew and was weaned, and Abraham made a great feast on the day that Isaac was weaned.

II. Memory Verse
   - 2 Peter 3:9
   - The Lord is not slow about His promise, as some count slowness, but is patient toward you, not wishing for any to perish but for all to come to repentance.

III. Language
   - Spelling/Handwriting
     - words to know: promise, laugh, eight, feast
     - spelling tips:
       - You have some big words today. The first is promise. It is spelled pro and mise, with a silent E.
       - The F sound in laugh is spelled with a G-H. The vowel sound is spelled A-U.
       - The word eight is the number eight. It's a homophone. It sounds like the word when you have finished eating. The word for the number eight has five letters. It starts with an E, and then has an I-G-H-T just like night and light.
       - The word feast is a noun. Except for the first letter, it is spelled just like the word beast.
   - Vocabulary/Grammar
     - wean (verse 8)
     - to gradually get used to not having something you've become dependent on

IV. Lesson
   - Today we have a fun topic, laughter. Go ahead, tickle someone.
   - Did you get someone to laugh? Did everyone else laugh too? That's because laughter is contagious.
   - What body systems do you think are involved in laughing?
     - The respiratory system is involved. Our diaphragm contracts and forces out the air causing the noises of laughter. Do you remember where your diaphragm is?

- It's under your lungs. Laugh and feel your belly move. That's your diaphragm at work.
- It can be hard to laugh on command, but faking it can lead to real laughter. Or, just keep tickling each other.
  - The muscular system is what is contracting your diaphragm.
    - Go ahead and laugh again. What other muscles do you feel contracting when you laugh?
      - A whole lot! Arms, legs, your whole body can get involved. (Tickling has actually been used as a form of torture because it forces sustained muscle contraction.)
    - Are the muscles involved in laughing working voluntarily or involuntarily?
      - Involuntarily; They just do it. It can even be hard to not laugh when you want to.
  - The other body system at work is the nervous system, which we haven't done a whole lesson on yet. That's your brain and the system of nerves that delivers the messages to and from your brain.
- What are things that make you laugh?
- Laughter isn't about humor. People laugh when they are just happy or feeling joyful or accepted, but people can also laugh because they are nervous or embarrassed.
  - Babies laugh long before they can talk. We don't learn to laugh. It's just part of being human.
  - Laughter is a social activity; it's something we do with others. We're more likely to talk to ourselves then laugh by ourselves.
- Laughter begins in the brain. Scientists don't know much about it. There is no laugh part of the brain. Different types of laughter can originate in different parts of the brain. Tickling, being embarrassed, and hearing a joke all send different signals to the brain but can all invoke laughter.
- How many times a day do you think you laugh? I'm not talking about big belly laughs, just any little laugh.
  - You might be surprised. A baby can laugh hundreds of times a day. An adult more like a dozen or two. You're probably in between.
  - Maybe you'd like to conduct a study today on how often you or your family members laugh. You can hang a tally sheet somewhere and try to keep track.
  - Laughter is associated with playing, so the more you play, the more you laugh.
- Do you like to laugh? Does it feel good?
  - You feel good because it's good for you! It's beneficial, meaning helpful, to your nervous system, circulatory system, muscular system, and your immune system, the system that fights sickness in your body.
    - Laughter helps your circulatory system by opening up your blood vessels more, increasing your blood flow.
    - Laughter helps your immune system by producing more cells which fight bad bacteria and viruses.
    - Laughter helps your nervous system by releasing *endorphins*, a chemical that stops pain signals, so people can feel less or no pain

when laughing. Some doctors prescribe laughter to help people who can't sleep because of pain!
- And as for your muscular system, it gives them a workout, increasing strength and tone.
- Abraham throws a feast to celebrate Isaac's first step in growing up. What is America's famous feast day?
  - Thanksgiving
  - Do you know when Thanksgiving is?
    - It's the fourth Thursday of November.
- Abraham Lincoln established Thanksgiving as an annual, national holiday, calling it a day to give thanks and praise to God and to seek His mercy for our country.
- Recall: Who established Thanksgiving as an annual, national holiday? What are some of the ways laughter is good for you?
  - President Abraham Lincoln
  - It helps your blood, your brain, your muscles, and your health.
- Explore more: How about find a story about Abraham Lincoln.

V. Discussion
- Has God ever made you laugh? Has He ever done a miracle or arranged circumstances for your family that just made you laugh?
- One of our laughing stories was when the phone repair man showed up at our house. Our phone hadn't worked for three days. We were in a foreign country and the government controlled the phones. To get it fixed meant spending the day at the government building to request to be put on the list for someone to come fix it. My husband was putting off taking care of it because who wants to spend the day like that when there's so much else to do? We were surprised by the repairman, who just showed up at our apartment, and asked him why he was at our house. He was just as surprised by our question and asked if our phone wasn't working. He thought it was very odd that our phone wouldn't be working and we'd be surprised that the repairman was there to fix it. Somehow the Lord got us on his fix-it list and our phone was working again. It made me laugh and it made the repair man laugh because I kept asking him why he had come.

VI. Writing
- Complete your worksheet for today. You are going to write a knock, knock joke.
- Here's an example.
  - Knock, knock.
  - Who's there?
  - Lettuce.
  - Lettuce who?
  - Lettuce in! It's cold out here!
- You will use periods, questions marks, and exclamation point.

**Day 79**

I. Read Genesis 21:9-16.
   9. Sarah saw Ishmael making fun of Isaac. He was Abraham's son, but had been born to Hagar the Egyptian.
   10. Sarah was upset so she said to Abraham, "Get rid of this maid and her son, for her son will not be an heir with my son Isaac."
   11. Abraham was distressed over this because Ishmael was his son.
   12. But God said to Abraham, "Do not be distressed over the boy and your maid; whatever Sarah tells you, listen to her. It is through Isaac that your descendants shall be named.
   13. And since Ishmael is your descendant, I will make his family into a nation also."
   14. So Abraham rose early in the morning and took bread and water and gave them to Hagar and sent her away with her son. And she left and wandered about in the wilderness of Beersheba.
   15. When the water was used up, she left the boy under one of the bushes.
   16. Then she went and sat down away from him, about a bowshot away, for she said, "Do not let me see the boy die." And she lifted up her voice and wept.

II. Memory Verse
   o 2 Peter 3:9
   o The Lord is not slow about His promise, as some count slowness, but is patient toward you, not wishing for any to perish but for all to come to repentance.

III. Language
   o Spelling/Handwriting
     - words to know: upset, listen, voice, rid
     - spelling tips:
       - <u>Upset</u> is made with the words up and set. Say the syllables separately to spell each part of the word.
       - The word <u>listen</u> has a silent letter T. It starts with the word list.
       - The word <u>voice</u> has the same vowel spelling pattern as your spelling word join. It ends with the same spelling pattern as your spelling words face and place.
       - The word <u>rid</u> is spelled just like it sounds.
   o Vocabulary/Grammar
     - distress (verse 11)
     - extreme sorrow or worry (noun); or to cause extreme sorrow or worry (verb)
     - Read verse 11. Is distress used as a verb or a noun in this verse?
       - verb

IV. Lesson
   o Today we read that Hagar sat a bowshot away from Ishmael. On Day 80 we'll learn that Ishmael becomes an archer. So, how far is a bowshot away? What causes the arrow to go farther or shorter distances? Let's learn a little about the physics of the bow and arrow.

- *Physics* is the branch of science that studies energy and how it interacts with matter, which is everything in the physical universe.
- What subject have we studied that is part of physics? What have we studied that has to do with energy?
  - light (Note: They can have other answers too.)
  - What is light?
    - moving energy
    - What is energy?
      - Energy is the ability to do work.
- Today it's the physics of archery.
  - There is more to it than we can learn about today, but we can learn some basics of what makes things move.
  - If energy is the ability to work, what is work? Any guesses?
    - *Work* is when a force moves an object, even if it's as small as an electron.
    - Here we go again. What is force?
      - *Force* is something that affects the motion of an object.
- Let's go through each of these.
  - Let's start with force. What is force?
    - something that affects the motion of an object
    - We've already learned about one force. What happens when you throw a ball up in the air?
  - Something changes its upward motion and pulls it back down. What force is that?
    - gravity
  - There was also a force that pushed the ball upward. That's called an applied force. You applied force to the ball to push it upward.
- Was work done when you threw the ball upward?
  - Yes, work is when a force moves an object. When you threw the ball upward, what was the object being moved?
    - the ball
  - What was the force?
    - You tossing the ball up was the applied force.
- Was work done when the ball fell back down after getting as high as it could go?
  - Yes! Work doesn't have to make you sweat. Work is a when a force moves an object. What is the force that moves the ball back down?
    - gravity
- See if you can answer this correctly. Think before you answer: work is a force moving matter. If you push against the wall, is work being done?
  - No, the wall doesn't move. It doesn't matter how hard you are working at pushing it.
- Pretend to shoot a bow and arrow. When is work being done?
  - Work is done when you pull back on the bowstring. You are applying a force that moves the arrow and bowstring back.
  - The bow string has to return to normal when you let go. Work is done when the string boings forward and moves the arrow forward.

- By the way, how far is a bowshot away? We don't know for sure. 200 yards (meters) was about the range of a medieval archer. The distance would have been less than that in Abraham's day because distances get farther as the bow improves. There are bows today that can shoot well over 1,000 yards (meters).
- Recall: What is energy? What is work? What is force?
  - the ability to do work
  - force moving an object
  - something that affects the motion of an object
- Explore more: Can you make a bow and arrow of sorts with maybe sticks and a rubber band?

V. Discussion
- Ishmael makes fun of Isaac, and Sarah kicks him out of the clan. When have you been made fun of and how did you handle it? How should you handle it?

VI. Writing
- Complete your worksheet for today. You are going to be thinking about nouns and verbs.
- A word can be a noun and a verb. Distress could be both depending on how you use it. If it's a thing, then it's a noun. If it's an action, then it's a verb.

**Day 80**

I. Read Genesis 21:14-21. This begins with the end of yesterday's reading.
    14 So Abraham rose early in the morning and took bread and water and gave them to Hagar and sent her away with her son. And she left and wandered about in the wilderness of Beersheba.
    15 When the water was used up, she left the boy under one of the bushes.
    16 Then she went and sat down away from him, about a bowshot away, for she said, "Do not let me see the boy die." And she lifted up her voice and wept.
    17 God heard the boy crying; and the angel of God called to Hagar from heaven and said to her, "What is the matter with you, Hagar? Do not fear, for God has heard the voice of the boy.
    18 Get up and go hold him by the hand, for I will make a great nation of him."
    19 Then God opened her eyes to see a well of water; and she went and got water and gave her son a drink.
    20 God was with the boy, and he grew; and he lived in the wilderness and became an archer.
    21 He lived in the wilderness of Paran, and his mother took a wife for him from the land of Egypt.

II. Memory Verse
    o 2 Peter 3:9
    o The Lord is not slow about His promise, as some count slowness, but is patient toward you, not wishing for any to perish but for all to come to repentance.

III. Language
    o Spelling/Handwriting
        • Test yourselves with the words from Day 76-79.
            ▪ yourself, pray, who, afraid
            ▪ thousand, please, clear, sister
            ▪ promise, laugh, eight, feast
            ▪ upset, listen, voice, rid
    o Vocabulary/Grammar
        • Test yourselves with the words from Day 76-79.
            ▪ integrity – the character quality of holding to strong moral principles
            ▪ restore – to bring something back to its normal condition
            ▪ wean – to gradually get used to not having something you've become dependent on
            ▪ distress – to cause extreme sorrow or worry

IV. Lesson
    o There was a lot of tension between Sarah and Hagar over Isaac and Ishmael because the firstborn son would inherit the father's money and position as the leader of the family clan. Being first born gave someone the rights of an heir, but the order we are born can affect a lot about who we become.
    o Birth order and its effect on us is a very interesting thing.
        • What's your birth order in the family? What's your birth order among just the other boys or girls among your siblings?

- Before I begin, this is, in part, just for fun. Don't let this lesson define who you are. You can defy expectations, just like God likes to do by choosing the least and the youngest to make the greatest.
- How do you think your experience growing up has differed from your siblings?
- Do you think you are treated differently than you siblings?
  - Let's see why those things might be.
- How do you think a firstborn's experience is different than a second born or sixth born?
  - The first born gets all the attention because there is only one kid. That's not the fault of the parents. It's just the way it is.
  - They might be treated more strictly as parents figure out how to parent.
  - They might have more expectations to speak early, walk early, etc. because the parent has no one else to focus on and is more hyper about making sure their kid is doing well.
- How do you think that affects the firstborn?
  - They have high expectations put on them and feel responsible for meeting those expectations.
- What changes when more kids come along?
  - Attention has to be shared. Again, that's not the parents' fault. It's just a fact.
  - Parents might be more relaxed and accept that kids will learn and develop and that they don't need to push to make it happen.
- Some things to note before you read the birth order descriptions.
  - Being born five years or more after a sibling can put you back to being more like a firstborn, though I would think this would be more so if your older sibling were at school and you got the full attention during the day.
  - Also, being the first girl or first boy, even if not the firstborn, is also considered to put you in firstborn position in terms of how it affects you.
  - Also, being a blended family, having adopted kids, etc., all changes things.
  - Plus, every family is different! These are generalizations. See how they fit you.
- Here are birth order descriptions.
  - First born
    - want to please people
    - leaders (since they were always looked up to by siblings)
    - responsible
    - achievers
    - cautious
  - Middle kids
    - adaptable
    - mediators
    - unique talents (wanting to be different from older siblings)
    - friendly
  - Youngest kids
    - outgoing
    - charmers
    - develop unique skills (wanting to be different from older siblings)
    - uncomplicated
    - fun-loving

- Only children
  - responsible
  - organized
  - comfortable as the center of attention
  - mature
  - leaders
o Recall: What social study topic did we study today? birth order
o Explore more: I tried to focus on the positive side of birth order. You can look at what struggles each group has. For instance, an only child can have a harder time in marriage as they aren't used to sharing their lives with someone else. How do you see that in your life? What can you do about it? (You always have a choice. Being born in a certain position in a family doesn't define who you are.)

V. Discussion
  o How do you think birth order has affected you? Do you think the birth order descriptions match you and your family? Why or why not?

VI. Writing
  o Complete your worksheet for today if you haven't already.
  o It has spelling and vocabulary to see what you remember.

**Day 81**

I. Read Genesis 21:22-24.
   22 Now it happened that king Abimelech and the commander of his army said to Abraham, "God is with you in everything you do."
   23 Please, swear to me here by God that you will treat me, my descendants, and our land well because I showed you kindness."
   24 Abraham said, "I swear it."

II. Memory
   o Job 19:25
   o As for me, I know that my Redeemer lives,
      And at the last He will take His stand on the earth.

III. Language
   o Spelling/Handwriting
      - words to know: happened, king, commander, army
      - spelling tips:
         - The word happened ends like most past tense verbs. Write hap-pen-ed.
         - The word king you have written before at the end of your spelling word making.
         - The word commander has just two more letters added onto your spelling word command. The "ER" at the end is spelled the most common way.
         - Army is the word arm with the letter we add at the end to make an E sound.
   o Vocabulary/Grammar
      - redeem (memory verse)
      - to get something or get back something in exchange for payment (verb)
         - If you gave someone a coupon for a free hug, they could redeem their coupon by giving it to you and they would get the hug in exchange.
         - Jesus is our Redeemer because He bought our lives by giving His.

IV. Lesson
   o Abimelech mentions his offspring, his children. What makes his children uniquely his?
   o Science can tell us what child belongs to which parent. They can look at a child's DNA and can compare it to parent DNA.
   o Have you heard of DNA? Have you seen a picture before like the one on the next page?
   o This picture shows the shape of DNA. The shape is called a *double helix*. DNA is long strands that look like a twisting ladder.
      - It is found in every cell of our body.
      - If you took all of the DNA in your body and put it end to end, it would reach to the sun and back several times!

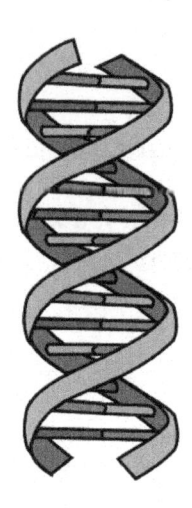

- What does DNA do?
    - DNA tells each cell what to do. It's the boss. There are over 200 types of cells in our bodies, like the cells that make our skin, and the cells that enable us to see, and the cells in our blood. Each has the same DNA code inside.
    - The DNA copies the right piece of information from itself, making RNA. The RNA delivers itself, the instructions, to the ribosome.
    - The ribosome follows the instructions to build the right kind of protein.
    - The protein has to be built in the right shape with the right chemicals at the right time in order to do its job.
    - The proteins then fulfill their calling, whatever they were designed to do, like maybe grow a new skin cell where you got cut.
    - Let's go over this again.
        - The DNA is the boss. It knows what to do.
        - The RNA is the messenger. It tells what to do.
        - A ribosome is the builder. It builds the workers.
        - Proteins are the robot workers; they do the job they were created to do.
    - Act out the process or draw a picture of it. The DNA knows what to do and has the information needed. (I need a new skin cell, done just like this.) The RNA takes that message to the ribosome. (Here's the kind of worker we need to build a skin cell.) The ribosome builds the worker. The worker produces the cell.
- DNA is in each and every cell in your body. It's found in the cell's nucleus. What else has a nucleus?
    - atoms
- Do you remember how many cells are in your body?
    - trillions
    - If each cell in your body were as big as a grain of salt, you'd be as big as a tractor trailer!
- Each of those cells has DNA inside. And each of the over 200 types of cells do different jobs in our bodies.
- Humans mostly are the same, so our DNA is about 99.9% the same. Our bodies need to follow the same instructions to live.
    - What do you think the .1% of DNA that is different controls in our bodies?

- That's the DNA that tells how we look: the color of our skin, our eyes, our hair, etc.
- That's the part of the DNA that is shared with our parents.
  - Each set of instructions from the DNA is called a *gene*. We get the "how we look" genes from our parents.
    - The DNA instructions in those first two cells that come together in a mother's womb give the instructions for new cells to be made with that same DNA, so those genes are built into us from the very beginning.
    - That DNA instructed more and more cells to be built, in the right place, at the right time, in the right way, to form the perfect you.
  - Recall: What shape is DNA? double helix; Where is DNA located? in the nucleus of every cell; What does DNA do? It gives the instructions for what needs to be done in your body.
  - Explore more: What do DNA and RNA stand for? What are nucleotides? What do amino acids have to do with ribosomes and proteins?

V. Discussion
  - Do you think you would ever want to join the army? Why or why not?

VI. Writing
  - Complete your worksheet for today.
  - Add double letters.

**Day 82**

I. Read Genesis 21:25-34. Abraham and Abimelech have made an agreement.
   25 But Abraham complained to Abimelech because his servants had seized Abraham's well.
   26 And Abimelech said, "I do not know who did that, and I hadn't heard anything about it before now."
   27 Abraham took sheep and oxen and gave them to Abimelech, and the two of them made a covenant promise to each other.
   28 Then Abraham set seven ewe lambs of the flock by themselves.
   29 Abimelech said to Abraham, "Why did you set these seven lambs by themselves?"
   30 Abraham said, "Take these seven ewe lambs as I sign that I dug this well."
   31 Therefore he called that place Beersheba, because there the two of them made a covenant promise.
   32 Abimelech and the commander of his army went back to the land of the Philistines.
   33 Abraham planted a tamarisk tree at Beersheba, and there he called on the name of the Lord, the Everlasting God.
   34 And Abraham stayed in the land of the Philistines for many days.

II. Memory Verse
   o Job 19:25
   o As for me, I know that my Redeemer lives,
     And at the last He will take His stand on the earth.

III. Language
   o Spelling/Handwriting
     • words to know: complain, know, hadn't, heard
     • spelling tips:
       ▪ Complain ends with the word plain as in not fancy. It has the same vowel spelling pattern as rain. The first syllable is written with only three letters.
       ▪ Know starts with a silent letter. It ends like your spelling words flow and window.
       ▪ The word hadn't is a contraction. It combines the words had and not. An apostrophe replaces the vowel in the word not.
       ▪ The word heard has the word ear inside of it, which is convenient since when you have heard something, you heard it with your ears.
   o Vocabulary/Grammar
     • seize (verse 25)
     • to take hold of suddenly and forcibly (verb, action verb)

IV. Lesson
   o Abraham sets aside seven ewe lambs. What are ewe lambs?
     • female baby sheep
     • And why do sheep have lambs for babies and not walruses?
   o The DNA from the parents is in the first two cells that begin the process of forming a baby in the womb. The DNA is replicated in the new baby that forms, giving the baby the appearance of its parents.

- So what makes the new baby a ewe instead of a ram, a male sheep. The answer is in the DNA, so let's look at it some more today.
  - What does DNA do?
    - It has the instructions.
    - What takes the instructions and delivers them?
      - RNA, the messenger
      - What does the RNA deliver the message to?
        - ribosome, the builder
        - What does the ribosome build?
          - protein, the worker that builds the cell that's needed
- One of those proteins wraps a piece of DNA around itself. The structure is called a *chromosome*.
- The DNA in the thread of chromosome has hundreds to thousands of sections. Those sections are the instructions. Each complete instruction from the DNA is called a *gene*. The chromosomes carry this gene information and use it to create new cells that are uniquely yours.
  - When new blood cells are formed, your genes (which are a piece of a chromosome which are a piece of DNA) make sure the new cells are of the right blood type for you.
  - When you grow new skin, which you do all the time, the genetic information in the chromosomes make sure it's the right kind and color of skin for you.
- Chromosomes are found in the nucleus of every cell. There are 23 pairs of them, how many chromosomes in all?
  - 46
- So, what makes a lamb a ewe instead of a ram?
  - 22 of the chromosomes are identical to its pair.
  - But there are 23 pairs of chromosomes.
  - One pair can be different. If the chromosomes making up the 23$^{rd}$ pair are identical to each other, then it's a female. (If you are a girl, all of your chromosomes are in identical pairs.)
  - If that last pair is made up of two different types of chromosomes (we call them X and Y), then it's a boy. That one little difference, makes a big difference.
- Speaking of identical, identical twins look identical because they have identical DNA. The original cell split into two, so they were literally created equal. One interesting note, though, they do not have identical fingerprints. Every single human in the world, ever, has a unique fingerprint. So God made a way for even identical twins to be their own unique person.
- Recap: Chromosomes are found in the nucleus of a cell. They are proteins that carry our genetic information, our genes, the information that makes our cells uniquely ours.
- Recall: How many pairs of chromosomes are in humans? What makes a lamb a ewe? What are genes? Where are genes? Where are the chromosomes?
  - 23 (Down Syndrome is when there is an extra chromosome.)
  - All 23 pairs of chromosomes are in identical sets.
  - Each set of instructions from the DNA.

- - They are sections of the chromosomes.
  - in the nucleus of each cell
- Sheep, by the way, have 54 pairs of chromosomes. Peas have 2; hermit crabs have 254.
- Explore more: It might be fun to look at your fingerprints. Scribble pencil onto a piece of paper. Push your finger into it. Then press your finger onto a clean piece of paper. See how they are different from each other.

V. Discussion
- What's unique about you? What information do you think is in your genes? There are stories about identical twins, separated at birth, who came together as adults and found they had so much in common, not just in how they looked, but in the music and foods they liked, little silly things they both did, etc. So, what do you think your genes say about you? How well do you know yourself? How would you describe yourself (not just in how you look)?

VI. Writing
- Complete your worksheet.
- You are going to work with contractions today like your spelling word, hadn't.

**Day 83** (Check Materials List)

I. Read Genesis 21:33 - 22:4.
   33 Abraham planted a tamarisk tree at Beersheba, and there he called on the name of the Lord, the Everlasting God.
   34 And Abraham stayed in the land of the Philistines for many days.
   1 It was after this time that God tested Abraham, and said to him, "Abraham!" And he said, "Here I am."
   2 God said, "Take your son, your only son, whom you love, Isaac, and go to the land of Moriah, and offer him there as a burnt offering on the mountain that I tell you."
   3 So Abraham got up early in the morning and saddled his donkey, and took two of his young men with him and Isaac his son; and he split wood for the burnt offering, and went to the place that God had told him.
   4 On the third day of the journey, Abraham saw the place from a distance.

II. Memory Verse
   - Job 19:25
   - As for me, I know that my Redeemer lives,
     And at the last He will take His stand on the earth.

III. Language
   - Spelling/Handwriting
     - words to know: street, computer, spray, truck
     - spelling tips:
       - I just chose these words today.
       - Street has a double letter for its vowel sound.
       - Computer has how many syllables?
         - 3
         - Remember that each syllable needs to have a vowel.
         - Computer starts with the same three letters as complain.
         - The second syllable is made with two letters.
         - The third syllable has three letters. (They are the same as the end of sister.)
       - Spray ends the same way as the word day.
       - Truck has two letters make the final sound.
   - Vocabulary/Grammar
     - offering (verse 3)
     - a gift, something offered (noun)
       - What is the adjective describing the noun, offering?
         - burnt

IV. Lesson
   - Abraham plants a tamarisk tree.
     - It's a deciduous tree. What does that mean?
       - It has leaves; the leaves shed in the fall.
     - The tamarisk is a tree that God designed to live in desert regions.
   - Do you remember any of the ways the cactus was built for the desert?

- It was mostly about water. It had a large stem and scales for holding in more water.
            - The tamarisk tree also has leaves. Its leaves are very small scales.
            - Do you remember how scales help desert plants?
                - They slow evaporation. When you want clothing to dry, you stretch it out in the sun. Scales are folded in to avoid having the sun hit the leaf.
    - Another name for it is the "salt cedar." The tamarisk thrives in *saline* soil, or salt-water soil.
        - Its leaves take in salt water and evaporation leaves behind salt on the leaves.
        - Thinking about what you know of the area of Israel we've been learning about, why do you think this was a good tree for Abraham to plant?
            - We know that Mount Sodom is a mountain of salt. Probably a lot of the surrounding areas had saline soil.
    - How does the salt water get into the leaves?
        - The water and salt are in the soil. It's the tree's roots that first take in the salty water from the soil.
        - Roots mostly grow horizontally, because the top part of the soil has the most oxygen.
            - The system of roots under the soil can be as big as the system of branches in the tree's crown.
            - It needs to be in order to support the tree, and all the kids that climb in it!
        - The water goes up from the roots into the tree trunk which has inside of it a system of tubes that carry the water and minerals from the soil up into the branches and finally to the leaves.
            - The tubes are kind of like drinking straws for the leaves.
        - Back down through the tubes goes sugar from the leaves.
    - Where did the sugar come from? That's for another day. But do you know where maple syrup comes from?
        - It comes from the sap of a maple tree. What do you think that sap is?
            - It's the sugar water traveling from the leaves down through the tubes in the tree trunk.
    - The tamarisk tree has very small pinkish or white flowers.
        - Since the flowers are so small, there are many of them and they produce lots of seeds, up to 500,000.
        - The seeds in the flowers have a small tuft of hair on the end of them, so they can float far distances through the air or on water.
            - Do you remember what it's called when seeds are scattered?
                - seed dispersal
    - Tamarisk seeds germinate very quickly. Do you remember what germination is?
        - It's the early growth of a seed plant.
        - The roots and shoot of a tamarisk tree can poke out within 24 hours, even if it's still floating along on the water and hasn't found a soil home yet.
    - Recall: What is saline? What takes the salt water in from the ground? Is a tamarisk tree deciduous or coniferous?
        - salt water

- the tree's roots
- deciduous, meaning it has leaves
  - Explore more: Find a stem of some sort to cut open and look inside. You can stick a celery stalk into a cup of water with food coloring in it to watch the celery slurp up the water in its "straws."

V. Discussion
- Is there anything in your life you feel like you couldn't give up if God asked you to?

VI. Writing
- Complete your worksheet for today. You are going to be writing pronouns.
- A pronoun replaces a noun. I wouldn't say, "Lee went to the store." I would say, "I went to the store." I replace my name with the pronoun I.
- Say a sibling's name or a friend's name and say that they are playing. Now replace their name with a pronoun.
- If you were going to use a pronoun instead of names to say who is reading and listening to this lesson right now, what would you say?
  - <u>We</u> are doing the lesson.

**Day 84**

I. Read Genesis 22:1-5. This is the same story from yesterday with another verse added.
 1. It was after this time that God tested Abraham, and said to him, "Abraham!" And he said, "Here I am."
 2. God said, "Take your son, your only son, whom you love, Isaac, and go to the land of Moriah, and offer him there as a burnt offering on the mountain that I tell you."
 3. So Abraham got up early in the morning and saddled his donkey, and took two of his young men with him and Isaac his son; and he split wood for the burnt offering, and went to the place that God had told him.
 4. On the third day of the journey, Abraham saw the place from a distance.
 5. Abraham said to his young men, "Stay here with the donkey. Isaac and I will go over there. We will worship and return to you."

II. Memory Verse
  - Job 19:25
  - As for me, I know that my Redeemer lives,
    And at the last He will take His stand on the earth.

III. Language
  - Spelling/Handwriting
    - verse 4
    - words to know: after, tested, split, wood
    - spelling tips:
      - After has five letters and two syllables, so it has at least two vowels.
      - Tested is the past tense of the verb to test. It ends like most past tense verbs.
      - Split is written just like it sounds.
      - Wood has a double letter making its vowel sound.
  - Vocabulary/Grammar
    - journey (verse 4)
    - a trip taking you from one place to another (noun)

IV. Lesson
  - Abraham probably used a simple machine to split the wood in today's reading. The simple machine is the wedge. There's a picture on the next page.
  - If we just grabbed hold of a log and pulled out on both sides, could we split it?
    - Unlikely! It takes a lot of force.
  - How does the wedge make it easier?
    - The wedge helps us by changing the direction of the force. We apply a downward force with the ax, helped by gravity, and the shape of the wedge pushes outward. The direction of the force is changed, pushing the wood out and splitting it.
  - What about the sharp edge of the ax? How does that help?
    - Its shape concentrates the force at a point, making it very strong on impact because the force hits in one place instead of being spread out.

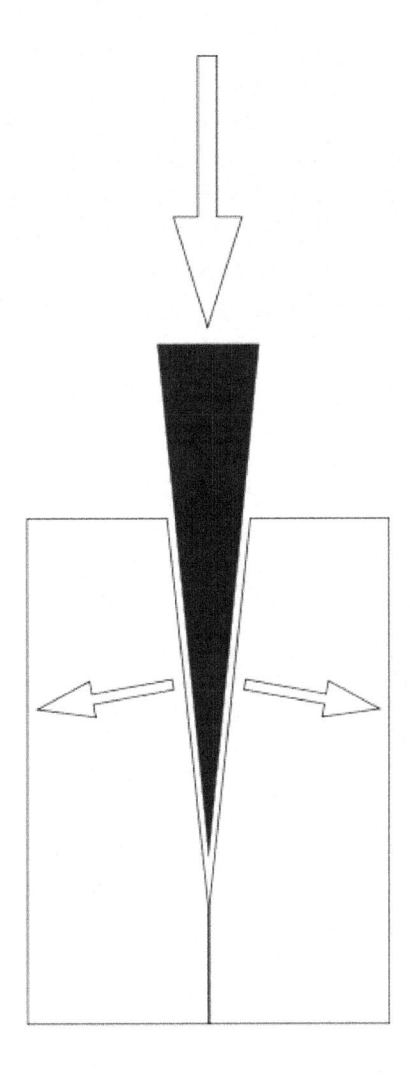

- Can you think of what in your home might be a wedge?
    - Some examples are: knives, sewing needles, scissors, doorstops, nails, forks.
    - Are any of those surprising to you? Can you see how they are all wedges?
    - What do they have in common?
        - They all have a point or an edge.
- Abraham splits the wood for a burnt offering. He says that they are going to worship on the mountain.
- What was his act of worship going to be?
    - sacrificing his son
    - Actually, the whole thing was an act of worship because he was obeying God's command.
- First, what is worship?
    - It's showing honor and love to God.
    - By that definition how is obedience worship?
        - Jesus said repeatedly that if we loved Him, we would obey Him. Obedience is showing our love for God.
        - It is honoring to obey without arguing or complaining.

- In the Old Testament there are offerings and sacrifices commanded by God that show honor to God.
  - But one offering was voluntary. It was the offering of thanksgiving.
  - What does it mean that it was voluntary?
    - It means that it wasn't required. People only did it when they chose to do it.
- Why do you think it's important that giving thanks is voluntary?
  - It shows that your heart is really thankful if you do it just because you want to.
- Recall: What type of simple machine is the ax? What is worship? What are some ways that God is worshiped in the Bible?
  - a wedge
  - showing honor and love to God
  - obedience, singing, dancing, giving
- Explore more: Learn about the different types of offerings in the Old Testament.

V. Discussion
- By this definition, do you worship God?
  - *Worship is to honor with extravagant love and extreme submission* (Webster's Dictionary, 1828).

VI. Writing
- Complete your worksheet for today, writing past tense verbs.
- You are going to write words in the past tense. Mostly we add ED onto the end of verbs to make them past tense. We talk today and we talked yesterday. We smile at each other today and smiled yesterday.
- Smile ends with an E, so we don't really add an ED onto the end, we just need to add the D.
- There are times we add a T, and there are times the word changes.
  - If we run today, what did we do yesterday?
    - We ran.
  - If we eat today, what did we do yesterday?
    - We ate.

**Day 85**

I. Read Genesis 22:5-9. (This is a continuation of the same story. You'll have to stay tuned for the exciting conclusion.)
- 5 Abraham said to his young men, "Stay here with the donkey, and I and the lad will go over there; and we will worship and return to you."
- 6 Abraham took the wood of the burnt offering and laid it on Isaac his son, and he took in his hand the fire and the knife. So the two of them walked on together.
- 7 Isaac spoke to Abraham his father and said, "My father!" And he said, "Here I am, my son." And he said, "Behold, the fire and the wood, but where is the lamb for the burnt offering?"
- 8 Abraham said, "God will provide for Himself the lamb for the burnt offering, my son." So the two of them walked on together.
- 9 Then they came to the place of which God had told him; and Abraham built the altar there and arranged the wood, and bound his son Isaac and laid him on the altar, on top of the wood.

II. Memory Verse
- o Job 19:25
  - As for me, I know that my Redeemer lives,
    And at the last He will take His stand on the earth.
- o Review last week's memory verse.
  - 2 Peter 3:9
  - The Lord is not slow about His promise, as some count slowness, but is patient toward you, not wishing for any to perish but for all to come to repentance.

III. Language
- o Spelling/Handwriting
  - Today you can write your memory verse.
  - Test yourselves on the words from Days 81-84.
    - happened, king, commander, army
    - complain, know, hadn't, heard
    - street, computer, spray, truck
    - after, tested, split, wood
- o Vocabulary/Grammar
  - Test yourselves on the words from Days 81-84.
    - redeem – to get something or get back something in exchange for payment
    - seize – to grab suddenly and forcefully
    - offering – a gift, something offered
    - journey – a trip taking you from one place to another

IV. Lesson
- o Can you find the wedge in today's reading?
  - Hint: It's in verse 6.
  - knife

- o Isaac says that they have brought along fire.
  - • Today, we're going to learn about fire and starting a fire.
- o Fires need three things. What are they?
  - • Oxygen, energy (which is usually heat), and some source of fuel (what you are going to burn, like wood)
- o Abraham arranges the wood for the fire. Why does wood have to be arranged? What should you try to do when you arrange wood for a fire?
  - • You need to make sure there is a flow of air so the fire is getting oxygen. If the wood is piled too tightly, there won't be airflow.
- o Stacking wood and allowing for oxygen to get in there takes care of two of the ingredients for fire. The hardest to come by is the heat. That's why some people carry fire with them. Once the fire is burning, it produces its own heat to keep the process going.
- o What are some ways that fire gets heat to start burning? In other words, how do you light a fire?
  - • Matches or flint rocks create an instant burst of heat.
  - • They need to be used on fuels that have a lower *combustion* temperature, the temperature that it will start burning at.
    - ▪ Combust means burn.
- o Once combustion takes place, you have a fire. What's combustion?
  - • burning
  - • Let's look more closely at what's happening when a fire is started.
- o When heat, oxygen, and fuel are present, the first thing that needs to happen is to wait for the heat to get hot enough to start the fire. It can seem like hard work sometimes to start a fire, if you don't have the right tools, but what would happen if you didn't need a lot of heat to start a fire?
  - • The world would be on fire all the time! Woods could just catch on fire because there is plenty of wood and oxygen present in the woods.

V. Lesson, cont.
- o The Bible isn't made up of isolated stories. The whole thing is the story of God's love for His people and how He is working it out so that they can be with Him forever.
- o The Old Testament isn't just about those individual people's lives. It's about God and what He's doing for you. There are symbols of Jesus throughout what we've read.
  - • Jesus is the ark that saves us from God's wrath.
  - • Jesus is our high priest like Melchizedek.
  - • The bread and the wine are symbols of Jesus' body and blood broken and spilled out for us.
  - • Do you recognize any similarities between Isaac and Jesus?
  - • Here are some:
    - ▪ Abraham is offering his only son as a sacrifice.
      - • God offered His only son as a sacrifice.
    - ▪ Abraham laid the wood that was going to burn Isaac on his back.
      - • Jesus was made to carry his own cross to his crucifixion.
    - ▪ Abraham says that God will provide the sacrificial lamb.
      - • Jesus was the Lamb of God. He was the lamb sacrificed on our behalf. He took the punishment for our sin, which was the death penalty.

- o  Right now, we are in the middle of the story. What major events are happening in the world? God is using those as part of His grand plan.
- o  Recall: To put out a fire you only have to remove one of the three ingredients. What are they and what are some examples of how you could remove them?
    - heat (blowing on the wick of a candle lowers the heat, throwing water on a fire cools it and removes the heat), oxygen (stomping on a fire, covering it, stop/drop/and roll), fuel (turning off the gas on the stove)
- o  Explore more: Light a fire. One fun thing to do is light a candle and then put a jar over it and watch it go out. You can lower the jar watch it start to go out and then lift it up to see the flame come back.

VI. Discussion
- o  God doesn't just work on a large scale. He knows each of us individually.
- o  How is God working in your life to bring you to Him or to make you more and more like Jesus?

VII. Writing
- o  Complete your worksheet if you haven't already.
- o  There is a place for practicing your spelling and vocabulary.

**Day 86**

I. Read Genesis 22:9-12.
9   Abraham and Isaac reached the place where God had sent them. Abraham built an altar there and arranged the wood, and bound his son Isaac and laid him on the altar, on top of the wood.
10  Abraham stretched out his hand and took the knife to kill his son.
11  But the angel of the Lord called to him from heaven and said, "Abraham, Abraham!" And he said, "Here I am."
12  He said, "Do not stretch out your hand against the boy, and do nothing to him. Now I know that you fear God, since you have not kept your only son from Me."

II. Memory Verse
- Hebrews 11:1
  Faith is being sure of what we hope for. It is being certain of what we do not see. (NIrV)

III. Language
- Spelling
  - verse 10
  - words to know: boy, hand, nothing, only
  - spelling tips:
    - The word boy has an "OY" sound spelled with a Y.
    - The word hand ends with the word and.
    - The word nothing says no thing.
    - The word only is the word on with an L-Y ending.
  - bind/bound (verse 9)
  - to tie something up tightly (verb)
  - This is another irregular past tense. I will bind the wood together into a bundle. I bound the wood into a bundle.

IV. Lesson
- We talked before about shelter and its importance for survival. We can look at another survival skill today, how to start a fire.
  - What are the three things necessary for a fire?
    - heat (energy), fuel, oxygen
  - If you were in the woods, what types of things would you look for for fuel?
  - When you start a fire, you usually use different kinds of fuel. It's good to choose different sizes of things. A log is good for burning for a longer time, but it's not easy to get burning. A leaf or thin twig is easier to get burning, but it won't burn for long.
    - It's also good to look for dry things, otherwise the heat energy will be used in evaporation before it can be used to start a fire.
    - If you are stuck in a wet area, you can look around for drier parts of trees. Start with a very, very small fire and keep your next size small pieces nearby to be dried out from the heat. You can a build a fire this way, little by little, adding on small pieces at a time until you have a fire going.

- That's fuel. To ensure oxygen you need to lightly pack your fuel. Start with the smallest and driest materials. Build a nest-like bundle of dried grasses, leaves and small twigs. Above it build a teepee of kindling, small branches. Once your fire is going, you can add on bigger kindling and then logs that will keep your fire going for a longer time.

- Now the hard part, the heat source. If you have matches or a lighter, you're good to go. Another tool is a flint and steel set. Flint creates a spark when struck by metal.
- Here are some methods you could use to start a fire in an emergency, an emergency, not for fun. A fire is not a toy to play with.
    - The most primitive method would be to spin a stick in a piece of wood. The rubbing produces heat which can start your fire. You make a notch in a piece of wood and put a small piece of twig in the hole. Over it place your stick which you spin between your hands to make it rub fast enough.
        - This is a hard method to use.
    - Another method involves metal and batteries. The easiest metal to use would be steel wool, but you can use metal paper clips and even a metallic gum wrapper.
        - The metal is rubbed against a battery (the part that makes the connection). A 9-volt battery is a good kind to use, and you could use your cell phone battery.
    - A final method involves sun light. The sun's energy warms us, right? Focusing that energy produces enough heat energy to start a fire.
        - You just need the sun and something that will focus the light. Some things that can be used are glasses, magnifying lenses, mirrors, cans, and water.
        - The goal for all of them is to direct the sunlight to a small point. Just like the wedge focuses all of the force on an edge making it more effective, a lens or mirror focuses all of the heat energy from the sun into one small point. All the heat concentrates in one spot, and it gets hotter and hotter, making it effective for starting a fire.

- Prepare a small nest of *tinder* (small, dry things that will easily combust or burn).
- Aim the sunlight at the tinder using your lens or mirror. You'll have to move to find the best distance.
  - The bottom of a can can be used as a mirror by shining it. You can shine it with things like sand or toothpaste, even chocolate can work.
  - Water can be used in something like a clear plastic bag. Fill the bag with some water. Tie it off into a ball.
  - In frozen conditions, you could even use ice as your water in a clear container to focus the sun's rays.
    - What are some things that you think you should be careful of when starting a fire?
      - Be careful not to burn yourself. Work away from yourself, such as when you are striking a flint.
      - Be sure to have a contained area to build your fire. You can build a wall of rocks around your fire to contain it in one area. A strong wind can spread your fire to nearby combustible materials, things that can burn easily. It's wrong to build a fire outside on a windy day in hot, dry weather. Why?
        - Dry things catch fire more easily and the wind can spread a spark, the heat needed to start a fire going.
      - Gasoline is highly combustible and is dangerous around any kind of fire.
      - And make sure you know how you would put it out before you light it.
  - Recall: What are good choices for tinder? Why is stacking kindling like a teepee a good idea? What are some ways to produce heat? What are some fire safety tips?
    - dry, small (leaves, grass, twigs)
    - It allows for oxygen flow.
    - rubbing, metal and batteries, sunlight
    - Know how to put out a fire. Keep fire away from materials that catch fire easily (especially gas). Make sure your fire is contained.
  - Explore more: It would be fun to heat up a spot using light and a magnifying lens or one of these other methods. Make sure to talk about safe places for fires to be and what you need to be careful about (like not really starting a fire while you are playing with concentrating light!)

V. Discussion
  - Do you have the fear of the Lord? Why or why not? How is it demonstrated in your life? Or how does your life demonstrate your lack of the fear of the Lord?

VI. Writing
  - Complete your worksheet for today.
  - You are going to be using the correct "to."
    - To is most commonly used as two letters, T-O, as in going to the store, or want to eat.

- Too with two O's means also or extra, something related to there being more. There are more O's in this one to help you remember that. I want some too! That's too much!
- The number two is spelled with a silent W.

**Day 87**

I. Read Genesis 22:13-14.
   13   Then Abraham looked up and saw a ram caught in the thicket by his horns; and Abraham went and took the ram and offered him up for a burnt offering in the place of his son.
   14   Abraham named that place The Lord Will Provide, and it is said to this day, "In the mount of the Lord it will be provided."

II. Memory Verse
   o   Hebrews 11:1
       Faith is being sure of what we hope for. It is being certain of what we do not see. (NIrV)

III. Language
   o   Spelling
       - words to know: looked, up, his, horns
       - spelling tips:
         ▪ The word <u>looked</u> is the past tense of your spelling word look. What two letters do you normally add onto a verb to make it past tense? Today you look great. Yesterday you looked great.
         ▪ The word <u>up</u> just has two letters.
         ▪ The word <u>his</u> ends with the word is.
         ▪ The word <u>horns</u> has the word or inside of it. It's a plural noun. There is more than one horn.
   o   Vocabulary
       - thicket (verse 13)
       - a dense group of shrubs, bushes or small trees (noun)
       - What does dense mean? Remember what density is?
         ▪ Density is how much stuff is in a place.
         ▪ If something is dense, then there is a lot of "stuff" in it.
         ▪ So, what is a dense group of shrubs and bushes?
           - a lot of them together in one place

IV. Lesson
   o   In today's story we have a ram caught in a thicket.
   o   What is a ram?
       - It's a male sheep.
   o   What do you remember about sheep?
       - They are mammals.
       - They follow each other blindly, meaning without thinking. They will just go with the flock wherever, even if it's into danger.
       - They have terrific peripheral vision. What does that mean?
         ▪ Peripheral vision is all that you can see to the side without turning your head. In fact, sheep's peripheral vision is so great that they can see behind them.
   o   What do you remember about mammals?

- warm blooded (Their body temperature stays the same no matter what environment they are in.)
- have hair
- give birth to babies instead of laying eggs
- moms give milk to their babies

o What else do you know about sheep? What about their hair?
- Their hair is wool. Those who raise sheep cut off the wool once a year in the spring. Cutting off a sheep's hair is called *shearing*.

o Let's learn a little about wool. Do you know how wool gets from a sheep's back to your back in the form of a sweater?
- After shearing, the wool is washed and washed and then picked over to clean out sticks and leaves and seeds that might be stuck in the sheep's wool.
- Wool is then carded, kind of like being combed. It can be done by hand or by machine. Here is a picture of a carding machine.

o We use machines to spin the wool into yarn. The first factories for spinning yarn and thread were built in the 1700s. By 1850 there were ten factories that made thread and cloth in the city of Lowell, Massachusetts.
- This was part of something called the Industrial Revolution, when people starting working in factories instead of working on farms.
- Factories liked to hire women and children because they could be paid less than men.
  - Children were given school in the evenings, but after working twelve hours they were too tired to stay awake for lessons.
  - At least seventy-five percent of the workers were women and were called the Lowell Mill Girls. They were paid half the wages of a man.
- As factories grew and grew and grew, technology advanced. The workers were expected to work faster and at more machines. It could be dangerous work, working too quickly near the fast spinning machines, especially when

you were exhausted from fourteen hours of work. If your hair got caught in a spinning spool of thread, you could be scalped!
- The workers got fed up with the life they were forced into by the rich bosses who controlled their lives and worked together to protest.
- The children of Lowell had others fighting for them.
    - A photographer named Lewis Hine took pictures of child workers to expose the harsh conditions they lived under.
    - In the 19th century, new laws were introduced to limit the number of hours factory employees could work and restrictions on child labor were put into place.
- Here is one of Lewis Hine's Lowell Mill Girls picture. The girl in the picture is twelve.

- Recall: What was the industrial revolution? How were the Lowell Mills a part of creating laws to protect workers? What's it called when sheep's wool is cut off?
    - moving people from an agricultural existence, working on farms, to living and working in cities because factories were being built and employed a lot of people
    - The Lowell Mill Girls protested (actually formed the first women's union) to fight how they were treated and the children were photographed to expose how they were being used by their profiteering bosses.
    - shearing
  o Explore more: Take a look at yarn to see how it's made up of lots of fibers spun together.

V. Discussion
- What part would you have played if you lived during the Industrial Revolution? Would you still be a farmer? Would you be a big boss, factory owner, mill worker, inventor of the new machinery, union director planning strikes?

VI. Writing
- Complete your worksheet for today.
- You are going to make a list of jobs you would like to do and jobs you would not like to do.
- Note: This isn't, "What do you want to be when you grow up?" I always avoid that with my kids. How could they possibly know where life will take them? This is just for fun. Let them say anything, and help them spell it. Try to encourage creativity. Would they want to design billboards? Swing on a trapeze? Run Amazon? The idea of this comes from my one son who one day announced, "I don't want to be a galley slave when I grow up." We all agreed that was a good idea! He made a list of jobs he didn't want when he grew up. It's become a joke in our family. Hopefully you have fun with it too.

**Day 88**

I. Read Genesis 22:15-19.
   15  Then the angel of the Lord called to Abraham a second time from heaven,
   16  and said, "By Myself I have sworn, declares the Lord, because you have done this thing and have not withheld your son, your only son,
   17  I will greatly bless you, and I will greatly multiply your descendants as the stars of the heavens and as the sand on the seashore; and your descendants will defeat their enemies.
   18  From among your descendants, all the nations of the earth will be blessed, because you have obeyed My voice."
   19  So Abraham returned to his young men who had been waiting, and they went together to Beersheba where Abraham lived.

II. Memory Verse
   o Hebrews 11:1
     Faith is being sure of what we hope for. It is being certain of what we do not see. (NIrV)

III. Language
   o Spelling/handwriting
     • words to know: done, Abraham, second, seashore
     • spelling tips:
       ▪ Done has the same vowel spelling pattern as your spelling word come.
       ▪ Abraham is a name so it begins with a capital letter. Spell each syllable. Each syllable only has one vowel, and they are all the same.
       ▪ Second ends like pond. Say it sec-ond to spell it. Each syllable has three letters.
       ▪ Seashore is a compound word, which means it's two words put together into one. What two words is it made up of?
   o Vocabulary
     • declare (verse 16)
     • to state clearly, to make known publicly (verb)

IV. Lesson
   o Abraham's descendants are going to number as the stars and as the sand. We're going to talk about sand.
   o How would you describe sand? What do you think it is?
     • Sand is mostly rocks. Here's a picture of some sand under a microscope.

- So if sand is really small rocks, where do you think it comes from?
  - Sand is created by erosion. Do you remember what erosion is?
    - Erosion is the gradual wearing away of land.
    - Rivers erode river banks and carry along little pieces of rock in them. Rocks are rolled along and worn down and deposited along the way. That's why riverbanks can be sandy.
    - Ocean waves wear away at rocks and carry along bits that break off and deposit them elsewhere.
    - Water in the ocean is always moving, and so it's always wearing away at the rock on the ocean floor.
    - The sand on beaches and on riverbanks doesn't stay put. It gets moved around by the water in its environment.
  - If rivers and oceans cause erosion that produces sand, why are deserts full of sand?
    - Of course, the first answer is because God made it so, but the second answer is erosion.
    - Water isn't the only way erosion occurs. Can you think of anything else that might cause erosion?
      - What happens to an eraser when you use it?
        - You rub and rub and pieces of it come off. It's being eroded in its own way.
      - What might cause rubbing in the desert?
  - Wind causes erosion in the desert. The rock is slowly worn away.
    - Wind carries off rocks that are small enough to be moved by wind.
    - Those rocks land and bang into rocks that stayed in place, chipping away at them.
    - Any tiny bits that break off can then be carried by the wind to chip away at other rocks.
- Recall: What creates sand? What is one way erosion occurs?
  - God ☺ and erosion
  - wind
- Abraham is told that all of the nations of the earth will be blessed because of his obedience. What are all the nations of the earth?
  - The number of official countries changes, so I couldn't even tell them all to you if I wanted to.
- Today you are going to learn some of the nations of the world. Use the key to find the countries on the map for Day 88 in your Map Book. (2 and 3 are tiny and harder to see.)
- Explore more: Try to find some of these on a globe or map that you have at home or play on Google Earth and go to a random place in each country.

V. Discussion
- Abraham is told that all the nations of the earth will be blessed because of his obedience.
- Did you ever think your obedience could make world-wide impact? It can! How does knowing that change your thoughts towards obedience in the little things?

231

- This reminds me of a story of a teenager who was kind to Japanese prisoners of war. Her parents had been missionaries who were killed by Japanese soldiers in WWII. She visited the prisoners and brought them gifts to show them love. She knew her parents would have wanted her to forgive them and to love them.
- A famous Japanese war hero found out about her and what she had done and it set him off investigating Christianity. He became an evangelist in Japan, leading thousands to Christ. It started with a teenager's obedience to love and forgive.
- This story is from the biography of Jacob Deshazer.

VI. Writing
- Complete your worksheet for today. You are going to be drawing a country and writing about it.
- Of the countries you found on the map today, which would you most like to visit? Why?

**Day 89**

I. Read Genesis 22:20-24.
20 It was after all these things that Abraham was told, "Your brother Nahor and his wife Milcah have had children.
21 Uz his firstborn and Buz his brother and Kemuel the father of Aram
22 and Chesed and Hazo and Pildash and Jidlaph and Bethuel."
23 Bethuel became the father of Rebekah; these eight Milcah bore to Nahor, Abraham's brother.
24 His concubine (kind of like Hagar was to Abraham), whose name was Reumah, had Tebah and Gaham and Tahash and Maacah.

II. Memory Verse
- Hebrews 11:1
  Faith is being sure of what we hope for. It is being certain of what we do not see. (NIrV)

III. Language
- Spelling/handwriting
  - verse 20
  - words to know: wives, lives, knives, shelves (Note: This has the word children, which they have already had as a spelling word. It is an irregular plural. They will practice another type of plural today for spelling and on their worksheet.)
  - spelling tips:
    - The word children is an irregular plural. Plurals are words that indicate more than one.
      - A regular plural is when the word follows the rules, like just add an S or ES.
      - The rule for your spelling words today is that when a word ends in F or FE, you take that off and add VES.
        - Write the plural of <u>wife, life, knife, and shelf.</u>
- Vocabulary/Grammar
  - allegiance
  - loyalty, a commitment to something

IV. Lesson
- We have another list of family today.
- We're going to talk about DNA some more and genetics, those genes carried around in our chromosomes that make each of us uniquely us.
  - Today we're going to talk about my favorite part of genetics. On Day 90 we'll practice it.
  - We get our genes, our genetic makeup, from our parents. But why then aren't you identical to your siblings? Let's find out.
- We've learned that a person's genes come from their parents. You get genes from your mom and from your dad. Their genes came from their parents, and so you are also getting parts of your grandparents' genes.

- You couldn't have all of your dad's genes and all of your mom's genes. You only need one set, and so what you get is a combination. The different combinations of those genes make you unique from your siblings.
  - A man named Mendel observed the regularity in how traits of what we look like were passed down from parent to children. Mendel noticed this not just in humans but in "parent" plants and "baby" plants.
    - If pollen from a white flower landed on a purple flower, the distinct genes from those two flowers would make up the genes of a new flower. Some baby flowers from these parents would be purple and some would be white, but it wouldn't be half and half. We're going to look at what in our genes shows which trait from our parents will be in us.
  - I'm using the word, *trait*; it's a distinguishing characteristic. You might have brown eyes. That's a trait. You might be stubborn. That's a trait.
    - For each of those unique things that make people different from one another we carry two pieces of information in our genes.
      - Our bodies do a lot of things in pairs!
      - From those two bits, a child gets one from the mother and one from the father.
        - One half of the gene that gives eye color comes from the mother and one half of the gene that gives eye color comes from the father.
        - It's that way for all of our genetic information that gives us our unique look, personality, and inherited abilities.
        - On the following page there is a picture of how this genetic information gets passed along.
          - We use capital letters and lowercase letters to show the two parts of the genetic information for both the mom and the dad.
          - You can see that there are four possible ways to combine the two pieces of information from both parents. There are four different outcomes possible in their children, for that one trait.
            - This happens for every single trait, not just hair color but hair texture and hair thickness, etc., so that there are many, many, many overall combinations of how all the traits could come together.
  - Recall: What is a trait and what are some examples?
    - a distinguishing characteristic
    - the color of a flower, how tall you grow, the shape of your nose, if you are talented at music, etc.

V. Discussion
  - Where do you get your physical traits from? Whose eyes do you have? Whose nose? Whose hair?
    - You could consider this "Explore More" and make a list. On Day 90 the question asks about non-physical traits.

VI. Writing
- o Complete your worksheet page for today.
- o Practice the plural spelling rule with F.

**Day 90**

I. Read Genesis 23:1-2.
    1  Sarah lived for one hundred and twenty-seven years.
    2  Sarah died in Hebron in the land of Canaan, and Abraham went in to mourn for Sarah and to weep and cry for her.

II. Memory Verse
- Hebrews 11:1
  Faith is being sure of what we hope for. It is being certain of what we do not see. (NIrV)
- Review last week's memory verse.
  - Job 19:25
  - As for me, I know that my Redeemer lives,
    And at the last He will take His stand on the earth.

III. Language
- Spelling/handwriting
  - Test yourselves on the words from Days 86-89.
    - boy, hand, nothing, only
    - looked, up, his, horns
    - done, Abraham, second, seashore
    - wives, lives, knives, shelves
- Vocabulary
  - Test yourselves on the words from Days 86-89.
    - bound – to tie together tightly
    - thicket – a dense group of shrubs, bushes or small trees
    - declare – to state clearly, to make known publicly
    - allegiance – loyalty, a commitment to something

IV. Lesson
- Today we're going to continue with how our genes determine our traits, our characteristics, the things that make each of us unique.
- What is DNA's job?
  - DNA is the boss of each cell. He gives the instructions.
- Genes are what we called each segment of the DNA.
  - Genes are the instructions the DNA gives out.
- Each gene has at least two variations. For instance, there are two genes that control eye color. One gene says either brown or blue, and one gene gives the instructions for either blue or green. Your eye color is the result of which of the two variations of each of those genes your instructions carry.
  - Genetics is very complex. There are billions and billions of people on the earth and each one is different. Even something as seemingly simple as eye color scientists don't fully understand how the genetics work beyond the basics.
- Let's do one example of genetics at work. We'll do more during the review week.
- Use your second worksheet for today to determine the genetic makeup of your new, pet dog.
  - (Note: Below are notes for the parent. Don't read them out loud.)

- They will first design a mom and a dad dog.
- Then they will choose randomly odd or even.
- Then you can explain to them what traits their puppy will have using the guidelines below.
- For the trait that they chose odd for, the mom trait chosen will be the dominant trait. For the traits that they chose even for, what was chosen for the dad will be the dominant trait.
    - As an example, for ears, if they chose long for dad and short for mom, and they chose "odd," then mom's trait, the short ears will be what the baby has.

V. Discussion
- What personality traits have you gotten from your grandparents?

VI. Writing
- Complete your worksheet for today if you haven't already.
- There is a place to practice spelling and vocabulary.

**Day 91**

I. Read Genesis 23:3-11.
   3   Then Abraham rose and spoke to the sons of Heth, saying,
   4   "I am a stranger here; give me a burial site that I may bury my dead out of my sight."
   5   The sons of Heth answered Abraham, saying to him,
   6   "Hear us, my lord, you are a mighty prince among us; bury your dead in the best of our graves; none of us will refuse you his grave for burying your dead."
   7   So Abraham rose and bowed to the people.
   8   And he spoke with them, saying, "If it is your wish for me to bury my dead out of my sight, then ask Ephron,
   9   that he may give me the cave at the end of his field; I will pay the full price."
   10  Ephron answered Abraham in the hearing of all who went in at the gate of his city, saying,
   11  "No, my lord, I give you the field, and I give you the cave that is in it. Let everyone know that I give it to you; bury your dead."

II. Memory Verse
   o   John 11:25
   o   Jesus said to her, "I am the resurrection and the life; he who believes in Me will live even if he dies."

III. Language
   o   Spelling/handwriting
       • verse 11
       • words to know: rose, spoke, give, here
       • spelling tips:
           ▪ The word rose ends with a silent E and has no Z.
           ▪ The word spoke is the past tense of speak. It also ends in a silent E.
           ▪ The word give also ends with a silent E, but it looks like it should say the long I sound.
           ▪ The word here also ends with a silent E!
   o   Vocabulary
       • refuse (verse 6)
       • to say no to doing something, or to refuse to give permission to do something

IV. Lesson
   o   Abraham is wanting to buy a cave. We read before about Lot and his daughters hiding out in a cave.
   o   How are caves formed inside of mountains? It's related to something we've already learned about. What do you think?
       • Caves can form in different ways, but they are basically made by erosion.
           ▪ Waves can pound away at a rock, and water (along with gritty sand) can erode away in cracks until the cracks become caves.
           ▪ Wind can do the same thing, carry along gritty sand that wears away in already existent cracks, until eventually there is a cave.
       • Why does Mount Sodom have caves? (hint: What is it made of?)

- It's made of salt and salt dissolves in water. Little by little exposure to water wears away at the mountain. Water gets into cracks and opens it up more and more.
- I've been in caves like the picture here with the big round stone and everything. They were in the Middle East, in Turkey, where my family lived for about seven years.

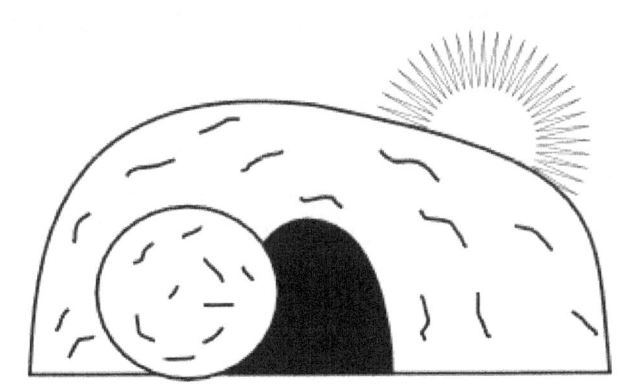

- Those caves were used for graves just like in the story.
- Abraham mourned when Sarah died, expressing his sadness.
- How are people supposed to mourn in your country? How are people supposed to act at a funeral when someone dies?
    - Are people expected to cry?
    - Are people expected to wear black?
- Christians sometimes call funerals "homegoing celebrations" and may wear "happy" colors instead of the traditional black. It's still normal to be sad and cry, even if you know someone is in heaven. And, it's okay not to cry.
- In many cultures there are different traditions for mourning.
    - Among the Roma we lived with in Macedonia, they had different cultural ideas about mourning. Roma are better known as Gypsies.
        - For the first twenty-four hours professional mourners were hired. Their job was to wail, loudly, so everyone knows how much the person was loved. (It doesn't make any sense to me, but it does to them.)
    - In Ghana, in Africa, they throw parties to celebrate the person who died. People eat, drink, and dance the night away. People donate money to the family of the deceased.
    - In Europe there are some cultures that expect a widow to mourn by wearing black, even for the rest of her life, or for at least two years.
    - In many cultures black is the color of mourning, and it is customary to bring food to the family in mourning.
    - In Turkey people are expected to bring sweets to the family and stay and sit with them.
    - In both Hinduism and Islam, it's considered wrong to be excessive in showing grief.
- In America we collectively show that we are mourning by hanging the American flag at half-mast.
- Recall: What are some differences in ways people morn? How does water create caves?

- celebrating and hiring professional wailers
- It creates caves through erosion. It can batter away at a rock or dissolve it.
    - Explore more: You could make your own cave by baking empty-tomb cookies.

V. Discussion
- Have you ever mourned the loss of someone or something? Was there anything or anyone who helped you through it?

VI. Writing
- Complete your workbook page for today.
- You are going to be identifying nouns today. Nouns are people, places, and things.
- A parent is a noun because it is a person. Brandon is a noun because he's a person too.

**Day 92**

I. Read Genesis 23:12-16.
12 And Abraham bowed before all of the people there.
13 He spoke to the owner of the field so that everyone could hear, saying, "I will give the price of the field, accept it from me that I may bury my dead there."
14 He answered Abraham, saying to him,
15 "My lord, listen; a piece of land worth four hundred shekels of silver, what is that between me and you? Bury your dead."
16 Abraham listened and weighed out four hundred shekels of silver, commercial standard.

II. Memory Verse
- John 11:25
- Jesus said to her, "I am the resurrection and the life; he who believes in Me will live even if he dies."

III. Language
- Spelling/handwriting
    - words to know: price, could, bowed, standard
    - spelling tips:
        - The word price follows the rule that a C followed by an E has its soft sound.
        - The word could has the same vowel spelling pattern as your spelling words ground and sprout.
        - The word bowed has the same vowel spelling pattern as your spelling word now and power.
        - The word standard starts with the word stand and ends with ARD.
- Vocabulary
    - standard (verse 16)
    - accepted as normal, or a level of quality (noun, adjective)

IV. Lesson
- Silver is weighed out as a measure, "commercial standard." That means there is a standard weight used in selling.
- When my family lived in Istanbul, we had a bazaar set up on our street every Sunday. Poles held up tarps for blocks and two rows of wooden tables lined the two sides of the street. There were clothes and school supplies for sale, but the majority of the bazaar sold food. Some things were sold by item, for instance six TL (Turkish Lira) for one tub of butter, but mostly, food was sold by weight.
    - You would ask for a kilogram of apples or whatever you wanted to buy. Some would give you a bag and you would choose your own. Others would choose for you. Always look for the booths where you can choose your own!
    - They would put your apples on the one side of the balance scale.

- They would put their commercial standard weight on the other side of the balance.
    - Weights could be for a half kilo, or for one or two kilos. A kilo is short for kilogram. It's a little more than two pounds.
- Then there are two types of sellers.
    - One would throw in an extra apple to tip the scale in your favor. The heavier side will be lower than the other. They didn't want to wait for the scale to be perfectly balanced, but they made sure you got your money's worth.
    - The other type of seller would work really hard to balance the scale. They would take out the big, beautiful apple that you chose carefully, and they would grab a smaller bruised one and throw it in to balance the scale out. They wanted to make sure you didn't get more than you paid for.
- There's another experience that's common at the bazaar. It's *haggling*, discussing the price to try to get the best deal for yourself.
- If I was ever offered a price by a smooth talker like Ephron, I would have haggled. In many parts of the Middle East, it is expected. You aren't told the "real" price. They expect you to make a lower offer. In some places the tourist books will tell you to offer one third of the price you were told. So if they said 30 dollars, you would say 10. They would say 25. You would say 15. Then you could agree on 20.
    - It's not that simple of course. You go back and forth. They say what great quality it is. You say you can get it cheaper elsewhere. They say it's beautiful. You say there are others just like it.
- Sometimes they will be staunch on their price and then you have to decide if you want to pay it. Sometimes you will get the lower price and they will look defeated!
    - This reminds me of another Bible verse.
- Recall: What does it mean to haggle? What tool is used in weighing?
    - a scale or balance scale
    - to argue the price of something to try to get the better deal (or just a fair deal)

- Explore more: Make a balance. You could use a long spoon or ruler over a chair and try to get it to balance.

V. Discussion
- What type of seller would you be? Making sure it's even or tipping the scale in favor of the other person?

VI. Writing
- Complete your worksheet for today.
- You are going to create compound nouns. Compound nouns are when two nouns come together to form one word, like rain and bow making rainbow.
- Note: some answers could be ball/cone, cake, boy/girl, ball, ground/pen

**Day 93**

I. Read Genesis 23:17-20.
   17 Ephron's field, the field and cave which was in it, and all the trees which were in the field, were officially given over
   18 to Abraham for a possession in the presence of all who were there.
   19 After this, Abraham buried Sarah his wife in the cave of the field facing Mamre (that is, Hebron) in the land of Canaan.
   20 So the field and the cave that is in it were given over to Abraham for a burial site.

II. Memory Verse
- John 11:25
- Jesus said to her, "I am the resurrection and the life; he who believes in Me will live even if he dies."

III. Language
- Spelling/handwriting
    - words to know: field, was, cave, facing
    - spelling tips:
        - <u>Field</u> follows the rule I before E.
        - The word <u>was</u> is one you just need to learn. It has one vowel. It ends with the word as.
        - The word <u>cave</u> ends with a silent E.
        - The word <u>facing</u> takes the silent E off of face to add its ending.
- Vocabulary
    - possession (verse 18)
    - something you have

IV. Lesson
- Today we're going to learn about the biome of fields. Do you remember the word biome? Do you remember what it means?
    - A biome is the broad characteristic of a major habitat, such as mountains are a biome and forests are a biome and fresh water is a biome.
    - Do you remember what a habitat is?
        - It's the home of a plant or animal.
- Abraham's in a field, so we're going to look at fields as a habitat.
    - I don't know what Abraham's field was like, specifically.
    - We've already looked at the desert as a biome. Today we'll look at grasslands as a biome.
- Fields are a type of grassland, the major biome. What do you know about fields or grasslands?
    - Obviously, they have grass.
    - They are often between forests and deserts. Grasslands often border deserts. This is because they get more rain than deserts to enable things to grow there and less rain than forests keeping so much from growing there.
    - There is grassland on every continent except Antarctica.

- Grasslands are used for farming, so in some areas, there is not much free, wild grassland.
- What animals live in the grasslands depends on where in the world you are. There could be zebras and lions and cheetahs and elephants if you are on the African *savannah*. Or foxes and prairie dogs and mice and skunks and deer in the American *prairies*. Grasslands have different names depending on where in the world you are.
    - Historically, bison ruled the prairies of America. They were hunted for food and for sport (just for fun) by those traveling west on the Oregon Trail. Bison roamed in huge herds making target practice easy. It's estimated that more than 20 million once roamed free in America. Now it's estimated that there are only 5,000 living in the wild in America. There are others in protected herds to keep them from dying out. As an example, you can pretend that you and your parent are the number of bison in the wild today. If there were 8,000 people in the room with you, that's how many bison there used to be.
    - Along with those animals are hundreds of bird, bug, and plant species.
- I told you how the savannah is the name of the grasslands in Africa and the prairie is the name of the grasslands in America. People living in grasslands are away from urban, city centers. What type of lifestyle do you think people have who live on the grasslands?
    - In some areas they are farmers. In some areas they are herders, living off of animals such as cows.
- Another famous grassland area in the world is named the Steppe.
    - The Steppe stretch across Asia and Europe. We'll look at maps of this area today.
    - Grasslands are usually found between forests and what?
        - deserts
    - Parts of the Eurasian Steppe were part of a famous trade route. Why do you think the steppes would make a good route for travelers who wanted to sell and buy goods?
        - Grasslands, like the Steppe, made for easier travel than forests or deserts.
    - Take a look at the maps for Day 93. The blue routes are the water routes for traders. We talked before how traders used rivers as highways. The red lines are what is known as the Silk Road because traders from China carried silk from China to trade in other lands.
        - You can see the Himalaya Mountains on the second map. The trade route had to make it past the highest obstacle in the world. You can also see a desert right in the path of the route.
        - Although the Steppes can have fierce winter winds, it still provided a better travel alternative to the desert or the forest or mountains.
- Recall: What is the name of the long strip of grasslands across Asia and Europe that enabled trade to be carried out over land? What are the grasslands in Africa called? What are the grasslands in America called?
    - the Steppe

- savannah
- the prairie
  o Explore more: Can you start reading a *Little House on the Prairie* book?

V. Discussion
  o What is it like where you live? How would you describe your habitat?

VI. Writing
  o Complete the worksheet for today.
  o You are going to be identifying animals that live in a grasslands biome.

**Day 94**

I. Read Genesis 25:1-11. (We're skipping the next story but will come back to it.)
 1  Abraham took another wife.
 2  She had six sons with Abraham.
 3-4 And they had many children.
 5  Now Abraham gave all that he had to Isaac;
 6  but to the sons of the others, Abraham gave gifts while he was still living, and sent them away from his son Isaac to the land of the east.
 7  Abraham lived one hundred and seventy-five years.
 8  Abraham breathed his last and died in a ripe old age, an old man and satisfied with life; and he was gathered to his people.
 9  Then his sons Isaac and Ishmael buried him in the cave with Sarah, facing Mamre,
 10 in the field which Abraham had purchased.
 11 It came about after the death of Abraham, that God blessed his son Isaac.

II. Memory Verse
- John 11:25
- Jesus said to her, "I am the resurrection and the life; he who believes in Me will live even if he dies."

III. Language
- Spelling/handwriting
  - words to know: gave, that, east, living
  - spelling tip:
    - The word <u>gave</u> has a silent E.
    - The word <u>that</u> is spelled just like it sounds.
    - The word <u>east</u> has the same spelling pattern as your spelling word beast.
    - The word <u>living</u> is made by taking the E off the end of the word live and adding I-N-G.
- Vocabulary
  - purchase (verb)
  - to buy

IV. Lesson
- We're going to use the story of Abraham buying the field and cave for today's lesson.
- Abraham pays for the field with silver. Look for silver on your periodic table. If you need a hint, it's in a group, which are the columns, with other metals used for payment. Some refer to this group as the coin metals.
  - It's just above gold on the chart and just under copper, both metals used as coins in history.
  - Silver is number 47 on the periodic table. What is its symbol?
    - Like gold it is a malleable metal, you can bend and shape it.
    - It can be melted and poured into molds.
      - The *melting point* is the temperature at which a solid turns to a liquid.
      - Do you remember that lava is melted rock?

- - The name of the melted rock under the earth's crust is *magma*.
  - Under the earth's crust is the *mantle* and it's made up of magma.
    - The mantle is the thickest layer of the earth. It is around 1800 miles (2900 kilometers) deep.
- Here's an image of the layers of the earth.

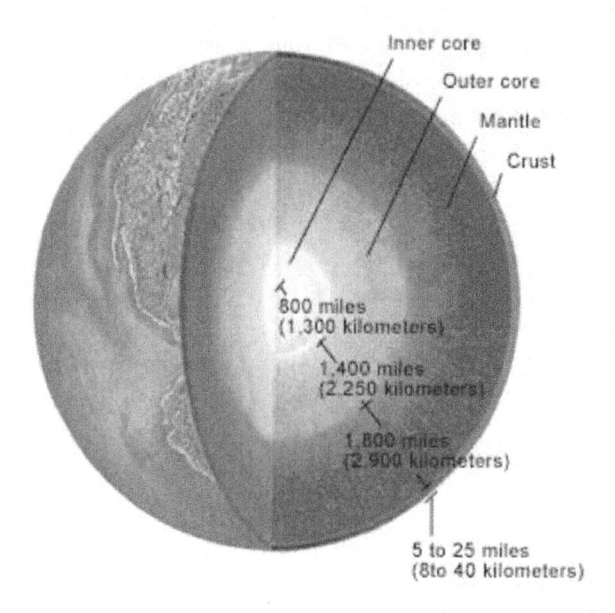

- Abraham paid with silver. The shekel was the weight that decided how much you paid of a certain metal, such as the coin metals like silver and gold and copper.
  - How do you think people paid for goods before there was a "commercial standard?"
    - People bartered for things. *Bartering* is trading. You make a deal. If you'll give me that, I'll give you this.
- Can you think of reasons why coins and then paper money are preferable?
  - I can think of a few reasons. For one, it set a standard of how much things are worth.
  - Maybe you are a leather worker, and you want a basket, but the basket maker doesn't want any leather. It made trade easier because everyone wanted what you had, money.
  - And also it was easier. Carrying around money is easier than hauling around an animal or 50 pounds of fruit or something!
- And speaking of easier, that's how paper money began, with a desire to make things easier.
  - Here's an image of ancient copper Chinese coins. Why do you think paper money would be easier?

- What if you were buying something very big and expensive? Those coins could get really heavy.
- The hole in the coin served two purposes from what I understand.
    - They were lined up on a square rod that would hold them in place so the edges could be sanded smooth.
    - Then the coins were threaded onto a string for easy carrying.
  - Recall: How did people buy before money? What are some reasons why money is preferable? What's the mantle like?
    - bartering
    - standard, easier to carry around, wanted/accepted by everyone
    - melted rock
  - Explore More: Maybe it would be fun to build a model of the earth's layers with colored playdough. You can cut it in half to see the layers.

V. Discussion
  - The Bible says that the love of money is the root of all sorts of evils (1 Timothy 6:10). What kinds of evil do you think comes out of the love of money? Do you ever find yourself loving money? How can you combat that to keep from falling into evil?

VI. Writing
  - Complete your workbook page.
  - Design money for your kingdom. In many countries there are pictures on coins and bills. What would your money look like in your country? What would it be called?

**Day 95**

I. Read Genesis 25:12-26.
- 12 Now these are the records of the generations of Ishmael, Abraham's son, whom Hagar the Egyptian, Sarah's maid, bore to Abraham;
- 13 and these are the names of the sons of Ishmael, by their names, in the order of their birth: Nebaioth, the firstborn of Ishmael, and Kedar and Adbeel and Mibsam
- 14 and Mishma and Dumah and Massa,
- 15 Hadad and Tema, Jetur, Naphish and Kedemah.
- 16 These are the sons of Ishmael and these are their names, by their villages, and by their camps; twelve princes according to their tribes.
- 17 These are the years of the life of Ishmael, one hundred and thirty-seven years; and he breathed his last and died, and was gathered to his people.
- 18 They settled from Havilah to Shur which is east of Egypt as one goes toward Assyria; he settled in defiance of all his relatives.
- 19 Now these are the records of the generations of Isaac, Abraham's son: Abraham became the father of Isaac;
- 20 and Isaac was forty years old when he took Rebekah, the daughter of Bethuel the Aramean of Paddan-aram, the sister of Laban the Aramean, to be his wife.
- 21 Isaac prayed to the Lord on behalf of his wife, because she was barren; and the Lord answered him and Rebekah his wife conceived.
- 22 But the children struggled together within her; and she said, "If it is so, why then am I this way?" So she went to inquire of the Lord.
- 23 The Lord said to her,

"Two nations are in your womb;
And two peoples will be separated from your body;
And one people shall be stronger than the other;
And the older shall serve the younger."

- 24 When her days to be delivered were fulfilled, behold, there were twins in her womb.
- 25 Now the first came forth red, all over like a hairy garment; and they named him Esau.
- 26 Afterward his brother came forth with his hand holding on to Esau's heel, so his name was called Jacob; and Isaac was sixty years old when she gave birth to them.

II. Memory Verse
- o John 11:25
    - Jesus said to her, "I am the resurrection and the life; he who believes in Me will live even if he dies."
- o Review last week's memory verse.
    - o Hebrews 11:1
    - o Now faith is the assurance of things hoped for, the conviction of things not seen.

III. Language
- o Spelling/handwriting
    - Test yourselves on the words from Days 91-94.
        - rose, spoke, give, here
        - price, could, bowed, standard

- field, was, cave, facing
- gave, that, east, living
- Vocabulary
  - Test yourselves on the words from Days 91-94.
    - refuse – to say no to doing something, or to refuse to give permission to do something
    - standard – accepted as normal, or a level of quality
    - possession – something you have
    - purchase – to buy

IV. Lesson
- Abraham's home town is Ur, in an area called Sumer. It's a city in southern Mesopotamia. The area is the oldest urban center of the world.
- What does urban mean?
  - it has to do with cities
- Sumerians developed city-states, which were cities and their surrounding areas each ruled by their own governments.
  - The city was walled off and centered around a temple. Priests of whatever gods they worshipped held considerable power and were the most educated.
  - The outlying areas around the walled city were farming areas that supplied the city with food.
  - The set up created the first ruling, elite classes of people.
  - Ur was one of the city-states.
- The Sumerians are maybe most famous for their writing system, called *cuneiform*. They wrote by making marks in a wet clay tablet. It would then be dried and would harden.

- Writing began out of necessity. They could track commerce, the buying and selling of things.
- Their writing system changed over time.
  - It began with numbers, using a system of 10s like we have today.

251

- It also began as written from top to bottom in columns. It used pictures as symbols for words.
- Later it switched to being written from left to right and phonetic letters were added, symbols for sounds, like a modern alphabet where the symbol D makes the sound "duh."
  - It developed into a way to keep records.
    - We can read in the Sumerian script about the creation of man and about the great flood and about the time when languages were confused.
    - Tablets with fragments of this story date back to 2000 BC. (date from http://www.icr.org/article/noah-flood-gilgamesh/)
  - The Sumerians are attacked by the Elamites and the Amorites in 1950 BC.
    - Always remember, history is full of real people. The Elamites and the Amorites are descendants of Noah. These are contemporaries of Abraham (meaning they lived at the same time). These aren't just stories. This was real life for real people.
  - In the 18th century BC, in the 1700s BC, there was a king of the Amorites named...Hammurabi.
    - He conquered the neighboring cities and brought them under his control instead of each having its own government. They paid taxes to him, and he offered protection.
    - He ruled from his capital city, Babylon.
    - Hammurabi built roads and canals, waterways. Easier transportation enabled him to more easily connect and rule over the various cities. It also enabled the development of a postal system, which means he made a way for mail to be delivered.
    - Not all of his progress was positive.
      - He is famous for his laws, but he divided his laws so that people were treated differently depending on if they were nobles or merchants (the sellers and traders) or farmers or slaves.
  - Recall: What people were the first to develop urban living? What famous king united the city-states under one ruler? In what area did all this take place? What is the name of the writing system developed by the Sumerians?
    - Sumerians
    - Hammurabi
    - Mesopotamia
    - cuneiform
  - Explore more: Write a set of laws. How should the world work?

V. Discussion
  - What do you think are the greatest accomplishments of your current president? What do you think are the greatest accomplishments of any leader of your country? What are some of the worst decisions of the current leader? What is one of the worst decisions of all time of any president from your country?

VI. Writing
- Complete your worksheet for today if you haven't yet.
- It's your spelling and vocabulary review.

**Day 96 (check Materials List)**

I. Read Genesis 25:27-26:5.
- 27 When the boys grew up, Esau became a skillful hunter, a man of the field, but Jacob was a peaceful man, living in tents.
- 28 Now Isaac loved Esau, because he had a taste for meat, but Rebekah loved Jacob.
- 29 When Jacob had cooked stew, Esau came in from the field and he was famished;
- 30 and Esau said to Jacob, "Please let me have some of that red stuff there; I am so hungry."
- 31 But Jacob said, "First sell me your birthright, the right to our father's inheritance."
- 32 Esau said, "Behold, I am about to die of hunger, so what use is the birthright to me?"
- 33 And Jacob said, "First swear to me"; so he swore to him, and sold his birthright to Jacob.
- 34 Then Jacob gave Esau bread and lentil stew; and he ate and drank, and rose and went on his way. Esau threw away his birthright without caring about it.
- 1 There was another famine in the land, so Isaac went to Gerar, to Abimelech king of the Philistines.
- 2 The Lord appeared to him and said, "Do not go down to Egypt; stay in the land I show you.
- 3 Live in this land, and I will be with you and bless you, for to you and to your descendants I will give all these lands, as I told your father Abraham.
- 4 I will multiply your descendants as the stars of heaven, and will give your descendants all these lands; and by your descendants all the nations of the earth shall be blessed;
- 5 because Abraham obeyed Me and kept My commandments."

II. Memory Verse
- o Review Joshua 24:15.
  - …Choose for yourselves today whom you will serve…but as for me and my house, we will serve the LORD.
- o Say Genesis 1:1 from memory.
  - In the beginning God created the heavens and the earth.

III. Language
- o Spelling
  - Have a spelling bee. (Parent: Read a word from Day 75's worksheet. Choose one they didn't have trouble with. Have them spell it out loud.)
  - If you want to do a spelling activity here are ideas.
    - Write words with sidewalk chalk.
    - Write words with invisible ink.
    - Write words by pressing down and then reveal them by coloring lightly over the words.
    - Color a page and then color over it in black. Write the words by scratching off the black.
    - Write the words with letters cut out of magazines.
    - Write the words with yarn.
    - Write the words in the air or on each other's back.

IV. Lesson
- o Complete the worksheet for Day 96.
- o You could try this out with our wheel and axle simple machine. Simple machines make work easier in different ways. Wheels and axles make work easier by making it so that less force is required. We don't have to use as much muscle to move an object when we use a simple machine.
- o Set up your experiment.
    - You'll need a broom, a table that a broom can reach across, string, bucket/basket with handle, a BIG book or heavy object that fits in the bucket/basket.
        - Lay a broom over a table with the broom part off the table on one side and the handle sticking off the end on the other side.
        - Tie a string to the broom handle and to the basket handle.
            - Tie the string tight and tape it to the broom handle after you tie it. We need it to wind around the broom handle when we turn it.
        - Put something heavy in the basket.
- o Here's a picture of our set up. We used a long-handled scrub brush.

- What's the axle?
    - the broom handle
    - We're going to use the broom end as the wheel.
- Holding the broom handle, turn it to try to lift the heavy basket.

255

- Now, hold onto the broom. If it has a plastic top across it, hold that. Otherwise, you need to create something to hold onto that's significantly wider than the handle. You could tape on a ruler or wooden spoon.
  - Turn the broom using your "wheel."
  - Is it easier? Why?
    - Both ways you are accomplishing the same work. You are moving the basket up.
    - With the wheel, you are turning over a greater distance so less force is needed to get the same work done.
- Now we are going to try another way to lift the book or whatever heavy object you are using. I'm going to say book.
  - Put the big book flat on the table. Try to lift it with one finger, enough so that you could hold onto the binding. You can't use a finger nail to get under it. That would be using a wedge, a simple machine!
  - Now we are going to try to lift the book with a wedge. Do you remember what a wedge does?
    - It's a simple machine that makes work easier by concentrating the force into one place and by changing the direction of the force.
  - Choose a wedge such as a long fork or a long spoon with a thin edge.
  - Slide it under the book. You are pushing in and the wedge is lifting the book up, even if just a little, but it's what you needed in order to lift the book.

**Day 97 (check Materials List)**

I. Read Genesis 26:6-11.
- 6 So Isaac lived in Gerar.
- 7 When the men of the place asked about his wife, he said, "She is my sister," for he was afraid to say, "my wife," thinking, "the men of the place might kill me to take Rebekah, because she is so beautiful."
- 8 It came about, after he had been there a long time, that Abimelech king of the Philistines looked out through a window, and saw that Isaac was caressing his wife Rebekah.
- 9 Then Abimelech called Isaac and said, "Certainly, she is your wife! How then did you say, 'She is my sister'?" And Isaac said to him, "Because I said, 'I might die because of her.'"
- 10 Abimelech said, "What is this you have done to us? One of the people might easily have taken your wife, and you would have made us guilty."
- 11 So Abimelech told all the people, saying, "He who touches this man or his wife will be put to death."

II. Memory Verse
- Review 2 Peter 3:9.
  - The Lord is not slow about His promise, as some count slowness, but is patient toward you, not wishing for any to perish but for all to come to repentance.
- Say from memory Psalm 150:6.
  - Let everything that has breath praise the Lord. Praise the Lord!

III. Language
- Spelling
  - Have a spelling bee. (Parent: Read a word from Day 75's worksheet. Choose one they didn't have trouble with. Have them spell it out loud.)
  - If you want to do a spelling activity here are ideas.
    - Write words with sidewalk chalk.
    - Write words with invisible ink.
    - Write words by pressing down and then reveal them by coloring lightly over the words.
    - Color a page and then color over it in black. Write the words by scratching off the black.
    - Write the words with letters cut out of magazines.
    - Write the words with yarn.
    - Write the words in the air or on each other's back.

IV. Lesson
- Complete the worksheet for Day 97.

**Day 98 (check Materials List)**

I. Read Genesis 26:12-22.
>12 Isaac sowed in that land and reaped in the same year a hundredfold. And the Lord blessed him,
>13 and Isaac became rich, and continued to grow richer until he became very wealthy;
>14 for he had possessions of flocks and herds and a great household, so that the Philistines were jealous of him.
>15 The Philistines had filled in all of his wells with dirt, all the wells that had been dug by his father's servants.
>16 Abimelech said to Isaac, "Go away from us, for you are too powerful for us."
>17 Isaac left and camped in the valley of Gerar, and settled there.
>18 Then Isaac dug again the wells of water which had been dug in the days of his father Abraham; and he gave them the same names which his father had given them.
>19 When Isaac's servants dug in the valley and found a well of flowing water,
>20 the herdsmen of Gerar quarreled with the herdsmen of Isaac, saying, "The water is ours!" So he named the well Esek, because they fought with him.
>21 Then they dug another well, and they argued over it too, so he named it Sitnah.
>22 He moved away from there and dug another well, and they did not argue over it; so he named it Rehoboth, for he said, "At last the Lord has made room for us, and we will be fruitful in the land."

II. Memory Verse
  - Review Job 19:25.
    - As for me, I know that my Redeemer lives,
      And at the last He will take His stand on the earth.
  - Say from memory Acts 17:28.
    - For in Him we live and move and exist, as even some of your own poets have said, "For we also are His children."

III. Language
  - Spelling
    - Have a spelling bee. (Parent: Read a word from Day 80's worksheet. Choose one they didn't have trouble with. Have them spell it out loud.)
    - If you want to do a spelling activity here are ideas.
      - Write words with sidewalk chalk.
      - Write words with invisible ink.
      - Write words by pressing down and then reveal them by coloring lightly over the words.
      - Color a page and then color over it in black. Write the words by scratching off the black.
      - Write the words with letters cut out of magazines.
      - Write the words with yarn.
      - Write the words in the air or on each other's back.

IV. Lesson
  - Complete the worksheet for Day 98.

**Day 99 (check Materials List)**

I. Read Genesis 26:23-35.
   23 Then Isaac went up from there to Beersheba.
   24 The Lord appeared to him the same night and said,

   "I am the God of your father Abraham;
   Do not fear, for I am with you.
   I will bless you, and multiply your descendants,
   For the sake of My servant Abraham."

   25 So he built an altar there and called upon the name of the Lord, and pitched his tent there; and Isaac's servants dug a well.
   26 Then Abimelech came to him from Gerar with his adviser and the commander of his army.
   27 Isaac said to them, "Why have you come to me, since you hate me and have sent me away from you?"
   28 They said, "We see plainly that the Lord has been with you; so we said, 'Let us make a covenant with you,
   29 that you will do us no harm, just as we have not touched you and have done to you nothing but good and have sent you away in peace. You are now the blessed of the Lord.'"
   30 Then he made them a feast, and they ate and drank.
   31 In the morning they arose early and exchanged promises; then Isaac sent them away and they left in peace.
   32 Now it came about on the same day, that Isaac's servants came in and told him about the well which they had dug, and said to him, "We have found water."
   33 So he called it Shibah, so the name of the city is Beersheba to this day.
   34 When Esau was forty years old, he married Judith and Basemath, both Hittites;
   35 and they were nothing but trouble to Isaac and Rebekah.

II. Memory Verse
   o Review Hebrews 11:1.
      • Now faith is the assurance of things hoped for, the conviction of things not seen.
   o Say from memory Romans 3:23.
      • For all have sinned and fall short of the glory of God.

III. Language
   o Spelling
      • Have a spelling bee. (Parent: Read a word from Day 80's worksheet. Choose one they didn't have trouble with. Have them spell it out loud.)
      • If you want to do a spelling activity here are ideas.
         ▪ Write words with sidewalk chalk.
         ▪ Write words with invisible ink.
         ▪ Write words by pressing down and then reveal them by coloring lightly over the words.
         ▪ Color a page and then color over it in black. Write the words by scratching off the black.
         ▪ Write the words with letters cut out of magazines.

- Write the words with yarn.
- Write the words in the air or on each other's back.

IV. Lesson
- Complete the worksheet for Day 99.

**Day 100**

I. Read Genesis 27:1-14.
1. It came about, when Isaac was old and nearly blind, that he called Esau and said to him, "My son." And he said to him, "Here I am."
2. Isaac said, "I am old and I do not know how much longer I will live.
3. Please take your gear, your quiver and your bow, and go out to the field and hunt game for me;
4. and prepare a savory dish for me such as I love, and bring it to me that I may eat, so that my soul may bless you before I die."
5. Rebekah was listening while Isaac spoke to Esau. So when Esau went to the field to hunt,
6. Rebekah said to her son Jacob, "I heard your father speak to your brother Esau, saying,
7. 'Bring me some meat you have hunted and prepare a savory dish for me, that I may eat, and bless you in the presence of the Lord before my death.'
8. Now, my son, listen to me as I command you.
9. Go to the flock and bring me two choice young goats, and I will prepare a meal just as your father loves.
10. Then you will bring it to your father, so that he may bless you before his death."
11. Jacob answered his mother Rebekah, "Esau my brother is a hairy man and I am a smooth man.
12. Perhaps my father will feel me, then he will know I am lying, and he will curse me instead of blessing me."
13. But his mother said to him, "Your curse be on me, my son; only obey my voice, and go, get them for me."
14. So he went and got them, and brought them to his mother; and his mother made food just the way his father loved it.

II. Memory Verse
- Review John 11:25.
  - Jesus said to her, "I am the resurrection and the life; he who believes in Me will live even if he dies."
- Say from memory 1 Corinthians 10:13.
  - No temptation has overtaken you but such as is common to man; and God is faithful, who will not allow you to be tempted beyond what you are able, but with the temptation will provide the way of escape also, so that you will be able to endure it.

III. Language
- Spelling
  - Have a spelling bee. (Parent: Read a word from Day 85's worksheet. Choose one they didn't have trouble with. Have them spell it out loud.)
  - If you want to do a spelling activity here are ideas.
    - Write words with sidewalk chalk.
    - Write words with invisible ink.
    - Write words by pressing down and then reveal them by coloring lightly over the words.
    - Color a page and then color over it in black. Write the words by scratching off the black.

- Write the words with letters cut out of magazines.
- Write the words with yarn.
- Write the words in the air or on each other's back.

IV. Lesson
- Complete the worksheet for Day 100.

**Day 101**

I. Read Genesis 27:15-29.
- 15 Then Rebekah took the best garments of Esau and put them on Jacob.
- 16 And she put the skins of the young goats on his hands and on the smooth part of his neck so that he would have hairy skin like Esau.
- 17 She also gave Jacob the food and the bread she had made.
- 18 Then Jacob came to his father and said, "My father." And he said, "Here I am. Who are you, my son?"
- 19 Jacob said to his father, "I am Esau your firstborn; I have done as you told me. Get up, please, sit and eat, that you may bless me."
- 20 Isaac said, "How is it that you have it so quickly?" And he said, "Because the Lord your God caused it to happen."
- 21 Then Isaac said to Jacob, "Please come close, that I may feel you, my son, whether you are really my son Esau or not."
- 22 So Jacob came close to Isaac his father, and he felt him and said, "The voice is the voice of Jacob, but the hands are the hands of Esau."
- 23 He did not recognize him, because his hands were hairy like his brother Esau's hands; so he blessed him.
- 24 And Isaac asked, "Are you really my son Esau?" And Jacob answered, "I am."
- 25 So he said, "Bring me the dish, that I may eat and bless you." And he brought it to him, and he ate; he also brought him wine and he drank.
- 26 Then his father Isaac said to him, "Please come close and kiss me, my son."
- 27 So he came close and kissed him; and when he smelled the smell of his garments, he blessed him and said,
  "See, the smell of my son
  Is like the smell of a field which the Lord has blessed;
- 28 Now may God give you of the dew of heaven,
  And of the fatness of the earth,
  And an abundance of grain and new wine;
- 29 May peoples serve you,
  And nations bow down to you;
  Be master of your brothers,
  And may your mother's sons bow down to you.
  Cursed be those who curse you,
  And blessed be those who bless you."

II. Memory Verse
- o Review 1 John 1:9.
  - If we confess our sins, He is faithful and just to forgive us our sins and to cleanse us from all unrighteousness. (KJV)
- o Say from memory Joshua 24:15.
  - Choose for yourselves today whom you will serve…but as for me and my house, we will serve the LORD.

III. Language
- Spelling
  - Have a spelling bee. (Parent: Read a word from Day 85's worksheet. Choose one they didn't have trouble with. Have them spell it out loud.)
  - If you want to do a spelling activity here are ideas.
    - Write words with sidewalk chalk.
    - Write words with invisible ink.
    - Write words by pressing down and then reveal them by coloring lightly over the words.
    - Color a page and then color over it in black. Write the words by scratching off the black.
    - Write the words with letters cut out of magazines.
    - Write the words with yarn.
    - Write the words in the air or on each other's back.

IV. Lesson
- Complete the worksheet for Day 101.
- In the early 19th century, America was quickly changing. They were in the middle of the Industrial Revolution. What was that?
  - It was a change in culture from an agricultural society to an urban society where people lived and worked in cities.
- New technology was bringing people to Lowell, Massachusetts, where factory growth exploded between 1820 and 1840.
  - The factories produced cotton thread and cotton fabric. Before this time people may have only owned two shirts. Factories were making cotton fabric cheaper and more available to people.
  - It was all possible because of machines. Machines cleaned the cotton, picking through it to take out sticks and seeds and such. Machines spun the cotton into threads. Water wheels (huge wheels on axles turned by a flowing river) were the tools that powered the machines in the factories.
  - Here is a picture of a water wheel that's not used any more.

**Day 102**

I. Read Genesis 27:30-40.
- 30 As soon as Isaac had finished blessing Jacob, and Jacob had hardly just left the room, that Esau his brother came in from hunting.
- 31 Then he also made savory food, and brought it to his father; and he said to his father, "Eat, that you may bless me."
- 32 Isaac, his father, said to him, "Who are you?" And he said, "I am your son, your firstborn, Esau."
- 33 Then Isaac shook violently, and said, "Who brought me food, so that I ate of all of it before you came, and blessed him? Yes, and he shall be blessed."
- 34 When Esau heard this, he cried out, "Bless me also, father!"
- 35 And Isaac said, "Your brother came and has taken away your blessing."
- 36 Then he said, "Is he not rightly named Jacob, for he has taken what was mine these two times? He took away my birthright, and now he has taken away my blessing." And he said, "Have you not reserved a blessing for me?"
- 37 But Isaac replied to Esau, "I have made him your master, and all his relatives I have given to him as servants; he will be satisfied with grain and new wine. What can I do, my son?"
- 38 Esau said to his father, "Do you have only one blessing, my father? Bless me, even me also." So Esau lifted his voice and wept.

- 39 Then Isaac his father answered and said to him,
  "Behold, you will live away from the fertile earth,
  And away from the dew of heaven from above.
- 40 "By your sword you shall live,
  And your brother you shall serve;
  But it shall come about when you become restless,
  That you will break his yoke from your neck."

II. Memory Verse
  - Review Romans 6:23.
    - For the wages of sin is death, but the free gift of God is eternal life in Christ Jesus our Lord.
  - Say from memory 2 Peter 3:9.
    - The Lord is not slow about His promise, as some count slowness, but is patient toward you, not wishing for any to perish but for all to come to repentance.

III. Language
  - Spelling
    - Have a spelling bee. (Parent: Read a word from Day 90's worksheet. Choose one they didn't have trouble with. Have them spell it out loud.)
    - If you want to do a spelling activity here are ideas.
      - Write words with sidewalk chalk.
      - Write words with invisible ink.
      - Write words by pressing down and then reveal them by coloring lightly over the words.

- Color a page and then color over it in black. Write the words by scratching off the black.
- Write the words with letters cut out of magazines.
- Write the words with yarn.
- Write the words in the air or on each other's back.

IV. Lesson
- Complete the worksheet for Day 102.

**Day 103**

I. Read Genesis 27:41-28:5.

    41  So Esau held a grudge against Jacob because of the blessing; and Esau said to himself, "After my father dies, then I will kill my brother Jacob."

    42  Now when the words of her elder son Esau were reported to Rebekah, she sent and called her younger son Jacob, and said to him, "Esau is planning to kill you.

    43  Now obey my voice, and flee to Haran, to my brother Laban!

    44  Stay with him a few days, until your brother is no longer so furious,

    45  and he forgets what you did to him. Then I will send and get you from there."

    46  Rebekah said to Isaac, "I am tired of living because of Esau's wives; if Jacob takes a Hittite wife, like these, what good will my life be to me?"

    1  So Isaac called Jacob and blessed him and said to him, "Do not take a wife from here.

    2  Go to the house of your mother's father; and from there take a wife from the daughters of Laban, your mother's brother.

    3  May God Almighty bless you and make you fruitful and multiply you, that you may become a company of peoples.

    4  May He also give you the blessing of Abraham, to you and to your descendants with you, that you may possess the land, which God gave to Abraham."

    5  Isaac sent Jacob away, and he went to Laban, the brother of Rebekah, Jacob's mother.

II. Memory Verse
- Review Genesis 1:4.
    - God saw that the light was good; and God separated the light from the darkness.
- Say from memory Job 19:25.
    - As for me, I know that my Redeemer lives,
    And at the last He will take His stand on the earth.

III. Language
- Spelling
    - Have a spelling bee. (Parent: Read a word from Day 90's worksheet. Choose one they didn't have trouble with. Have them spell it out loud.)
    - If you want to do a spelling activity here are ideas.
        - Write words with sidewalk chalk.
        - Write words with invisible ink.
        - Write words by pressing down and then reveal them by coloring lightly over the words.
        - Color a page and then color over it in black. Write the words by scratching off the black.
        - Write the words with letters cut out of magazines.
        - Write the words with yarn.
        - Write the words in the air or on each other's back.

IV. Lesson
- Complete the worksheet for Day 103.

**Day 104**

I. Read Genesis 28:6-17.
- 6 Esau saw that Isaac had blessed Jacob and sent him away to take a wife,
- 7 and that Jacob had obeyed his father and his mother and had gone.
- 8 So Esau saw that his Hittite wives displeased his father Isaac;
- 9 and Esau went to Ishmael, and married as well, Mahalath, Ishmael's daughter.
- 10 Then Jacob left and went toward Haran.
- 11 He came to a certain place and spent the night there, because the sun had set; and he took a stone and put it under his head, and lay down to sleep.
- 12 He had a dream and saw a ladder was set on the earth with its top reaching to heaven; the angels of God were going up and down on it.
- 13 The Lord stood above it and said, "I am the Lord, the God of your father Abraham and the God of Isaac; the land on which you lie, I will give it to you and to your descendants.
- 14 Your descendants will also be like the dust of the earth, and you will spread out to the west and to the east and to the north and to the south; and in you and in your descendants shall all the families of the earth be blessed.
- 15 Behold, I am with you and will keep you wherever you go, and will bring you back to this land; for I will not leave you until I have done what I have promised you."
- 16 Jacob woke up and said, "The Lord is in this place, and I did not know it."
- 17 He was afraid and said, "How awesome is this place! This is none other than the house of God, and this is the gate of heaven."

II. Memory Verse
- o Review Genesis 26:4.
    - I will multiply your descendants as the stars of the heaven, and will give your descendants all these lands; and by your descendants all the nations of the earth shall be blessed.
- o Review Hebrews 11:1.
    - Now faith is the assurance of things hoped for, the conviction of things not seen.

III. Language
- o Spelling
    - Have a spelling bee. (Parent: Read a word from Day 95's worksheet. Choose one they didn't have trouble with. Have them spell it out loud.)
    - If you want to do a spelling activity here are ideas.
        - Write words with sidewalk chalk. Write words with invisible ink.
        - Write words by pressing down and then reveal them by coloring lightly over the words.
        - Color a page and then color over it in black. Write the words by scratching off the black.
        - Write the words with letters cut out of magazines.
        - Write the words with yarn.
        - Write the words in the air or on each other's back.

IV. Lesson
- o Complete the worksheet for Day 104.

**Day 105**

I. Read Genesis 28:18-29:8.
- 18 Jacob got up early in the morning, and took the stone that he had put under his head and set it up as a pillar and poured oil on top of it.
- 19 He called the name of that place Bethel; however, the name of the city had been Luz.
- 20 Then Jacob made a vow, saying, "If God will be with me and will keep me safe on this journey that I take, and will give me food to eat and clothes to wear,
- 21 and I return to my father's house in safety, then the Lord will be my God.
- 22 This stone, which I have set up as a pillar, will be God's house, and of all that You give me I will surely give a tenth to You."

- 1 Then Jacob went on his journey, and came to the land of the sons of the east.
- 2 He looked, and saw a well in the field with three flocks of sheep lying there beside it, for from that well they watered the flocks. The well was covered with a large stone.
- 3 When all the flocks were gathered there, they would then roll the stone away and water the sheep, and then put the stone back in its place over the well.
- 4 Jacob said to them, "My brothers, where are you from?" And they said, "We are from Haran."
- 5 He said to them, "Do you know Laban the son of Nahor?" And they said, "We know him."
- 6 And he said to them, "Is it well with him?" And they said, "It is well, and here is Rachel his daughter coming with the sheep."
- 7 He said, "Behold, it is still high day; it is not time for the livestock to be gathered. Water the sheep, and go, pasture them."
- 8 But they said, "We cannot, until all the flocks are gathered, and they roll the stone from the mouth of the well; then we water the sheep."

II. Memory Verse
- o Review 2 Corinthians 1:20.
    - For as many as are the promises of God, in Him they are yes; therefore also through Him is our Amen to the glory of God through us.
    - (All the promises of God are yes and amen in Christ Jesus.)
- o Say from memory John 11:25.
    - Jesus said to her, "I am the resurrection and the life; he who believes in Me will live even if he dies."

III. Language
- o Spelling
    - Have a spelling bee. (Parent: Read a word from Day 95's worksheet. Choose one they didn't have trouble with. Have them spell it out loud.)
    - If you want to do a spelling activity here are ideas.
        - Write words with sidewalk chalk.
        - Write words with invisible ink.
        - Write words by pressing down and then reveal them by coloring lightly over the words.
        - Color a page and then color over it in black. Write the words by scratching off the black.

- Write the words with letters cut out of magazines.
- Write the words with yarn.
- Write the words in the air or on each other's back.

IV. Lesson
- Complete the worksheet for Day 105.

**Day 106**

I. Read Genesis 29:9-20.
- 9   Rachel came with her father's sheep; she was a shepherdess.
- 10  When Jacob saw Rachel and the sheep of Laban his mother's brother, Jacob went up and rolled the stone from the mouth of the well and gave water to the flock of Laban his mother's brother.
- 11  Then Jacob kissed Rachel, and lifted his voice and wept.
- 12  Jacob told Rachel that he was a relative of her father and that he was Rebekah's son, and she ran and told her father.
- 13  So when Laban heard the news of Jacob his sister's son, he ran to meet him, and embraced him and kissed him and brought him to his house. Then he told Laban about all these things.
- 14  Laban said to him, "Surely you are family." And he stayed with him a month.
- 15  Then Laban said to Jacob, "Because you are my relative, should you work for me without being paid? Tell me, how would you like to be paid?"
- 16  Now Laban had two daughters; the name of the older was Leah, and the name of the younger was Rachel.
- 17  Leah's eyesight was poor, but Rachel was beautiful of form and face.
- 18  Now Jacob loved Rachel, so he said, "I will serve you seven years for your younger daughter Rachel."
- 19  Laban said, "It is better that I give her to you than to give her to another man; stay with me."
- 20  So Jacob served seven years for Rachel and the time flew by quickly because of his love for her.

II. Memory Verse
- o  Learn Jeremiah 29:11.
- o  "For I know the plans I have for you," declares the Lord, "plans to prosper you and not to harm you, plans to give you hope and a future."

III. Language
- o  Handwriting/Spelling (Note: The words this week come from various places in Genesis.)
    - words to know: kissed, quick, love, another
    - spelling tips:
        - The word kissed is the past tense of kiss which has a double letter.
        - Quick ends with two letters that make the K sound together. The second letter just about always follows the first.
        - The word love is not spelled like it sounds. It ends with a silent E and looks like it should say L-OE-V.
        - The word another has how many syllables?
            - 3
            - The last two have the same spelling pattern as your spelling word brother.
- o  Vocabulary
    - weep (verse 11 - wept)

- to cry intensely (verb)

IV. Lesson
- o We're just going to travel around the globe this week, visiting a continent each day. Today we'll go to Africa. Find Africa on the map of the world in the front of your Map Book.
- o The first African country we'll look at is Chad.
  - Chad is located in the center of Africa. Try to find it on the Africa map in your map book for Day 106. It's under Libya which is on the northern coast of Africa.
  - The northern part of Chad is part of the Sahara Desert and gets little rain. The southern part of the country has grassland good for grazing animals.
  - There are a lot of well-known African animals, such as lions, giraffes, hippos, rhinos, elephants, and crocodiles, living in Chad, but only in small numbers because of poaching, meaning people hunt the animals.
  - Chad has about 14 million people, but they are not spread evenly over the country; most people live in the south, while the north is almost empty.
  - There are many languages spoken in Chad, but the two official ones are French and Arabic.
  - There are several different religions practiced in Chad. A little over half of the people are Muslim; about 22% are Catholic; about 18% are Protestant; and many Chadians practice their ancient traditions involving belief in spirits. There are many missionaries in Chad, both Christian and Muslim. The different groups generally get along without serious problems here, unlike in neighboring Nigeria.
  - Chad is a very poor country. About 80% of the people live in extreme poverty.
  - Education is a problem here; only about 25% of the people are literate. That means that three out of every four people cannot read.
- o The next country we'll look at is a tiny, little-known but very beautiful country that is completely surrounded by another country!
  - The land of Lesotho is unusual in several ways among African countries. Its name is pronounced "Leh-SOO-too."
  - Lesotho is in the middle of South Africa. You can find those two countries at the southern, bottom, tip of the continent.
  - Lesotho is the highest country in the world; the whole country is up in the mountains. Because of its high mountains and cool climate, it is sometimes called "the Switzerland of Africa."
  - Lesotho only has about 2 million people. It is unusual among African countries in that there is only one ethnic group or tribe, called the Basotho.
  - The two official languages of Lesotho are English and Sesotho, which is the language of the Basotho people. The language uses a complicated system of changes in tone of voice, which change the meaning of words.
  - Because of the cold climate, the traditional clothing of Lesotho revolves around a thick wool blanket, which can be seen everywhere, in every season, and is worn differently for men and for women.

- About 90% of the people of Lesotho consider themselves Christian. The sad fact, though, is that it seems that for many people this is a part of their culture but doesn't really impact their lifestyle.
- Because of the very high rates of disease (HIV/AIDS), life expectancy is only 42 years in Lesotho. There are also about 100,000 orphans, which is a huge number for such a small country.
- About 40% of the people live in extreme poverty and only about 5% of the people use the internet.
  - The Kenyan flag is on the map book page for today, Day 106. Our friends from Kenya taught us this simple bread recipe. They eat it daily. It's called Ugali.
    - 4 cups of water
    - 1 cup of yellow cornmeal
    - Mix and boil.
    - Stir and mush constantly until it pulls away from side of pan without sticking.
    - Cover and let stand.

V. Discussion (from your reading over the review weeks)
  - What is your birthright as a Christian? (What is birthright?)
  - Do you take advantage of your position?

VI. Writing
  - Complete your workbook page for today.
  - You are going to find Africa. This is on a different page than your spelling.

**Day 107**

I. Read Genesis 29:21-30.
21 Jacob said to Laban, "My time is completed; present me with my wife."
22 Laban gathered all the men of the place and made a feast.
23 Now in the evening Laban took his daughter Leah, and brought her to him in the dark; and Jacob joined himself to her.
24 Laban also gave his maid Zilpah to his daughter Leah as a maid.
25 So it came about in the morning that Jacob was surprised that it was Leah! And he said to Laban, "What is this you have done to me? Was it not for Rachel that I served with you? Why then have you deceived me?"
26 But Laban said, "It is not the practice in our place for the younger sister to marry before the firstborn.
27 Spend a week with this one, and we will give you the other daughter also for serving me another seven years."
28 Jacob did so and completed a week with Leah, and Laban gave him his daughter Rachel as his wife.
29 Laban also gave his maid Bilhah to his daughter Rachel as her maid.
30 So Jacob joined with Rachel also, and he loved Rachel more than Leah, and he served with Laban for another seven years.

II. Memory Verse
- Practice Jeremiah 29:11.
- "For I know the plans I have for you," declares the Lord, "plans to prosper you and not to harm you, plans to give you hope and a future."

III. Language
- Handwriting/Spelling
  - words to know: my, all, dark, years (Note: They have one page for the week with space for all of their spelling words. Look for the first Day 106 page.)
  - spelling tips:
    - The word <u>my</u> is a type of pronoun. Instead of saying, "Lee's book," I would say, "My book."
    - The word <u>all</u> has a double letter.
    - The word <u>dark</u> has the same spelling pattern for the middle sound as your words hard and farm.
    - The word <u>years</u> is a plural noun. It's the plural of your spelling word year. Plural means more than one.
- Vocabulary
  - complete – total, having all the parts, finished (adjective)

IV. Lesson
- We're traveling around the globe this week, visiting a continent each day. Today we'll go to Asia. Find Asia on the map of the world in the front of your Map Book.
- Take a look at Asia in your Map Book for Day 107. There are two maps.
- Asia is very diverse. There are northern countries such as Kazakhstan and Mongolia, the islands of Southeast Asia such as Indonesia and the Philippines, and the desert nations of the Middle East such as Saudi Arabia.

- Let's learn a little about Asian nations.
- I lived in Turkey for about seven years, so I think we should start there. It isn't on your first map, but it's on the left of your second map for Day 107 if you want to start by finding it.
    - Turkey is a large and ancient country. Some say even part of the Garden of Eden was located there. In fact, several parts of the Bible can be mapped in Turkey, including the early churches and where Noah's ark landed.
    - Turkey is a "bridge" from Europe to Asia. The city of Istanbul is divided by water and part of the city stands on each continent.
    - Turkey has always been a desirable country because it is surrounded on many sides by water. It has a long history of being invaded.
    - Turkey became a Muslim nation when the Ottomans attacked and took control in 1299.
    - The language in Turkey is called Turkish.
    - Their money is called the Turkish Lira. One lira is about 60 US cents, though it changes constantly. This is their new money. They changed from their old system where one dollar equaled more than one million lira!
    - The crescent moon and star on Turkey's flag are symbols of Islam.
- My favorite recipe I learned in Turkey is lentil soup.
    - One onion
    - One carrot, grated
    - One cup red lentils
    - Tomato paste
    - Salt
    - Chop onion. Cook onion in a tablespoon of oil for a few minutes. Add a tablespoon of tomato paste. Continue to stir for a couple minutes. Pour in six cups of water. Add red lentils and grated carrot. Cover and boil over low heat about an hour. Salt to taste.
- The eastern part of Asia is mostly Islamic. Asia is the birth place of the largest religions of the world. Muslims, Christians, and Jews all consider Jerusalem in Israel to be a sacred place to their religion. Everything we've been reading about in Genesis has taken place in Asia.
- America has been at war in the Islamic Middle East a number of times, vying for power and control. America has fought in Afghanistan, Iraq, and Kuwait.
- Islamic, Muslim countries don't allow other religions to practice freely. Neither do communist countries. One of the communist countries of Asia is Laos.
    - Laos is located in southeast Asia. Look for it on your maps. It's between Vietnam and Thailand under (south of) China.
    - It's a small, mountainous country composed of lots of different ethnic groups speaking a variety of languages.
    - The capital of Laos is Vientiane. It's a small, relatively peaceful city.
    - About 50% of the people of Laos are Lao. That's the name of their ethnic group. Their language is also called Lao and is closely related to Thai, spoken next door in Thailand. The Lao people are the dominant ones in Laos and often tend to look down on the other ethnic groups.
    - Most of the people of Laos are Buddhists. There are many Buddhist temples throughout Laos, and the sight of Buddhist monks dressed in their orange

robes is common. Every Buddhist male is expected to serve as a monk for a period of time.
- Laos is a very poor country. Many of the people rely on small-scale farming to support themselves.

V. Discussion
- o Laban really seems like a cheat. Have you ever been cheated? What happened? What did you do about it?

VI. Writing
- o You are going to complete your worksheet for today. There is a separate page for spelling and for the map.
- o Color the continent of Asia as close as you can.

**Day 108**

I. Read Genesis 29:31-30:8.
- 31  The Lord saw that Leah was unloved, and He allowed her to have children, but Rachel could have none.
- 32  Leah had a son and named him Reuben. She said, "The Lord has seen my sorrow; now my husband will love me."
- 33  Then she had another son and said, "The Lord has heard that I am unloved. He has given me this son also." So she named him Simeon.
- 34  She had another son and said, "Now this time my husband will become attached to me, because I have given him three sons." So he was named Levi.
- 35  And she had another son and said, "This time I will praise the Lord." So she named him Judah. Then she stopped having children.
- 1  Now when Rachel saw that she had no children, she became jealous of her sister; and she said to Jacob, "Give me children, or I will die."
- 2  Jacob's anger burned against Rachel, and he said, "Am I in the place of God, who has kept you from having children?"
- 3  She said, "Here is my maid Bilhah, go to her that through her I too may have children."
- 4  So she gave him her maid Bilhah as a wife, and Jacob went to her.
- 5  Bilhah had a son.
- 6  Then Rachel said, "God has heard my voice and has given me a son." So she named him Dan.
- 7  Rachel's maid Bilhah had a second son.
- 8  So Rachel said, "I have wrestled with my sister, and I have won." And she named him Naphtali.

II. Memory Verse
- o Practice Jeremiah 29:11.
- o "For I know the plans I have for you," declares the Lord, "plans to prosper you and not to harm you, plans to give you hope and a future."

III. Language
- o Handwriting/Spelling  (Note: Remember that the spelling is on the first Day 106 worksheet.)
    - words to know: unloved, allow, none, have
    - spelling tips:
        - <u>Unloved</u> is the opposite of loved. That's what adding UN to the front of a word does. It turns it into its opposite.
        - <u>Allow</u> is the words all and ow put together. Think of your spelling words: now, power, and town when spelling ow.
        - <u>None</u> is the word one with an N in front.
        - <u>Have</u> ends with a silent E and looks like it should say hay-v.
- o Vocabulary
    - sorrow (verse 32)
    - intense sadness (sorrow)

IV. Lesson
- o We're traveling around the globe this week, visiting a continent each day. Today we'll go to South America.
- o Find South America on the map of the world in the front of your Map Book. Then look at South America in your Map Book for Day 108.
- o The first country we'll look at is Brazil. It's huge, covering nearly half of South America.
    - Brazil is the largest country in South America, and the fifth largest country in the world both in size and in population.
        - Over 206 million people live there.
    - Brazil is the home of the Amazon River, the world's second longest.
    - There are a variety of different climates in Brazil. The northern part is mostly tropical rain forest; the central part is more grassland; and the southern part is mountainous and some areas have cool winters and even snow.
    - Scientists estimate that there are nearly 4 million different types of plants and animals in Brazil.
        - Some especially interesting animals include jaguars, sloths, capybaras (the world's largest rodent), the anaconda (the world's largest snake), the Goliath spider (second largest spider), pink dolphins, poison dart frogs, and about 75 different species of apes and monkeys.
    - Brazil is estimated to have over 50 native tribes which are uncontacted (meaning they have little or no contact with the outside world), living mostly in the Amazon region.
    - The official language of Brazil is Portuguese, which was brought over to the New World by the explorers from Portugal who settled here. Portuguese is similar to Spanish. There are also about 180 languages spoken by the native tribes.
- o Another country of South America, one which touches Brazil, is Paraguay.
    - Paraguay is located very centrally in South America, and is sometimes referred to as the "Heart of South America" in Spanish.
    - The land is mostly grassy plains, wooded hills, or marshes.
    - The weather of Paraguay is influenced by winds. Between October and March, warm winds blow from the Amazon region to the north; from May to August, cold winds blow from the Andes mountains to the northwest.
    - The population of Paraguay is only about 7 million. Its capital city is called Asunción and has only about half a million people.
    - Spanish is the official language of Paraguay, along with a native language called Guarani, which most people speak.
    - About 90% of the people are Roman Catholic.
    - The people of Paraguay are known for being very happy and easygoing.
    - A relatively high percentage of the population is very poor.
- o Recipe from Brazil – Moqueca de Peixe – Brazilian Fish Stew
    - 2 lbs white fish (ex: tilapia) 1 ½ T salt 2 T lime juice 2 T garlic, mashed 3 tomatoes, seeded* 1 onion 2/3 c cilantro 1/3 c scallions 2 T palm oil 1 can (~1 c) coconut milk
    - Mix the salt, garlic, and lime juice and rub over the fish. (You can use either fish fillets or cuts with bone.) In a small bowl or on a large cutting board, mix

the seasoning: thinly slice the tomatoes and onions, and chop the cilantro and scallions. Mix together and mash slightly to release the flavors. In a larger bowl or casserole, layer the fish and seasoning: place the fish in single layers with the tomato/onion mix spread between each layer. Cover tightly and let marinade for at least 30 min. Heat the palm oil in a large pan (or Dutch oven) over medium heat. Add all the fish and seasoning, cover, and simmer until fish flakes easily (10-20 min). Remove from heat and gently stir the coconut milk into the broth that has formed (stir around the fish to avoid flaking). Serve with white rice.
- *Note: It really is necessary to seed the tomatoes; otherwise, the final dish will be too watery.

V. Discussion (from the review weeks)
- It would seem that Jacob was the one who was supposed to receive the blessing. He becomes the father of the nation of Israel. Did Rebekah do the right thing or the wrong thing?
    - This is tricky stuff. God can use even sinful actions of men (or women) to accomplish His goals. It doesn't make their actions right, though.
    - What maybe could she have done differently to ensure Jacob received the blessing? Was it her responsibility to make sure Jacob was the one blessed?
    - What about Jacob? He had the choice between disobeying his mother and lying to his father. Is it okay to disobey when someone asks you to sin? Did he do right or wrong? What do you think he should have done?

VI. Writing
- Complete your worksheet for today.
- Find South America.

**Day 109**

I. Read Genesis 30:9-24.
   9  When Leah saw that she was no longer having children, she took her maid Zilpah and gave her to Jacob as a wife.
  10  Leah's maid Zilpah had a son.
  11  Then Leah said, "How fortunate!" So she named him Gad.
  12  Leah's maid Zilpah had a second son.
  13  Then Leah said, "Everyone will call me happy for having so many sons." So she named him Asher.
  ...
  17  God gave Leah a fifth son.
  18  Then Leah said, "God has given me my due because I gave my maid to my husband." So she named him Issachar.
  19  Leah conceived again and had a sixth son to Jacob.
  20  Then Leah said, "God has given me a good gift; now my husband will stay with me, because I have six sons." So she named him Zebulun.
  21  Afterward she had a daughter and named her Dinah.
  22  Then God remembered Rachel, and God opened her womb.
  23  She had a son and said, "God has taken away my shame."
  24  She named him Joseph, saying, "May the Lord give me another son."

II. Memory Verse
- Practice Jeremiah 29:11.
- "For I know the plans I have for you," declares the Lord, "plans to prosper you and not to harm you, plans to give you hope and a future."

III. Language
- Handwriting/Spelling
  - verse 24
  - words to know: longer, having, named, days
  - spelling tips:
    - The word <u>longer</u> has an -ER ending. Remember there is always a vowel in every syllable. It's never just R.
    - <u>Having</u> is have with an -ING ending. What has to happen to the silent E at the end of have?
    - <u>Named</u> is the word name with an extra letter.
    - The word <u>days</u> has the same vowel spelling pattern as say and away.
- Vocabulary
  - fortunate (verse 11)
  - good things happening that were unexpected, things going in your favor that you couldn't control (adjective)

IV. Lesson
- We're traveling around the globe this week, visiting a continent each day. Today we'll go to Europe.

- Find Europe on the map of the world in the front of your Map Book. Then look at Europe in your Map Book for Day 109. There are two maps. The one has writing that's too small, but it shows how many countries there are very clearly.
- The first country of Europe we'll talk about is one that our family visited. We got to spend some time living in a small house far from any towns in the beautiful land of Finland.
  - Finland is located in the northern part of Europe in the region known as Scandinavia.
  - The population of Finland is about five and a half million people. Most of them are known as Finns and speak a language called Finnish. It is very different from other European languages.
  - The country is mostly flat and covered with coniferous forests called taiga.
    - A coniferous forest is a forest full of pine trees, Christmas trees.
  - Much of Finland has long, cold winters and short summers.
  - The northern part of Finland is called Lapland. Reindeer are common there.
  - Finland is a member of the European Union, or the EU, and uses the euro, the same currency used by many other European countries.
  - The system of education in Finland is considered to be one of the best in the world. Some of its characteristics include: less homework, more play time, more independent exploration, more individual attention from teachers…sounds a little like homeschooling, doesn't it?
  - Finland also has one of the highest standards of living in the world, meaning the country's people are generally very prosperous compared to other countries, including the US.
- Now let's look at another, smaller country in Europe. This is a place I lived in for about six years, and I like to call it my favorite place in the world. I'm talking about Macedonia.
  - Macedonia is located in southeastern Europe, just north of Greece. It is on the so-called "Balkan Peninsula."
    - Try to find it on the map. Macedonia is just above Greece, which is the peninsula to the east (right) of Italy.
  - Macedonia is only about the size of Vermont and only has about two million people (less than Houston, Texas).
  - Macedonia is landlocked (surrounded on all sides by land). It is mostly mountainous and generally has warm, dry summers and cold, moderately snowy winters. Some high mountain areas have long winters with lots of snow.
  - The population of Macedonia is very diverse. The majority of the people are ethnically Macedonian, but there is a large minority of ethnic Albanians and smaller minorities of Turkish and Roma (Gypsy) people.
  - The ethnically Macedonian people are Eastern Orthodox Christian, but the Albanian, Turkish, and Roma people are mostly Muslim.
  - Our family mostly lived and worked with the Roma people, also known sometimes as the Gypsies. Right outside of Skopje is the largest Roma settlement in the world.
  - If you spend time with people in Macedonia, you'll quickly realize that relationships are more important to them than time. Just going to get your

hair cut or get an oil change can take a long time (hours even) because people like to take their time and talk, drink tea or coffee, talk some more...
- Here's a recipe from Macedonia.
  - "Selsko Meso" (Village Meat)
  - Two medium onions
  - Half pound stew meat
    - I use two pounds for 10 of us (7 are adults/teens).
  - Use a wide and deep pan. Use plenty of oil. I use olive oil. Turn it up to high heat on the stove.
  - Brown mushrooms in oil and remove.
  - Chop onions and cook in oil to brown a little. Remove.
  - Add half a pound of stew beef and let brown.
  - Add two drinking cups of water.
  - Bring to boil and simmer for about two hours. Check to make sure water doesn't all disappear.
  - Add a tablespoon of chopped parsley at the end. Salt to taste. They use lots! Actually, they use Vegeta.

V. Discussion (from your reading over the review weeks)
- Do you see God's blessing as important as Jacob did? What do you have in your life because of God's blessing? Is there anything that we have because of ourselves and not because God first gave to us?

VI. Writing
- Complete your worksheet for today.
- Find South America.

**Day 110**

I. Read Genesis 30:25-35.
- 25 It came about when Rachel had given birth to Joseph, that Jacob said to Laban, "Send me away, that I may go to my own place and to my own country.
- 26 Give me my wives and my children for whom I have served you, and let me leave."
- 27 But Laban said to him, "If it pleases you, stay with me; I know that the Lord has blessed me because you were with me."
- 28 Laban continued, "Tell me what I can pay you."
- 29 But Jacob said to him, "You yourself know how I have served you and how your herds and flocks have grown under my care.
- 30 You didn't have much before I came here, and now it has increased, and the Lord has blessed you wherever I have been. But now, I want to provide for my own household."
- 31 So Laban said, "What can I give you?" And Jacob said, "Do not give me anything. If you will do this one thing for me, I will again keep your flock:
- 32 let me pass through your entire flock today, removing from there every speckled and spotted sheep and every black one among the lambs and the spotted and speckled among the goats. I will take those and I will take them as my pay.
- 33 So my honesty will answer for me. You will know if I have told the truth or have cheated you. If you find any sheep or goats that are not speckled and spotted among the lambs, you can consider them stolen."
- 34 Laban said, "Good, let that be our deal."
- 35 So Joseph removed on that day the striped and spotted male goats and all the speckled and spotted female goats, every one with white in it, and all the black ones among the sheep, and gave them into the care of his sons.

II. Memory Verse
- o Test yourselves on Jeremiah 29:11.
- o "For I know the plans I have for you," declares the Lord, "plans to prosper you and not to harm you, plans to give you hope and a future."

III. Language
- o Handwriting/Spelling
  - Test yourselves on words from Days 106-109. There is a spot on the first Day 106 page in your workbook.
    - kissed, quick, love, another, my, all, dark, years, unloved, allow, none, have, longer, having, named, days
- o Vocabulary
  - Test yourselves on words from Days 106-109. There's no place in the workbook for this today. Maybe you could act out the words or demonstrate them somehow.
    - weep – to cry intensely
    - complete – total, having all the parts, finished
    - sorrow – intense sadness
    - fortunate – good things happening that were unexpected, things going in your favor that you couldn't control

IV. Lesson
- We're traveling around the globe this week, visiting a continent each day. Today we'll go to North America.
- The first North American country we'll be talking about is the southern neighbor of the US: Mexico.
    - The official name of Mexico is the "United Mexican States."
    - Mexico has a large population, with over 120 million people.
    - Mexico is made up of 31 states, plus Mexico City, which forms its own state.
    - Spanish is the official language of Mexico, and there are also many American Indian languages used by millions of people.
    - Most Mexicans are Catholic, and Mexico is the world's second largest Catholic country after Brazil.
- The next country we'll be talking about might surprise you: Nicaragua! You may be thinking, "But that's not in North America!" Well, technically it is...Nicaragua is a small country in what we call Central America, which is not actually a continent, but is part of the North American continent.
    - Nicaragua is the largest country in Central America.
    - The country is full of amazing natural beauty. About a fifth of the country is protected land, as in national parks and nature reserves.
    - Nicaragua has lots of mountains and at least 19 active volcanoes.
    - The capital and largest city of Nicaragua is called Managua.
    - Spanish is Nicaragua's official language. Some people of African descent on the eastern coast speak English or English Creole (which means English mixed with other languages).
    - Nicaragua has a population of about 6 million. The people are a mixture of European, Native Americans, Africans, and even Asians.
    - About 5% of the people are members of the Miskito Native American tribe and speak their own language.
    - Most of the people in Nicaragua are Roman Catholic. Catholic bishops have a lot of influence in the country, and most towns honor patron saints, who are believed to talk to God on behalf of the people.
    - There are annual fiestas, or celebrations, honoring the patron saint of a particular area. The most important religious festival all over the country is called La Purisma; it is a week of festivities in early December dedicated to the Virgin Mary. Fancy altars are built to honor her in homes and businesses.
    - The currency used in Nicaragua is called the cordoba. The symbol used for this currency is C$.
    - The cuisine of the west coast of Nicaragua uses a lot of local fruits and corn; the cuisine of the east coast uses a lot of seafood and coconut. Corn, rice, and beans are very common ingredients. Most people eat meat only on special holidays, since most people cannot afford it.
    - Nicaragua is a very poor country. It is the second poorest country in the Western Hemisphere after Haiti.
    - Nicaragua faces dangers from earthquakes, volcanic eruptions, landslides, and hurricanes.
    - The Nicaraguan people especially value family and politeness. They are often very eager to avoid offending anyone.

- Look at the next page in the Map Book and find each continent and about where each country is that you've learned about this week: Kenya, Sudan, Turkey, Laos,…

V. Discussion
- Jacob was faithful for many years but is getting fed up. What are his good qualities? Would he make a good husband?
- What qualities would make a good husband? (Boys can think of these for themselves, who they need to become to be good husbands, or you can flip it around and say what qualities you should look for in a wife.)

VI. Writing
- Complete the worksheet for today.
- There is a place for spelling and for finding North America.

**Day 111**

I. Read Genesis 24:1-9. (We've jumped back to the story we skipped. It's the story of Rebekah.)
1. Now Abraham was very old; and the Lord had blessed Abraham in every way.
2. Abraham said to his oldest servant, who was in charge of all that Abraham owned, "Please place your hand under my thigh,
3. and I will make you swear by the Lord, the God of heaven and the God of earth, that you will not take a Canaanite wife for my son, from here where I live,
4. but you will go to my country and to my relatives, and take a wife for my son Isaac."
5. The servant said to him, "Suppose the woman is not willing to follow me back here; should I take your son there?"
6. Then Abraham said to him, "Do not take my son back there!
7. The Lord, the God of heaven, who took me from my father's house and from the land of my birth, and who spoke to me and who swore to me, saying, 'To your descendants I will give this land,' He will send His angel before you, and you will take a wife for my son from there.
8. But if the woman is not willing to follow you back, then you will be free from this oath; only do not take my son back there."
9. So the servant placed his hand under the thigh of Abraham his master, and swore to him concerning this matter.

II. Memory Verse
- Learn Deuteronomy 31:8.
- "The LORD is the one who goes ahead of you; He will be with you. He will not fail you or forsake you. Do not fear or be dismayed."

III. Language
- Handwriting/Spelling
  - words to know: very, way, under, follow
  - spelling tips
    - The word <u>very</u> has four letters and only one is a vowel. It's the letter E.
    - The word <u>way</u> has the same spelling pattern as day.
    - The word <u>under</u> has how many syllables?
      - 2
      - Every syllable must have a vowel.
    - The word <u>follow</u> has the same ending as window.
- Vocabulary
  - swear, swore, oath
  - These are promises that have to be kept as if something bad might happen to you if you didn't. The New Testament teaches that we should not swear, but that we should just mean what we say. If we say that we'll do something, then it should mean that we will do it without needing to make promises.

V. Lesson
- There was a body part mentioned in today's reading. What was it?
  - thigh

- Today we're going to do some *anatomy*, the study of the structure of living things.
- We have learned a little human anatomy. Do you remember where your femur is?
    - It's your thigh bone.
    - Why did we learn its name? What makes it special?
        - It's the longest bone in the body.
    - We learned bicep. Can you flex your biceps?
        - Those are muscles.
    - Do you remember where Achilles was weak?
        - It was in the back of his heel.
        - Your Achilles tendon is that hard line that comes up from your heel.
    - Do you remember what tendons do?
        - They connect bone and muscle.
    - Do you remember how muscles move?
        - The muscle fibers stack up when the muscle contracts (which pulls on the tendon, which pulls on the bone).
- On the next page is a diagram of a human skeleton drawing with some labels. Where are the ribs and the spine?
- Recall: Sing "Head and Shoulders."
    - Cranium, Clavicle, Patella, Phalanges, Patella, Phalanges
    - repeat
    - eyes, ears, mandible, and nose
    - Cranium, Clavicle, Patella, Phalanges, Patella, Phalanges
- Explore More: There are probably online games to build skeletons that you could play with. Learn other bones or teach the ones you know to others. Use them around the house instead of head, knee, etc.

V. Discussion
- What do you think about arranged marriages and love marriages? Is one better than the other? Is there a way to combine the two?

VI. Writing
- Complete the worksheet.
- There is an activity to match the bones.

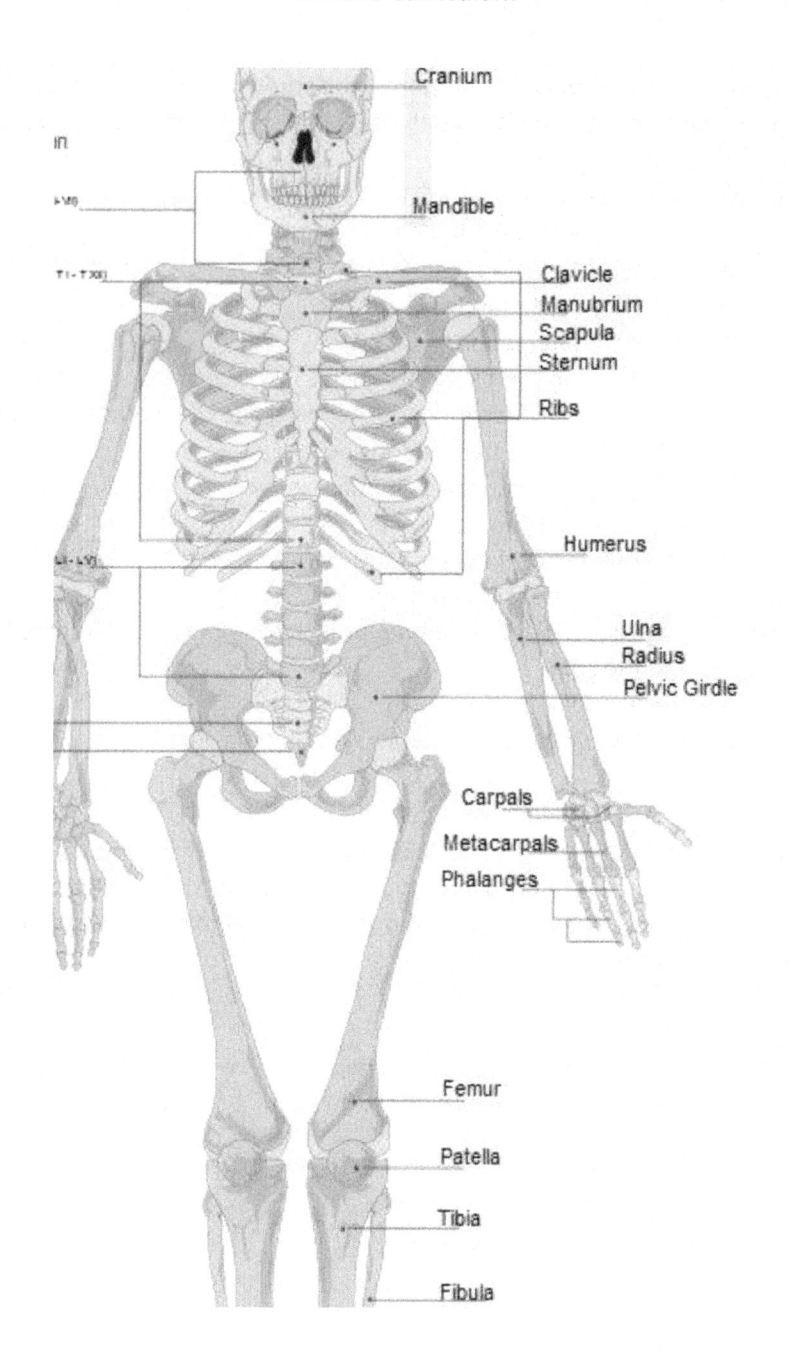

**Day 112 (check Materials List)**

I. Read Genesis 24:10-21.
- 10 Then Abraham's servant took ten camels from the camels of his master, and set out with a variety of good things from Abraham; and he went to Mesopotamia, to the city of Nahor.
- 11 He made the camels kneel down outside the city by the well of water at evening time, the time when women go out to draw water.
- 12 He said, "O Lord, the God of my master Abraham, please grant me success today, and show lovingkindness to my master Abraham.
- 13 I am standing by the spring, and the daughters of the men of the city are coming out to get water;
- 14 now may it be that the girl to whom I say, 'Please let down your jar so that I may drink,' and who answers, 'Drink, and I will water your camels also'—may she be the one whom You have chosen for Your servant Isaac; and I will know that You have shown lovingkindness to my master."
- 15 Before he had finished speaking, Rebekah who was the daughter of Abraham's brother Nahor, came out with her jar on her shoulder.
- 16 The girl was very beautiful, a virgin, and she went down to the spring and filled her jar and came up.
- 17 Then the servant ran to meet her, and said, "Please let me drink a little water from your jar."
- 18 She said, "Drink, my lord"; and she quickly lowered her jar to her hand, and gave him a drink.
- 19 Now when she had finished giving him a drink, she said, "I will draw also for your camels until they have finished drinking."
- 20 So she quickly emptied her jar into the trough, and ran back to the well to draw, and she got water for all his camels.
- 21 Meanwhile, the man was watching her in silence, to see if the Lord had made his journey successful or not.

*Note: Did you notice that God sent Rebekah before the servant even finished his prayer?

II. Memory Verse
- o Learn Deuteronomy 31:8.
- o "The LORD is the one who goes ahead of you; He will be with you. He will not fail you or forsake you. Do not fear or be dismayed."

III. Language
- o Handwriting/Spelling
  - words to know: jar, lower, filled, drink
  - spelling tips:
    - For the word <u>jar</u> has the same vowel spelling pattern as your spelling words farm and hard.
    - The word <u>lower</u> has the same vowel spelling as your spelling word flow.

- The word <u>filled</u> is the past tense of the verb to fill. Fill has a double letter. Then you add on two letters to make it past tense, to tell you it is already filled.
- The word <u>drink</u> has five letters and one vowel. The INK sound is made like the ING sound. Just the last letter is changed.

- Vocabulary
  - trough (verse 20)
  - It's what the animals are drinking out of. It's a long container open on top.

IV. Lesson
- In today's reading, we read about the servant and the camels taking a drink. We learned about several of the body's systems earlier this year, but let's learn another today, the digestive system.
- The *digestive system* is the body system that takes in food and drink, uses it in our bodies, and discards waste from our bodies.
  - What is the first part of the digestive system if what it does is take in food and drink?
    - Our mouths are the first part. What different things are happening in your mouth when you eat that are helping you swallow and continue on the digestive process?
      - There are teeth chewing the food, a tongue moving around the food, and *saliva*, your spit, is at work breaking down your food and making it easier to swallow.
- Once you swallow food, where does it go?
  - Down your throat, right? When you breathe in through your mouth where does the air go?
    - Down your throat. There are two different paths down from your mouth. One leads to the lungs and one leads to the stomach.
    - If you've ever choked on food, it's because a piece started heading down the lung path, which we call the wind pipe. When you cough, that air is pushing out whatever you got stuck in your wind pipe.
  - The path down to your stomach is your *esophagus*. There are muscles that act as gatekeeper to keep air out of the stomach and food out of the lungs.
    - We can swallow air when we eat. Do you know what happens when you swallow air?
      - You burp it out.
- We've moved from the mouth through the esophagus down to the stomach. What do you think happens in your stomach?
  - The stomach stores food while it's being broken down further into a mushy, liquidy mixture.
  - That breaking down of food is a chemical process. There is an acid in your stomach (like vinegar and lemon juice are acids); it's called gastric acid, and it eats at the food to break it down. It also can kill harmful bacteria that might have been eaten.
  - Once the food is ready (in maybe 2 to 5 hours depending on what you ate), it is moved on to your intestines.

- Do you know where your stomach is?
    - It's not in your belly. That's where your intestines work.
    - Your stomach is actually just a little ways below your heart. Here's a picture.

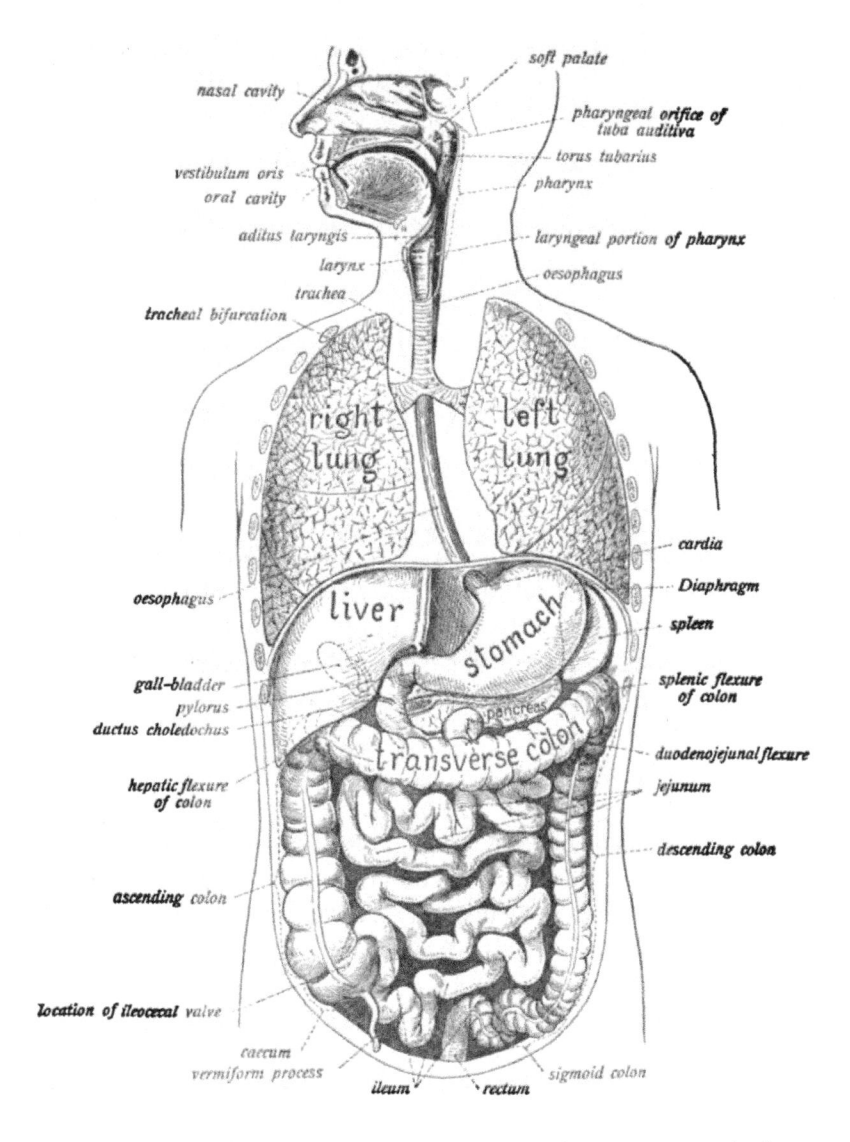

- As I said, what's in your belly is your intestines. There are two, the large and the small intestines.
    - In the picture we see the word colon. The colon is the tube part of the large intestines. You can see that it wraps around the small intestines.
    - What you can't see is how long those squiggly tubes are. Want to make a guess?
        - The large intestine is much shorter. It's about five feet long and four inches around. (nearly 10 centimeters around and 1.5 meters long)
        - The small intestine is smaller only in that it's about two inches around (4 centimeters), but it's about 22 feet long by the time you're an adult. (about 6.5 meters)
        - Measure out 22 feet. That's what is wrapped up inside of you. Amazing isn't?

- o The small intestine comes first. Your food can spend about four hours there as it turns into a very watery mixture. This allows the nutrients from your food, all the good stuff, the vitamins, minerals and proteins to get absorbed into your blood, making your blood healthy.
- o What's leftover, the stuff your body can't use, is passed onto your large intestines. There's one last chance in the colon for any leftover liquid to be absorbed into the blood. If all of the liquid is being absorbed, what's leftover?
  - Poop. It's what is produced at the end when the digestive system has completed its job.
- o Recall: What's the scientific word for spit? What's the esophagus? What's the body system that takes in and uses food?
  - saliva
  - the tube that carries food from the mouth to the stomach
  - digestive system
- o Explore More: You can talk about what's happening when you eat lunch today. Digestion starts in the mouth.

V. Discussion
- o Learning how hard your body has to work to digest and how what you eat and drink goes into your blood (which supplies every other part of your body with what it needs to function), does it make think twice about how you eat?
  - What foods do you think make your body function best?
  - What foods do you think hinder how your body functions?

VI. Writing
- o Today there is a trough on their page.
- o They are going to think of what the animals could do to the trough. These will be prepositions. It's just a first introduction to the idea. A preposition shows location.
- o The animals could get in the trough, walk around the trough, hide under the trough, sit on the trough, drink out of the trough, etc.
  - In, around, under, on, and out are all prepositions.
- o The worksheet doesn't use the word preposition. You'll have to. You can also play prepositions together. Get behind a chair. Sit on the chair. Walk around the chair. Stand by the chair. Put the chair between you. Walk away from the chair.

**Day 113**

I. Read Genesis 24:22-32. What story are we in the middle of? What's happening?
- 22 When the camels had finished drinking, Abraham's servant took a gold ring and two gold bracelets for her wrists that were valuable,
- 23 and said, "Whose daughter are you? Please tell me, is there room for us to stay in your father's house?"
- 24 She said to him, "I am the daughter of Bethuel, granddaughter of Nahor."
- 25 Again she said to him, "We have plenty of both straw and feed, and room for you."
- 26 Then the man bowed low and worshiped the Lord.
- 27 He said, "Blessed be the Lord, the God of my master Abraham, who has shown His lovingkindness and His truth; the Lord has guided me to the house of my master's brothers."
- 28 Then the girl ran and told her mother and all who were there.
- 29 Now Rebekah had a brother whose name was Laban; and Laban ran outside to the man at the spring.
- 30 When he saw the ring and the bracelets on his sister's wrists, and when he heard what his sister Rebekah had said, he went to the servant, who was standing by the camels at the spring.
- 31 And he said, "Come in, blessed of the Lord! Why do you stand outside since I have prepared a place for you and the camels?"
- 32 So Abraham's servant went with him into the house. Then Laban unloaded the camels, and he gave straw and feed to the camels, and water to wash his feet and the feet of the men who were with him.

II. Memory Verse
- o Practice Deuteronomy 31:8.
- o "The LORD is the one who goes ahead of you; He will be with you. He will not fail you or forsake you. Do not fear or be dismayed."

III. Language
- o Handwriting/Spelling
    - words to know: when, straw, feed, wash
    - spelling tips:
        - The word when starts with W-H to make the W sound.
        - The word straw ends with AW to make the vowel sound.
        - The word feed has a double letter to make the vowel sound.
        - The word wash has an A for its vowel sound.
- o Vocabulary
    - valuable (verse 22)
    - worth a lot (adjective)

IV. Lesson
- o Today we're going to make a family tree.
- o God, Adam, Eve, Seth, Cain, Abel, then a break but under Seth: Methuselah, Lamech, Noah, and his sons: Shem, Ham, Japheth
    - From Japeth we get the tribes of Gog and Magog.

293

- From Ham come the Canaanites and Amorites.
- From Shem come the Elamites and a son named, Arphaxad, who is the great, great, great, great, great grandfather of Terah.
  - Terah is the father of Abraham, Sarah (by a different mother), Nahor and Haran.
  - Can you add Hagar, Ishmael, and Isaac?
  - Haran has Lot and Milcah and Iscah.
    - From Lot come the Moabites.
  - Can you use today's reading to add on Rebekah and Laban? (The Nahor mentioned in verse 24 is Abraham's brother. Nahor marries Milcah and they have Bethuel.)
  - Then you can add Jacob and his sons.
  - Explore More: What else can you fill in?

V. Discussion
  - Your lineage starts with Adam and Noah as well. We are all related. If you were related to the orphan or the widow or the homeless man, how would you treat them? Is there someone you don't like? Can you see them as part of your family?
  - When we become Christians, we become part of God's family. Do you see yourself as one family with other believers?

VI. Writing
  - Your worksheet today should already be completed.
  - You could go back to your family tree on Day 45 and think of adjectives to describe those listed there.

**Day 114**

I. Read Genesis 24:33-49. We're continuing the story of Rebekah today.
   33  When food was set before Abraham's servant to eat, he said, "I will not eat until I have told you why I have come." And Laban said, "Go ahead."
   34  So he said, "I am Abraham's servant.
   35  The Lord has greatly blessed my master, so that he has become rich; and He has given him flocks and herds, and silver and gold, and servants and maids, and camels and donkeys.
   36  Now Abraham and his wife Sarah had a son in their old age, and he has given him all that he has.
   37  My master made me swear, saying, 'You must not take a wife for my son from the daughters of the Canaanites, in whose land I live;
   38  but you must go to my relatives, and take a wife for my son.'
   39  I said to my master, 'Suppose the woman does not return with me.'
   40  He said to me, 'The Lord, before whom I have walked, will send His angel with you to make your journey successful, and you will take a wife for my son from my relatives;
   41  you will be free from my oath if they do not give her to you.'
   42  "So I came today to the spring, and said, 'O Lord, the God of my master Abraham, if now You will make my journey on which I go successful;
   43  I am standing by the spring, and may it be that the maiden who comes out to draw, and to whom I say, "Please let me drink a little water from your jar";
   44  and she will say to me, "You drink, and I will give water to your camels also"; let her be the woman whom the Lord has appointed for my master's son.'
   45  "Before I had finished speaking in my heart, Rebekah came out with her jar on her shoulder, and went down to the spring, and I said to her, 'Please let me drink.'
   46  She quickly lowered her jar from her shoulder, and said, 'Drink, and I will water your camels also'; so I drank, and she watered the camels also.
   47  Then I asked her, and said, 'Whose daughter are you?' And she said, 'The daughter of Bethuel, Nahor's son'; and I put the ring on her nose, and the bracelets on her wrists.
   48  And I bowed low and worshiped the Lord, and blessed the Lord, the God of my master Abraham, who had guided me in the right way to find a wife for my master's son.
   49  So now if you are going to deal kindly with my master, tell me; and if not, let me know, that I may go elsewhere."

II. Memory Verse
   o Practice Deuteronomy 31:8.
   o "The LORD is the one who goes ahead of you; He will be with you. He will not fail you or forsake you. Do not fear or be dismayed."

III. Language
   o Handwriting/Spelling
     • words to know: go, ahead, rich, greatly
     • spelling tips:
       ▪ The word go is just two letters.
       ▪ The word ahead is the words a and head combined.
       ▪ The word rich is spelled just like it sounds. Do you remember what two letters make the CH sound?

- The word <u>greatly</u> starts with your spelling word great and ends with the same spelling pattern as your spelling words family, early, and only.
    - Vocabulary
        - successful (verse 40)
        - getting what you wanted, accomplishing what you set out to do (adjective)

IV. Lesson
- Today's lesson is in answered prayer.
- What does the servant pray in our Bible story?
- Who does the servant's prayer affect?
    - It affected Rebekah, Isaac, their families, their future children Esau and Jacob and all of Israel that comes from Jacob, including Jesus.
- Some prayers we may never know the impact of.
    - I'm going to tell stories of answered prayers today.
- I told you one example earlier about George Washington Carver. Do you remember his prayer?
    - Of course, he prayed lots of things over his lifetime, but one thing he specifically prayed and asked God was why He created the peanut. He would get up at four in the morning and ask God, "What do you want me to discover today?"
    - He discovered three hundred uses for the peanut and one hundred uses for the sweet potato.
- Why is that a big deal?
    - Cotton farming had ruined the soil in southern America. All of the nutrients were taken out of the soil and crops weren't growing well. Freed slaves often just kept growing cotton because that's all they knew.
    - George convinced these farmers to grow peanuts and sweet potatoes so that they would have nourishing food from what they grew and because those crops would put nutrients back into the soil.
    - The problem was that no one wanted to buy their crops. With his discoveries he was able to create a large demand for their crops. Factories wanted peanuts instead of just cotton because they could make so many products out of them such as oil, flour, and soap.
- People agree that George Washington Carver did more than anyone else to restore the South after the terrible Civil War. He especially helped former slaves, like himself, to create a living.
    - He was born a slave. When he was a baby, his mother was kidnapped and he never saw her again. He was raised as the child of his owners.
    - His prayers affected a whole country and the families of former slaves not only those alive then but their children and grandchildren. And who knows how having a successful farm affected those future generations?
    - This is what was written about George Washington Carver when he died. "He could have added fortune to fame, but caring for neither, he found happiness and honor in being helpful to the world."
- And by his prayers he helped his whole world.
- How about another George, George Müller. He lived in England in the 1800s.

- He became a Christian in college. His father refused to continue to pay for his schooling because he wanted to become a missionary. George prayed and asked God to provide the money for tuition to continue at school.
  - An hour later he was offered a job tutoring. It paid his expenses.
- George Müller is most famous for running orphanages, taking in Britain's street children. He cared for more than 10,000 orphans during his life.
- He prayed for everything, for the building, for the furniture, for the food, for the clothing, etc. but on the first day, no children showed up. He realized he had taken that for granted! He prayed for children, and they came. The rest, as they say, is history.
- The most famous story of his answered prayers comes from a time when the orphanage ran out of food.
  - George ordered all of the children to go and sit in the dining room anyway. They prayed and thanked God for their meal. There was a knock on the door. A baker hadn't been able to sleep the night before thinking that the orphans needed food and had gotten up and made bread for the children. Then there was someone else at the door. A milk delivery wagon broke in front of the orphanage. The milk was given to the children so it wouldn't spoil. The children were fed.
- How many lives were affected by George Muller's prayers? We can never know. All of those ten thousand orphans, what would have become of them if they had lived on the street? Their lives changed direction completely and who knows what they each went on to contribute to the world.
- Recall: Who were the two men whose prayers changed the world? What did they do?
  - George Washington Carver, George Muller
  - helped save the southern economy and raise African Americans up from poverty, took care of more than 10,000 orphans
- Explore More: I'm sure you could find books on these two great men or online videos.

*At the end of the lesson I included a story of a child's answered prayer, just because. ☺ There are millions of stories of answered prayers. This story is from the site praybold.org and is printed with permission from their site.

V. Discussion
- What are your family's stories of answered prayer?
- We discussed before how an act of obedience can change the world. What about a prayer? If you believed your prayers could change the world, what would you be praying for?

VI. Writing
- Complete your worksheet for today.
- You are going to write sentence with lots of adjectives.
- The answered-prayer story is on the next page.

## A LITTLE GIRL'S PRAYER

*(As told by Helen Roseveare, a doctor missionary from England to Zaire, Africa)*

One night I had worked hard to help a mother in the labor ward; but in spite of all we could do she died leaving us with a tiny premature baby and a crying two-year-old daughter. We would have difficulty keeping the baby alive, as we had no incubator (we had no electricity to run an incubator) and no special feeding facilities.

Although we lived on the equator, nights were often chilly with treacherous drafts. One student midwife went for the box we had for such babies and the cotton wool the baby would be wrapped in. Another went to stoke up the fire and fill a hot water bottle. She came back shortly in distress to tell me that in filling the bottle, it had burst. Rubber perishes easily in tropical climates.

"And it is our last hot water bottle!" she exclaimed.

As in the West it is no good crying over spilled milk, so in Central Africa it might be considered no good crying over burst water bottles. They do not grow on trees, and there are no drugstores down forest pathways.

"All right," I said, "Put the baby as near the fire as you safely can; sleep between the baby and the door to keep it free from drafts. Your job is to keep the baby warm."

The following noon, as I did most days, I went to have prayers with many of the orphanage children who chose to gather with me. I gave the youngsters various suggestions of things to pray about and told them about the tiny baby. I explained our problem about keeping the baby warm enough, mentioning the hot water bottle. The baby could so easily die if it got chills. I also told them of the two-year-old sister, crying because her mother had died.

During the prayer time, one ten-year-old girl, Ruth, prayed with the usual blunt conciseness of our African children. "Please, God," she prayed, "send us a water bottle. It'll be no good tomorrow, God, as the baby will be dead, so please send it this afternoon."

While I gasped inwardly at the audacity of the prayer, she added by way of corollary, "And while You are about it, would You please send a dolly for the little girl so she'll know You really love her?"

As often with children's prayers, I was put on the spot. Could I honestly say, "Amen"? I just did not believe that God could do this. Oh, yes, I know that He can do everything. The Bible says so. But there are limits, aren't there? The only way God could answer this particular prayer would be by sending me a parcel from the homeland. I had been in Africa for almost four years at that time, and I had never, ever received a parcel from home.

Anyway, if anyone did send me a parcel, who would put in a hot water bottle? I lived on the equator!

Halfway through the afternoon, while I was teaching in the nurses' training school, a message was sent that there was a car at my front door. By the time I reached home, the car had gone, but there, on the verandah, was a large twenty-two pound parcel! I felt tears pricking my eyes. I could not open the parcel alone, so I sent for the orphanage children. Together we pulled off the string, carefully undoing each knot. We folded the paper, taking care not to tear it unduly. Excitement was mounting. Some thirty or forty pairs of eyes were focused on the large cardboard box.

From the top, I lifted out brightly colored, knitted jerseys. Eyes sparkled as I gave them out. Then there were the knitted bandages for the leprosy patients, and the children looked a little bored. Then came a box of mixed raisins and sultanas-that would make a nice batch of buns for the weekend. Then, as I put my hand in again, I felt the... could it really be? I grasped it and pulled it out-yes! A brand-new, rubber hot water bottle! I cried. I had not asked God to send it; I had not truly believed that He could.

Ruth was in the front row of the children. She rushed forward, crying out, "If God has sent the bottle, He must have sent the dolly, too!"

Rummaging down to the bottom of the box, she pulled out the small, beautifully dressed dolly. Her eyes shone! She had never doubted!

Looking up at me, she asked, "Can I go over with you, Mummy, and give this dolly to that little girl, so she'll know that Jesus really loves her?"

That parcel had been on the way for five whole months! Packed up by my former Sunday school class, whose leader had heard and obeyed God's prompting to send a hot water bottle, even to the equator. And one of the girls had put in a dolly for an African child-five months before -- in answer to the believing prayer of a ten—year—old to bring it "that afternoon."

**Day 115**

I. Read Genesis 24:50-67. Today we're finishing the chapter and the story of Rebekah's marriage to Isaac.
- 50 Then Laban and Bethuel replied, "The matter comes from the Lord; so we cannot say anything about it.
- 51 Here is Rebekah, take her and go, and let her be the wife of your master's son, as the Lord has spoken."
- 52 When Abraham's servant heard their words, he bowed himself to the ground before the Lord.
- 53 The servant brought out articles of silver and articles of gold, and garments, and gave them to Rebekah; he also gave valuable things to her brother and to her mother.
- 54 Then he and the men who were with him ate and drank and spent the night. When they got up in the morning, the servant said, "Let me go to my master."
- 55 But her brother and her mother said, "Let the girl stay with us a few days, say ten; afterward she may go."
- 56 He said to them, "Don't keep me, since the Lord has blessed my way. Let us go to my master."
- 57 And they said, "We will call Rebekah and ask her what she wishes to do."
- 58 Then they called Rebekah and said to her, "Will you go with this man?" And she said, "I will go."
- 59 So they sent away their sister Rebekah and her nurse with Abraham's servant and his men.
- 60 They blessed Rebekah and said to her,
  "May you, our sister,
  Become thousands of ten thousands,
  And may your descendants possess
  The gate of those who hate them."
- 61 Then Rebekah left with her maids, and they mounted the camels and followed the man. So the servant took Rebekah and left.
- 62 Now Isaac had come back, for he was living in the Negev.
- 63 Isaac went out to meditate in the field toward evening; and he lifted up his eyes and looked, and saw that camels were coming.
- 64 Rebekah looked, and when she saw Isaac she got down from the camel.
- 65 She said to the servant, "Who is that man walking in the field to meet us?" And the servant said, "He is my master." Then she took her veil and covered herself.
- 66 The servant told Isaac all the things that he had done.
- 67 Then Isaac brought her into his mother Sarah's tent, and he took Rebekah, and she became his wife, and he loved her; and Isaac was comforted after his mother's death.

II. Memory Verse
- o Test yourselves on Deuteronomy 31:8.
- o Find it in the Bible.
- o "The LORD is the one who goes ahead of you; He will be with you. He will not fail you or forsake you. Do not fear or be dismayed."
- o Do you know what Genesis 1:1-5 is?

III. Language
- o Handwriting/Spelling
  - Test yourselves with words from Days 106-109.
    - very, way, under, follow
    - jar, lower, filled, drink
    - when, straw, feed, wash
    - go, ahead, rich, greatly
- o Vocabulary
  - Test yourselves with the words from Days 106-109.
    - swear, swore, oath – promises that must be kept as if something bad might happen to you otherwise
    - trough – a long container open on top, used for animals to drink out of
    - valuable – worth a lot
    - successful – getting what you wanted, accomplishing what you set out to

IV. Lesson
- o We're going to talk a little more about George Washington Carver.
- o Carver was the name of the family who owned George's mother. He was treated well, raised like a son in their home after George's mother was kidnapped and sold.
  - He chose the name Washington himself when he wasn't receiving mail. He had to distinguish himself from a white man named George Carver who kept getting his mail. He named himself after the first president of the United States.
- o He learned to read and write at home, but wanting to go to school, he had to move west to Kansas from his home in Missouri to find a school that taught black children.
  - He worked as a cook and by doing housework, whatever it took, to be able to attend these schools, while he was still a kid.
  - He graduated from a high school in Kansas even though he constantly faced discrimination, people treating him wrongly because his skin was dark.
  - He was accepted at a college in Kansas. He was turned away when he showed up because they saw that he was an African American.
  - He became the first black student at Iowa State College. He had to sleep in an office and eat in the basement with the kitchen staff to maintain segregation from the white students. He started a laundry business to put himself through school.
- o Why did Carver work so hard to go to school? Why did he take jobs and work just to be able to go to school? Why did he not give up when the college rejected him? Why did he not give up when he was treated poorly compared to the other students? Why was education that important to him? Any thoughts?
- o Slaves were freed right around the time George Washington Carver was born. It was good timing for George to be born, but of course, it was God was behind it. George had the chance to go to school. Before slaves were freed, there had been a law that made it illegal for anyone to teach a slave to read.
  - Why? Why wouldn't they want a slave to be able to read? Why was it important to them to have uneducated slaves?

- Why do you think it would be easier to control slaves who were uneducated?
  - George Washington Carver got his master's degree and became a professor. He eventually accepted a position at a school for only African American students. It was called Tuskegee University. The students there were required to build their own buildings.
    - Why? What benefit would that bring?
      - It taught them skills, and it taught them to be diligent workers. They learned to love to work.
  - How did they learn to love work?
    - They learned by working. Working gave them valuable tools for life, and it gave them pride in what they accomplished.
  - The students also did their own farming to produce their own food and did all the cleaning and such around the university campus.
  - Why were the students willing to work so hard to be able to go to school?
  - What makes education so valuable?
  - What makes education so dangerous that it had to be kept from slaves?
    - Every piece of information is power. Every word you learn how to use is a tool for persuasion. Every math concept you learn is a tool for discovery. Every history lesson learned is a tool for freedom. Every science lesson learned is a tool for creating. Every piece of art and music explored is a new way of thinking opened in your mind.
    - Education is power.
  - Missionaries have lost their lives to give people knowledge of God's Word. The knowledge of God's Word is the most powerful of all. It's the power to be saved!
  - Explore More: You could learn about Booker T. Washington who founded Tuskegee.

V. Discussion
  - Do you see education as valuable? Do you see education as dangerous to those in power? Are you taking advantage of your education?
  - Maybe not everything interests you, but you learn all you can, and then you take the things that interest you and learn everything possible. Become a master at it. Change the world.
  - Get a high five and/or hug if you decide you want to change the world. ☺
  - Do you want more explanation about the value of education?
    - Words are tools for persuasion. Abraham Lincoln credited an author for starting the Civil War by writing her book *Uncle Tom's Cabin*, which showed the cruelty of slavery.
    - Math is a tool for discovery. Math shows us patterns. It can help us uncover faults and scams, and it can reveal to us future direction by following the outcome of those patterns.
    - History is a tool for freedom. The saying goes, "Those who don't know history are bound to repeat it." Knowing history frees us to make better choices.
    - Science is a tool for discovery. George Washington Carver is an example.

VI. Writing
  - Complete your worksheet for today if it's not already finished.
  - You have spelling and vocabulary on your page for today.

**Day 116**

I. Read Genesis 37:1-11. (We're moving into Joseph's story now.)
1. Jacob lived where his father had, in the land of Canaan.
2. These are the records of the generations of Jacob.
   Joseph, when he was seventeen, was a shepherd with his brothers. Joseph told their father about some wrong things his brothers had done.
3. Now Israel (Jacob) loved Joseph more than all his sons, because he was the son of his old age; and he made him a tunic of many colors.
4. His brothers saw that their father loved him more than all of them; so they hated him and could not be friendly to him.
5. Then Joseph had a dream, and when he told it to his brothers, they hated him even more.
6. He said to them, "Please listen to this dream I had;
7. we were binding sheaves in the field, and my sheaf rose up and stood tall; and your sheaves gathered around and bowed down to mine."
8. Then his brothers said to him, "Are you actually going to rule over us?" So they hated him even more for his dreams and for his words.
9. Now he had still another dream, and told it to his brothers, and said, "I have had another dream; and behold, the sun and the moon and eleven stars were bowing down to me."
10. He told the dream to his father and to his brothers; and his father rebuked him and said to him, "What is this dream that you have had? Will I and your mother and your brothers actually come to bow ourselves down before you to the ground?"
11. His brothers were jealous of him, but his father kept it in mind.

II. Memory Verse
- Learn Romans 8:28.
- And we know that God causes all things to work together for good to those who love God, to those who are called according to His purpose.

III. Language
- Handwriting/Spelling
  - words to know: more, many, colors, stood
  - spelling tips:
    - The word <u>more</u> has the word OR inside of it and ends with a silent E.
    - The word <u>many</u> ends with the word any.
    - The word <u>colors</u> is plural. There is more than one color. It has the word OR inside of it as well.
    - The word <u>stood</u> has the same vowel sound as your spelling words good and food.
- Vocabulary
  - rebuke (verse 10)
  - to scold; to tell someone their behavior is wrong in a sharp manner (action verb)
  - As a noun, a rebuke is the words expressed when someone scolds.

IV. Lesson
- o Joseph is given a varicolored tunic. Here's a picture of a *tunic*. It's basically like a short dress, but it was masculine, manly attire back then. Why do you think men wore dresses, robes, etc. Why didn't people wear pants?
  - My guess is that it was a lot simpler to make. They didn't have sewing machines. Pants have to be fitted and kept up. They weren't using buttons and zippers. They were also probably cool in the desert heat.
- o Joseph's tunic had a lot of colors. What do you think was special about that?
  - Most clothing was probably just the color it came as. It was a lot of work to dye cloth or thread, and a lot of work means it was expensive. This was not even just a dyed tunic. It was woven together with a variety of colors or it was sewed together from a variety of cloths. It was not something any of his brothers would ever own.
- o Today we're going to learn a little about dying cloth in the ancient world. People have been dying cloth for all of recorded history. Why do you think people like to wear colors?
  - I think it affects how people feel.
  - We've talked about turning cotton into thread and turning wool into yarn. That thread and yarn can get color from dying, or it can be made into clothing and then dyed.
- o Dying cloth, up until the Industrial Revolution was in full swing, meant taking a color found in nature and applying it to the cloth.
- o Let's say you decide you want to turn your shirt brown and you choose a brown chocolate chip cookie as your dye.
  - What happens if you smear a chocolate chip cookie on your clothes?
    - Some of it would just brush off as crumbs. Some of it would turn your clothes brown in that spot.

- What happens after it is washed (hopefully)?
  - The brown comes out.
- One problem with using a chocolate chip cookie is that it only colored your shirt in a small area. When you dye cloth, you want to dye the whole thing.
- Can you think of things people had to figure out in order to dye clothing? What were two other problems they had to overcome? (Note: Think of the results of rubbing chocolate chip cookie on your shirt.)
  - They had to find color that would stick to the fabric.
  - They had to find color that wouldn't just come off when it got wet.
  - So, they had to get the dye color to stick and to stay stuck.
- Where do you think their dye came from?
  - It came from plants and animals.
  - Did you ever peel and grate carrots and end up with orange fingers?
- The first dyes were just plants rubbed into wool. (They had sheep. They didn't have cotton farms. Wool was the main source for threads for fabric.)
- Later dyes were boiled in water with the textile. This enabled the whole cloth to be more evenly dyed.
- Boiling was done with animal dyes such as the purple that came from sea snail.
  - You may know that purple is considered the color of royalty. Can you guess how a color might have come to be worn only by royalty? (Hint: It could be worn by anyone wealthy.)
    - It was really expensive to make. Supposedly it took 12,000 snails to make enough dye to color the trim on the edge of a cloak.
  - This kind of dye was special because the color remained and even was said to get better with age instead of fading.
- Do you remember the two problems people had to overcome in order to dye clothing?
  - They had to make it stick and stay.
- Most dyes didn't stay as well as the royal purple color. They needed what we call a *mordant*.
  - Modern day mordants include alum if you want to try this at home.
  - Ancient mordants included old urine. When mixed with the dye, the color would then stick and stay on the wool.
- Recall: What were two problems that cloth dyers had to overcome?
  - making the color stick and then keeping it there so it wouldn't be washed out
- Explore More: You could try to turn something a color. Do you have a white rag? Try boiling it with some colorful veggies.

V. Discussion
- Have you ever been jealous of someone? Who? Why?
- How did you react to feeling jealous?

VI. Writing
- Complete your worksheet for today.
- You are going to be writing sentences. Make sure they start with capital letters and end with correct punctuation.

**Day 117 (check Materials List)**

I. Read Genesis 37:12-21.
   12  Then Joseph's brothers took their father's flock to Shechem to find land for the animals to graze.
   13  Israel said to Joseph, "Aren't your brothers in Shechem? I will send you to them." And Joseph said to him, "I will go."
   14  Then Israel said to him, "Go now and see how your brothers and the flock are doing, and bring word back to me." So he sent him from the valley of Hebron, and Joseph reached Shechem.
   15  A man found him wandering in the field. The man asked him, "What are you looking for?"
   16  Joseph said, "I am looking for my brothers; please tell me where they are with the flock."
   17  The man said, "They have moved from here; I heard them say, 'Let us go to Dothan.'" So Joseph went after his brothers and found them at Dothan.
   18  When they saw him from a distance and before he got close, they made a plan to put him to death.
   19  They said to one another, "Here comes this dreamer!
   20  Let's kill him and throw him into one of the pits; and we will say, 'A wild beast ate him.' Then let's see what will become of his dreams!"
   21  But Reuben heard this, he rescued Joseph by saying, "Let's not take his life."

II. Memory Verse
   o  Practice Romans 8:28.
   o  And we know that God causes all things to work together for good to those who love God, to those who are called according to His purpose.

III. Language
   o  Handwriting/Spelling
      • words to know: brothers, animals, flock, father's
      • spelling tips:
         ▪ The word brothers is the plural of your spelling word brother.
         ▪ The word animals is the plural of your spelling word animal.
         ▪ The word flock is a collective noun. Even though it's talking about a lot of sheep, it's just one thing. It ends with two letters making the K sound, like your spelling words back and truck.
         ▪ The word father's is not plural. It is talking about something that belongs to the father. It's father's flock. We add an apostrophe S to show that something belongs to someone. We'll practice that on our worksheet today.
   o  Vocabulary
      • graze (verse 12)
      • to eat grass or crops in a field, to eat little by little throughout the day

IV. Lesson
   o  There's an imaginary wild beast in today's reading. What wild beasts would have lived where they were? What do you think?

- Some animals that Joseph might have encountered are goats, lions, antelopes, bears, crocodiles, ostriches, cheetahs, ox, and deer.
  - Which of those animals do you think would have been willing to eat Joseph?
    - lions, bears, crocodiles, cheetahs
  - Let's look at lions today. Let's start with their scientific classification. What is scientific classification?
  - It's the way we organize living things into categories.
    - What kingdom would lions belong to? (hint: bacteria, plants…)
      - animal kingdom
    - Is a lion a vertebrate or an invertebrate?
      - vertebrate
      - What does that mean?
        - It means that the animal has a spine, a backbone.
    - What class does a lion belong to? (hint: not reptile, not fish, not bird…)
      - mammal
    - What order does a lion belong to? (hint: What does it eat? not a herbivore)
      - carnivore
    - What family does a lion belong to? (hint: not canine…)
      - feline (cat)
    - A lion's genus is panther.
    - The species of lion we're talking about today is the Persian Lion or the Asiatic Lion.
      - Can you guess where Asiatic Lions live? (Note: If they can't guess, you could show them the word. It's easier to see the connection than to hear it.)
        - Asiatic means of Asia.
  - Right now, these lions only live in India. They are *endangered*, meaning there are not many left.
  - The species is in danger of going *extinct*, not existing anymore, but they are protected now. There were fewer than 200 left, but their numbers are increasing.
  - Take a guess at how tall and long an Asiatic lion can be.
    - Asiatic lions can stand three and a half feet tall, to the shoulder (over 100 cm), and can be nearly ten feet (3 m) long, including the tail.
    - Stand up and figure out about how big that would be.
  - Guess how much a lion weighs?
    - The male weighs around 400 pounds (175 kilos) and the female weighs around 250 pounds (115 kilos).
  - What do you think they eat besides Josephs?
    - Lions are carnivores, so they eat meat, other animals.
    - They hunt in groups and work together to get meals of deer, antelope, boars, bulls, and many other animals.
    - It's the female lions that do most of the hunting.
  - The male lions are the ones with manes, the hair around their heads. They defend their territory and their family.
    - Like other animals, lions mark their territory with urine. The scent lets other animals know it's not their turf and to stay away.

- o Lions live in *prides*, like fish swim in schools. A pride is a family group. It can have a few males and several females and then all of their cubs.
  - Lions are the only felines that live in family groups.
- o Recall: What carnivore, vertebrate, mammal were we learning about today? What is the name of their family group? What do we call animals that are in danger of becoming extinct?
  - lions
  - a pride
  - endangered
- o Explore More: Watch a video or read a book on lions.

V. Discussion
- o Just a note of something I wanted to share with you: I told you that lions live in prides. Fish swim in schools. We call it a pod of whales. The most fascinating is a murder of crows!
- o If you could travel anywhere in the world, where would it be? Why?

VI. Writing
- o Complete your worksheet for today.
- o We add an apostrophe S to show that something belongs to someone.

**Day 118**

I. Read Genesis 37:19-25.
- 19 They said to one another, "Here comes this dreamer!
- 20 Let's kill him and throw him into one of the pits; and we will say, 'A wild beast ate him.' Then let's see what will become of his dreams!"
- 21 But Reuben heard this, he rescued Joseph by saying, "Let's not take his life."
- 22 Reuben said to them, "Don't hurt him. Throw him into this pit, but don't hurt him." He planned to rescue him and take him back home safely.
- 23 So it came about, when Joseph reached his brothers, that they took Joseph's tunic of many colors that was on him;
- 24 and they took him and threw him into the pit. Now the pit was empty, without any water in it.
- 25 Then they sat down to eat a meal. While they were eating, a caravan of Ishmaelites was coming from Gilead, with their camels bearing aromatic gum and balm and myrrh, on their way to bring them down to Egypt.

II. Memory Verse
- Practice Romans 8:28.
- And we know that God causes all things to work together for good to those who love God, to those who are called according to His purpose.

III. Language
- Handwriting/Spelling
  - words to know: dreams, pits, don't, one
  - spelling tips:
    - The word dreams is a plural noun. It has the same vowel spelling as your spelling words seas and beast.
    - The word pits is spelled just like it sounds. Say it carefully. It is a plural noun. There is more than one pit.
    - The word don't has an apostrophe. It's a contraction. It's the words do and not put together.
    - The word one you've spelled at the end of the word everyone.
- Vocabulary
  - balm (verse 25)
  - a cream used for medicine, a sweet smell, or anything that heals or soothes (noun)

IV. Lesson
- In our reading today, there are traders bearing aromatic gum and balm and myrrh. Let's learn what we can about those things.
- For one, they all can be very fragrant, sweet smelling.
- Balms are often thought of as medicine, but it could be a sweet-smelling lotion or even a kind of plant that is used in seasoning.
- When it says gum, it's not talking about bubble gum, but it does usually refer to a sticky substance. In other translations, instead of "aromatic gum" it says "spices."

- o   This gum is taken from trees, and in fact, myrrh is a type of gum. It's used as a perfume, or in medicine, or to burn to produce a sweet smell.
- o   Since we're talking about aromatics, things that give off fragrant or sweet-smelling aromas, let's learn about smell. What are we actually smelling? How does a smell get from something into our noses? Where do those smells come from? Any ideas?
- o   What goes into our eyes that allows us to see?
    - light
- o   When we smell, we are taking in molecules. We breathe in molecules that are in the air. That's the beginning of our body's *olfactory system*, what we know as our sense of smell.
    - Molecules of the scent are in the air we breathe.
        - Those molecules could be in something like smoke that is carrying them into the air.
        - Those molecules could also be in what's evaporating off of substances.
            - Evaporation is happening in the oven when dinner is cooking, which is why we smell it after a while.
        - Why don't we smell windows?
            - They aren't releasing anything into the air.
- o   Most of your nose is dedicated to cleaning the air before it gets to your lungs, but a small portion of it, about 5%, (remember that's five balloons out of the hundred) is dedicated to smells.
    - But in just that small location in our noses, we have 40 million neurons ready to receive molecules. We call those neurons olfactory receptor neurons.
    - Each smell triggers a different set of neurons.
        - People can distinguish between thousands and thousands of smells.
- o   Those neurons are part of our nervous system which means those olfactory receptors send their signals straight to the brain.
    - In the brain different reactions are triggered.
    - What are different reactions to smells that you can think of?
        - There's disgust and wanting to flee away from it.
        - There's a delicious smell that can literally trigger your body to make your mouth start watering.
        - There's a sweet smell that makes you feel good and warm inside.
        - Smells can trigger feelings. They can make us feel peaceful or excited.
        - Smells can also trigger memories. Your brain can connect a smell today to a memory from years before.
- o   We can get used to smells. Since smells trigger so much activity in our brain, if we continue to smell something, our neurons will stop sending signals to our brain about it, so we aren't overwhelmed by the continuous reaction to it.
    - The smell hasn't gone away. You've just gotten over it.
- o   Recall: What are we breathing in that enable us to register a smell? What system takes in molecules and identifies them as scents?
    - molecules
    - olfactory system
- o   Explore More: You could try some smell experiments. You can test each other's sense of smell by blindfolding each other and putting out things for each other to smell and

guess what it is. Make sure you don't mix smells. Keep things separate. You could also put out three shirts that have been worn for at least a few hours and see if you can tell which one is yours by the scent. (We each have a unique scent, like a fingerprint!)

V. Discussion
- Reuben told them to throw him in a pit in order to save him. Why? Did he have another choice?

VI. Writing
- Complete your worksheet for today.
- Make words plural.

**Day 119**

I. Read Genesis 37:25-28. We're continuing our story. Do you remember where Joseph is? (in the pit)

  25 Then they sat down to eat a meal. While they were eating, a caravan of Ishmaelites was coming from Gilead, with their camels carrying aromatic gum and balm and myrrh, on their way to bring them down to Egypt.
  26 Judah said to his brothers, "What profit is it for us to kill our brother and cover it up?
  27 Let's sell him to the Ishmaelites and not kill him. He is our brother after all." And his brothers listened to him.
  28 Then some Midianite traders passed by, so they pulled Joseph up and lifted him out of the pit, and sold him to the Ishmaelites for twenty shekels of silver. And the traders brought Joseph into Egypt.

II. Memory Verse
  o Practice Romans 8:28.
  o And we know that God causes all things to work together for good to those who love God, to those who are called according to His purpose.

III. Language
  o Handwriting/Spelling
    • words to know: meal, eating, silver, while
    • spelling tips:
      ▪ The word meal has the same vowel spelling pattern as your spelling word dreams.
      ▪ The word eating is your spelling word eat with an ING ending.
      ▪ The word silver has two syllables. Remember that every syllable must have a vowel.
      ▪ The word while ends with a silent E and has two letters making the first sound, just like your spelling words which, when, and who.
  o Vocabulary
    • profit (verse 26)
    • to get a benefit, often refers to money (verb)
    • As a noun it means the thing you got, such as an advantage or the money you made.

IV. Lesson
  o Our Ishmaelite traders are traveling by camel. Let's learn about the camel today.
  o We talked about desert plants before. What's special about the plants that are able to survive in the desert?
    • They have to be able to live without a lot of water. What are some of the ways they do that? Do you remember what helps the cactus?
      ▪ Plants, like the cactus, have a really large stem to store lots of water.
      ▪ Plants have scales instead of open leaves to slow evaporation.
  o How do you think a camel is like a cactus?
    • Did you say that they both store water? This is a trick question! Many people believe that camels store water in their hump. That's not true, though. Their

humps are fat. I'll tell you about that in a second. So, how is a camel like a cactus?
- The cactus and the camel were both created to limit evaporation.
  - That hump of fat keeps all of the camel's fat away from its body. Why do walruses have fat, blubbery bodies?
    - It keeps them warm with insulation. Camels don't need help staying warm in the desert. Keeping the fat away from their bodies keeps them cooler so they don't sweat and lose water.
- Camels are mammals. Are mammals warm blooded or cold blooded?
  - warm blooded
  - What does that mean?
    - Its body temperature doesn't depend on the temperature of the air surrounding it.
  - When you get hot, you sweat to cool off. The sweat evaporates off of you.
  - When your body temperature goes up a degree, how do you feel?
    - sick
  - Camels are quite unique in that their body temperature can go up over ten degrees during the day (6 degrees Celsius). He doesn't need to sweat to cool off because his body is okay with its temperature rising to that extent.
- Camels can go months without drinking. When they get the chance to drink, they can drink and drink and drink and drink and drink! But it's not being stored, just replacing all the water they've used up.
  - Their digestive system conserves water. Their intestines take out all of the water until the camel's poop comes out completely dry. This is convenient for their owners who can use it as fuel for their fires.
- Camels get water from plants that they eat, but they aren't herbivores. They are omnivores. In fact, they are everything-ores. They can and will eat just about anything. They've been known to eat their owners' tents.
  - They can eat cactus and other thorny desert plants. Their mouths are so tough that thorns don't poke through the skin in their mouths.
- Let me tell you one last way camels were created to survive in the desert. They have an extra eyelid. It moves across the eye horizontally. It is *transparent*, which means that the camel can see through it. Why do think that eyelid might be needed by a camel?
  - It protects the camel's eye from sand. It can help clear sand out too, if it's already gotten in there.
- The traders bringing the camels are coming from Gilead. You can see where that is on Day 117. Do you remember what balm is?
  - It's a cream or something that can be used for healing.
- There is a song called, "There Is a Balm in Gilead," which is a well-known traditional African-American spiritual.
  - Here are the traditional lyrics for its chorus:
    There is a balm in Gilead
    To make the wounded whole;
    There is a balm in Gilead
    To heal the sin-sick soul.

- o Recall: What's in a camel's hump? Why doesn't a camel sweat easily? What does a camel eat? Why is the camel's extra eyelid transparent?
    - fat
    - It can handle a raised body temperature.
    - most anything
    - so they can see through it
- o Explore More: You can listen to the song online. You can also look for pictures of the different types of camels.

V. Discussion
- o What songs give you hope? What songs encourage you?
- o If you were to write a spiritual, what would it be about?

VI. Writing
- o Complete your writing worksheet page for today.

**Day 120**

I. Read Genesis 37:29-36.
29 Reuben returned to the pit, and Joseph was not in there; so he tore his clothes.
30 He went back to his brothers and said, "The boy isn't there; where am I to go?"
31 So they took Joseph's tunic, killed a male goat, and dipped the tunic in the blood;
32 and they took the many-colored tunic and brought it to their father and said, "We found this; see if it is your son's tunic or not."
33 Then Jacob checked it and said, "It is my son's tunic. A wild beast has eaten him; Joseph has surely been torn to pieces!"
34 So Jacob tore his clothes and mourned for many days.
35 Then all his sons and all his daughters tried to comfort him, but he refused to be comforted. And he said, "Surely I will die mourning for my son." So his father wept for him.
36 Meanwhile, the Midianites sold Joseph in Egypt to Potiphar, Pharaoh's officer, the captain of the bodyguard.

II. Memory Verse
- Test yourselves on Romans 8:28.
  - And we know that God causes all things to work together for good to those who love God, to those who are called according to His purpose.
- Find it in the Bible.
- Review Jeremiah 29:11.
  - "For I know the plans I have for you," declares the Lord, "plans to prosper you and not to harm you, plans to give you hope and a future."

III. Language
- Handwriting/Spelling
  - Test yourselves on words from Day 116-119.
    - more, many, colors, stood
    - father's, brothers, animals, flock
    - dreams, pits, don't, one
    - meal, while, eating, silver
- Vocabulary
  - Test yourselves on words from Day 116-119.
    - rebuke – to scold; to tell someone their behavior is wrong in a sharp manner
    - graze – to eat grass or crops in a field, to eat little by little throughout the day
    - balm – a cream used for medicine, a sweet smell, or anything that heals or soothes
    - profit – to get a benefit, often refers to money

IV. Lesson
- Joseph is thrown into a pit. It's a dried up well. Why is it dry? Why is there lots of rain in some parts of the world and practically none in others? Any guesses? Let's see what we can find out.

- Before we can talk about rain, we need to remember what we've learned about water.
  - What makes up a water molecule?
    - Hydrogen and oxygen atoms, specifically two hydrogen atoms and one oxygen atom. How do you write a water molecule with the symbols for hydrogen and oxygen?
      - $H_2O$
  - What are the solid, liquid, and gas forms of $H_2O$?
    - ice, water, and water vapor
    - Ice is made up of water molecules. The water you drink is made up of water molecules. The clouds are formed with water molecules. It's all the same water molecules.
  - What is different about the water molecules that make them appear solid sometimes or a gas sometimes?
    - The difference is in the temperature and how much the molecules are moving.
    - When molecules have a lower temperature, are they moving faster or slower?
      - slower
      - Are they in a solid or a gas when they are moving very slowly?
        - solid
    - When molecules get warmer, they start moving more, and the solid becomes a liquid.
    - When the temperature gets even higher, the molecules get really excited and start moving around a lot. Then what form do they take?
      - a gas
  - Water heats up and enters the air.
    - The air gets full of water. We feel sticky when it's humid out, when there is lots of water in the air, because our sweat can't evaporate easily since the air is already so full of water. It's dense. There's not much room left to squeeze in more water vapor.
  - The water is in the air, where does warm air go?
    - Hot air rises.
    - What happens when it gets high enough?
      - It cools. What happens when water molecules cool?
        - They slow down and condense into a solid. What happens when those solids get together?
          - It rains.
  - Take a look at the water cycle picture on Day 120 in your Map Book.
  - Once you've followed all the arrows on your water cycle diagram, look at the map on the next page. It shows how much precipitation, mostly rain and snow, each country gets.
    - Those two countries with the most rainfall are Colombia, in South America, and Papua New Guinea.
    - Make observations.
  - Recall: What happens to water molecules when they evaporate?

- They turn into water vapor and are in the air. Warm air rises. When it gets higher and cools, it condenses and forms back into water droplets. There's no end! It's a cycle! The droplets collect and then gravity pulls them down as rain (or snow).
  - Explore More: You could make rain. There are different ways to do it. The simplest is to boil water in a pot with a glass lid. Watch the water condense into drops on the lid. (There is another map in the Map Book that didn't make it into these lessons if you want to take a look.)

V. Discussion
  - Do you believe God controls the weather specifically or generally? Did He create the weather patterns and set them in place and then let His creation do its thing, or does He control specific weather each day? Or does He do both? When? Do you know stories of when God seemed to specifically control weather? (We know in the Bible how God speaks to the storm and it stops at that moment. Matthew 8)

VI. Writing
  - Complete the workbook page for today if you haven't already.
  - There is a spelling and vocabulary review.

**Day 121**

I. Read Genesis 39:1-9. (I've left out chapter 38.)
1. Joseph had been taken down to Egypt; and Potiphar, an Egyptian officer of Pharaoh, the captain of the bodyguard, bought him from the Ishmaelites, who had taken him down there.
2. The Lord was with Joseph, so he became a successful man. And he was in the house of his Egyptian master.
3. Now his master saw that the Lord was with him and that the Lord caused Joseph to prosper in everything he did.
4. Joseph was favored by his master and became his personal servant. He made Joseph overseer over his house, and he put Joseph in charge of everything in his house.
5. It came about that from the time he put Joseph in charge over all that he owned, the Lord blessed the Egyptian's house on account of Joseph, so that the Lord's blessing was on everything in the house and in the field.
6. So he left everything in Joseph's charge, and because Joseph was there, he did not concern himself with anything other than what he was going to eat.
Joseph was handsome.
7. His master's wife looked with desire at Joseph, and she said, "Lie with me."
8. But he refused and said to his master's wife, "My master does not concern himself with anything in the house, and he has put me in charge of all that he owns.
9. There is no one greater in this house than I, and he has kept nothing from me except you, because you are his wife. How could I do this great evil and sin against God?"

\*Note if you want to explain: Potiphar's wife is sinning. She is an adulteress, a woman who wants to act like she's married to someone she's not. She sinned when she first desired for him to lie in bed with her. That's called lust. None of us are to lust after anyone we aren't married to. We guard our eyes from immodesty, and we take thoughts captive so that we won't desire what isn't ours. In the day the Lord gives you a husband or wife, you will be free to look at them and touch them and kiss them and have all the pleasure of a husband and wife. And after we marry, we keep our eyes and our touches for our husband or wife only. Joseph refuses and knows he wouldn't only be sinning against Potiphar but against God.

II. Memory Verse
- Learn Micah 6:8.
- He has told you, O man, what is good;
And what does the Lord require of you
But to do justice, to love kindness,
And to walk humbly with your God?

III. Language
- Handwriting/Spelling
  - words to know: taken, down, house, anything
  - spelling tips:
    - The word <u>taken</u> starts with the word take which has the same vowel spelling pattern as your spelling word made.

- The word <u>down</u> has the same spelling pattern as your spelling word town.
- The word <u>house</u> has the same vowel spelling pattern as your spelling word out and ends with a silent E.
- The word <u>anything</u> is the words any and thing combined. It's a compound word.
          - Vocabulary
             - prosper (verse 3)
             - to succeed financially or physically (action verb)

IV. Lesson
  - We're going to learn about ancient Egypt for a couple of days. Let's look at where we are in history. In a few weeks we'll work on a timeline of what we talked about this year.
  - Abraham was around 2000 BC. What does BC stand for?
      - before Christ
  - Does the time of Joseph's story come after or before Abraham's story?
      - after
  - Are the year numbers of when Joseph lived going to be smaller or bigger than 2000?
      - The year numbers will be smaller. Before Christ we count down the year numbers to 1 BC. Then we just jump to 1 AD and start counting up again.
  - There are a lot of dates out there about Egypt and Joseph. It seems his story fits into Egypt's Middle Kingdom in the years from 2000-1550 BC.
  - What do you think is the most famous feature of Egypt?
      - You probably said the pyramids because even if you didn't know anything else, you probably knew about the pyramids.
          - Do you know the name of the most famous pyramid?
              - The Great Pyramid of Giza
  - The pyramid of Giza was built during the Old Kingdom period, during Abraham's time and before Joseph's time.
  - What was so special about the pyramid in Giza?
      - Earlier pyramids were what we call step pyramids. When you build a pyramid out of Legos or blocks, they are step pyramids. If your legs were long enough, you could walk up the pyramids like steps.
      - Do you know what was different about this Great Pyramid?
          - Its sides were smooth.
              - It was covered in completely smooth limestone, fitted exactly to keep the slope of the pyramid.
          - It was the tallest man-made object in the world for thousands of years. It was about 480 feet tall (147 meters). It was an astonishing engineering feat.
              - Its cap was covered in gold.
  - The pyramids weren't like your block towers. They were open on the inside. They had rooms and passageways. They were built as tombs for the Pharaohs, the kings of Egypt.
  - The pyramids have attracted archeologists, those who study the past from what we can still physically find of it.

- A big find was in 1922 when the tomb of the famous King Tut was found. King Tutankhamen was a pharaoh of the New Kingdom, coming after the days of Moses.
- He died young and left no heir and his general took over. He's famous because his gold-covered tomb was found. He was buried with many pure gold objects. His outer coffin was pure gold. And a wonderfully preserved mask that was placed over him was preserved and is displayed for the world.
  o Following are some pictures of King Tut.
  o Recall: What biblical patriarch lived when the pyramids were first built? What is the name of the pyramid that was made with smooth sides?
    - Abraham
    - The Great Pyramid of Giza
  o Explore More: Look at pictures of the pyramids and build your own.

The pictures following:

1. Howard Carter, the archeologist who found King Tut's tomb, carefully cleaning off the inner coffin which was ornately made to look like the Pharaoh.

2. A pharaoh in maybe the 1300s BC, King Tut was a boy king whose gold-encrusted tomb fascinated the world. The picture is of the gold mask that he was buried with.

V. Discussion
- Have you ever been filled with desire for something you can't have? What did you do about it? What choice do you have in such a situation? How can you prevent being in that situation?
- It's a common trick of the enemy to cause us to feel addicted to something. We feel we just have to have it. We never need anything but Jesus, so when you feel that way, remember it's the devil's trick. Don't let him trick you. Wise up. Repent, which means change your mind, and ask God for help. Confess your struggle to your parents who will pray for you and encourage you. It's not sin to be tempted, but it's sin when you let it control you. Taking the steps of confessing and repenting are the first steps to getting free from a controlling desire.

VI. Writing
- Complete your workbook page for today.
- Make compound words.

**Day 122**

I. Read Genesis 39:9-18.
   9  There is no one greater in this house than I, and he has kept nothing from me except you, because you are his wife. How could I do this great evil and sin against God?"
   10 As she spoke to Joseph day after day, he did not listen to her.
   11 It happened one day that he went into the house to do his work, and none of the men of the household was there inside.
   12 She caught him by his garment, saying, "Lie with me!" And he left his garment in her hand and ran outside.
   13 When she saw that he had left his garment in her hand and had run outside,
   14 she called to the men of her household and said to them, "See, he came in to me to lie with me, and I screamed.
   15 When he heard me scream, he left his garment beside me and ran outside."
   16 So she left his garment beside her until his master came home.
   17 Then she spoke to him with these words, "The Hebrew slave, whom you brought to us, came in to me to make sport of me;
   18 and as I raised my voice and screamed, he left his garment beside me and ran outside."

II. Memory Verse
   o  Practice Micah 6:8.
   o  He has told you, O man, what is good;
      And what does the Lord require of you
      But to do justice, to love kindness,
      And to walk humbly with your God?

III. Language
   o  Handwriting/Spelling
      • words to know: beside, outside, run, ran
      • spelling tips:
         ▪ The words beside and outside are both compound words with the word side in them. The word side ends with a silent E.
         ▪ The words run and ran are different forms of the same verb.
   o  Vocabulary
      • garment (verse 12)
      • a piece of clothing (noun)

IV. Lesson
   o  We're going to continue with ancient Egypt. Do you know what hieroglyphics are?
      • Do you remember the form of writing we learned about that was used by the Sumerians in Mesopotamia?
         ▪ cuneiform
   o  Hieroglyphics are written with hieroglyphs. They are picture words. They were written on all sorts of surfaces in the early years of the pharaohs.
      • Hieroglyphs have been found on bones, pottery, and walls.
   o  Like cuneiform, and all languages, it was simplified over time.

- Pictures represented words, but over time a simplified symbol came to represent a sound, so that words could be formed by putting the sounds together.
  o This simplified writing was able to be written on their form of paper. Do you know what it was?
    - It was made from papyrus, a plant found along the Nile.
      - The stalks of the plant were slightly decomposed in water and then layered upon each other and smashed together and then dried.
    - Other cultures bought papyrus paper from the Egyptians. What are some of the reasons that paper would be better than clay tablets for writing on?
      - It wouldn't break when dropped. It was lighter to carry. It was easier to store as it didn't take up as much space.
  o According to Mr. Donn, papyrus was also used to make "baskets, sandals, mats, rope, blankets, tables, chairs, mattresses, medicine, perfume, food, and clothes." (egypt.mr.donn.org/papyrus.html)
    - Papyrus could grow ten feet tall. Can you picture how it could be used for some of those purposes? Which ones can't you imagine?
  o The Egyptians invented more than papyrus paper for writing. They were an agricultural society, so they made ways to make their farming work easier.
    - They used irrigation ditches that carried water from the Nile to their farmland. They invented a simple tool, a bucket on a pole weighted at the other end, that would make getting water out of the Nile and into those ditches easier.
  o They had a tool that would measure the level of the Nile flood and made a plow that could be pulled by oxen. You saw picture of it when we learned about oxen (Day 77).
  o They also invented different types of clocks.
    - They made obelisks (ob-e-lisks) which were basically just straight, four-sided statues. Here's a picture (by David Monniaux). (The Washington Monument in Washington, D.C. is this shape.)
    - How do you think it helped tell time?
      - It cast shadows. It's like a sun dial. Over time it developed and markings were made around it to show where the shadow would fall throughout the day.
    - A nighttime clock was also developed. It was a water clock. It was a bowl with rows of holes in it. How do you think it worked?
      - The water ran out of the holes. As the water lowered in the bowl, you could see by the markings how many hours had passed since it had been filled.
    - Why is this a better nighttime clock than daytime clock?
      - I would think evaporation in the heat of the day would throw off the timing.
  o Recall: What were some of the Egyptians' inventions?

- clocks, agricultural tools (plow drawn by oxen), papyrus paper
  - Explore More: Place a stick in the yard or tape a ruler to a walkway and watch the shadow change. What does the shadow look like at different times of day? Or, design your own clock of sorts.

V. Discussion
  - Joseph had to endure a lot of temptation. Sometimes it's necessary to flee from temptation. Joseph ran away when he had to.
  - Do you face a strong temptation? You might be pulled to the TV, internet, video games, or snacks, for instance. You never want something controlling your actions. If you have strong urges for something that you give into, then those feelings are controlling your actions. How can you flee that temptation and get it away from you?

VI. Writing
  - Complete your worksheet for today.
  - You are going to write past tense sentences.

**Day 123**

I. Read Genesis 39:19-23.
19 When Joseph's master heard his wife say, "This is what your slave did to me," he got very angry.
20 So Joseph's master took him and put him into the jail, the place where the king's prisoners were held.
21 But the Lord was with Joseph and was kind to him, and gave Joseph favor with the chief jailer.
22 The chief jailer put Joseph in charge of all the prisoners who were in the jail. Joseph was responsible for everything that was done there.
23 The chief jailer did not supervise anything that Joseph was in charge of because the Lord was with Joseph and he prospered.

II. Memory Verse
- Practice Micah 6:8.
- He has told you, O man, what is good;
  And what does the Lord require of you
  But to do justice, to love kindness,
  And to walk humbly with your God?

III. Language
- Handwriting/Spelling
  - words to know: Joseph, Joseph's, king, king's
  - spelling tips:
    - The name Joseph starts with a capital letter. Why?
      - All names begin with a capital letter.
      - There are two letters that write the "joe" syllable of the name.
      - There are four letters that write the second syllable, the last syllable, the "seff."
      - The last two letters are P-H. PH together make the F sound.
    - The word Joseph's shows that something belongs to Joseph. It was Joseph's garment.
    - The word king you have already had as a spelling word.
    - The word king's is the possessive. Something belongs to the king. It's the king's prisoners.
- Vocabulary
  - supervise (verse 23)
  - to keep watch over someone while they work (action verb)

IV. Lesson
- We're going to learn about the justice system.
- Why does Joseph get thrown in jail?
  - He was accused of doing wrong.
  - Was it a true accusation?
    - No! But it didn't matter.

- In the Bible we are given the instruction that no one is to be found guilty on the testimony of just one witness (Deuteronomy 17). That means that you can't assume someone did something wrong just because one person said so. Let's define a few words.
    - guilty and innocent – Do you know what these words mean?
        - Guilty means you did something wrong.
        - Innocent means you didn't do something wrong.
        - However, in the justice system, guilty means it was decided that you did something wrong and innocent means it was decided that you didn't do something wrong.
        - Can you tell the difference?
            - Unfortunately, in any justice system you can be found guilty and actually be innocent and can be declared innocent when you are actually guilty.
- We learned a little about Old Testament justice. There were laws in place to make sure wrong was punished in order to protect everyone else. Who wrote the justice system code of law that had messy housewives thrown in the Euphrates?
    - Hammurabi
    - His law did have many similarities to God's law given to Moses for the Israelites, but it didn't have justice for all. Different people were treated differently under the law. What was considered just and fair was determined by your rank in society.
    - In America that isn't supposed to happen. They say justice is blind. What do you think that means?
        - It means that laws apply to everyone, no matter who you are.
- What happens when you get arrested in America?
    - You are told what your rights are in a language you understand and are taken to jail.
    - You wait for a trial, up to six months.
    - The trial is between you and whoever is accusing you of wrongdoing. There are lawyers speaking for each side.
    - A jury listens to the lawyers and to the witnesses and decides the verdict, guilty or innocent.
    - If the verdict is guilty, then the judge gives the *sentencing*, meaning decides what the punishment will be.
- Recall: Go over these words: verdict, guilty, innocent, sentence, justice, trial, jury.
- Explore More: Act out a trial. You need a judge, lawyers, and jury. Use a stuffed animal for the *defendant*, the person accused of the crime, and you can add stuffed animals to the jury if you like. Act out multiple roles if necessary.
    - The prosecutor, the lawyer for the accuser, should accuse the defendant of the crime and tell the jury why they think the defendant is guilty.
    - The lawyer for the defendant should tell the jury why the defendant is innocent.
    - The jury decides the verdict, whether guilty or innocent.
    - If the defendant is found guilty, the judge decides the sentence, the punishment.

V. Discussion
- o Are you responsible enough to not be supervised like Joseph? Do you get your chores and schoolwork done thoroughly and on time so that no one has to come and check and remind you what needs to be done?
- o That should be a goal: to be known as responsible. Do you think an employer would want to hire someone with a reputation for being responsible to get his work done well and on time?

VI. Writing
- Complete your worksheet.
- You are going to be writing apostrophes.

**Day 124**

I. Read Genesis 40:1-4.
1. Then the cupbearer and the baker for the king of Egypt upset the king of Egypt.
2. Pharaoh was furious with his two officials, the chief cupbearer and the chief baker.
3. So he put them in the house of the captain of the bodyguard, in the jail, the same place where Joseph was in prison.
4. The captain of the bodyguard put Joseph in charge of them, and he took care of them. They were in jail for a while.

II. Memory Verse
- Review Micah 6:8.
- He has told you, O man, what is good;
  And what does the Lord require of you
  But to do justice, to love kindness,
  And to walk humbly with your God?

III. Language
- Handwriting/Spelling
  - words to know: baker, body, guard, bodyguard
  - spelling tips:
    - To turn a verb into a profession, we normally add E-R to the end of it. The verb to bake already ends with an E, so you just need to add an R to turn it into baker.
    - The word body has four letters. The final letter usually makes the E sound when it's on a word that has more than one syllable. You used it to write your spelling words only and greatly.
    - The word guard has a tricky spelling. There is a U after the G. Then it uses the vowel spelling pattern you used in words like jar and dark.
    - The word bodyguard is a compound word.
- Vocabulary
  - furious (verse 2)
  - really angry (adjective)

IV. Lesson
- When America's Constitution was written in 1787, there was debate about what should be included. A compromise was the Bill of Rights. They were not in the Constitution, but they were added as amendments.
- Let's start learning those first ten amendments, the Bill of Rights. They were written to protect the freedom of the people, to protect them from their government.
- The First Amendment may be the most important of all. It says that the government cannot establish a religion, and it can't stop anyone from practicing their religion. It also says that we have the right to gather together peacefully in protest and to say and write what we want without the government stopping us.
  - Where I lived in the Middle East for a number of years, the government would arrest people who said anything bad about it. Many journalists were thrown in jail for just reporting the truth about the government. While the

- American government shows favor to news people who are nicer to them, they can't stop people from complaining about them.
- The Second Amendment says that no one can stop people from owning guns.
- The Third Amendment just says that you can't be forced to have a soldier stay in your home.
- The Fourth Amendment says that the police or government agent can't search your home and can't take anything from you without a *warrant*, a special permission that can only be given if there is good reason to search your home, like maybe you are a suspected thief and they want to search your home for what was stolen.
- The Fifth Amendment states several things.
  - One is that you can't be made to be a witness against yourself. They can't ask you if you did it or not unless you decide you are willing to answer their questions.
  - The Fifth Amendment also ensures what we know as *due process*. That just means that you have to be accused and have a trial and be found guilty before giving out a sentence. They can't just put you in jail without having gone through the justice process.
- The Sixth Amendment is about trials.
  - You have to have your trial within six months or they have to drop your case and let you go free. That's in every case except a murder trial.
  - You have to have a jury that hasn't already made up their mind about you being guilty or innocent. They have to assume the person is innocent until they are proven guilty.
  - The Sixth Amendment is also the one that gives you the right to have a lawyer.
- The Seventh Amendment ensures a trial by jury and that a judge can't overrule a decision by the jury.
- The Eighth Amendment protects against excessive fines and the use of cruel punishment against prisoners.
- The Ninth Amendment says there are other rights that need to be protected that aren't each specifically listed in the Bill of Rights.
- The Tenth Amendment says that any power not given the government by the Constitution belongs to the states and the people. This amendment protects people from the government taking too much power.
- Why do we need a Bill of Rights? Do we need to be protected from our government? These were written by America's government leaders when America was first beginning. They were breaking away from their previous government.
  - The Bill of Rights keeps the government from having the power to do whatever it wants. They have to respect the rights of the people.
- Recall: What is an amendment? What is the Constitution?
  - an addition to the US Constitution
  - It is the highest law in America.
- Explore More: It might be fun to try to violate rights and defend rights. Stand on a chair and make a speech. Throw each other in prison, etc.

V. Discussion
- o If you had the power to do absolutely anything you wanted to do with no fear of punishment in any way, what would you do?

VI. Writing
- Complete your worksheet for today.
- Remember your rights!

**Day 125**

I. Read Genesis 40:5-8. Where is Joseph? (Answer: prison)
   5   Then the cupbearer and the baker for the king of Egypt, who were confined in jail, both had a dream the same night, each man with his own dream and each dream with its own interpretation.
   6   When Joseph came to them in the morning and observed them, behold, they were dejected.
   7   He asked Pharaoh's officials who were with him in confinement in his master's house, "Why are your faces so sad today?"
   8   Then they said to him, "We have had a dream and there is no one to interpret it." Then Joseph said to them, "Do not interpretations belong to God? Tell it to me, please."

II. Memory Verse
   - Say from memory, Micah 6:8.
     - He has told you, O man, what is good;
       And what does the Lord require of you
       But to do justice, to love kindness,
       And to walk humbly with your God?
   - Find it in the Bible.
   - Review Romans 8:28.
     - And we know that God causes all things to work together for good to those who love God, to those who are called according to His purpose.

III. Language
   - Handwriting/Spelling
     - Test yourselves on your words from Days 121-124.
       - taken, down, house, anything
       - outside, beside, run, ran
       - Joseph, Joseph's, king, king's
       - baker, body, guard, bodyguard
   - Vocabulary
     - Test yourselves on your words from Days 121-124.
       - prosper – to succeed financially or physically
       - garment – a piece of clothing
       - supervise – to keep watch over someone while they work
       - furious – really angry

IV. Lesson
   - Let's learn about dreams. When do you dream?
     - You dream when you are sleeping. We all dream every night even if you don't remember any dreams when you wake up.
   - Scientists have labeled our sleep in different stages.
   - The deepest level of sleep we get to quickly once we fall asleep.
     - Our muscles relax.
     - Much of our brain goes to sleep. We stop thinking things over. Our brain still functions, keeping us alive, but it's not too active.

- It's hard to wake up someone who is in a deep sleep. If they get woken up, they may feel all confused for a bit.
- This is when you grow too. While you are in a deep sleep, your body builds bone and muscle and does repairs.
- We do dream during this phase of sleep, but it's not very exciting. Usually we dream about doing the things we did during the day. This is when sometimes some people sleep walk or talk. They are replaying activities they did during the day. Our brain decides what's important to remember and what we can forget.
- We spend about 75% of our sleep in the deep sleep stage.
    o About every hour and a half…how long is that in minutes?
    o About every 90 minutes, we enter what is known as REM sleep. The word REM, written R-E-M stands for Rapid Eye Movement.
        - Our eyes move really fast under our eyelids, but the rest of our body doesn't move at all. We are paralyzed. Our muscles don't work. Maybe this is to keep us from sleep walking and acting out the crazy dreams of REM sleep!
        - While our brains have less activity during deep sleep, the brain during REM sleep is almost as active as a waking brain. There is one part of the brain that is still asleep. It's the part of the brain that makes connections to predict what's going to happen.
        - That's part of what makes REM dreams seem crazy. In real life we know that if this happens, then this is the outcome, but without that knowledge during sleep, our brains can let unpredictable things occur.
    o Our dreams are actually important. They help in a few ways.
        - Dreams let us process our emotions. It's important to handle our emotions. Replaying the emotion we are feeling in a different situation allows our minds to detach the strong emotion from what we experienced in real life.
        - Dreams are strongly associated with memory and emotions. Scientists can scan people's brains and see what parts of the brain are most active. We are remembering things that are important and letting go of things that aren't important during our dreams.
        - Dreams can also help us solve problems. Our crazy dreams let us try out different situations and see how to solve our problems.
            ▪ Studies have shown that when people are presented with a puzzle to figure out, those who are allowed to nap are more likely to figure it out than those who just keep thinking about it, trying to figure out the puzzle.
            ▪ People who learn something new are more likely to remember it twelve hours later if they learned it in the evening and then slept than those who learned it in the morning and tried to recall it at the end of the day.
            ▪ When trying to make a decision or to solve a problem, it might be really good advice to "sleep on it."
        - In a related way, dreams can help us solve problems we haven't had yet. We can practice what we would do in a certain situation and figure out the best response, even if we aren't aware we are doing it. It's just in our brains somewhere.

- o We do know that God can speak through dreams, but we all dream every night, and every dream isn't from God. He made our bodies and mind to work through things in our dreams in a way where our "thinking" brain can't get in the way. In that way we can learn from our dreams.
- o Mendeleev came up with the form of the periodic table in a dream. It was on his mind. He had been working and working on it. His brain was able to put the pieces of the puzzle together while he slept.
- o Recall: What is the stage of sleep called when we have crazy dreams and aren't sleeping as deeply? REM sleep
- o Explore More: What dreams do you remember having? Can you figure out what they mean? (There's often a real emotion attached to dreams, even if the substance is crazy.)

V. Discussion
- o What dreams do you remember having? Do you think they had a meaning? Can you relate them to any of the descriptions from the lesson?

VI. Writing
- Complete your worksheet for today if you haven't already.
- It's a review of your spelling and vocabulary.

**Day 126 (check Materials List)**

I. Read Genesis 40:16-23.
16 When the chief baker saw that Joseph had given a good interpretation to the cup bearer, he said to Joseph, "I also had a dream. There were three baskets of white bread on my head.
17 In the top basket there were all sorts of baked food for Pharaoh, and the birds were eating them out of the basket on my head."
18 Then Joseph answered and said, "This is the interpretation: the three baskets are three days.
19 Within three more days, Pharaoh will hang you, and the birds will eat the flesh off you."
20 And it came about on the third day, which was Pharaoh's birthday, that he had a feast for all his servants.
21 He restored the chief cupbearer to his job, and he again put the cup into Pharaoh's hand;
22 but he hanged the chief baker, just as Joseph had told them.
23 Yet the chief cupbearer did not remember Joseph and did not mention him.

II. Memory Verse
- Learn Psalm 55:22.
- Cast your burden upon the LORD and He will sustain you; He will never allow the righteous to be shaken.

III. Language
- Handwriting/Spelling
  - words to know: cup, job, told, off
  - spelling tips:
    - Cup is spelled just like it sounds.
    - Job is spelled just like it sounds.
    - Told is your spelling word old with one extra letter.
    - Off is spelled with three letters and one is a double letter.
- Vocabulary
  - interpretation (verse 16, 18)
  - the explanation of something's meaning (noun)
  - The action verb form of the word is interpret. You can interpret a dream or interpret the meaning of a phrase in another language.
  - Someone who interprets is an interpreter, which is also a noun, a person. The interpretation is a noun; it's a thing.

IV. Lesson
- We learned a little about grain and yeast earlier. We're going to learn about bread today.
- Let's try to stretch back and remember about grain. We talked about grain because early Mesopotamian society was an agricultural society. What does that mean?
  - They were farmers.
- Their lives revolved around grain in many ways. Grain was grown, harvested, threshed to knock off the grains of wheat from the rest of the plant, and then winnowed to separate out the pure grain by using the wind to blow the rest away.

- Once you have grain, what do you think needs to happen to make bread?
    - The grain is ground into flour. Some people today do that at home with an appliance in their kitchen, but it can also be done by grinding it between two large flat rocks.
        - That kind of flour is known as whole grain. It's made from the whole wheat grain.
    - To make bread the flour has to be mixed with at least water and then heated to bake. Flour and water (with a little salt) is a very basic cracker. It's the simplest form of bread.
    - In the Bible it's called unleavened bread. Do you know what that means?
- It means that there is no leaven in the bread, nothing to make it rise and not be flat. What do you add to make bread rise?
    - You usually add yeast. You can also add baking soda or baking powder.
- Baking soda is scientifically known as sodium hydrogen carbonate. What elements does it sound like it's made of?
    - It sounds like it's made from a sodium atom and a hydrogen atom and a carbon atom. That's not exactly right, though. It has all of those, but it also has three oxygen atoms.
    - We often use baking soda in cookies to make them puff up when they bake.
    - The baking soda releases carbon dioxide when it interacts with an acid such as sour cream, lemon juice, or even brown sugar. Those gas bubbles get caught in the dough and cause it to rise and fill kind of like a balloon.
- Baking powder is just baking soda already mixed with an acid. It just needs a liquid to set off the chemical reaction. The liquid makes the acid and baking soda combine and the reaction of the chemicals releases carbon dioxide. Like blowing up a balloon, the carbon dioxide fills the cake or bread or biscuit dough or whatever with gas, filling it and making it puff up.
    - You can make leavened bread by just mixing flour, water, and baking powder. You can then bake it, or in a yummier way, fry it in a pan covered in oil. I would add a little salt though!
- Yeast works in the same way in that the chemical reaction produces carbon dioxide which fills up the bread dough making it rise. When you punch down bread dough, you are just releasing the trapped carbon dioxide.
    - We mentioned yeast when we learned about fermentation. Do you remember what fermentation is?
        - It's the breakdown of a substance by yeast or other such organism.
        - I said organism. Yeast is alive!
        - It mixes with sugar to produce the carbon dioxide and then the yeast dies when it is cooked.
- Recall: What kingdom does yeast belong to? What does baking soda need to react with to produce carbon dioxide? What does yeast use to produce carbon dioxide? What does carbon dioxide have to do with leavened bread, bread that rises and isn't flat?
    - the fungus kingdom
    - acid
    - sugar

- The carbon dioxide is what causes the bread dough to rise by filling it with gas bubbles.
    - Explore More: You could make leavened and unleavened bread. When you see bubbles. They are carbon dioxide.

V. Discussion
    - What are your family birthday traditions?

VI. Writing
    - Complete your workbook page for today.
    - You are going to write molecule names like sodium hydrogen carbonate.
        - $NaHCO_3$

**Day 127**

I. Read Genesis 41:1-13.
    1   It happened, that after two full years, Pharaoh had a dream, where he was standing by the Nile.
    2   Up from the Nile there came seven cows, fat and good looking; and they grazed in the marsh grass.
    3   Then seven other cows came up after them from the Nile, ugly and gaunt, and they stood by the other cows on the bank of the Nile.
    4   The ugly and gaunt cows ate up the seven fat cows. Then Pharaoh woke up.
    5   He fell asleep and dreamed a second time; seven ears of grain came up on a single stalk, plump and good.
    6   Then seven ears, thin and scorched by the east wind, sprouted up after them.
    7   The thin ears swallowed up the seven plump and full ears. Then Pharaoh woke up and realized that it was a dream.
    8   In the morning he was troubled about his dreams, so he sent and called for all the magicians of Egypt, and all its wise men. And Pharaoh told them his dreams, but there was no one who could interpret them for Pharaoh.
    9   Then the chief cupbearer spoke to Pharaoh, saying, "I have forgotten to mention something.
    10  Pharaoh was furious with his servants, and he put me in jail, both me and the chief baker.
    11  We had a dream on the same night, he and I; each of us dreamed his own dream.
    12  A Hebrew youth was with us there, a servant of the captain of the bodyguard, and we told the dreams to him, and he interpreted our dreams for us.
    13  And everything happened just as he interpreted for us. My job was restored and the baker was hung."

II. Memory Verse
    o   Learn Psalm 55:22.
    o   Cast your burden upon the LORD and He will sustain you; He will never allow the righteous to be shaken.

III. Language
    o   Handwriting/Spelling
        • words to know: full, standing, grass, wind
        • spelling tips:
            ▪ The word <u>full</u> has a double letter at the end.
            ▪ <u>Standing</u> begins just like your spelling word standard.
            ▪ The word <u>grass</u> also ends with a double letter.
            ▪ The word <u>wind</u> is spelled just like it sounds.
    o   Vocabulary
        • gaunt (verse 4)
        • scrawny looking, especially looking thin from hunger (adjective)

IV. Lesson
    o   In Pharaoh's dream he saw fat cows and gaunt cows. Let's learn about cows today. Cows are the cousin of what animal we already learned about?
        • oxen

- Cows are in what kingdom?
  - the animal kingdom
- Do you think they are vertebrates or invertebrates?
  - vertebrates, meaning they have a backbone
- What class do you think they belong to? (For example: reptile, insect, mammal, fish, bird…)
  - They are mammals.
- Some people say that cows have four stomachs. This isn't really true, but they do have four compartments in their digestive system.
  - Two of those compartments can hold massive amounts of food. I read 50 gallons. (That's nearly 200 liters.) One of the compartments is called the rumen. When we ruminate on something, we're thinking long and hard about it.
    - They can eat forty pounds (18 kilos) of food and drink a bathtub worth of water each day.
      (from https://www.aipl.arsusda.gov/kc/cowfacts.html)
    - What do you think cows eat?
      - They eat things like grass, hay, and corn.
      - Are they carnivores, herbivores, or omnivores?
        - They are herbivores. They only eat plants.
  - Food gets into the digestive compartments through the esophagus. Do you remember what your esophagus is?
    - It's the tube that takes food down from the mouth.
  - Cows will also send partially digested food back up the esophagus and will keep chewing on it.
    - This is called chewing the cud and cows can chew the cud for a lot of the day.
    - Food can get through our digestive system in a few hours; it can take a couple of days for food to work through a cow's digestive system.
- Dairy cows provide more than 90% of the world's milk supply. One cow can give up to 25 gallons of milk a day. (That's nearly 100 liters.)
  - What other food do we get from cows?
    - beef
- Cows are an honored animal in the Hindu religion. They have festivals where they decorate cows and celebrate them as symbols of their religion and there are laws about killing cows.
- Recall: Do cows have four stomachs? What does it mean that cows chew their cud? Why are cows so important to the world?
  - No, they do have four compartments to their digestive system.
  - They spit up into their mouth food that was already partially digested and keep chewing it.
  - They make the milk we drink.
- Explore More: You could learn about cow cloning.

V. Discussion
- The president has a Cabinet, a collection of men and women who give him advice on different areas of the life of the country. One is over the department of education. One is over the department of agriculture. One is over the department of

transportation. One is over security, etc. Which department do you think is the most important? Why?

VI. Writing
- o Complete your worksheet for today.
- o You will be writing sentences. Every sentence starts with a capital letter. Every sentence ends with punctuation. Every sentence has a subject, something it's about. Subjects are nouns. Every sentence has a verb. The subject has to do or be something.
- o You are going to find those parts of your sentences.

**Day 128**

I. Read Genesis 41:14-32.
14 Then Pharaoh sent and called for Joseph, and they quickly brought him out of the dungeon; and when he had shaved and changed his clothes, he came to Pharaoh.
15 Pharaoh said to Joseph, "I have had a dream, but no one can interpret it; and I have heard it said about you, that when you hear a dream you can interpret it."
16 Joseph then answered Pharaoh, saying, "It is not me; God will give Pharaoh an answer."
17 So Pharaoh spoke to Joseph, "In my dream, I was standing on the bank of the Nile;
18 and seven cows, fat and good looking came up out of the Nile, and they grazed in the marsh grass.
19 Seven other cows came up after them, poor and very ugly and gaunt, such as I had never seen for ugliness in all the land of Egypt;
20 and the lean and ugly cows ate up the first seven fat cows.
21 Yet when they had eaten them, it could not be seen that they had eaten them because they were just as ugly as before. Then I woke up.
22 I also saw in my dream, seven ears of grain, full and good, came up on a single stalk;
23 and as well, seven ears, withered, thin, and burnt by the east wind, sprouted up after them;
24 and the thin ears swallowed the seven good ears. Then I told the dreams to the magicians, but there was no one who could explain it to me."
25 Now Joseph said to Pharaoh, "Pharaoh's dreams are the same; God has told Pharaoh what He is about to do.
26 The seven good cows are seven years; and the seven good ears are seven years; the dreams are one and the same.
27 The seven lean and ugly cows that came up after them are seven years, and the seven thin ears burnt by the east wind will be seven years of famine.
28 It is as I have said: God has shown to Pharaoh what He is about to do.
29 Seven years of great abundance are coming in all the land of Egypt;
30 and after them seven years of famine will come, and all the abundance will be forgotten in the land of Egypt, and the famine will take everything from the land.
31 So the abundance will be lost because of the famine that will follow because it will be very severe.
32 Having the dream twice means that the matter is set, and God will quickly make it happen."

II. Memory Verse
- Practice Psalm 55:22.
- Cast your burden upon the LORD and He will sustain you; He will never allow the righteous to be shaken.

III. Language
- Handwriting/Spelling
  - words to know: ugly, quickly, lost, twice
  - spelling tips:
    - The word ugly ends like your spelling words early and greatly.
    - The word quickly ends the same way. You've had quick as a spelling word already.

- The word <u>lost</u> has one letter for the vowel sound.
- The word <u>twice</u> ends like your spelling word price.
- o Vocabulary
  - abundance (verse 29 and 30)
  - a lot of something (noun)

IV. Lesson
- o In Pharaoh's dream he's told of a time of abundance and a time of famine.
- o Do you remember any of the causes of famine?
  - It could be a crop failure. What would cause crops to fail and not grow properly?
    - extreme weather (droughts—Do you know what a drought is? flooding, severe storms)
    - disease
    - bugs (like the boll weevil that ate cotton plants)
  - A crop failure might mean there wasn't enough food for everyone or that since there was less food available it cost too much for poorer people to buy any.
- o Now let's look at abundance from a scientific perspective. If disease, extreme weather and bugs could cause famine, what do you think would cause abundance, lots and lots of crops, plenty of food for everyone?
  - Let's look at the opposite of each of the things that would cause famine.
- o Disease-What's the opposite of disease?
  - health
  - If disease can cause a crop failure, then healthy plants would be part of an abundant crop.
  - What do plants need to be healthy?
    - sun, water, good soil full of nutrients
    - Healthy soil would contribute to healthy plants.
  - Fertilizers are used to create soil that plants thrive in. Some people make healthy soil by creating *compost*.
    - You make compost by mixing soil with dead leaves and grass and any leftover vegetable and fruit scraps that you have. You can add in other food trash such as egg shells.
    - It all decomposes and breaks down into the soil. All of the nutrients from the food gets into the soil and then can get into the plants.
      - Some fertilizers are made from chemicals, but then the chemicals can get into the plants which then get into our bodies when we eat them. They might make nice looking food, but it's not necessarily the healthiest food.
- o We have healthy plants living in healthy soil. The next cause of a crop failure is extreme weather. What would be the opposite of extreme weather?
  - The opposite would be regular intervals of rain and sun, neither too much.
    - When there isn't enough rain, then farmers use irrigation techniques. We've used that word before. Do you remember what irrigation is? The ancient Mesopotamians used irrigation ditches.

- Irrigation is getting water to your crops. They dug ditches to make waterways from the rivers to their crops.
- Now farmers use pipes to carry water and sprinkler systems to simulate rain falling.
      - The last on the list was bugs. Bugs can be bad for crops if they eat them, especially if swarms of a certain type of bug eat only a certain type of plant, and they all come together to the same part of a country at the same time. It can devastate a crop.
        - It would seem the opposite of bugs would be no bugs, however, bugs can be good for crops. Earthworms are good for soil. They are practically making their own compost down there.
        - Ladybugs, especially baby ladybugs, are good for gardens. They only eat bugs that eat plants. They are guardians of gardens.
        - Centipedes do the same and hunt only bugs that eat and harm plants.
          - Why is a centipede called a CENTipede?
            - There are 100 CENTs in a dollar. There are 100 years in a CENTury.
            - CENT means 100, so centipedes have 100 legs.
      - Recall: What is compost? What is irrigation? What are some things that make for an abundant crop?
        - It's soil mixed with natural things that would make it healthier such as grass and banana peels, natural things that have decomposed.
        - watering crops
        - perfect weather, healthy soil, helpful bugs
      - Explore More: Start a compost pile.

V. Discussion
  - As Christians we can trust God to meet all of our needs. We never have to be powerless, and we can always rely on Jesus.
  - We also need to remember that no government acts on its own. God is in control. God can bring about abundance and prosperity. God can bring about poverty and famine. Either way, God is acting in love! When God brings hard times, it's a way to turn us to Him.
  - Do you trust that God loves you even when things seem bad?

VI. Writing
  - Complete your worksheet for today.
  - Draw a picture of a plant getting all it needs to grow healthy.

**Day 129**

I. Read Genesis 41:33-40. This starts with Joseph talking to Pharaoh. He just finished giving the dream interpretation.
- 33 "Now let Pharaoh look for a wise man and set him over the land of Egypt.
- 34 Let Pharaoh appoint overseers in charge of the land, and let the leaders collect a fifth of the crops that grow in the land of Egypt in the seven years of abundance.
- 35 Then let them gather all the food of these good years that are coming, and store up the grain for food in the cities under Pharaoh's authority, and let them guard it.
- 36 Let the food be stored for the seven years of famine which will come in the land of Egypt, so that the famine will not destroy the land."
- 37 The idea seemed good to Pharaoh and to all his servants.
- 38 Pharaoh said to his servants, "Can we find another man like Joseph, who has a divine spirit?"
- 39 So Pharaoh said to Joseph, "Since God has told you of all this, there is no one as wise as you.
- 40 You will be over my house and will be honored; only I will be greater than you."

II. Memory Verse
- o Practice Psalm 55:22.
- o Cast your burden upon the LORD and He will sustain you; He will never allow the righteous to be shaken.

III. Language
- o Handwriting/Spelling
  - words to know: wise, set, charge, third (Third is from Gen. 40.)
  - spelling tips:
    - The word wise ends with a silent E and has no Z.
    - The word set is spelled just like it sounds.
    - The word charge ends with the last two letters in your spelling word image. You have written the AR sound in your spelling words such as hard and farm.
    - The word third starts just like your spelling word thirty.
- o Vocabulary
  - appoint (verse 34)
  - to set someone in charge over something, or to choose a time or place for something (verb)

IV. Lesson
- o Joseph is going to store up grain during the years of abundance so that there will be food during the years of famine.
- o Today we're going to learn about food storage. We learned about Egyptians storing organs from bodies by dehydrating them.
- o Let's look first at dehydration as a storage technique. To *dehydrate* is to take the water out of something. It's the opposite of hydrating. You hydrate yourself when you drink water. You are dehydrated when you are in need of a drink of water.
  - The dried herb seasonings you have in your kitchen are dehydrated. That's how they can sit on your shelf for months without going bad.

343

- The tea leaves in your tea bags are dehydrated leaves.
- Raisins are dehydrated grapes. Grapes go bad. Raisins don't.
o So what keeps the dehydrated food from spoiling?
- It must have to do with the lack of water.
- Living things need water.
- Yeast is a living thing right? It's in the fungus family and so is mold.
- Mold is the stuff that grows on old food that you let sit around too long. It's a living thing, and it's working on eating your food, decomposing it.
o Mold, yeast, and other fungi such as mushrooms are called *decomposers*. Their job is to break down things that have died.
- Decomposing things that have died makes them useful to our world. It brings them down into the soil, and then they can be used again by plants and in turn by the animals who eat plants.
- Remember how everything is interdependent? We all rely on each other. We rely on decomposers to make our soil richer for better plants which we animals then eat.
o Since decomposers, such as mold, are living things too, they need water. Without water, they can't live. Dried food doesn't make a good habitat for them.
o We've talked about living things needing water. We've talked about plants needing water, sun, and soil (its food), but we haven't mentioned the obvious. Living things need air.
- Food can be packed in tightly so that little air is present. Without air, living things will die.
- One storage technique is vacuum packing. It sucks the air out of the container so that those little living cells of the fungus kingdom can't get at the food.
o What about Joseph's grain storage?
- We aren't told how he did it, but huge silos have been found among ancient Egypt's remains. A *silo* is a large cylindrical building, like a huge can for holding grains. The ones found in Egypt are 20 feet across and 25 feet tall (6 meters/7.6 meters).
  - If you can't imagine that, it's like four tall kids lying end to end and then five tall kids standing on top of each other.
- Silos are still used. It's an efficient way to store grain.
- Even without extra special techniques, why was Joseph's attempt at storing massive amounts of grain successful?
  - We're told repeatedly that God blessed everything that Joseph did.
o Recall: What are two types of techniques used for preserving food? Why do those techniques keep food from decomposing? What is the name of the type of building that is often used to store grain?
- dehydration and vacuum packing
- They make the food an unfit habitat for the decomposers like mold that spoil food.
- silo
o Explore More: Look through your kitchen and think about what types of preservations you can find. Do you have raisins? Do you have sealed bags?

V. Discussion
- Are you a saver, a spender, or a giver?

VI. Writing
- Complete your worksheet for today.
- You are going to be writing sentences again today.
- What do all sentences have?
  - capital letter
  - ending punctuation
  - noun (subject)
  - verb

**Day 130**

I. Read Genesis 41:41-49.
   41  Pharaoh said to Joseph, "I have set you over all of Egypt."
   42  Then Pharaoh took off his signet ring from his hand and put it on Joseph's hand, and put expensive garments on him and put a gold necklace around his neck.
   43  He had Joseph ride in his second chariot and called to everyone, "Bow the knee!" And Pharaoh set Joseph over all of Egypt.
   44  Pharaoh said to Joseph, "Though I am Pharaoh, without your permission no one will raise his hand or foot in all of Egypt."
   45  Then Pharaoh named Joseph Zaphenath-paneah; and he gave him Asenath, the daughter of Potiphera priest of On, to be his wife. And Joseph was over the whole land of Egypt.
   46  Joseph was thirty years old when he was before Pharaoh, king of Egypt. And Joseph went through the whole land of Egypt.
   47  During the seven years of abundance the land produced crops abundantly.
   48  So Joseph gathered a portion of all the food and placed the food in the cities; he placed in every city the food from its own surrounding fields.
   49  This is how Joseph stored up grain in great abundance like the sand of the sea, until he stopped measuring it, because it was too much to measure.

II. Memory Verse
   o  Say from memory Psalm 55:22.
      • Cast your burden upon the LORD and He will sustain you; He will never allow the righteous to be shaken.
   o  Find it in the Bible.
   o  Review Micah 6:8.
      • He has told you, O man, what is good; and what does the Lord require of you, but to do justice, to love kindness, and to walk humbly with your God?

III. Language
   o  Handwriting/Spelling
      • Test yourselves on the words from Days 126-129.
         ▪ cup, job, told, off
         ▪ full, standing, grass, wind
         ▪ ugly, lost, quickly, twice
         ▪ wise, set, charge, third
   o  Vocabulary
      • Review your words from Days 126-129.
         ▪ interpretation – the explanation of something's meaning
         ▪ gaunt – scrawny looking, especially looking thin from hunger
         ▪ abundance – a lot of something
         ▪ appoint – to set someone in charge over something, or to choose a time or place for something

IV. Lesson
   o  We're going to review what we've learned of simple machines and look at one of them in a new way.
   o  What are simple machines? What do they do for us in general?

- Simple machines are tools that make work easier.
    o Do you remember the scientific definition of work?
        - It's a force moving an object.
        - Is picking up a piece of paper work?
            - Yes, the force applied by your hand is moving the paper.
        - Is throwing a ball up in the air work?
            - Yes, the force applied by your hand is moving the ball.
        - Is the ball falling back down work?
            - Yes, the force of gravity is moving the ball down.
        - Is your whole family pushing against the side of your house trying to get it to move work?
            - No, the house doesn't move, so no work was accomplished on the house. No work is accomplished if an object isn't moved.
    o We learned about the wheel and axle with the well, the screw, and the wedge when we talked about Abraham's ax.
    o Today we read about Joseph getting to ride in a chariot. Here's a picture of a chariot. What simple machine that we've learned about is at work?

- the wheel and axle
- The work is done by the horse pulling the chariot. The horse applies the force. The bigger the wheel the less force would be needed to pull the chariot.
    - Now look at the picture of the old bicycle. Why is the wheel so big?

- Did you say it required less force to go the same amount of distance?
    - That's true, but it also did something else.
    - If they applied the same amount of force then what would happen?
        - They would go so much farther for the same amount of force.
        - The distance increased and the force stayed the same meaning this bicycle allowed them to go really fast.
- The chariot was a symbol of power. Rulers rode in chariots. Warriors rode in chariots.
- Here are verses 42 and 43 from today's reading.
    - Then Pharaoh took off his signet ring from his hand and put it on Joseph's hand, and clothed him in garments of fine linen and put the gold necklace around his neck. He had him ride in his second chariot; and they proclaimed before him, "Bow the knee!"
- When people are told to bow before Joseph, what does that symbolize?
    - Bowing symbolized their respect for and submission to Joseph.
- Pharaoh had Joseph dressed in expensive clothing and a gold necklace. What does that symbolize?
    - I would say wealth and power.
    - There's an expression, "The clothes make the man." What do you think that might mean?
        - Not only do people respond to us differently depending on how we dress, but we respond differently too.
        - When we get really dressed up, we behave differently than when we are in jeans and sweats.
    - Workers wear uniforms because it gives them respect for their position. People respond differently.
    - People give more respect to people in white lab coats, like a doctor would wear, even if the person isn't a doctor.

- Even more interesting, people act smarter (as in scoring better on activities) when wearing what they believe is a doctor's lab coat.
- When people saw Joseph, they responded to his new attire. It made him look important, and he was treated as someone important.
  - Pharaoh also gives Joseph a signet ring. The symbol on the ring was Pharaoh's own. It meant that Joseph had Pharaoh's authority.
    - The signet ring was a symbol of authority.
  - Can you think of any symbols today? What do you picture when you picture someone with authority and power? What do they look like? What do they have?
  - How is this a symbol of authority?

  - Recall: Why might it a good idea to get dressed in the morning instead of trying to do your school work in your pajamas? What did Joseph's wearing Pharaoh's signet ring mean to people? What do simple machines do for us?
    - We act differently depending on how we are dressed.
    - It meant that Joseph had Pharaoh's authority.
    - They make work easier.
  - Explore More: What are symbols of power? Why do presidential candidates wear red ties? Look at pictures of the president speaking or presidential candidates. What symbols are present? Look at toy cars, wagons, bikes, whatever you have with wheels. Find the axles. Watch the wheels and axles turn. What makes the axle turn?

V. Discussion
  - Do you judge people by how they look? Do you think the same about someone who looks homeless and someone who is dressed beautifully?
  - James 2:2-4 For if a man comes into your assembly with a gold ring and dressed in fine clothes, and there also comes in a poor man in dirty clothes, and you pay special attention to the one who is wearing the fine clothes, and say, "You sit here in a good place," and you say to the poor man, "You stand over there, or sit down by my footstool," have you not made distinctions among yourselves, and become judges with evil motives?
  - If those two people came to your church one Sunday, would you invite one of them home for lunch?

VI. Writing
  - Complete your workbook page for today if you haven't already.
  - There are places to practice your spelling and vocabulary.

**Day 131**

I. Read Genesis 41:50-42:13. During our final review weeks, we're going to read through the rest of Joseph's story to the very end of Genesis.

50 Before the famine came, two sons were born to Joseph and his wife, Asenath, the daughter of Potiphera priest of On.
51 Joseph named the firstborn Manasseh, saying, "God has made me forget all my trouble and all my father's household."
52 He named the second Ephraim, saying, "God has made me fruitful in the land of my affliction."
53 When the seven years of abundance ended,
54 and the seven years of famine began, just as Joseph had said, then there was famine in all the lands, but in all the land of Egypt there was bread.
55 So when all the land of Egypt was famished and starving, the people cried out to Pharaoh for bread; and Pharaoh said to all the Egyptians, "Go to Joseph and do whatever he tells you."
56 When the famine had reached everywhere, Joseph opened all the storehouses and sold grain to the Egyptians.
57 The people from everywhere came to Egypt to buy grain from Joseph, because the famine was severe.

Chapter 42
1 Now Jacob saw that there was grain in Egypt.
2 He said, "I have heard that there is grain in Egypt; go down there and buy some for us, so that we may live and not die."
3 Then ten brothers of Joseph went down to buy grain from Egypt.
4 But Jacob did not send Joseph's brother Benjamin, afraid that something might happen to him."
5 So the sons of Israel came to buy grain along with everyone else.

6 Joseph ruled over the land; he was the one who sold the grain. And Joseph's brothers came and bowed down to him with their faces to the ground.
7 When Joseph saw his brothers he recognized them, but he disguised himself and spoke to them harshly. "Where have you come from?" And they said, "From the land of Canaan, to buy food."

8 Joseph recognized his brothers, but they did not recognize him.
9 Joseph remembered the dreams which he had about them. He tested them saying, "You are spies; you have come to look at the undefended parts of our land."
10 Then they answered, "No, my lord. We are your servants. We have come to buy food.
11 We are all sons of one man; we are honest men, your servants are not spies."
12 Joseph responded, "No. You are spies, and you have come to look at the undefended parts of our land!"
13 But they said, "Your servants are twelve brothers in all, the sons of one man in the land of Canaan. The youngest is with our father today, and one is dead."

II. Memory Verse
- Can you say from memory? Deuteronomy 31:8

- o Find it in the Bible.
  - The LORD is the one who goes ahead of you; He will be with you. He will not fail you or forsake you. Do not fear or be dismayed.
- o Review Joshua 24:5.
  - [If it is disagreeable in your sight to serve the LORD,] choose for yourselves today whom you will serve: [whether the gods which your fathers served which were beyond the River, or the gods of the Amorites in whose land you are living;] but as for me and my house, we will serve the LORD.

III. Language
  - o Spelling
    - Have a spelling bee. (Parent: Read a word from Day 90's worksheet. Choose one they didn't have trouble with. Have them spell it out loud.)
    - If you want to do a spelling activity here are ideas.
      - Write words with sidewalk chalk.
      - Write words with invisible ink.
      - Write words by pressing down and then reveal them by coloring lightly over the words.
      - Color a page and then color over it in black. Write the words by scratching off the black.
      - Write the words with letters cut out of magazines.
      - Write the words with yarn.
      - Write the words in the air or on each other's back.

IV. Lesson
  - o Complete the worksheet for Day 131.

**Day 132**

I. Read Genesis 42:14-38.
14 Joseph said again, "You are spies;
15 by this you will be tested: you shall not go from this place unless your youngest brother comes here!
16 You will stay in prison while one of you goes to get your brother that your words may be tested, whether there is truth in you. But if not, I will know you are spies."
17 So he put them all together in prison for three days.

18 After three days Joseph said to them,
19 "If you are honest men, let one of your brothers be confined in your prison; but as for the rest of you, go and take grain home,
20 and bring your youngest brother back here to me, to show your words are true, and you will not die." And they did so.
21 The brothers said to one another, "We are guilty because we saw Joseph's distress when he pleaded with us, but we would not listen because of that this is happening to us now.
22 Reuben said, "Didn't I tell you, 'Don't sin against the boy'; and you wouldn't listen?"
23 They did not know that Joseph understood because he was using an interpreter.
24 Joseph turned away and wept. But when he returned to them, he took Simeon and bound him before their eyes.
25 Then Joseph gave orders to fill their bags with grain and to put back their money into their sacks, and to give them what they need for the journey home.

26 They loaded their donkeys with the grain and departed.
27 When they came to a place to spend the night, one of the brothers opened his sack to give his donkey something to eat, and he saw his money in his sack.
28 He said to his brothers, "My money has been returned to me." And their hearts sank, and they turned trembling to one another, asking, "What has God done to us?"

29 When they arrived home in Canaan, they told their father all that had happened to them.
30 "The man, the lord of the land, spoke harshly to us and thought we were spies.
31 But we told him, 'We are honest men; we are not spies.
32 We are twelve brothers; one is no longer alive, and the youngest is with our father in the land of Canaan.'
33 The man, the lord of the land, said to us, 'By this I will know that you are honest men: leave one of your brothers with me and take grain to feed your households, and go.
34 But bring your youngest brother to me that I may know that you are not spies. Then I will give your brother back to you, and you may trade in the land.'"

35 Now as they were emptying their sacks, they saw that they all had their bundle of money still in their sack; they were dismayed.
36 Their father Jacob said to them, "You have caused me to grieve my children: Joseph is no more, and Simeon is no more, and you would take Benjamin!"
37 Then Reuben spoke to his father, "You may put my two sons to death if I do not bring Benjamin back to you; put him in my care, and I will return him to you."
38 But Jacob said, "Benjamin will not go with you; his brother is dead, and he alone is left. I would die if something happened to him."

II. Memory Verse
- Practice Jeremiah 29:11.
- Find it in the Bible.
    - "For I know the plans I have for you," declares the Lord, "plans to prosper you and not to harm you, plans to give you hope and a future." (NIV)
- Review 2 Peter 3:9.
    - The Lord is not slow about His promise, as some count slowness, but is patient toward you, not wishing for any to perish but for all to come to repentance.

III. Language
- Spelling
    - Have a spelling bee. (Parent: Read a word from Day 90's worksheet. Choose one they didn't have trouble with. Have them spell it out loud.)
    - If you want to do a spelling activity here are ideas.
        - Write words with sidewalk chalk.
        - Write words with invisible ink.
        - Write words by pressing down and then reveal them by coloring lightly over the words.
        - Color a page and then color over it in black. Write the words by scratching off the black.
        - Write the words with letters cut out of magazines.
        - Write the words with yarn.
        - Write the words in the air or on each other's back.

IV. Lesson
- Complete the worksheet for Day 132.

**Day 133**

I. Read Genesis 43:1-22.
1. Now the famine was severe.
2. It came about when Jacob's family had finished eating the grain which they had brought from Egypt, that their father said to them, "Go back, buy us a little food."
3. Judah spoke to him. "The man solemnly warned us, 'Do not come back unless your brother is with you.'
4. If you send our brother with us, we will go down and buy you food.
5. But if you do not send him, we will not go; for the man said to us."
6. Then Israel said, "Why did you treat me so badly by telling the man that you had another brother?"
7. But they said, "The man asked about our relatives, saying, 'Is your father still alive? Have you another brother?' So we answered his questions. Could we possibly know that he would say, 'Bring your brother down'?"
8. Judah said to his father Israel, "Send the lad with me and we will go, that we may all live and not die.
9. You may hold me responsible for Benjamin. If I do not bring him back to you, then blame me.
10. If we had not waited so long, by now we could have returned twice."

11. Then their father Israel said to them, "If it must be, then do this: take some of the best products of the land in your bags, and carry them down to the man as a present, a little balm and a little honey, aromatic gum and myrrh, pistachio nuts and almonds.
12. Take double the money, and take back the money that was returned in your sacks; perhaps it was a mistake.
13. Take your brother also, and return to the man;
14. and may God Almighty grant you compassion in the sight of the man, so that he will release to you your other brother and Benjamin. And as for me, if I am bereaved of my children, I am bereaved."
15. So the men took this present, and they took double the money, and Benjamin; then they went down to Egypt and stood before Joseph.

16. When Joseph saw Benjamin with them, he said to his house steward, "Bring the men into the house, and slay an animal and prepare it; for the men are to dine with me at noon."
17. So the man did as Joseph said, and brought the men to Joseph's house.
18. Now the men were afraid, because they were brought to Joseph's house; and they said, "It is because of the money that was returned in our sacks the first time that we are being brought in, that they can take us for slaves with our donkeys."
19. So they came near to Joseph's house steward, and spoke to him at the entrance of the house,
20. and said, "Oh, my lord, we came down the first time to buy food,
21. and when we stopped for the night, we opened our sacks, and all of each man's money was in his sack. So we have brought it back.
22. We have also brought down other money to buy food; we do not know who put our money in our sacks."

II. Memory Verse
- Practice Romans 8:28.
- Find it in the Bible.
    - And we know that God causes all things to work together for good to those who love God, to those who are called according to His purpose.
- Review Job 19:25.
    - As for me, I know that my Redeemer lives,
      And at the last He will take His stand on the earth.

III. Language
- Spelling
    - Have a spelling bee. (Parent: Read a word from Day 90's worksheet. Choose one they didn't have trouble with. Have them spell it out loud.)
    - If you want to do a spelling activity here are ideas.
        - Write words with sidewalk chalk.
        - Write words with invisible ink.
        - Write words by pressing down and then reveal them by coloring lightly over the words.
        - Color a page and then color over it in black. Write the words by scratching off the black.
        - Write the words with letters cut out of magazines.
        - Write the words with yarn.
        - Write the words in the air or on each other's back.

IV. Lesson
- Complete the worksheet for Day 133.

**Day 134**

I. Read Genesis 43:23-44:9.

23 He said, "Be at ease, do not be afraid. Your God and the God of your father has given you treasure in your sacks; I had your money." Then he brought Simeon out to them.
24 Then the man brought the men into Joseph's house and gave them water, and they washed their feet; and he gave their donkeys fodder.
25 So they prepared the present for Joseph's coming at noon; for they had heard that they were to eat a meal there.

26 When Joseph came home, they brought into the house to him the present and bowed to the ground before him.
27 Then he asked them about their welfare, and said, "Is your old father well? Is he still alive?"
28 They said, "Your servant our father is well; he is still alive." They bowed down in homage.
29 As he lifted his eyes and saw his brother Benjamin, his mother's son, he said, "Is this your youngest brother?" And he said, "May God be gracious to you, my son."
30 Joseph hurried out for he was deeply stirred over his brother, and he sought a place to weep; and he entered his chamber and wept there.
31 Then he washed his face and came out; and he controlled himself and said, "Serve the meal."
32 So they served him by himself, and them by themselves, and the Egyptians who ate with him by themselves, because the Egyptians could not eat bread with the Hebrews, for that is loathsome to the Egyptians.
33 Now they were seated before him, in order of their ages, and the brothers looked at one another in astonishment.
34 He took portions to them from his own table, but Benjamin's portion was five times as much as any of theirs. So they feasted and drank freely with him.

Chapter 44
1 Then he commanded his house steward. "Fill the men's sacks with food, as much as they can carry, and put each man's money in the mouth of his sack.
2 Put my cup, the silver cup, in the mouth of the sack of the youngest, and his money for the grain." And he did as Joseph commanded.
3 As soon as it was light, the men were sent away with their donkeys.
4 They had just gone out of the city when Joseph said to his house steward, "Follow the men; and when you find them, say to them, 'Why have you repaid evil for good?
5 Is not this the cup of my lord? You have done wrong in doing this.'"

6 So he overtook them and spoke these words to them.
7 They said to him, "Why does my lord speak such words? Far be it from your servants to do such a thing.
8 The money which we found in the mouth of our sacks we have brought back to you from the land of Canaan. How then could we steal silver or gold from your lord's house?
9 Whoever has the cup, let him die, and we will be my lord's slaves."

*Does it confuse you that Joseph would hide the cup in Benjamin's bag and accuse him of stealing? He's testing his brothers to see if they had repented, to see if they had changed. Would they be willing to abandon their brother? Did they despise Benjamin, the favorite, the way they despised Joseph?

II. Memory Verse
- o Practice Micah 6:8
- o Find it in the Bible.
    - He has told you, O man, what is good;
      And what does the Lord require of you
      But to do justice, to love kindness,
      And to walk humbly with your God?
- o Review Hebrews 11:1.
    - Now faith is the assurance of things hoped for, the conviction of things not seen.

III. Language
- o Spelling
    - Have a spelling bee. (Parent: Read a word from Day 90's worksheet. Choose one they didn't have trouble with. Have them spell it out loud.)
    - If you want to do a spelling activity here are ideas.
        - Write words with sidewalk chalk.
        - Write words with invisible ink.
        - Write words by pressing down and then reveal them by coloring lightly over the words.
        - Color a page and then color over it in black. Write the words by scratching off the black.
        - Write the words with letters cut out of magazines.
        - Write the words with yarn.
        - Write the words in the air or on each other's back.

IV. Lesson
- o Complete the worksheet for Day 134.

**Day 135**

I. Read Genesis 44:10-34. We're starting with the brothers being accused of stealing.
10  So he said, "Let it also be as you said; whoever has the cup will be my slave, and the rest of you will be innocent."
11  Then they hurried, each man lowered his sack to the ground, and each man opened his sack.
12  He searched, beginning with the oldest and ending with the youngest, and the cup was found in Benjamin's sack.
13  Then they tore their clothes, and when each man loaded his donkey, they returned to the city.

14  When Judah and his brothers came to Joseph's house, he was still there, and they fell to the ground before him.
15  Joseph said to them, "What is this deed that you have done? Do you not know that such a man as I can indeed practice divination?"
16  So Judah said, "What can we say to my lord? What can we speak? And how can we justify ourselves? God has found out our sin; we are my lord's slaves, both we and the one in whose possession the cup has been found."
17  But he said, "Far be it from me to do this. The man who had the cup, he will be my slave; but as for you, go up in peace to your father."

18  Then Judah approached him, and said, "Oh my lord, may your servant please speak a word in my lord's ears, and do not be angry with your servant; for you are equal to Pharaoh.
19  My lord asked his servants, saying, 'Have you a father or a brother?'
20  We said to my lord, 'We have an old father and a little child of his old age. Now his brother is dead, so he alone is left of his mother, and his father loves him.'
21  Then you said to your servants, 'Bring him down to me that I may see him.'
22  But we said to my lord, 'The lad cannot leave his father, for if he should leave his father, his father would die.'
23  You said to your servants, however, 'Unless your youngest brother comes down with you, you will not see my face again.'
24  Thus it came about when we went up to your servant my father, we told him the words of my lord.
25  Our father said, 'Go back, buy us a little food.'
26  But we said, 'We cannot go down. If our youngest brother is with us, then we will go down; for we cannot see the man's face unless our youngest brother is with us.'
27  Your servant my father said to us, 'You know that my wife bore me two sons;
28  and the one went out from me, and I said, "Surely he is torn in pieces," and I have not seen him since.
29  If you take this one also from me, and he is harmed, I will die from sorrow.'
30  Now, therefore, when I come to your servant my father, and the lad is not with us, since his life is bound up in the lad's life,
31  when he sees that the lad is not with us, he will die. We will kill him with sorrow.
32  For your servant said, 'If I do not bring him back to you, then let me bear the blame forever.'

33 Now, therefore, please let your servant remain as a slave instead of the lad, and let the lad go up with his brothers.

34 For how shall I go up to my father if the lad is not with me—for fear that I see my father die?"

II. Memory Verse
- Practice Psalm 55:22.
- Find it in the Bible.
  - Cast your burden upon the LORD and He will sustain you; He will never allow the righteous to be shaken.
- Review John 11:25
  - Jesus said to her, "I am the resurrection and the life; he who believes in Me will live even if he dies."

III. Language
- Spelling
  - Have a spelling bee. (Parent: Read a word from Day 90's worksheet. Choose one they didn't have trouble with. Have them spell it out loud.)
  - If you want to do a spelling activity here are ideas.
    - Write words with sidewalk chalk.
    - Write words with invisible ink.
    - Write words by pressing down and then reveal them by coloring lightly over the words.
    - Color a page and then color over it in black. Write the words by scratching off the black.
    - Write the words with letters cut out of magazines.
    - Write the words with yarn.
    - Write the words in the air or on each other's back.

IV. Lesson
- Complete the worksheet for Day 135.

**Day 136**

I. Do you remember what a remnant is? It's what's left over. In biblical terms it means that God always has a group of His people. It will never happen that all of the Jews or that all of the Christians will be killed off. God will always preserve a remnant of His people. Read Genesis 45:1-20.

1. Then Joseph could not control himself before all those who stood by him, and he cried, "Have everyone go out from me." So there was no man with him when Joseph made himself known to his brothers.
2. He wept so loudly that the Egyptians heard it, and the household of Pharaoh heard of it.
3. Then Joseph said to his brothers, "I am Joseph! Is my father still alive?" But his brothers could not answer him, for they were scared by his presence.

4. Then Joseph said to his brothers, "Please come closer to me." And they came closer. And he said, "I am your brother Joseph, whom you sold into Egypt.
5. Do not be angry with yourselves, because you sold me here, for God sent me before you to preserve life.
6. The famine has lasted two years, and there are still five years in which there will be no harvesting.
7. God sent me before you to preserve for you a remnant in the earth, and to keep you alive by a great deliverance.
8. It was not you who sent me here, but God; and He has made me a father to Pharaoh and lord of all his household and ruler over all the land of Egypt.
9. Hurry and go up to my father, and say to him, 'Thus says your son Joseph, "God has made me lord of all Egypt; come down to me, do not delay.
10. You will live in the land of Goshen, and you will be near me, you and your children and your children's children and your flocks and your herds and all that you have.
11. There I will also provide for you, for there are still five years of famine to come, and you and your household will be in poverty."'
12. Your eyes see, and the eyes of my brother Benjamin see, that it is my mouth which is speaking to you.
13. Now you must tell my father of all my splendor in Egypt, and all that you have seen; and you must hurry and bring my father down here."
14. Then he fell on his brother Benjamin's neck and wept, and Benjamin wept on his neck.
15. He kissed all his brothers and wept on them, and afterward his brothers talked with him.

16. Now when the news was heard in Pharaoh's house that Joseph's brothers had come, it pleased Pharaoh and his servants.
17. Then Pharaoh said to Joseph, "Say to your brothers, 'Load your beasts and go to the land of Canaan,
18. and take your father and your households and come to me, and I will give you the best of the land of Egypt and you will eat the fat of the land.'
19. Now you are ordered, 'Take wagons from the land of Egypt for your little ones and for your wives, and bring your father and come.
20. Do not concern yourselves with your things, for the best of all the land of Egypt is yours.'"

II. Memory Verse
- o Can you say from memory Romans 3:23?
- o Find it in the Bible.
    - For all have sinned and fall short of the glory of God.

III. Language
- o Spelling
    - Have a spelling bee. (Parent: Read a word from Day 90's worksheet. Choose one they didn't have trouble with. Have them spell it out loud.)
    - If you want to do a spelling activity here are ideas.
        - Write words with sidewalk chalk.
        - Write words with invisible ink.
        - Write words by pressing down and then reveal them by coloring lightly over the words.
        - Color a page and then color over it in black. Write the words by scratching off the black.
        - Write the words with letters cut out of magazines.
        - Write the words with yarn.
        - Write the words in the air or on each other's back.

IV. Lesson
- o Complete the worksheet for Day 136.

**Day 137**

I. Read Genesis 45:21-46:16.

21 The sons of Israel did as they were told; Joseph gave them wagons as Pharaoh commanded, and gave them what they needed for the journey.
22 To each of them he gave changes of garments, but to Benjamin he gave three hundred pieces of silver and five changes of garments.
23 To his father he sent as follows: ten donkeys loaded with the best things of Egypt, and ten female donkeys loaded with grain and bread and sustenance for his father on the journey.

24 So he sent his brothers away, and as they departed, he said to them, "Don't argue on the way."
25 They went up from Egypt, and came to the land of Canaan to their father Jacob.
26 They told him, saying, "Joseph is still alive, and indeed he is ruler over all the land of Egypt." But he was stunned, and he did not believe them.
27 When they told him all the words of Joseph that he had spoken to them, and when he saw the wagons that Joseph had sent to carry him, the spirit of their father Jacob revived.
28 Then Israel said, "It is enough; my son Joseph is still alive. I will go and see him before I die."

Chapter 46
1 So Israel set out with all that he had, and came to Beersheba, and offered sacrifices to the God of his father Isaac.
2 God spoke to Israel in visions of the night and said, "Jacob, Jacob." And he said, "Here I am."
3 He said, "I am God, the God of your father; do not be afraid to go down to Egypt, for I will make you a great nation there.
4 I will go down with you to Egypt, and I will also bring you up again; and Joseph will close your eyes."

5 Then Jacob left from Beersheba; and the sons of Israel carried their father Jacob and their little ones and their wives in the wagons which Pharaoh had sent to carry him.
6 They took their livestock and their property to Egypt, and Jacob and all his descendants with him:
7 his sons and his grandsons with him, his daughters and his granddaughters, and all his descendants he brought with him to Egypt.

8 Now these are the names of the sons of Israel, Jacob and his sons, who went to Egypt: Reuben, Jacob's firstborn.
9 The sons of Reuben: Hanoch and Pallu and Hezron and Carmi.
10 The sons of Simeon: Jemuel and Jamin and Ohad and Jachin and Zohar and Shaul the son of a Canaanite woman.
11 The sons of Levi: Gershon, Kohath, and Merari.
12 The sons of Judah: Er and Onan and Shelah and Perez and Zerah (but Er and Onan died in the land of Canaan). And the sons of Perez were Hezron and Hamul. [Note: Jesus is from the tribe of Judah. He ancestors are Judah, Perez and Hezron.]
13 The sons of Issachar: Tola and Puvvah and Iob and Shimron.
14 The sons of Zebulun: Sered and Elon and Jahleel.

15 These are the sons of Leah, whom she bore to Jacob in Paddan-aram, with his daughter Dinah; he had thirty-three sons and daughters.
16 The sons of Gad: Ziphion and Haggi, Shuni and Ezbon, Eri and Arodi and Areli.

II. Memory Verse
- Practice 1 Corinthians 10:13.
- Find it in the Bible.
    - No temptation has overtaken you but such as is common to man; and God is faithful, who will not allow you to be tempted beyond what you are able, but with the temptation will provide the way of escape also, so that you will be able to endure it.

III. Language
- Spelling
    - Have a spelling bee. (Parent: Read a word from Day 90's worksheet. Choose one they didn't have trouble with. Have them spell it out loud.)
    - If you want to do a spelling activity here are ideas.
        - Write words with sidewalk chalk.
        - Write words with invisible ink.
        - Write words by pressing down and then reveal them by coloring lightly over the words.
        - Color a page and then color over it in black. Write the words by scratching off the black.
        - Write the words with letters cut out of magazines.
        - Write the words with yarn.
        - Write the words in the air or on each other's back.

IV. Lesson
- Complete the worksheet for Day 137.

**Day 138**

I. Read Genesis 46:17-34.
17 The sons of Asher: Imnah and Ishvah and Ishvi and Beriah and their sister Serah. And the sons of Beriah: Heber and Malchiel.
18 These are the sons of Zilpah, whom Laban gave to his daughter Leah; and she gave him sixteen people.
19 The sons of Jacob's wife Rachel: Joseph and Benjamin.
20 Now to Joseph in the land of Egypt were born Manasseh and Ephraim, whom Asenath, the daughter of Potiphera, priest of On, bore to him.
21 The sons of Benjamin: Bela and Becher and Ashbel, Gera and Naaman, Ehi and Rosh, Muppim and Huppim and Ard.
22 These are the sons of Rachel, who were born to Jacob; there were fourteen people in all.
23 The sons of Dan: Hushim.
24 The sons of Naphtali: Jahzeel and Guni and Jezer and Shillem.
25 These are the sons of Bilhah, whom Laban gave to his daughter Rachel, and she bore these to Jacob; there were seven people in all.
26 All the people belonging to Jacob, who came to Egypt, his direct descendants, not including the wives of Jacob's sons, were sixty-six people in all,
27 and the sons of Joseph, who were born to him in Egypt were two; all the people of the house of Jacob, who came to Egypt, were seventy.

28 Now he sent Judah on ahead to Joseph, to point out the way to Goshen; and they came into the land of Goshen.
29 Joseph prepared his chariot and went up to Goshen to meet his father Israel; as soon as he appeared before him, he fell on his neck and wept a long time.
30 Then Israel said to Joseph, "Now let me die, since I have seen your face, that you are still alive."
31 Joseph said to his brothers and to his father's household, "I will go up and tell Pharaoh, and will say to him, 'My brothers and my father's household, who were in the land of Canaan, have come to me;
32 and the men are shepherds, for they have been keepers of livestock; and they have brought their flocks and their herds.'
33 When Pharaoh calls you and says, 'What is your occupation?'
34 you should say, 'Your servants have been keepers of livestock from our youth even until now, both we and our fathers,' that you may live in the land of Goshen; for every shepherd is loathsome to the Egyptians."

II. Memory Verse
- Practice 1 John 1:9
- Find it in the Bible.
    - If we confess our sins, He is faithful and just to forgive us our sins and to cleanse us from all unrighteousness. (KJV)

III. Language
- o Spelling
    - Have a spelling bee. (Parent: Read a word from Day 90's worksheet. Choose one they didn't have trouble with. Have them spell it out loud.)
    - If you want to do a spelling activity here are ideas.
        - Write words with sidewalk chalk.
        - Write words with invisible ink.
        - Write words by pressing down and then reveal them by coloring lightly over the words.
        - Color a page and then color over it in black. Write the words by scratching off the black.
        - Write the words with letters cut out of magazines.
        - Write the words with yarn.
        - Write the words in the air or on each other's back.

IV. Lesson
- o Complete the worksheet for Day 138.

**Day 139**

I. Read Genesis 47:1-19.
1. Joseph went and told Pharaoh, "My father and my brothers and their flocks and their herds and all that they have, have come out of the land of Canaan; they are in the land of Goshen."
2. He took five men from among his brothers and presented them to Pharaoh.
3. Pharaoh said to his brothers, "What is your occupation?" So they said to Pharaoh, "Your servants are shepherds, both we and our fathers."
4. They said to Pharaoh, "We have come to live in the land, for there is no pasture for your servants' flocks, for the famine is severe in the land of Canaan. Please let your servants live in the land of Goshen."
5. Then Pharaoh said to Joseph, "Your father and your brothers have come to you.
6. The land of Egypt is yours to use as you please; let your father and your brothers live in the best of the land, in the land of Goshen; and if you know that your brothers are skilled, put them in charge of my livestock."

7. Then Joseph brought his father Jacob and presented him to Pharaoh; and Jacob blessed Pharaoh.
8. Pharaoh asked Jacob, "How many years have you lived?"
9. So Jacob answered, "My years are one hundred and thirty, few and unpleasant and not as many as my fathers lived during the days."
10. Jacob blessed Pharaoh and went out from his presence.
11. So Joseph settled his father and his brothers and gave them part of the land of Egypt, in the best of the land, in the land of Rameses, as Pharaoh had ordered.
12. Joseph gave his father and his brothers and all his father's household food, according to how many children they had.

13. Now there was no food in all the land, because the famine was so severe. The land was no longer fertile. Everyone struggled.
14. Joseph took all the money that was used to buy grain, and Joseph brought the money into Pharaoh's house.
15. When everyone had spent all of their money, all the Egyptians came to Joseph and said, "Give us food, for why should we die in your presence? Our money is gone."
16. Then Joseph said, "Give us your livestock, and I will give you food in exchange, since your money is gone."
17. So they brought their livestock to Joseph, and Joseph gave them food in exchange for the horses and the flocks and the herds and the donkeys; and he fed them with food in exchange for all their livestock that year.
18. When that year ended, they came to him the next year and said to him, "We will not hide from my lord that our money is all spent, and the cattle are my lord's. There is nothing left for my lord except our bodies and our lands.
19. Why should we die before your eyes, both we and our land? Buy us and our land for food, and we and our land will be slaves to Pharaoh. So give us seed, that we may live and not die, and that the land may not be empty."

II. Memory Verse
- Practice Romans 6:23.

- o Find it in the Bible.
  - For the wages of sin is death, but the free gift of God is eternal life in Christ Jesus our Lord.

III. Language
- o Spelling
  - Have a spelling bee. (Parent: Read a word from Day 90's worksheet. Choose one they didn't have trouble with. Have them spell it out loud.)
  - If you want to do a spelling activity here are ideas.
    - Write words with sidewalk chalk.
    - Write words with invisible ink.
    - Write words by pressing down and then reveal them by coloring lightly over the words.
    - Color a page and then color over it in black. Write the words by scratching off the black.
    - Write the words with letters cut out of magazines.
    - Write the words with yarn.
    - Write the words in the air or on each other's back.

IV. Lesson
- o Complete the worksheet for Day 139.

**Day 140**

I. Read Genesis 47:20-48:4.
- 20 So Joseph bought all the land of Egypt for Pharaoh, because every Egyptian sold his field, because the famine was so severe. Then Pharaoh owned all the land.
- 21 As for the people, he moved them to the cities in Egypt.
- 22 Only the land of the priests he did not buy, because the priests received their land from Pharaoh, and they lived off the land which Pharaoh gave them. So, they did not sell their land.
- 23 Then Joseph said to the people, "I have bought you and your land for Pharaoh; now, here is seed for you, and you may plant.
- 24 At the harvest you shall give a fifth to Pharaoh, and four-fifths shall be your own for seed of the field and for your food and for those of your households and as food for your little ones." [Note: In balloons, that's 20 balloons for Pharaoh, 80 for the people.]
- 25 So they said, "You have saved our lives! Let us find favor in the sight of my lord, and we will be Pharaoh's slaves."
- 26 Joseph made it a law that is valid to this day, that Pharaoh should have the fifth; only the land of the priests did not become Pharaoh's.
- 27 Now Israel lived in the land of Egypt, in Goshen, and they gained property in it and the family grew numerous.
- 28 Jacob lived in the land of Egypt seventeen years, so the length of Jacob's life was one hundred and forty-seven years.
- 29 When Israel knew he would die soon, he called his son Joseph and said to him, "Please, if I have found favor in your sight, place now your hand under my thigh and deal with me kindly and faithfully. Please do not bury me in Egypt,
- 30 but when I lie down with my fathers, carry me out of Egypt and bury me in their burial place." And he said, "I will do as you have said."
- 31 He said, "Swear to me." So he swore to him. Then Israel bowed in worship at the head of the bed.

Chapter 48
- 1 It was after this time that Joseph was told, "Your father is sick." So, he took his two sons Manasseh and Ephraim with him.
- 2 When Jacob was told, "Your son Joseph has come to you," Israel collected his strength and sat up in the bed.
- 3 Then Jacob said to Joseph, "God Almighty appeared to me at Luz in the land of Canaan and blessed me,
- 4 and He said to me, 'Behold, I will make you numerous, and I will give this land to your descendants after you for an everlasting possession.'

II. Memory Verse
- o Practice Genesis 26:4.
- o Find it in the Bible.
  - I will multiply your descendants as the stars of the heaven, and will give your descendants all these lands; and by your descendants all the nations of the earth shall be blessed.

III. Language
- o Spelling
    - Have a spelling bee. (Parent: Read a word from Day 90's worksheet. Choose one they didn't have trouble with. Have them spell it out loud.)
    - If you want to do a spelling activity here are ideas.
        - Write words with sidewalk chalk.
        - Write words with invisible ink.
        - Write words by pressing down and then reveal them by coloring lightly over the words.
        - Color a page and then color over it in black. Write the words by scratching off the black.
        - Write the words with letters cut out of magazines.
        - Write the words with yarn.
        - Write the words in the air or on each other's back.

IV. Lesson
- o Complete the worksheet for Day 140.

**Day 141**

I. Read Genesis 48:5-22. Jacob (Israel) is speaking to Joseph.
- 5 "Your two sons, who were born in Egypt before I came, are mine; Ephraim and Manasseh shall be mine, as Reuben and Simeon are.
- 6 But your children that have been born after them are yours; their inheritance will be under their brothers.
- 7 As for me, when I came, Rachel died in the land of Canaan on the journey, when there was still some distance; and I buried her there on the way to Bethlehem. It broke my heart."
- 8 When Israel saw Joseph's sons, he said, "Who are these?"
- 9 Joseph said to his father, "They are the sons God has given me." So he said, "Please bring them to me so that I may bless them."
- 10 Israel eyes were not good because of his age so that he could not see. Then Joseph brought the children close to him, and he kissed them and hugged them.
- 11 Israel said to Joseph, "I never expected to see your face, and God has let me see your children as well."
- 12 Then Joseph took them from his knees and bowed with his face to the ground.
- 13 Joseph took them both, Ephraim with his right hand toward Israel's left, and Manasseh with his left hand toward Israel's right, and brought them close to him.
- 14 But Israel stretched out his right hand and laid it on the head of the younger son, Ephraim, and his left hand on Manasseh's head, crossing his hands, even though Manasseh was the firstborn.
- 15 He blessed Joseph, and said,

    "The God before whom my fathers Abraham and Isaac walked,
    The God who has been my shepherd all my life to this day,
- 16 The angel who has redeemed me from all evil,
    Bless the lads;
    And may my name live on in them,
    And the names of my fathers Abraham and Isaac;
    And may they grow into a multitude in the midst of the earth."

- 17 When Joseph saw that his father laid his right hand on Ephraim's head, it upset him; and he took his father's hand to move it to Manasseh's head.
- 18 Joseph said to his father, "No, my father, this one is the firstborn. Place your right hand on his head."
- 19 But his father refused and said, "I know, my son, I know; he also will become a people and he also will be great. However, his younger brother will be greater than he, and his descendants will become a multitude of nations."
- 20 He blessed them that day, saying,

    "All Israel will bless others saying,
    'May God make you like Ephraim and Manasseh!'"

    Thus, he put Ephraim before Manasseh.
- 21 Then Israel said to Joseph, "I am about to die, but God will be with you and bring you back to the land of your fathers.
- 22 I give you one portion more than your brothers, which I took from the Amorites with my sword and my bow."

II. Memory Verse
- For the last time, say Genesis 1:1-5.

III. End of the Year Activities
- This week you are going to plan out the rest of your school year. I want you to be part of making the plan. We should have a plan for history and social studies. We should have a plan for science. We should have a plan for writing. We should have a plan for vocabulary. We should have a plan for spelling.
- First let's play a noun game.
  - Play the picnic game. You say, "I'm going on a picnic and brought an apple."
  - You pick anything to bring that starts with an A.
  - Then the next person says it but chooses to bring something that starts with a B.
  - Then it's your turn again, and you will bring something that starts with a C.
- Today, let's plan out spelling.
  - Use your worksheet page today to list activities that you would enjoy to practice spelling.
  - You can use any of the spelling words from the year which are listed in the back of this book.

**Day 142**

I. Read Genesis 49:1-15.
1  Then Jacob called his sons and said, "Gather together that I may tell you what will happen to you in the days to come.
2  "Gather together and hear, O sons of Jacob;
   And listen to your father Israel.
3  "Reuben, you are my firstborn;
   My power and the beginning of my strength,
   More than the others in dignity and in power.
4  "Uncontrolled as water, you will not be greater than the others,
   Because you went to your father's bed;
   Then you defiled it—he went up to my couch.

5  "Simeon and Levi are brothers;
   Their swords are used for violence.
6  "Let my soul not listen to their advice;
   Let not my glory be joined with them;
   Because when they were angry, they killed men,
   And in their selfishness, they hurt oxen.
7  "Their anger is cursed because it is fierce;
   And their wrath because it is cruel.
   I will keep them apart in Jacob,
   And scatter them in Israel.

8  "Judah, your brothers will praise you;
   You will rule over your enemies;
   Your brothers will bow down to you.
9  "Judah is a lion cub;
   From the prey you have gone up.
   He crouches; he lies down as a lion,
   And as a lion, who dares to get him riled up?
10 "The scepter will always be with Judah,
   The ruler's staff will be held by him,
   And all people will obey him.
11 "He ties his foal to the vine,
   And his donkey's colt to the best vine;
   He washes his garments in wine,
   And his robes in the juice of grapes.
12 "His eyes are dull from wine,
   And his teeth white from milk.

13 "Zebulun will live at the seashore;
   And his city will be a haven for ships,
   And he will be toward the city of Sidon.

14 "Issachar is a strong donkey,
   Lying down between the sheepfolds.

15 "When he saw that a resting place was good
And that the land was pleasant,
He bowed his shoulder to carry burdens,
And became a slave.

II. Memory Verse
- o If you want to keep working on memory verses, see how many you can comfortably review a day. Reviewing four a day would take a week to get through them all. Reviewing them two a day would take two weeks to go through them all. You can review one a day and still review them every twenty days and get through them all several times before the new school year starts.

III. Review Activities
- o Grammar
  - Play the add-on game. Today you will play with action verbs. What's an action verb?
    - It's something we do.
  - To play the first person lists something they will do today at the park. They will say an action verb that starts with the letter A.
    - Example: "Today at the park I'm going to Astound."
  - The next person says the same thing but has to say a word that starts with the letter B.
    - Whoever wants to make it harder should repeat the whole list each time from the beginning as well as add their new word to the end of the list.
  - Continue until you get to Z!
- o Today you are going to make a plan about how you are going to review vocabulary.
  - Use your worksheet to make your plan.
  - The list of your words is at the end of this book.

**Day 143**

I. Read Genesis 49:16-33.

16 "Dan will judge his people,
As one of the tribes of Israel

17 "Dan will be a serpent in the way,
A horned snake in the path,
That bites the horse's heels,
So that his rider falls backward.

18 "For Your salvation I wait, O Lord.

19 "As for Gad, raiders will raid him,
But he will raid at their heels.

20 "As for Asher, his food will be rich,
And he will produce royal dainties.

21 "Naphtali is a doe set loose,
He gives beautiful words.

22 "Joseph is a fruitful branch,
A fruitful branch by a spring;
Its branches run over a wall.

23 "The archers bitterly attacked him,
And shot at him and harassed him;

24 But his bow remained firm,
And his arms were ready,
From the hands of the Mighty One of Jacob
(From there is the Shepherd, the Stone of Israel),

25 From the God of your father who helps you,
And by the Almighty who blesses you
With blessings of heaven above,
Blessings of the deep that lies beneath,
Blessings of the breasts and of the womb.

26 "The blessings of your father
Have gone beyond the blessings of my ancestors
Up to the highest edge of the everlasting hills;
May they be on the head of Joseph,
And on the crown of the head of the one distinguished among his brothers.

27 "Benjamin is a hungry wolf;
In the morning he eats his prey,
And in the evening, he divides his catch."

28 All these are the twelve tribes of Israel, and this is what their father said to them when he blessed them. He blessed them, each one with the blessing appropriate to him.

29 Then he said to them, "I am about to be gathered to my people; bury me with my fathers in the cave that is in the field of Ephron the Hittite,

30 in the cave, which Abraham bought along with the field from Ephron the Hittite for a burial site.
31 There they buried Abraham and his wife Sarah, there they buried Isaac and his wife Rebekah, and there I buried Leah—
32 the field and the cave that is in it, purchased from the sons of Heth."
33 When Jacob finished giving this command to his sons, he drew his feet into the bed and breathed his last, and was gathered to his people.

II. Memory Verse
- Continue work on memory verses if you so choose.

III. Language
- Grammar
  - Play the add-on game. Today you will play with adjectives. What's an adjective?
    - It describes a noun.
  - To play the first person lists something that describes the puppy they saw at the park. They will say an adjective that starts with the letter A.
    - Example: "Today at the park I saw a puppy that was Amazing."
  - The next person says the same thing but has to say a word that starts with the letter B.
    - Whoever wants to make it harder should repeat the whole list each time from the beginning as well as add their new word to the end of the list.
  - Continue until you get to Z if you can!
- Today you are going to make a plan about how you are going to review writing.
  - Use your worksheet to make your plan.

**Day 144**

I. Read Genesis 50:1-11.
1. Then Joseph fell on his father's face and cried over him and kissed him.
2. Joseph commanded his servants the physicians to embalm his father. So the physicians embalmed Israel.
3. Now forty days were required for it, for such is the period required for embalming. And the Egyptians cried for him seventy days.
4. When the days of mourning for him were past, Joseph spoke to the household of Pharaoh, saying, "If you are pleased with me, then please speak to Pharaoh, saying,
5. 'My father made me swear, saying, "Behold, I am about to die; in my grave which I dug for myself in the land of Canaan, there you must bury me." So, please let me go up and bury my father; then I will return.'"
6. Pharaoh said, "Go up and bury your father, as he made you swear."
7. So Joseph went up to bury his father, and with him went up all the servants of Pharaoh, the elders of his household and all the elders of the land of Egypt,
8. and all the household of Joseph and his brothers and his father's household; they left only their little ones and their flocks and their herds in the land of Goshen.
9. There also went up with him both chariots and horsemen; and it was a very great company.
10. When they came to the threshing floor of Atad, which is past the Jordan river, they mourned there with very great and sorrowful cries; and he spent seven days mourning for his father.
11. Now when the inhabitants of the land, the Canaanites, saw the mourning, they said, "This is a difficult mourning for the Egyptians." So, it was named Abel-mizraim.

*Note: What did they do to Israel (Jacob)? They embalmed him. They dehydrated him and made him a mummy!

II. Memory Verse
- Continue work on memory verses if you so choose.

III. Language
- Grammar
    - Play the apostrophe game. One person names a person and an object. (Note: This would be a good part for the parent, but you could take turns.)
    - The next person puts them together. Jump like an apostrophe (dolphin) where it goes.
    - Example: Mike bike, Mike's bike, jump when you say the S. Make your body shape like an apostrophe.
- Today you are going to make a plan about how you are going to review science.
    - Use your worksheet to make your plan.
    - The list of your lesson topics is at the end of this book.

**Day 145**

I. Read Genesis 50:12-26.
- 12 His sons did for him as he had commanded them;
- 13 his sons carried him to the land of Canaan and buried him in the cave of the field, which Abraham had bought along with the field for a burial site from Ephron the Hittite.
- 14 After he had buried his father, Joseph returned to Egypt, he and his brothers, and everyone who had gone up with him.
- 15 When Joseph's brothers saw that their father was dead, they said, "What if Joseph bears a grudge against us and pays us back in full for all the wrong which we did to him!"
- 16 So they sent a message to Joseph, saying, "Your father commanded before he died, saying,
- 17 'You must say to Joseph, "Please forgive, I beg you, the sin of your brothers, for they did you wrong."' And now, please forgive." And Joseph cried when they spoke to him.
- 18 Then his brothers came and fell down before him and said, "We are your servants."
- 19 But Joseph said to them, "Do not be afraid. Am I God?
- 20 As for you, you meant evil against me, but God meant it for good in order to bring all this about, to keep many people alive.
- 21 So do not be afraid; I will provide for you and your little ones." So he comforted them and spoke kindly to them.
- 22 Now Joseph stayed in Egypt, he and his father's household, and Joseph lived one hundred and ten years.
- 23 Joseph saw the third generation of Ephraim's sons; also the sons of Machir, the son of Manasseh.
- 24 Joseph said to his brothers, "I am about to die, but God will surely take care of you and bring you up from this land to the land which He promised on oath to Abraham, to Isaac and to Jacob."
- 25 Then Joseph made the sons of Israel swear, saying, "God will surely take care of you, and you will carry my bones up from here."
- 26 So Joseph died at the age of one hundred and ten; and he was embalmed and placed in a coffin in Egypt.

*Note: Joseph recognizes that God was in control the whole time, even when things appeared horribly wrong. He knew that God worked it out so that Joseph could keep his family alive through the famine. God always preserves a remnant, right? God was doing much more though. One of the truths God spoke to Abraham was that his descendants would be strangers in a land that wasn't their own and would be enslaved and oppressed there. Joseph's moving his family to Egypt sets the stage for that prophecy to be fulfilled.

II. Lesson
- o Grammar
    - Play the apostrophe game. One person names two words that can be combined into a contraction. (Note: This would be a good part for the parent, but you could take turns.)
    - The next person puts them together. Jump like an apostrophe (dolphin) where it goes.
    - Examples: can not, can't; she will, she'll
- o Today you are going to make a plan about how you are going to review social studies.

- Use your worksheet to make your plan.
- The list of your lesson topics is at the end of this book.

III. Bible
- We skipped a section of Genesis if you want to be reading it over these ending weeks.
- Genesis 29:36 through all of chapter 36.

Course Descriptions

Students will develop their writing skills with practice of grammar and spelling skills while adding to their vocabulary. They will study the geography and history of the world as well as learn about modern-day government and economics. They will learn more about how the world works through the study of physics, chemistry, earth science, and biology.

Junior Edition Scope and Sequence

Spelling

| | |
|---|---|
| 1 | God, earth, over, light |
| 2 | dry, seas, good, there |
| 3 | morning, plants, fruit, seed |
| 4 | night, heaven, sign, season |
| 5 | review |
| 6 | great, fifth, which, parents |
| 7 | each, beast, ground, kind |
| 8 | rule, image, likeness, fish |
| 9 | food, surface, male, sky |
| 10 | review |
| 11 | shrub, sprout, rain, mist |
| 12 | dust, garden, place, tree |
| 13 | name, gold, land, flow |
| 14 | die, saying, want, because |
| 15 | review |
| 16 | bone, join, sleep, ashamed |
| 17 | sew, open, piece, together |
| 18 | children, head, face, command |
| 19 | station, look, become, might |
| 20 | review |
| 21 | Cain, came, brother, farm |
| 22 | hard, said, away, find |
| 23 | father, city, tents, two |
| 24 | tools, seven, time, also |
| 25 | review |
| 26-35 | Review Weeks |
| 36 | mighty, twenty, forever, sons |
| 37 | animal, every, saw, eyes |
| 38 | end, people, them, rooms |
| 39 | seventeen, alive, wives, life |
| 40 | review |
| 41 | Noah, remember, were, water |
| 42 | made, window, bird, foot |
| 43 | clean, again, eat, thing |
| 44 | myself, never, making, between |
| 45 | review |
| 46 | everyone, same, words, let's |
| 47 | passed, pitched, child, Lot |
| 48 | donkeys, woman, tell, severe |
| 49 | before, family, are, well |
| 50 | review |

| | |
|---|---|
| 51 | return, went, out, meet |
| 52 | old, three, year, you |
| 53 | maid, wrong, power, your |
| 54 | angel, spring, sees, trouble |
| 55 | review |
| 56 | nine, twelve, Sarah, next |
| 57 | trees, sitting, heat, day |
| 58 | visit, wife, come, back |
| 59 | ten, thirty, fifty, forty-five |
| 60 | review |
| 61-70 | Review Weeks |
| 71 | sun, safe, town, fire |
| 72 | from, lived, everything, salt |
| 73 | early, been, with, smoke |
| 74 | now, took, dead, dream |
| 75 | review |
| 76 | yourself, pray, who, afraid |
| 77 | thousand, please, clear, sister |
| 78 | promise, laugh, eight, feast |
| 79 | upset, listen, voice, rid |
| 80 | review |
| 81 | happened, king, commander, army |
| 82 | complain, know, hadn't, heard |
| 83 | street, computer, spray, truck |
| 84 | after, tested, split, wood |
| 85 | review |
| 86 | boy, hand, nothing, only |
| 87 | looked, up, his, horns |
| 88 | done, Abraham, second, seashore |
| 89 | wives, lives, knives, shelves |
| 90 | review |
| 91 | rose, spoke, give, here |
| 92 | price, could, bowed, standard |
| 93 | field, was, cave, facing |
| 94 | gave, that, east, living |
| 95 | review |
| 96-105 | Review Weeks |
| 106 | kissed, quick, love, another |
| 107 | my, all, dark, years |
| 108 | unloved, allow, none, have |
| 109 | longer, having, named, days |
| 110 | review |
| 111 | very, way, under, follow |

| | |
|---|---|
| 112 | jar, lower, filled, drink |
| 113 | when, straw, feed, wash |
| 114 | go, ahead, rich, greatly |
| 115 | review |
| 116 | more, many, colors, stood |
| 117 | father's, brothers, animals, flock |
| 118 | dreams, pits, don't, one |
| 119 | meal, while, eating, silver |
| 120 | review |
| 121 | taken, down, house, anything |
| 122 | outside, beside, run, ran |
| 123 | Joseph, Joseph's, king, king's |
| 124 | baker, body, guard, bodyguard |
| 125 | review |
| 126 | cup, job, told, off |
| 127 | full, standing, grass, wind |
| 128 | ugly, lost, quickly, twice |
| 129 | wise, set, charge, third |
| 130 | review |
| 131-140 | Review Weeks |

Vocabulary

1. surface – the outer layer of something
2. separate – to move things apart
3. produce – to make, to cause to come into existence
4. govern – to rule, to be in control over a group of people
5. review
6. multiply – to increase a lot, to become more and more quickly
7. creep – to move slowly and carefully, especially in the hopes of not being noticed
8. synonym – word of similar meaning
9. subdue – to bring under control
10. review
11. mist – a cloud of tiny water droplets near the earth's surface
12. form – to create something, to put things together into a shape
13. flow – to move smoothly and continuously
14. command – to give an order
15. review
16. ashamed – feeling very embarrassed and guilty over something you did that was bad
17. serpent – snake
18. deceive – make someone believe something that isn't true
19. to station – to place someone in a particular place for a particular purpose
20. review
21. wanderer – someone who wanders - To wander means to move around, not really with any specific direction.
22. vengeance – revenge
23. presence – being there, whether seen or not
24. strike – to hit suddenly with a lot of strength
25. review

26-35. Review Weeks

36. renown – fame, lots of people know you and talk about you
37. corrupt – doing something wrong to get what you want
38. establish – to create something intended to last
39. righteous – doing what is right
40. review
41. decrease – to become less or to make something become less
42. remove – to take away, to get rid of
43. require – to need, to say that something has to be done
44. descendants – all the children that are born from you and from your children, etc.
45. review
46. babble – to talk nonstop in a way that you aren't even listened to or understood
47. accumulate – to gather, to get more and more
48. severe – intense, extreme
49. sustain – support physically or mentally

| | |
|---|---|
| 50 | review |
| 51 | deliver – to rescue, save |
| 52 | heir – the person who will inherit property, money, or position title after a person leaves a position or dies |
| 53 | prevent – to keep something from happening |
| 54 | authority – the person or organization in power, in control, with the right to give orders |
| 55 | review |
| 56 | intercept – blocking something from getting to where it's supposed to go |
| 57 | opposite – having a position on the other side, or being completely different |
| 58 | deny – refuse |
| 59 | return – to go back to where you came from, to bring back something you took from a place |
| 60 | review |
| 61-70 | Review weeks |
| 71 | inhabitant – someone who lives in a place |
| 72 | pillar – a tall, relatively thin structure that is used to support a building or decorate it |
| 73 | furnace – a metal stove where something is burned to produce heat |
| 74 | settle – to stay in one place |
| 75 | review |
| 76 | integrity – the character quality of holding to strong moral principles |
| 77 | restore – to bring something back to its normal condition |
| 78 | wean – to gradually get used to not having something you've become dependent on |
| 79 | distress – to cause extreme sorrow or worry |
| 80 | review |
| 81 | redeem – to get something or get back something in exchange for payment |
| 82 | seize – to grab suddenly and forcefully |
| 83 | offering – a gift, something offered |
| 84 | journey – a trip taking you from one place to another |
| 85 | review |
| 86 | bound – to tie together tightly |
| 87 | thicket – a dense group of shrubs, bushes or small trees |
| 88 | declare – to state clearly, to make known publicly |
| 89 | allegiance – loyalty, a commitment to something |
| 90 | review |
| 91 | refuse – to say no to doing something, or to refuse to give permission to do something |
| 92 | standard – accepted as normal, or a level of quality |
| 93 | possession – something you have |
| 94 | purchase – to buy |
| 95 | review |
| 96-105 | Review Weeks |
| 106 | weep – to cry intensely |
| 107 | complete – total, having all the parts, finished |

| 108 | sorrow – intense sadness |
| 109 | fortunate – good things happening that were unexpected, things going in your favor that you couldn't control |
| 110 | review |
| 111 | swear, swore, oath – promises that must be kept as if something bad might happen to you otherwise |
| 112 | trough – a long container open on top, used for animals to drink out of |
| 113 | valuable – worth a lot |
| 114 | successful – getting what you wanted, accomplishing what you set out to |
| 115 | review |
| 116 | rebuke – to scold; to tell someone their behavior is wrong in a sharp manner |
| 117 | graze – to eat grass or crops in a field, to eat little by little throughout the day |
| 118 | balm – a cream used for medicine, a sweet smell, or anything that heals or soothes |
| 119 | profit – to get a benefit, often refers to money |
| 120 | review |
| 121 | prosper – to succeed financially or physically |
| 122 | garment – a piece of clothing |
| 123 | supervise – to keep watch over someone while they work |
| 124 | furious – really angry |
| 125 | review |
| 126 | interpretation – the explanation of something's meaning |
| 127 | gaunt – scrawny looking, especially looking thin from hunger |
| 128 | abundance – a lot of something |
| 129 | appoint – to set someone in charge over something, or to choose a time or place for something |
| 130 | review |

131-140  Review Weeks

| Lesson | |
|---|---|
| 1 | light is moving energy, energy is ability to work |
| 2 | continents and oceans |
| 3 | seeds (germination, decompose) |
| 4 | sun lights and warms, equator (atoms, hemispheres) |
| 5 | birds (vertebrates, warm-blooded), living things |
| 6 | fish, salmon, sea monsters (fossils) |
| 7 | insects, ant diligence (diligent, invertebrate, antennae, thorax, abdomen) |
| 8 | arachnids and interdependence (scorpions) |
| 9 | mammals (instinct, peripheral vision) |
| 10 | moon, rest (orbit) |
| 11 | water cycle (evaporation, condensation) |
| 12 | compass rose, Far East, breath in oxygen (lungs and diaphragm) |
| 13 | circulatory system, map key |
| 14 | what's necessary for a plant to grow, civilization, Fertile Crescent |
| 15 | classification, grain |
| 16 | bones, marriage |
| 17 | rivers |
| 18 | reptiles, snakes |
| 19 | habitats/biomes, AD/BC |
| 20 | deserts, nomads |
| 21 | tundra, Antarctica |
| 22 | myths, dinosaurs, Achilles |
| 23 | gazelle, domesticated animals |
| 24 | bronze, iron, gold, Bronze Age |
| 25 | moon, solar system, false religion |
| 26-35 | Review Weeks |
| 36 | muscular system |
| 37 | muscular system |
| 38 | density |
| 39 | boats |
| 40 | floods |
| 41 | evaporation, Noah's ark |
| 42 | fresh water |
| 43 | states of matter, safety in Christ |
| 44 | rainbows |
| 45 | ancestors |
| 46 | steel, skyscrapers |
| 47 | shelter, Abraham's travels |
| 48 | famine |
| 49 | sustainability |
| 50 | tar pits |

| | |
|---|---|
| 51 | calories |
| 52 | rivers |
| 53 | conceive |
| 54 | springs, Arabs |
| 55 | name meanings |
| 56 | just laws  (Hammurabi Code) |
| 57 | hospitality |
| 58 | old age |
| 59 | the remnant |
| 60 | simple machines, hanging gardens |
| 61-70 | Review Weeks |
| 71 | bowing |
| 72 | atoms and molecules |
| 73 | refugees |
| 74 | caves |
| 75 | periodic table/punishment |
| 76 | earth's orbit |
| 77 | oxen, Oregon Trail |
| 78 | laughter |
| 79 | work |
| 80 | birth order |
| 81 | DNA |
| 82 | chromosomes |
| 83 | tamarisk tree (saline, roots) |
| 84 | worship, wedge |
| 85 | fire, God's story |
| 86 | how to start a fire (survival style) |
| 87 | sheep, wool, Lowell Mills |
| 88 | sand, erosion, countries |
| 89 | genetics |
| 90 | genetics |
| 91 | caves, mourning |
| 92 | commerce |
| 93 | grasslands, the Silk Road |
| 94 | silver, money |
| 95 | Sumerians, Hammurabi |
| 96-105 | Review Weeks |
| 106 | Africa, Lesotho, Chad |
| 107 | Asia, Turkey, Laos |
| 108 | South America, Brazil, Paraguay |
| 109 | Europe, Macedonia, Finland |
| 110 | North America, Canada, Mexico |

| | |
|---|---|
| 111 | bones, anatomy review (clavicle, cranium, patella, phalanges, mandible) |
| 112 | digestive system |
| 113 | family tree of Jacob |
| 114 | answered prayer |
| 115 | George Washington Carver (the importance of education) |
| 116 | dying cloth |
| 117 | lions |
| 118 | smell |
| 119 | camels |
| 120 | water cycle |
| 121 | pyramids |
| 122 | Egyptian inventions |
| 123 | justice system |
| 124 | Bill of Rights |
| 125 | dreams |
| 126 | leaven, chemical reactions |
| 127 | cows |
| 128 | healthy plants |
| 129 | food storage |
| 130 | simple machines, wheel and axle, symbols |
| 131 - | Review |

Workbook

| | |
|---|---|
| 1 | sentences (capitalize first word, ending punctuation) |
| 2 | find verbs, N&S America |
| 3 | Africa, write a sentence |
| 4 | Asia, nouns and verbs |
| 5 | spelling and vocabulary review |
| | |
| 6 | subject, predicate, draw a fish |
| 7 | things as nouns, draw an insect |
| 8 | synonyms, draw an arachnid |
| 9 | identify mammals |
| 10 | spelling and vocabulary review |
| | |
| 11 | water cycle diagram, correcting sentences |
| 12 | compass rose, write a sentence |
| 13 | map with key, spelling heart |
| 14 | commands, vocabulary drawing |
| 15 | spelling and vocabulary review |
| | |
| 16 | nouns – places |
| 17 | rivers, spelling/drawing serpent |
| 18 | write a question, venomous snake |
| 19 | Put the years in order, Draw an animal in its habitat. |
| 20 | spelling and vocabulary review |
| | |
| 21 | nouns – people, peninsula |
| 22 | write a sentence, peninsula |
| 23 | plural nouns |
| 24 | plural nouns/spelling, design a tool |
| 25 | spelling and vocabulary review |
| 26 | |
| 27 | |
| 28 | |
| 29 | |
| 30 | |
| 31 | |
| 32 | |
| 33 | |
| 34 | |
| 35 | |
| 36 | write a sentence, muscular system |
| 37 | adjectives |

| | |
|---|---|
| 38 | fill in the missing letter, draw low population density |
| 39 | fill in the silent E, design a boat |
| 40 | spelling and vocabulary review |
| 41 | names, capital letters |
| 42 | remove the silent E |
| 43 | states of matter |
| 44 | write a sentence, draw a rainbow |
| 45 | spelling and vocabulary review |
| 46 | apostrophes |
| 47 | map of Abraham's travels |
| 48 | contractions |
| 49 | un/sustainable practices |
| 50 | spelling and vocabulary review |
| 51 | capitalize names of places |
| 52 | EE vowel spelling pattern |
| 53 | writing sentences |
| 54 | state |
| 55 | spelling and vocabulary review |
| 56 | nouns, verbs, sentences |
| 57 | opposites |
| 58 | nouns, verbs, sentences |
| 59 | thank you note |
| 60 | spelling and vocabulary review |
| 61 | |
| 62 | |
| 63 | |
| 64 | |
| 65 | |
| 66 | |
| 67 | |
| 68 | |
| 69 | |
| 70 | |
| 71 | OW |
| 72 | pillars, nouns |
| 73 | names, proper nouns |
| 74 | question and answer sentences |
| 75 | spelling and vocabulary review |
| 76 | earth's orbit |
| 77 | oxen |
| 78 | knock, knock jokes |
| 79 | nouns and verbs |

| | |
|---|---|
| 80 | spelling and vocabulary review |
| 81 | double letters |
| 82 | contractions |
| 83 | subject pronouns |
| 84 | past tense |
| 85 | spelling and vocabulary review |
| 86 | to, too, two |
| 87 | jobs |
| 88 | country |
| 89 | plurals |
| 90 | spelling and vocabulary review |
| 91 | nouns (people, places, things) |
| 92 | animals in the grasslands |
| 93 | compound words |
| 94 | designing money |
| 95 | spelling and vocabulary review |
| 96 | |
| 97 | |
| 98 | |
| 99 | |
| 100 | |
| 101 | |
| 102 | |
| 103 | |
| 104 | |
| 105 | |
| 106 | Find Africa. |
| 107 | Find Asia. |
| 108 | Find South America. |
| 109 | Find Europe. |
| 110 | Find North America. |
| 111 | Find the bones. |
| 112 | prepositions |
| 113 | family tree |
| 114 | adjectives in a sentence |
| 115 | spelling and vocabulary review |
| 116 | sentence writing |
| 117 | possessives |
| 118 | plurals |
| 119 | ING |
| 120 | spelling and vocabulary review |
| 121 | compound words |

| | |
|---|---|
| 122 | past tense sentences |
| 123 | apostrophe |
| 124 | draw a picture of one of your rights |
| 125 | spelling and vocabulary review |
| 126 | write molecule names |
| 127 | sentences |
| 128 | draw a plant getting all it needs to be healthy |
| 129 | sentences |
| 130 | spelling and vocabulary review |
| 131 | |
| 132 | |
| 133 | |
| 134 | |
| 135 | |
| 136 | |
| 137 | |
| 138 | |
| 139 | |
| 140 | |
| 141 | Spelling |
| 142 | Vocabulary |
| 143 | Writing |
| 144 | Science |
| 145 | History |

If you find a mistake in any of our books, please contact us through genesiscurriculum.com to let us know.

# Thank you for using the Genesis Curriculum. We hope you had a great year of learning together.

Genesis Curriculum also offers:

> GC Steps: This is GC's preschool and kindergarten curriculum. There are three years (ages three through six) where kids will learn to read and write as well as develop beginning math skills.

> A Mind for Math: This is GC's elementary school learning-together math program based on the curriculum's daily Bible reading. Children work together as well as have their own leveled workbook.

> Rainbow Readers: These are leveled reading books. They each have a unique dictionary with the included words underlined in the text. They are also updated to use modern American spelling.

Look for more years of the Genesis Curriculum using both Old and New Testament books of the Bible. Find us online to read about the latest developments in this expanding curriculum.

**GenesisCurriculum.com**

Made in the USA
Monee, IL
17 December 2019